THE

PRESENT STATE

OF

ECCLESIASTICAL ARCHITECTURE

IN

ENGLAND.

BY

A. WELBY PUGIN, ARCHITECT.

WITH

Thirty-six Illustrations.

REPUBLISHED FROM THE DUBLIN REVIEW.

LONDON:

CHARLES DOLMAN, 61, NEW BOND STREET.

1843.

RICHARDS, PRINTER, ST MARTIN'S LANE.

m. a.

ON THE PRESENT STATE OF

ECCLESIASTICAL ARCHITECTURE
IN ENGLAND.

ARTICLE THE FIRST.
From the Dublin Review, No. XX.
May 1841.

A 2

ECCLESIASTICAL ARCHITECTURE IN ENGLAND.

ART. II.—*Elevation of the Cathedral Church of St. Chad, Birmingham.* By A. W. Pugin. London: 1840.

THE revival of our ancient parochial church architecture is a subject which occupies much attention at the present time; after three centuries of demolition and neglect, the solemn structures raised by our Catholic ancestors are being gradually restored to somewhat of their original appearance,* and buildings which but a few years since were considered as unsightly and barbarous erections of ignorant times, are now become the theme for general eulogy, and models for imitation. To the English Catholic there is no class of religious edifices of greater interest than the ancient parish churches of this country. They are admirably suited to the present wants and necessities of the Church, nor is it possible to adopt, consistently, any other models for the greater portion of our ecclesiastical buildings.

However glorious, magnificent, and edifying as were the great cathedral and abbatical churches, wonderful monuments of piety and zeal, we cannot turn to them in our present condition as objects of imitation. To rival them is wholly out of the question; to produce a meagre and reduced copy would be little better than caricaturing past glories. They were, in fact, the crowning result of Catholic piety and zeal, when it covered the face of the land, when all hearts and hands were united in the great work of rearing piles to God. These vast and sumptuous churches were, however, only the result of a long series of humble endeavours; they were the flowers of that faith which had been sown and cultivated by other means.

It is, in fact, by parish churches, that the faith of a nation is to be sustained and nourished; in them souls are engrafted to the Church by the waters of baptism; they are the tribunals of penance, and the seats of mercy and forgiveness. In them is the holy Eucharistic sacrifice continually offered up, and the sacred body of our Lord received by the faith-

---

* Among these restorations, none is more deserving of praise than that of the Temple church, London. The whole of the unsightly fittings of the last century have been removed, the marble caps and shafts beautifully restored, the whole of the vaulted ceiling diapered and painted, and many of the windows are being filled with stained glass, which, in design and execution, may vie with some of the richest windows of antiquity.

ful; there the holy books are read, and the people instructed; they become the seat and centre of every pious thought and deed; the pavement is studded with sepulchral memorials, and hundreds of departed faithful repose beneath the turf of the consecrated enclosures in which they stand. Each Catholic parish church is the history of the adjacent county; the family chantry, with its baronial monuments and heraldic bearings, the churchman's brass, the crusader's tomb, the peasant's cross, the storied windows, are all evidences of a long series of men and events; and valuable indeed are the national records furnished by many of even the humblest churches of this land; and even now, desecrated and despoiled as they are, still is there a traditionary reverence for these monuments of ancient piety left among the people.

Are not village spires, the church bells, the old porches, the venerable yew trees, the old grey towers, subjects on which writers and poets love to dwell? and Catholic feeling has never been so obscured in this land but that many have been found to view these holy spots with pious reverence; and what is truly consoling, the traditional form of the old buildings, although dreadfully debased and disfigured, has never been totally abandoned.* If the English Catholic body avail themselves of this feeling of attachment to the old parish churches which exists among a great body of the people, wonderful good may be produced; but if they neglect the means they are bound to employ to turn this feeling to the restoration of the old faith, then it will be found extremely inimical to the revival of religion.

A vast body of uninformed but excellently intentioned people, especially in agricultural districts, oppose the progress

---

* There are many interesting examples of this fact to be found in England. In that stronghold of Christian architecture, Oxford, we find colleges and buildings erected during the reigns of James and Charles, with the arrangement and features of the ancient buildings. At St. John's college are some beautiful groined ceilings of a very late date. The hall of Lambeth Palace, erected *since the restoration* by Archbishop Juxon, has buttresses, tracery windows, battlements, a lovre, a dais with a bay window, open framed roof, and all the characteristics of a refectory of the 15th century.

At Westminster Abbey the end of the north transept was almost rebuilt in the 17th century.

The font and cover at Durham Cathedral, set up in the time of Charles 1st, are carried up to a great height with niches, buttresses, and pinnacles.

The details of all these works are debased, and Italian monstrosities appear occasionally; but still these, and numberless other examples which might be adduced, fully prove that England long clung with a sort of lingering love to her ancient architecture.

of Catholicism from Catholic motives. They look upon the old church as the true one, they are not sufficiently instructed to draw a distinction between that same old church under Catholic or Protestant ministration, and they equally despise and avoid the dissenting conventicle, built by some independent preacher, or the *dissenting-looking* conventicle, erected in fact for the celebration of the very rites for which the old church was built, but with which it does not appear to have the slightest connexion, as an admirable writer in the *British Critic* beautifully expresses himself; " Grecian temple, Catholic cathedral, Corinthian portico, Norman doorway, pilaster and pinnacle, cannot differ so much or so essentially as the notions of a church, a preaching house, and a house of prayer. If then," he continues, "one could ensure the greatest technical accuracy in details, still if the Genevan principle of a house of God instead of the Catholic be adopted, the result must be an architectural monster." Such is the language of one, who, although unfortunately separated from us in communion, is evidently united in taste with the ancient faithful of this land ; and it is lamentable that few among us appear to feel the truth of these observations. Modern Catholics have frequently abandoned *Catholic architecture* for the *Genevan*, and even make light of this melancholy decay, and speak of the architecture of the house of God and the formation of his sanctuary, on which our Catholic ancestors bestowed the greater part of their lives and goods, as a thing indifferent, dependent on mere whim and idea. Now it is scarcely less important to adhere to the traditions of the Church as regards the arrangements of material buildings, than as to any other matters connected with the celebration of the divine mysteries; for it is impossible that these latter can be performed in accordance with the rituals and intentions of the Church, if the former are disregarded ; and yet it is a melancholy fact, that even a great portion of the clergy seem utterly unconscious of the close connexion between the two.

The most ardent supporters of the modern temple or conventicle style, who have cast away without the least compunction, not only the splendours but the *proprieties and essentials* of church architecture, affect great horror of what they term innovation in matters of much less importance. They regard the reduction of a shovel-ended stole to its ancient and reasonable shape, or the unstarching of a crimped surplice and restoring its graceful and ample folds, in the light of an almost mortal sin; while they sever every link between themselves and Catholic practice and antiquity in the style and arrangement of their churches. Surely this must arise from want of due reflection or information on these matters.

Can it be imagined that the Church in all ages, would have defined with such scrupulous exactness every thing connected with the celebration of the divine office, had not such precautions been considered necessary to ensure a becoming and solemn performance of the sacred rites? The Church, moreover, appointed proper officers, such as archdeacons, and rural deans, to act under the bishop, and see that the intentions and regulations of the Church were properly carried out, and to report on the state of the various churches in the diocess.

There are yet existing visitations of the twelfth century, where the slightest defect or irregularity in the fabric or ornaments is carefully noted down, with directions for amendment; yet all these excellent regulations to preserve uniformity and discipline, established by the wisdom of the ancient Churchmen, are accounted as foolishness by many Catholics of these days. To assert the importance of adhering to ancient tradition in these matters, is sufficient to draw forth ridicule, and even censure. It is lamentable to hear the sentiments which are expressed on ecclesiastical architecture by many who should be most ardent in reviving it in all its ancient purity, but who do not even bestow as much consideration on it as on the construction of their stables. The principal part of our modern churches are the result of mere whim and caprice. Those who build them are regulated neither by ecclesiastical nor architectural authority; hence a new Catholic church is almost certain to be a perfect outrage on ecclesiastical propriety and architectural taste. It is impossible to say, before it is erected, whether the building will look most like an auction room or a methodist meeting; whether it will have any symbol of Christianity about it, or be quite plain; whether it will be a caricature of pointed or of Grecian architecture; whether it will have any characteristics of a Catholic church at all, if we except its extremely offensive appearance, which, grievous as it may be, is become a very distinguishing mark of a Catholic building.

Formerly, the word *church* implied a *particular sort of edifice invariably erected on the same principle*; it might be highly ornamented, or it might be simple; it might be large or small, lofty or low, costly or cheap, but it was arranged on a certain *regulated system. Churches built hundreds of miles apart, and with the difference of centuries in the period of their erection, would still exhibit a perfect similarity of purpose, and by their form and arrangement attest that the same faith had instigated their erections, und the same rites were performed within their walls.* But now, alas, the case is widely different; anything may be built and called a church; any style, any plan, any detail. No sooner is a new building of this kind determined upon, than there is a muster of committee-men to adjust preliminaries, and decide on plans. These are men generally ignorant of every thing connected with these matters; which the result of their labours but too plainly proves. Some Protestant builder,—a matter-of-fact one-idea Roman-cement man, whose highest achievement in architectural art has been the erection of a market-house, or modernizing the front of an hotel—is not uncommonly considered as a fit and proper person to design and carry out an edifice intended for those very rites which produced the erection of every truly fine church in the land. Of course this individual, who is perfectly destitute of any idea of what the church should be like, eagerly catches at the suggestions of the committee-men, who are far from backward in having a say on these occasions. One has seen a new chapel lately opened, which he thinks extremely *neat and pretty*, but would propose that the altar should stand in a sort of alcove; a second, however, objects to this latter proposition, as he proves that those who would sit in the *last seat of the gallery could not look down on the top of the altar;* this is declared to be a fatal objection, and the altar is decided to stand against a flat wall, where *it can be well seen on three sides.* A hints that something in the Gothic style would look well; but B declares it to be all *expensive gingerbread.* C, who has been to Rome, laughs outright at such a barbarism as pointed architecture, and asks A sarcastically if he ever saw a Grecian portico; talks with equally extravagant praise of St. Peter's and the Parthenon, the two most opposite buildings in the world, and concludes with an eulogium on classical taste and refinement, and the barbarisms of the old Catholics. A ventures to reply, that there was something very grand about the old churches, notwithstanding, and offering some remarks about antiquity, is cut short by a loud laugh and general cry, "Oh, we're *all for the modern now;*" in which the one-idea Roman-cement man heartily joins, and compels him to be silent. After some further conversation about a marble altar from abroad, candlesticks of the newest Parisian fashion, and some other foreign novelties, the meeting separates, and a building is commenced, which in due time is finished, and opened with a band of theatricals, who, as the bills announce, have *kindly consented* to sing the praises of God—it might perhaps be added, as is sometimes seen on benefit bills, (*for that day only*), which would be an additional inducement for a full audience. This is a true picture of the manner in which many Catholic churches have been, and, what is worse, are still, being built; yet, perhaps, close by such an abortion stands the old parish church of the town. Although simple in its architecture, Catholic is indelibly stamped on its venerable exterior. Heretical violence has stripped it of its most beautiful ornaments; Protestant churchwardens have fattened on its old leaded roof and spire; it is curtailed of its fair proportions, and disfigured by some unsightly modern additions, which have been tacked on to its ancient walls; yet, in spite of these memorable disadvantages, it still tells its tale,—it is Catholic from foundation to tower top. Melancholy is it to think that this venerable pile should have been alienated from the ancient faith; but thrice melancholy is it that those who should ever regard it with veneration, and strive to imitate its beauties, should pass it by unheeded and despised; and as if in mockery of its venerable grandeur, raise a conventicle-looking structure under its very walls, where the assemblage of architectural monstrosities becomes a standing proof of the degeneracy of modern times.

It is very probable that many well-disposed persons have been led to approve, or at least tolerate, these miserable erections, from a mistaken idea that nothing could be accomplished in the pointed style under an immense cost. Now so far from this being the case, *this architecture has decidedly the advantage on the score of economy ;* it can be accommodated to *any materials, any dimensions,* and *any locality.* The erroneous opinions formed on this subject are consequent on the unfortunate results attending the labours of those who, when about to build in the pointed style, take some vast church for their model; and then, without a twentieth part of the space, or a hundredth part of the money, try to do something like it. This is certain to be a failure. Had they, on the contrary, gone and examined some edifice of antiquity, corresponding in *scale and intention to the one they wished to erect,* they would have produced a satisfactory building at a reasonable cost. Some persons seem to imagine that every pointed church must be a cathedral or nothing: this has even been cited as a reason why the proposed new Catholic church at York should *not* be Gothic, on account of its vicinity to the cathedral. Nothing can be more absurd: no one would think for an instant of attempting to rival the extent or richness of that glorious pile; but were there not above thirty parochial churches anciently in York? and did their builders think it expedient to depart from Catholic architecture in the design, on account of the stupendous cathedral? Certainly not. There were many buildings among them, and small ones too, *equally perfect and beautiful for the purpose for which they were intended as the minster itself.* Architecture to be good must be consistent. A parish church, to contain a few hundred persons, must be very differently arranged from a metropolitan cathedral; and if this principle be understood, and acted upon, the Catholics of York may erect an edifice suitable to their present necessities, which would not be unworthy of William de Melton or Walter Skirlaw

Churches must be regulated in their scale and decorations (as was the case formerly) by the means and numbers of the people; it being always remembered that the house of God should be as good, as spacious, as ornamented, as circumstances will allow. Many a humble village church, of rubble walls and thatched roof, has doubtless formed as acceptable an offering to Almighty God (being the utmost the poor people could accomplish) as the most sumptuous fabric erected by their richer brethren. Everything is relative; a building may be admirable and edifying in one place, which would be disgraceful in another. As long as the Catholic principle exists, of dedicating the best to God, be that great or little, the intention is the same, and the result always entails a blessing. But this does not afford the slightest ground for a pretext, urged by some wealthy persons in these days of decayed faith, that it does not matter how or where God is worshipped, and that four walls are equally well adapted for the purpose with the most solemn piles. God expects, and it is beyond contradiction His due, that we should devote to His honour and service a large portion of the temporal benefits we enjoy. While, therefore, it would be both absurd and unjust to expect more than what the station and means of persons enable them to contribute towards the erection of churches, it is a horrible scandal, and a fearful condemnation, that many persons of wealth and influence do oppose the Catholic principle, of making the house of God the centre of earthly splendour; and instead of contributing to this great and holy work, try to excuse their conduct by urging the miserable arguments of Protestants on these matters. While for the gratification of their own personal vanity, or the indulgence of their luxury, no expense can be too profuse, it is lamentable to look around on the various buildings used for Catholic worship in this land, and to see how few among them are at all fitted, either by their arrangement or decoration, for the sacred purposes for which they are intended.

We will not speak of chapels built fifty years ago, since it may with justice be urged that those were times of persecution; but we will turn to those churches which have been raised within a few years, and without the existence of any other restrictions than those which either the miserable parsimony or ignorance of the builders have imposed on them. In London itself, what are termed the *fashionable* chapels are uglier and more inconvenient than many Protestant chapels of ease; so ill-constructed as to arrangement, as to expose the sacred mysteries to unnecessary interruptions and publicity; so confined in their dimensions, that not a hundredth part of the people can squeeze in to hear mass; so meagre in decoration, that many Protestant churches are infinitely more elegant; and yet to these places, Sunday after Sunday, will Catholics of wealth, influence, and station, be driven in their carriages; and will appear, or actually are, perfectly satisfied with the building wherein they assemble to worship God, when the very entrance halls of their dwellings are more handsomely furnished, and the sideboards of their dining rooms are ten times more costly than the altar. In many country missions the case is even more deplorable; for we may find chapels destitute not only of the ornaments, but the essentials for the holy sacrifice, and even, horrible to name, the blessed Eucharist, the fountain of grace, received in a vessel of meaner material than what is generally used for the domestic table. The altar, composed only of a few boards, neglected, decayed, and dirty; candlesticks of the commonest description, holding an almost expiring wick; trash and trumpery, in the shape of paper pots of artificial flowers, are stuck about to make up a show, and the whole presents the chilling aspect of combined neglect, bad taste, and poverty.

But there is another sort of chapel, especially in large towns, which presents an equally offensive and distressing appearance, although from different causes; in these the evil does not proceed from either poverty or neglect, but from the ill-judged expenditure of money by pious but uninformed persons. In these places, societies of ladies are frequently formed for adorning the altar: the principal and ostensible object of such a sisterhood is admirable, but the manner in which the affair is carried out is generally lamentable. These well-meaning ladies transfer all the nicknackery of the work-room, the toilette-table, and the bazaar, to the altar of God. The result is pitiable;—cut papers of various colours, pretty ribbons, china pots, darling little gimcracks, artificial flowers, all sorts of trumpery, are suffered to be intruded not only into the vicinity of the seat of most holy mysteries, but actually in the presence of the blessed sacrament itself, insulting to the majesty of religion and distracting to every well-regulated and informed mind. The pranks these well-intentioned but ill-judged devotees are allowed to practise are truly extraordinary. Their intentions are excellent; they wish to work for the good and advancement of religion, although they unknowingly hinder it, by rendering its externals childish and ridiculous in appearance. But why should not their efforts be turned into a good channel? let them embroider frontals of altars, which are susceptible of every variety of ornament and design; they should be varied for every festival, and have appropriate subjects and emblems worked on them for each. The orpheys and hoods of copes, and the crosses of chasubles, would be an ample field for the exertions of the most indefatigable needle-women; and beautiful church ornaments might they produce, if they would quit the Berlin pattern and pole-screen style, and imitate the ancient and appropriate embroidery. We are greatly indebted to the ladies of the middle ages for much beautiful church needlework; but pure taste was then generally diffused, and *all worked in accordance with the regulations and traditions of the Church*, which were strictly enforced; and we may hope that such will again be the case, when Catholic art is better and more extensively understood.

But to return: there is another class of chapels, belonging to private mansions and families, which are generally in a most disgraceful state. Often has the butler a well-furnished pantry, the housekeeper her spacious storeroom, the cook his complete *batterie de cuisine*, all, in fact, well provided except the chapel and the chaplain: no pittance can be too small for the latter, nothing too mean or paltry for the former. There are some exceptions; but collectively they are quite unworthy of their sacred purpose; it would be invidious to name examples of either class, but we may mention some defects nearly common to them all, and leave the application of the remarks to those who may feel deserving of them.

The origin of these private chapels may be traced to both necessity and devotion. First: necessity, which during the times of persecution precluded the possibility of the public celebration of the Divine mysteries, and obliged the priests of the Church to seek privacy and concealment: hence the houses of those families who retained the ancient faith answered the purposes of parochial churches, and thus true religion was preserved by these means throughout the land. Secondly: the devotion of pious persons, who were anxious to have the consolations of religion under their very roof. Private chapels and chaplains are undoubtedly very ancient, and it is a practice which if properly carried out cannot be too much commended. It must be admitted, however, that it is a great privilege to have the same holy rites performed under one's own roof for which the most extensive piles in Christendom have been raised. The presence of the Lord of Hosts is no ordinary honour, and yet, strange to say, these reflections, if ever they are made, seem to produce but little effect on the minds of those who ought to be most sensibly touched by them. To *keep up a chapel* in these days is considered a *merit instead of a privilege;* a man is not accounted liberal who keeps a cook to administer to his appetite, a butler to provide him drink, and, in fine, a vast number of persons to attend and supply all he requires; this all passes by, nor is it of course considered any way meritorious; but to support a chaplain to administer the sacraments—without which all food, all raiment, all wealth, all state, is utterly dead and unprofitable— is thought in these days something very great and very praiseworthy. Out on such contradiction! the world does not in all its varieties exhibit such specimens of inconsistency as are to be found between the faith and practice of modern Catholics. If a visitor of fashion announces his intention of honouring their mansions with a visit, what preparations, what uncovering of holland, what setting up of wax lights; while the most holy sacrament of our Lord's body, deserted and forlorn, is left in a mean receptacle, without lamp or honour, in some half-furnished, half-dilapidated, and decayed chamber, which the owner of the house consents to give up to God, out of his vast and sumptuous residence; and while the commonest articles of food are served up on massive silver, by footmen in costly liveries, a miserable bit of plated ware is the earthly tabernacle for the sacred body of our Lord, and a cast-off gown is considered sufficiently good for a vestment wherein to offer up the adorable sacrifice. When a new private chapel is decided on, how often is some outhouse or adjacent stable converted into a sanctuary for the Lord of Hosts. Many private chapels have bed rooms *over* them, which is strictly forbidden ; others are situated directly over the meanest offices of the house ; and few indeed are there which have been arranged with the slightest reference to the sanctity of their purpose.

We cannot dismiss this part of our subject without referring to a chapel recently erected in the north, which is an instance much to be regretted of the foreign and novel ideas which exist among some of our most distinguished English Catholics. Money was lavished on this building with a zeal and devotion which would have done honour to days of livlier faith ; the endowment also was ample ; everything was done in a fine spirit, but with most mistaken ideas of Catholic architecture. A plaster imitation of Italian design has been erected on the soil of that county which can boast a Rivaulx, a Fountains, a Beverley, a York,—a county whose face is studded with Catholic remains of every style, from the severe lancet to the elaborate perpendicular. Alas ! Catholic England, how art thou fallen, when thine own children forget the land of their fathers, and leave thy most beauteous works unnoticed and despised, to catch at foreign ideas, unsuited to their country, and jarring with its national traditions.

The long exclusion of the English Catholics from the an-cient ecclesiastical edifices, and the necessity which existed till lately of a foreign education, have undoubtedly produced this lamentable departure from the traditions and feelings of their ancestors. It is therefore of the highest importance to set forth the beauty and fitness of the ancient churches, and the necessity of adhering strictly to them as the models for our imitation. The majestic cathedral and celebrated ruin may occasionally arrest the attention of the modern Catholic traveller, but how few think on the interesting claims on their attention which *almost every rural church possesses !* how often do they pass unheeded the old grey tower and moss-covered chancel, when within their walls might be found many a memorial of old Catholic faith, which would not have sur-vived the attacks of fanaticism and novelty in a more conspi-cuous spot. It is beyond even a doubt that the rural popu-lation of England were ardently attached to the faith of their fathers, and that but trifling changes were made in the inter-nal decorations of the churches, till the ascendency of the Cal-vinists and fanatics under Cromwell; and even in the present day many of these ancient and holy edifices may be found tolerably perfect in their original internal arrangement.*

We will now consider what is to be regarded as forming a complete Catholic parish church for the due celebration of the divine office and administration of the sacraments, both as regards architectural arrangement and furniture. The building should consist of a nave, with a tower or belfry. A southern porch, in which a stoup for hallowed water should be provided; at the western end of the nave, and usually in the south aisle, a stone font with a wooden cover fastened with a lock, and near it an ambry in the wall for the oleum cate-chumenorum and holy chrism. The chancel at the eastern end should be separated from the nave by an open screen sup-porting the rood and rood loft, ascended by a staircase in the wall.

Wooden seats, with low backs, and placed wide enough apart to admit of kneeling easily, may be fixed in the nave and aisles, allowing alleys of sufficient width for the passage of processions. A stone or wooden pulpit sufficiently elevated may be erected in a convenient position in the nave.

The chancel floor should be raised at least one step above the nave, and the upper step on which the altar stands three steps above the floor of the chancel. The altar should consist of one slab of stone (marked with five crosses, and a cavity for relics) raised on solid masonry or stone pillars.

---

* Those churches which are situated in parishes too poor to admit of heavy rates, are invariably found in the best preservation. In wealthy towns, the parish churches have been considered as stock jobs, by which each ignorant shop-keeper, as he attains the office of warden, might enrich his pockets at the expense of the ancient fabric. In these buildings, the havoc which each trade has made in its turn may easily be traced. The carpenter has removed the carved and painted timbers of the roof, with the massive covering of lead, and set up a flat pitched slated covering in their stead, erected a few galleries, and *inclined planes* for seats; the painter has marbled and grained all the oak work left; while the glazier has carefully removed the stained windows, and replaced them by neat and uniform lights; the plasterer has stuccoed the chancel ceiling, and coloured down the stone work; the smith has lined the walls with stove piping, and set up a host of cast-iron furnaces; and each of these worthies is certain to record their achievements in some too legible inscription on the walls. St. Margaret's church, at Lynn, is a forcible illustration of this system. This magnificent fabric has been completely gutted of its ancient features. New roofs, new ceilings, new pavements, new pews, even plaster Italian ornaments stuck up to mask the old work. Immense sums have been expended to destroy every internal ornament and arrangement, simply on account of the *town being rich enough to bear the expense of these enormities*; for but a few miles from this very place are some most beautiful churches, secured by their poverty and ne-glect, where the carved angels yet enrich the oak-beamed roof, where the low-back sculptured benches yet remain; the fonts with their pinacled covers; the chancels divided off by the old traceried screens, on which the painted enrich-ments may still be descried, and so many of the ancient features left, that were it not for the unsightly reading-desks, and the decayed tables in place of the old and solemn altars, one would almost seem transported into some sacred edifice of the old time.

On the epistle side of the altar a sacrarium should be fixed, with a basin and waste pipe, with a stone shelf for the cruets. On the same side, and corresponding to the width of the three steps ascending to the altar, three niches should be built, partly in the thickness of the wall, and partly projecting, with canopies, and convenient seats for the priest, deacon, and sub-deacon. Opposite to these an arched tomb, to serve as the sepulchre for holy week. Adjoining the chancel, a sacristy or revestry for keeping the vestments and ornaments; or, in any small churches an almery may be provided for this purpose on the gospel side of the altar, within the chancel. An image of the saint in whose honour the church is dedicated, should be set up in the chancel. Where there are lateral aisles, they should be terminated towards the east by altars, either erected against the wall, and protected by open screen-work, or in chapels, eastward of the aisles, divided off from the church by screens. That these arrangements may be the better understood, we have subjoined four plans of Catholic churches now erecting in exact conformity with the ancient traditions.—(See Plates I, II, III, and below.)

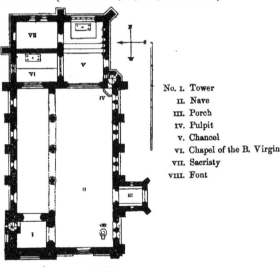

No. I. Tower
II. Nave
III. Porch
IV. Pulpit
V. Chancel
VI. Chapel of the B. Virgin
VII. Sacristy
VIII. Font

ST. MARY'S, STOCKTON ON TEES.

Having thus generally noticed the requisites for a church, we will now proceed to consider these in detail.

B

OF THE POSITION OF THE CHURCH.

A church should be so placed that the faithful face the east while at prayer. Such has been the practice of the Church from the earliest period, and very few are the examples of any deviation from this rule. The chancel should consequently be turned towards the east; and all the altars in the church should be so placed, that the celebrant, while officiating, looks towards the same quarter.*

Independent of all Christians turning towards the same point, being a beautiful figure of the unity of the Church, those learned writers, Durandus, Gavantus, and Cardinal Bona, have adduced the following reasons for this rule:—

1. That the apostles turned towards the east while at prayer.

2. That the Holy Spirit descended on them from the east on Pentecost.

3. That we should all turn towards the Holy Land, where our Lord was born.

4. That as our Lord was the great light of the world, we should turn towards the brightest quarter of the world, as a figure of his glory.

5. That as our Lord was crucified looking towards the west, the roods, placed in the same position, face the faithful.

6. That the star appeared in the east to the three wise men at the birth of our Lord.

7. To distinguish the faithful from infidels or heretics, who, being without faith or unity, turn in any direction.

8. That according to the traditional belief of the Church, our Lord will come from the east to judge the living and the dead.

But independent of these mystical and pious reasons, the ancient and canonical position is the most judicious that could have been chosen. How beautifully do the rays of the rising sun, streaming through the brilliant eastern windows of the choir or chancel, darting their warm and cheerful light to the very extremity of the nave, correspond to the hymn appointed to be sung at prime.

> " Jam lucis orto sidere,
> Deum precemur supplices,
> Ut in diurnis actibus,
> Nos servet a nocentibus."

* An inspection of a plan of an old cruciform church would readily shew how strictly this principle was adhered to in the arrangement of the various altars, whether in the transepts, extremities of aisles, or lateral chapels of apsics.

Then as the day advances, from the whole southern side a flood of light is poured into the building, gradually passing off towards evening, till all the glories of a setting sun immediately opposite the western window light up the nave with glowing tints, the rich effect being much increased by the partial obscurity of the choir end at the time.

Now this beautiful passage of light from sunrise to sunset, with all its striking and sublime effects, is utterly lost in a church placed in any other than the ancient position. In short, there are both mystical and natural reasons for adhering to antiquity in this practice, a departure from which can only be justified under the most urgent necessity.*

OF THE CHURCHYARD.

The inclosure within which a church was erected was set apart by solemn consecration for the burial of the faithful.†

And however objectionable places for interment may be in the midst of crowded cities, still it must be allowed that nothing can be more calculated to awaken solemn and devout feelings, than passing through the resting-place of the faithful departed. How often is the pious Christian moved to pray for his deceased brother, when he sees graven on his tomb,—" Of your charity pray for my soul"! What a train of profitable reflections, what holy meditations, may not be suggested by a sepulchral cross! In days of faith, prayer formed the link of communion between the living and the departed. Truly might it be said in time of old, when such pious respect was paid to the memorials and sepulture of the dead, "Oh, grave, where is thy victory! Oh, death, where is thy sting!"

Men formerly visited and knelt by tombs and graves; now they would shun them, and try and banish them from their sight as things odious and dreadful, and in accordance with the spirit of the times, which strives to make churches like

---

* We occasionally find examples of ancient churches, which, from the localities in which they have been erected, deviate from the usual position of west to east. These are, however, to be regarded as exceptions to the rule, and they can only serve as authorities for equally difficult scites.

† The first prayer in the beautiful office of the consecration of a cemetery is as follows:—

"Omnipotens Deus, qui es custos animarum et tutela salutis, et fides credentium, respice propitius ad nostræ servitutis officium, ut ad introitum nostrum purgetur bene✝dicatur, sancti✝ficetur, et consecretur hoc cœmeterium, ut humana corpora hic post vitæ cursum quiescentia, in magno judicii die simul cum felicibus animabus mereantur adipisci vitæ perennis gaudia. Per Christum Dominum nostrum. Amen."

B 2

assembly-rooms, gay and comfortable, with carriage drives and covered porticos to set down the company:—the very remembrance of death is to be excluded, lest the visitors to these places might be shocked at the sight of tombs. Hence burying the dead is become a marketable matter, a joint-stock concern, an outlay of unemployed capital; and a large pleasure-ground, sufficiently distant from the town, is staked out by some speculators; in which, according to the prospectuses issued, every religion may have a separate parterre, with any class of temple, from the synagogue to the meeting-house.

However these sort of modern arrangements may suit the unitarian and the infidel, we hope and trust the Catholic church will still be surrounded by its consecrated inclosure, with its winding path, and its tombs, where the pious Christian may recite a *De Profundis* and a *requiem,* as he wends his way to the house of prayer, and still may the branches of the solemn yew tree* overshadow its arched porch. It was customary to erect a stone cross, raised on steps, on the south-western side of the church to mark the hallowed ground; and the shafts of these crosses, some of which were even Saxon, still remain in various churchyards, although the upper part has almost in every instance been destroyed by Protestant fanaticism. Wooden crosses, with the name of the deceased, and an invocation for prayer painted or cut on them, were erected over the graves of the faithful, in place of the hideous upright slabs, with bad poetry, pompous inscriptions, and ludicrous cherubs, now so much in vogue. These sepulchral crosses are still set up on the Continent in villages, and such retired places as have yet remained in happy ignorance of urns, pedestals, broken pillars, and all the adopted Pagan emblems of mortality,† for which modern designers have abandoned the ancient and touching memorials of departed Christians.‡

---

* The branches of yew trees served anciently for palms in the procession of Palm Sunday.

† So blindly do artists of the present day adopt the ornaments and ideas of ancient paganism, that a stuff has recently been manufactured at Lyons intended for copes, to be used in funeral offices, in which the *poppy, emblem of eternal sleep,* has been introduced in lieu of those appropriate figures by which the joyful mystery of the resurrection (a Christian's brightest hope) was formerly represented.

‡ In an old English office-book belonging to the Scarisbrick family of Lancashire, the illuminated borders at the office for the dead are particularly curious. The whole of the ceremonies connected with a burial service are most accurately depicted. The convoy, the hearse, and lights in the church, the celebration of the holy Eucharist, the recitation of the office, and the churchyard with the grave, are all introduced. In this latter we have a perfect delineation of the

Besides these, some graves were covered with coped slabs,
gradually diminishing at the lower end, with floreated crosses
sculptured on them, and the inscription cut on each side of
the stems; and there are some instances of a later date, of
regular altar tombs, with panelling and shields round them,
having been erected in churchyards, of which there are examples at Glastonbury, Lavenham (Suffolk), and Bury St.
Edmund's. Several of the Catholic churches now erecting
will have cemeteries round them, disposed in the ancient
manner, and from which all modern funeral monstrosities will
be rigidly excluded.

OF THE EXTERNAL FORM AND DECORATION OF THE CHURCH.

The most striking and characteristic external feature of a
church is its tower or spire. This is so attached to the popular notion of such a building, that any religious edifice
wanting this essential mark would never generally receive any
other appellation than that of chapel. Towers, attached to
parochial churches, are most ancient in this country; they
appear to have been erected from a very early period, and
several Saxon examples yet remain. It is a feature of ecclesiastical architecture which the establishment never abandoned
even in its most degenerate period.

A church tower is a beacon to direct the faithful to the
house of God; it is a badge of ecclesiastical authority, and it
is the place from whence the heralds of the solemnities of the
church, the bells, send forth the summons. Let no one
imagine that a tower is a superfluous expense,* it forms an
essential part of the building, and should always be provided
in the plan of a parochial church.

A tower to be complete, should be terminated by a spire:
every tower during the finest periods of pointed architecture
either was, or was intended to be, so finished; a spire is in
fact an ornamental covering to a tower; a flat roof is contrary
to every principle of the style, and it was not till the decline
of the art that they were adopted. The vertical principle,

---

stone cross, the wooden crosses at the head of the graves, and all the interesting
characteristics of an Anglo-Catholic parochial cemetery of the 15th century.

* If funds are not sufficient, the tower may be the last part of the building
completed; but due preparation should be made with regard to walls and foundations from the *beginning*, so that it may always be carried up when means will
allow of its completion. This is the principle on which all the ancient churches
were built. The *plan on which they were commenced was originally good*, and then
they were gradually completed as the funds permitted.

emblematic of the resurrection, is a leading characteristic of Christian architecture, and this is nowhere so conspicuous or striking as in the majestic spires of the middle ages. The position of towers in parochial churches are various; they are generally placed at the west end of the nave, rising directly from the ground. This we will illustrate by three examples of Catholic churches now erecting;—the first is St. Giles's, Cheadle; the second the large parochial church of St. George's-in-the-fields; the third St. Oswald's, near Liverpool. —(See Plates IV, V, and VI.)

In cruciform parish churches, the tower is sometimes placed at the intersection of the nave and transepts, but of this we have no revived example at present.

We occasionally find the tower placed at the extremity of an aisle, and this expedient is usually resorted to in churches built in towns and confined situations, where there would not be sufficient space for a tower to project at the western end. Of this we give two examples;—the church of St. Wilfrid, now erecting at Hulme, near Manchester, and the church of St. Mary's, building at Stockton-on-Tees.—(See Plates VII and VIII.) To those whose ideas of architectural beauty are formed on the two and two system of modern building, this argument will appear very singular; but building for the sake of uniformity never entered into the ideas of the ancient designers; they regulated their plans and designs by localities and circumstances; they made them *essentially convenient and suitable to the required purpose, and decorated them afterwards.*

To this we owe all the picturesque effects of the old buildings: there is nothing artificial about them,—no deception,— nothing built up to make a show,—no sham doors and windows to keep up equal numbers,—their beauty is so striking because it is *natural.* The old builders did not think it necessary to build up a high wall to hide a roof, nor disguise a chimney into a flower pot; they made these essential parts of a building ornamental and beautiful: *this is the true spirit of pointed design, and until the present regular system of building both sides of a church exactly alike be broken up, no real good can be expected.* One of the greatest beauties of the ancient churches is this variety. It is impossible to see both sides of a building at once; how much more gratifying is it, therefore, to have two varied and beautiful elevations to examine, than to see the same thing repeated. A southern porch does not necessarily demand a northern one; a vestry on one side does not require an opposite one to keep up uniformity; a chantry chapel may be erected at the extremity of one aisle, without any necessity of raising up a building to look like it at the end of the other. A tower, if the locality require it, may be built on one side or corner of a church, without any obligation of building up another opposite.[*]

How many magnificent examples do we find among the ancient churches of towers placed in these positions, the entrances through them serving for southern porches. In very small churches, of exceedingly simple design, we occasionally find belfreys, in the form of perforated gables, or turretted projections, carved up at the end walls, and surmounted by stone crosses. These sort of belfreys are frequently found in ancient chapels, of which there is a beautiful instance yet remaining at Glastonbury. Among the revived Catholic buildings, some of the smallest have belfreys of this description, of which we give for examples,—St. Mary's on the Sands, Southport, Lancashire; St. Ann's, Keighley, Yorkshire,—(for which see Plate IX); and St. Mary's, Warwick Bridge, Cumberland.

ST. MARY'S CHURCH, WARWICK BRIDGE.

It was usual to place a small belfrey of this description on the eastern gable of most parish churches; in which the Sanctus bell was rung to warn the faithful who might be in the vicinity of the church, that the holy mysteries were being celebrated. A very rich belfry for this purpose is to be placed on the east gable of St. Giles's church, now erecting at Cheadle.

---

[*] We are glad to perceive that the architect of the new Protestant church at Leeds has ventured to place his tower on the side of the building. This is certainly an advance towards better things.

OF THE PORCH.

The next part of the sacred edifice we have to consider is
the porch. It was generally built to the southward, and in
the second bay of the nave from the north end; there are
several examples, however, of northern porches, and some few
western ones, especially in situations much exposed to the
wind of the sea coast.* Porches in England frequently consist of two stories, the upper room having been appropriated
formerly to the purposes of a library, a school, or muniment
room: occasionally these apartments appear to have been
occupied by the sacristan, and they are sometimes provided
with tracery apertures, through which the church would be
watched at night.

Porches were, and ought now to be used for the following
purposes :—

1. The insufflations of baptism were performed in the porch,
where the child was exorcised previous to being admitted into
the sacred building.

2. Women were churched in the porch after child-bearing.

3. The first part of the marriage service was performed in
the porch.

4. Penitents assisted at mass in the porch during Lent.

Holy water stoups were generally hollowed out of the porch
walls, and frequently built in niches on either side of the external arch, as at Bury St. Edmund's; all stoups for hallowed
water should be placed *outside* the building. The custom of
Christians sprinkling themselves with this water, is only a
modification of the ancient custom of actually washing the
hands and mouth, as an emblem of purification before prayer,
which was generally practised in the early ages of the Church.
It was for this purpose that large fountains and basins were
placed near the entrance of great churches, many of which yet
remain, as at St. Peter's at Rome, and several of the French
cathedrals, Lyons, Chartres, &c. This custom among Christians is mentioned by St. John Chrysostom,† Eusebius, and

* At Cromer church, Norfolk, there are three magnificent porches, which
have been suffered to go to shameful decay. At Cley church, Norfolk, there is
a beautiful western porch; also at Snetisham church in the same county. At
King's Sutton church, Oxon, there is an elegant western porch of the early part
of the 15th century, with effigies of the builders kneeling on each side of a niche,
which anciently contained an image of the patron saint of the church.

† St. John Chrysostom in his " Homily on St. John,"—" Manus lavamus in
ecclesiam ineuntes." The same in the Homily on St. Matthew"—" In ecclesia
hunc morem obtinere cernimus apud multos, ut vestibus puris in templum ineant
et ut manus lavent."

other writers of antiquity. Hallowed water was only taken on *entering* a church formerly, and never on leaving it. There is a regular ceremonial for presenting hallowed water to persons of distinction *on their entering* a church, but nothing of the kind was ever thought of on their departure. De Moleon, in his *Voyage Liturgique*, mentions several cathedral churches in France where the custom of taking holy water was strictly confined to entering. The original intention of this custom, which was to purify the soul *previous to commencing prayer*, having in a great measure been lost sight of, it is become usual to take the water on entering or leaving a church, indifferently. But Le Brun, who stands high as a writer on ecclesiastical or liturgical antiquities, thus speaks on this subject: " Those who are in the habit of taking hallowed water on leaving a church, are more moved to do so by the mere sight of the *bénitier* than by any consideration of the real intentions of the Church; in this matter of which (he continues) the *curés de paroisse* neglect to instruct them."

Porches were frequently used as places of sepulture, even by persons of distinction. The great Talbot, Earl of Shrewsbury, directed his body to be buried in the porch of the parish church of Whitchurch.

From these remarks it will be seen that porches were not considered by our Catholic forefathers as mere places for scraping feet and rubbing shoes, but as a portion of the sacred edifice peculiarly devoted to the performance of solemn rites, and to be entered with due respect and reverence.

It may be proper to remark in this place, that the practice of selling books of devotion, rosaries, &c. in the porches of the churches, but too frequent on the Continent, is a great abuse; such traffic is *strictly forbidden by the decrees of many synods and councils*, and those who tolerate the abuse are liable to severe ecclesiastical censures. That great champion of Catholic antiquity, Father Thiers,* who flourished during the

---

* The principal works of this great Theologian and learned Rubrician are as follows:—

1. " Dissertation sur les Autels."—2. " Dissertation sur les Jubés;"—an admirable work, setting forth the antiquity and intention of roods and choir screens, and denouncing those innovators who ventured to remove them during the last century, and whom he most appropriately designates as Ambonoclasts.—3. " Dissertation sur le Clôture des Chœurs."—4. " Sur les Superstitions," in 4 vols.; a most learned and laborious work, in which all the abuses which have existed at various times in the celebration of rites and ceremonies are separated from the decrees of the Church on those matters, and forms a most edifying and interesting exposition of true Catholic practices.—5. " Dissertation sur les Perukes," in

last century, openly denounced the chapter of Chartres cathedral for suffering two women to retail objects of devotion under the porches of that glorious church, which were intended for holy purposes; and at the time he published a most learned treatise on the use and intention of this portion of the church, and brought forward such overwhelming proofs of the irregularity of the practice, from the highest authorities, that the chapter, to their great mortification, were compelled to own their fault.

It cannot be urged in palliation of this great abuse, that the things sold are intended for holy purposes. The church has decreed that *nothing whatever shall be sold, either under the porches or within the edifice.* The dovesellers, whom our Lord cast out of the temple, traded only *in offerings;* and the profanation of the holy place is equally great by the traffic in candles, from which abuse so much scandal continually arises. We cannot, however, hope for any improvement in these respects from our foreign brethren, while they have so little feeling for the sanctity of the temple of God as to erect shoe stalls between the buttresses, and heap filth against the entrances, of the most glorious monuments of Christian antiquity. But we trust that the English Catholic churches will at least be preserved from these horrible profanations.

---

which the writer treats on all the coverings of the head used in the church, mitres, caps, callottes, amices; and also the antiquity of shaving the heads of persons devoted to the clerical state; on praying with the head uncovered, and the irregularity of ecclesiastics wearing wigs or false hair.—6. "Sur la Clôture des Religieuses."—7. "Sur les Porches des Eglises."—8. "Sur la Larme de Vendôme," a false relic formerly exposed at the church of Vendôme; a beautiful treatise on the Catholic doctrine touching the veneration of relics, and the abuses of the same.—9. "Sur l'Exposition du très Saint Sacrément;" in this work the discipline of the Church relative to the reservation and veneration of the blessed Eucharist, from the earliest ages down to the last century, is fully described, with the form and materials of the various vessels used for this sacred purpose; a work admirably calculated to set forth the sanctity and majesty of this most holy sacrament, and the antiquity of the Catholic doctrine touching the blessed Eucharist.—10. "Sur un Inscription dans une Eglise de Rheims en honneur de St. François;" a censure on an extravagant inscription set up by a Franciscan in a church at Rheims in honour of St. Francis (afterwards defaced by order of the archbishop), with an exposition of Catholic doctrine relative to the veneration and invocation of saints.

Those who are thoroughly acquainted with the works of this holy and learned writer, must be well instructed in ecclesiastical antiquity; for so great was his erudition and research, that he appears to have examined every source of information on this all-important subject. His works are now exceedingly scarce, for although approved of by the holy see, he was too sincere a writer, and fearless exposer of abuses for the corrupt age in which he lived. Acing on that grand principle expressed in these words,—" falsitas non debet tolerari sub velamine pietatis,"—he became one of the greatest witnesses of Catholic truth against the innovation of revived Paganism and Protestant error.

OF THE FONT.

On proceeding through the southern porch, and entering the church, the first object that arrests our attention is the font. Nor is its position so near the entrance without a sufficient reason. We have previously remarked that the exorcisms of baptism were performed in the porch; the priest then leads the catechumen, not yet regenerated by the waters of baptism, into the church, but far removed from the seat of the holy mysteries, the chancel; nor is he allowed *to approach the sanctuary till the all-important sacrament of baptism has been administered to him.* *

The font may be made either of stone or lead, sufficiently large to admit of immersion, with a wooden cover secured by a lock, to protect the baptismal water from any profanation. These covers were occasionally carried up with canopies and pinnacles to a great height, either suspended from the roof by a counterweight, or a portion of the tabernacle work made to open on the side.†

The new fonts at St. Mary's, Derby, St. Chad's, Birmingham, and Stafford, have covers of this description, surmounted by the appropriate emblem of a dove descending with rays. The font of St. Giles's, Cheadle, will stand within an enclosed baptistry at the western end of the south aisle, and will be furnished with a richly floreated canopy of the decorated period. When the importance of the holy sacrament of baptism, and necessity of administering it with becoming solemnity is considered, it would seem almost impossible that any Catholic church should be unprovided with a regular font. It is a lamentable fact, however, that this most essential piece of church furniture is seldom to be found in modern Catholic churches,—a jug and basin, such as might be used by puritans and fanatics, being often the only substitute, and these in places where silver tea services are being subscribed for the clergyman. But the poorest church should be provided with a regular stone font, and as it is possible to erect one under £10, the expense cannot be an obstacle to their general

* How often in these days of decayed discipline is the whole baptismal service performed within the sanctuary, destroying all the mystical illusions of the ancient arrangement, and admitting a soul under the curse of original sin, at once into the holy of holies. This, among other departures from ancient usages, has arisen in a great measure from the impracticability of following ancient rites in the modern conventicles built for Catholic worship.

† At Sudbury church, Suffolk, Selby church, Lincolnshire, Fosdyke church, Lincolnshire, and St. Peter's, Norwich, are fine examples of canopied covered fonts. The latter is peculiarly beautiful in its design.

restoration. Each of the churches engraved in this article is provided with fonts, canonically placed, corresponding in style and ornament to that of the building, and for the most part these churches have been completed for considerably less sums than the plastered and cemented assembly-rooms raised for Catholic worship in later times, which are deficient in every requisite for the sacred purpose for which they have been erected.

OF THE NAVE AND AISLES.

These form the portion of the edifice in which the faithful assist during the celebration of the holy mysteries. Nave is undoubtedly derived from the word *navis*, or ship, a figure often used with reference to the church. Aisle is derived from the French, and signifies wing or side, and can be only applied with propriety to the lateral portions of the building. Middle aisle is a contradiction of terms; side aisle becomes tautology. In the ancient arrangement of the faithful, the men were placed in the upper part of the nave, and the women behind at the lower end; but, by the custom of later times, the women were placed on the gospel side, and the men on the epistle. The appropriation of particular seats and distinction of places was strictly forbidden among the two classes.*
Seats were used in the *parochial* churches in England from a very early period, and many of these remain tolerably perfect at the present time. They were very low, and wide apart, for the greater convenience of kneeling, open at both ends, and sometimes most beautifully ornamented with carving.†
The pulpit should be placed in some convenient part of the nave, either against a pillar, or by the chancel arch. The ancient churches were generally provided with a pulpit of wood or stone, many fine examples of which are yet to be

---

* By a decree of the synod of the diocese of Exeter in 1284, no one should claim any seat in a church; but whoever first entered a church for the purpose devotion, might choose at his pleasure a place for praying.
† At Little Walsingham church, Norfolk, the whole of the ancient seats remain quite perfect; the backs are enriched with perforated tracery of varied design, and the ends are carried up into foliated finials.
On the seats of Warksworth church, Oxon, the creed is carved in a string course round the backs, and on the ends a representation of the Annunciation of our blessed Lady, and other mysteries, with the pious donor of the seats represented kneeling at prayer, with a scroll and a scripture.
The lords of the manor had occasionally a sort of pew, like a chantry chapel, of which there is a fine example at Lavenham church, Suffolk, and the patron of the church was usually permitted to sit within the chancel; but both these customs may be considered as departures from pure discipline.

found. It is to be remarked that the pulpits were far different from the cumbrous rostrums used for the purpose in the present day, and we need hardly observe that the monstrosity of a reading-desk is a pure Protestant introduction. In the view of the nave of Southport church, as well as Cheadle, it will be seen that the pulpits are fashioned precisely on the old models, corbeled out, and ascended by the rood stairs, and not so large as to form a prominent feature.

At the eastern end of the nave, over the great chancel arch, the Doom or Last Judgment was usually depicted. The reason for placing this awful and certain event so conspicuously before the people is too obvious to need any comment. Most of these edifying paintings were defaced, under Edward the Sixth, as superstitious, but one has been newly discovered at Coventry, which, although very late and coarse in execution, is exceedingly curious.

At the eastern end of the aisles should be small altars; that on the southern side was usually dedicated in honour of our blessed Lady.* These altars should be protected by open screens enclosing chapels, called percloses. There are many remains of such screens and enclosures in old parish churches, but the altars have been invariably destroyed.

OF THE CHANCEL SCREEN, ROOD, AND ROOD LOFT.†

From the earliest ages there has been a separation between priest and people, between the sacrifice and the worshippers, in every church. They have been various in materials, in construction, and in arrangement, but have always existed in some form or other.‡ In parish churches, these screens were generally built of wood, and consisted of open tracery panels,

---

* It may be proper in this place to notice a very common error, of speaking of churches and altars as being dedicated *to* such a saint. The Church has never sanctioned the dedication of a church to *any* saint; they *are all dedicated to God*, (but according to a most ancient and laudable custom), *in honour* of certain saints, by whose names they are distinguished.

† It is worthy of remark that the first rood erected in England since their destruction by act of Parliament, was set up in the private chapel of Ambrose Lisle Phillipps, Esq. of Grace Dieu Manor, a zealous restorer of Anglo-Catholic antiquity. In this chapel most solemn service is performed on Sundays and festivals, the Gradual chaunted from the Lettern, and the whole office sung by men and choristers in the devotional and sublime plain chant, the only music sanctioned by the Church.

‡ In a continuation of this article, it is proposed to enter fully into the history of rood lofts, when describing the arrangements of cathedral and conventual churches, where they were used for more solemn purposes than in the parochial ones.

from about three feet from the floor, with an entrance capable
of being closed by doors with open panels; their height varies
from eight to fifteen feet, according to the scale of the church,
and their breadth extends the whole width of the chancel
arch, or in a choir church the breadth of the nave.* The
carving on many of these screens is most varied and elaborate,
and independent of the important mystical reasons for their
erection, they form one of the most beautiful features of the
ancient churches, and impart much additional effect to the
chancel when seen through them. Like other parts of the
interior, these screens were enriched with painting and
gilding, and on the lower panels it was customary to figure
saints and martyrs on diapered grounds.†

THE ROOD LOFT

Was a gallery partly resting on the screen, and running across
the whole of its width, frequently supported on arched canopied
work rising from the screen. The ascent to these lofts in
large churches was usually by two staircases; but in small
parish churches one was considered sufficient. It was carried
up either in the pier of the chancel arch, or in a small turret
outside the wall, and communicated with the rood loft by
a narrow gallery, of which there are several examples at
Stamford. We will not refer in this place to the use of these
rood lofts or *jubés* in large buildings, but confine our remarks
to their purpose in parochial churches.

Their first and most important use was to serve as an elevated place from whence the holy Gospel might be sung to
the people, according to a most ancient and universal practice
of the Church, of singing the holy Gospel from a raised place.‡

---

* Many of the large parish churches had regular choirs with stalls, as at St.
Peter's, Norwich; St. Mary's, Coventry; Long Melford church, Suffolk. In
these churches there were no arched divisions between the nave and choir, the
separations consisted only in the screen and rood loft over it.

† It is not unusual for modern artists to decry the ancient system of decorating churches with much painting; but those who raise these objections seem to
forget that what is technically termed keeping, is quite as requisite *in a building*
as *in a picture.* The moment colour is introduced in the windows, the rest of
the ornaments must correspond,—the ceiling, the floor, all must bear their part
in the general effect. A stained window in a white church is a mere spot, which,
by its richness, serves only to exhibit in a more striking manner the poverty of
the rest of the building.

In the old churches, the azure and gilt ceiling, the encrusted tiles of various
colours, the frescoes on the walls, the heraldic charges, the costly hangings of
the altars, the variegated glass, all harmonized together, and formed a splendid
whole, which can only be produced by the combined effect of all these details;—
omit any of them, and the unity of the design is destroyed.

‡ The ambones of the ancient Basilicas served for this purpose.

2. The whole of the Passion of our Lord was sung from the rood loft;* the Gradual and other parts of the mass were chanted, and small organs fixed on the rood loft.

3. Lessons were read from the rood loft in many churches, and holy days announced to the people.

4. On great feasts, lights were set up in the rood loft, and at Christmas and Whitsuntide it was decorated with boughs and evergreens. Immediately in the centre of the loft stood the rood or cross, with an image of our Lord crucified, and on either side the blessed Virgin and St. John. The cross was usually floreated,† and terminated at the extremities with quatrefoils, and emblems of the four evangelists; on the reverse of which the four doctors of the Church were not unfrequently carved.

To illustrate these screens and roods, we have figured various churches, either completed or in course of erection.

The first is the interior of St. Mary's, Southport,‡ (see Pl. X)

---

* "There was a fair rood loft, with the rood, Mary and John of every side, and with a fair pair of organs standing thereby; which loft extended all the breadth of the church. And on Good Friday, a priest there standing by the rood sang the Passion."—*Records of Long Melford Church.*

† It is worthy of remark, that the ancient crosses were all richly decorated, in order to set forth that the very instrument on which our divine Redeemer suffered an ignominious death had become the emblem of his glorious victory over sin and its punishment, and should therefore be ornamented as the figure of this great triumph and our redemption. The old mystical school of Christian painters invariably figure our Lord with *extended* arms on the cross,—not through ignorance of drawing, but to represent the Son of God embracing the sins of the whole world. Not unfrequently, too, do we find the figure of the blessed Virgin and St. John much smaller in proportion than that of our Lord. This was done solely for the purpose of expressing the majesty of God. If we only examine attentively the productions of the ages of faith, we shall find that they convey a profound mystical meaning; and many conventional modes of representing the sacred things, that have been described by modern upstarts as proofs of barbarous ignorance, are in fact the most convincing proofs of the piety and wisdom of those who produced them. Their productions are addressed to the *understanding*, not merely *to the eye*, and there is more edification to be gained from a Saxon cross, with its enamelled emblems, than in all the anatomical crucifixions of modern times, in which the whole efforts of the artists appear to have been directed towards producing a distorted representation of a dying malefactor, instead of the overpowering sacrifice of the Son of God. It *is much safer to treat those holy mysteries in a conventional and emblematic manner, than to aim at unattainable realities.* The celebrated Crucifixion of Rubens is painful, not to say disgusting; certainly not edifying. The Christian artists have enveloped every incident of our Lord's life and suffering with a spiritual and mystical form, calculated to impress the mind with deep veneration for the sacred truths they represent. Sooner or later Christian art will be appreciated as it deserves, and the semipagan representations of the last three centuries, (in which *sacred things have only been made a vehicle to exhibit the lascivious art of modern painters,* who scrupled not, when professing to embody the blessed Virgin herself, to select their models from the profligate and abandoned) will sink into the abhorrence they deserve.

‡ This building, which possesses every requisite for a parochial church,—

of which an exterior prospect is given on Plate IX. This church being exceedingly small, the chancel screen is merely surmounted by the rood without any loft; the screen as well as the cross are diapered and painted from ancient examples. The second is the name of St. Alban's church at Macclesfield, just completed. (See Pl. XI.) Here is a regular rood loft, ascended from a staircase in the southern chapel, twelve feet from the chancel floor, surmounted by a cross, with the usual accompaniments. The images of this rood are of ancient German work of the 15th century, and were removed from their original position during the invasion of the French.

The eastern window seen through the screen, is filled with rich stained glass, given by John the present Earl of Shrewsbury, a great benefactor to this church. In the tracery are angels, habited in albs, bearing scrolls with various scriptures, and shields with emblems of our Lord's passion; the Talbot lion is also introduced in the quatrefoils.

In the centre light is an image of St. Alban, protomartyr of England, standing under a canopy; the other lights are filled with quarried glass interspersed with emblems.

The sedilia and dossell of altar are of stone; this latter consists of a row of canopied niches, richly carved and filled with images of apostles.

On either side of the screen hang two damask curtains of crimson, and a frontal is suspended before the altar. At the end of the southern aisle is a chapel dedicated in honour of our blessed Lady, and divided off by an open screen in a stone arch. The church is capable accommodating from eight hundred to one thousand persons, and its total cost, with the tower complete, will be about 6000*l.*

The third example is a transverse section of the great church now erecting in St. George's Fields, London (see Pl. XII); shewing the great rood screen and loft,[*] with the screens and chapels terminating the aisles. The width of the nave is 28 feet, the aisles 18 feet; and the length, exclusive of chancel and tower, 160 feet; the chancel will be 43 feet in depth, with stalls on either side, and the side chapel 20. The great chancel window will be filled with the genealogy of our Lord, on the root of Jesse, in rich stained glass, the gift of

---

nave, chancel, rood and screen, stone altar, sedilia, sacrarium, southern porch, stoups for hallowed water, font and cover, bell, turret, organ and loft, open seats, stone pulpit, stained glass, and is capable of holding 300 persons,—has been erected for 1500*l.*, including every expense.

[*] This rood loft is ascended by two staircases, which will be seen by reference to the plan. These staircases terminate outside in pinnacled turrets.

the Earl of Shrewsbury; and every detail of the building will be carried out in the style of the time of Edward III. A great part of the church will be left open, without seats, and three thousand persons may be easily accommodated on the floor. No galleries of any description will be introduced, but all the internal arrangements will be strictly a revival of those which were anciently to be found in the large parochial churches of England.

The fourth example is a section of a small, simple, but complete church, lately erected at Dudley,* (see Pl. VII)

---

* This church, which is calculated to hold six hundred parishioners in the nave and aisles, stands on a declivity on the south-east side of the castle. The sacred edifice is surrounded by a cemetery, in which a stone cross is erected, and at the western extremity of the land a small simple parsonage house is now erecting, to which will be added a school.

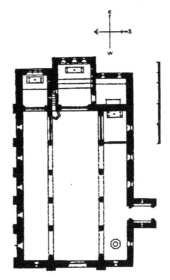

ST. MARY'S, DUDLEY.

The references of the plan will shew that this church possesses every canonical requisite for its sacred purpose. The eastern windows are filled with stained glass of a mosaic pattern, interspersed with emblems and subjects: in the chancel are ancient images of our blessed Lady and St. Thomas of Canterbury; while the vestry is furnished with a complete set of sacred vessels and ornaments, of which the following is an inventory:—a processional cross, wit Mary and John; a

which will be dedicated in honour of our blessed Lady and that glorious martyr St. Thomas of Canterbury.

The fifth example is a view of the interior of St. Giles's, Cheadle, now erecting, (see Pl. XIII.) Over the great chancel arch will be seen the Doom painted on the wall; at the eastern end of the aisles are screens inclosing chapels with altars; the pulpit is placed on the gospel side of the chancel arch; the rood loft is supported by arched ribs over the screen, and is ascended by the staircase which leads to the pulpit.

This church, which is being raised at the sole charge of the Earl of Shrewsbury, will be a perfect revival of an English parish church of the time of Edward I; decidedly the best period of pointed architecture. The floor will be entirely laid with encrusted tiles; every window will be filled with painted glass; and the smallest ornaments will be finished with scrupulous regard to correctness of style. We refer the reader to the plan, and west elevation of this church, at Plates I & IV; also to the engraving of the chancel, at Plate XVI.

OF THE CHANCEL.

We now come to the place of sacrifice, the most sacred part of the edifice; and well may we exclaim, when passing beneath the image of our Redeemer, and through the separating screen of mystic import, into this holy place, "O quam terribile est locus iste." The ancient chancels were truly solemn and impressive, and those who have souls to appreciate the intentions of the old Catholic builders, must be edified with their wisdom and propriety, in keeping the seat of the holy mysteries at a reverential distance from the people, and in setting forth the dignity and privilege of the priestly office, by separating the ministers who are offering up the holy sacrifice from the worshippers. "Cancellos qui circumstant altaria presbyteri tantum et clerici ingrediantur: neque ullo modo ibi seculares maxime dum divina mysteria celebrantur admitti debent," says Merati in his Commentaries on Gavantius;

---

holy water vat and asperge for processions; a silver gilt chalice, with an enamelled foot of the thirteenth century; a ditto ciborium, with an ancient foot; a pair of cruets; a copper gilt thurible; a pair of triple candlesticks, for the high altar; a pair of small ditto, for chapel of blessed Virgin; a small tower, for the reservation of the blessed sacrament; a basin and pricket, for a light for the high altar; a set of vestments, of each colour; an apparelled alb and a plain alb; a frontal for the high altar; a ditto of velvet and gold embroidery, for the altar of Lady chapel; a set of altar cloths; corporal cases; an ornamented cross, for the altar. The whole cost of this building, including all the abovementioned ornaments, vestments, stained glass, architect's charges, and every expense, was 3165l.; which fully proves for how moderate a sum a real Catholic church may be erected, if the funds are judiciously employed.

and if the mysteries of religion are to be held in reverence by the people, the old traditions and observances must be restored and enforced. Of all lamentable innovations, the wretched recesses substituted for chancels in modern churches are the most horrible: the altars are not only crowded up by seats, but *actually overlooked,* and the sanctity of the sacrifice itself partially disregarded. If these barriers round the holy place were considered necessary in days of faith, how doubly are they wanted at the present time! Churches are now built on exactly the same principle as theatres, to hold the greatest number of persons in the smallest possible space; and the only difference in the arrangement is the substitution of an altar and altarpiece for the proscenium and drop-scene. What is the consequence? Catholic feeling is soon lost among the people: there is not even a corner for holy meditation or retired reflection; they are filled and emptied like dissenting meeting-houses. The worshipper is either in a mob, or in the odious and Protestant distinction of a private pew. The humblest old Catholic church, mutilated as it may have been, is ten times more impressive than these staring assembly-rooms, which some persons, in these days, consider the most appropriate erections for Catholic worship.

The first view of a chancel is that of St. Wilfred's church, now erecting at Hulme, near Manchester.* (See Pl. XIV.) Here the altar is of a very early form, the front being open, and the top slab supported by stone pillars, three in number, gilt and painted. Under the altar is deposited a shrine† with relics, round which a velvet curtain is occasionally drawn.‡

---

* This church, as may be seen on reference to the plan, (Pl. III) consists of a nave and two aisles, with a tower at north-western corner. Eight hundred persons may be seated in the body of the church, besides a considerable open space left at the lower end. The eastern chapels are divided off, by open screens, from the aisles, and also from the side arches of chancel. The font is placed near the southern porch. At the south-eastern end is the sacristy, communicating from the chapel of the blessed Virgin, and fitted up with almeries and all requisite fittings. Attached to the church, by a small cloister, is a large and commodious parsonage house for the residence of the clergy. The church, house, enclosure of ground, and all internal fittings, as well as every essential ornament for divine service, also architect's commission, will not exceed the cost of £5000.

† Shrines were very frequently placed under the ancient altars; a custom which probably originated from celebrating on the tombs of martyrs. Under the high altar of Bayeux Cathedral, previous to the great revolution, were five shrines of silver gilt; and the frontal of the altar, which was also of silver parcel gilt, was made to open on certain great festivals, like two doors, to show the reliquaries.

‡ The curtains hung in front of shrines, under the ancient altars, are undoubtedly the origin of antependiums or frontals, for we find examples of such curtains in the earliest records of altars, which were made to run on a rod fixed immediately under the slab.

c 2

Behind the altar is a succession of lancet stone arches, the panels
of which are richly diapered and ornamented with Christian
emblems : the painted window over them, as well as the cathe-
rine-wheel window at the top, will be filled with mosaic stained
glass, with subjects occasionally introduced in small medallion
and quarterfoils. The sedilia and sacrarium are of stone, and
taken out of the thickness of the wall. The eastern wall of the
chancel is four feet in thickness, and the deep splays of the window will be enriched with painted scrolls, in the early style.

A second example is the chancel of St. Mary's, Uttoxeter,
(see Pl. XV,) a small church recently completed. Here the
altar is of the ancient triptic form,* with doors to be closed
during the latter part of Lent; in the centre is a picture of
our blessed Lady, copied from one of the true Christian school;
on either side are two damask curtains, hung on rods, between
which and the altar stand two large candlesticks to hold
tapers, lit from the Sanctus to the Communion. The front of
the altar is of stone, gilt and painted, with the Crucifixion in
the centre, and the emblems of evangelists in the angles. The
rood is here supported by an arch beam, with angels bearing
tapers. Before the altar hang three lamps, one of which is
kept constantly burning, and the other two lit during the
celebration of mass. The sedilia are three stone recesses, divided by shafts, and diapered at the back; opposite to these
is an arched recess, for the sepulchre in holy week. The
three lancet windows over the altar are filled with stained
glass, of an early character, and at the western end is a rose
window, very richly glazed.

---

* These triptics were usually placed over altars in the Continental churches;
as at Cologne Cathedral, and several of the German churches, particularly those
of St. Lawrence and St. Sebald's ; at Nuremberg they will remain in the most
perfect state. The old form remained in use long after the cessation of pointed
architecture in these countries, and even down to the time of Rubens. There is
a most splendid enamelled triptic of the twelfth century in the Museum of St.
Mary's College, Oscott, and the form was commonly employed for all religious
pictures, and not unfrequently in wood and ivory carvings. In carved triptics
for altars, the sculptured figures are placed immediately over the altar, and the
doors are decorated with painting only ; in these latter, the pious donors were
frequently painted kneeling at prayer, with their patron saints standing behind
them. Although these triptics were not very generally placed over altars in
England, still we have instances of their having been used at Melford Church,
Suffolk. " At the back of the high altar was set up the story of Christ's Passion,
fair gilt and beautifully set forth to cover and keep clean all which *were very fair
painted boards, made to shut to, which were opened upon high and solemn feast
days.* In Durham Cathedral there was also, standing against the wall, a most
curious fine table, with *two leaves to open and shut,* comprehending the Passion of
our Lord Jesus Christ, richly cut and fine lively colours, which table was always
locked up but on principal days."—*Rites of Durham.*

The third example is the church of St. Giles, Cheadle, (see Pl. XVI.) The whole of the ceiling will be richly painted with azure panels and gilt stars; the string course supporting the ribs is charged with shields and inscriptions. In the stone niches on each side of the window are images of our blessed Lady and St. Giles. Over the altar is a stone screen of tabernacle work, with images of apostles, and our blessed Lord in the centre; on the altar are a pair of candlesticks and an altar cross, with rich hangings, and frontals of various colours. The sacrarium is here formed by a fourth compartment added to the sedilia, which are surmounted by gables and pinnacles, richly foliated. On the north side is an arched tomb for the sepulchre; and the floor will be paved with encrusted tiles, charged with armorial bearings.

OF THE SEDILIA.

On the epistle side of the altar, either on the ascent of the steps leading up to the altar, or on the level pavement, three arched recesses are invariably built, for the officiating priest, deacon, and sub-deacon to sit in during the chanting of the Gloria and Credo.* These sometimes consist of three simple arches, supported either by corbels or shafts; and occasionally we find them richly decorated with canopies and groining. In parochial churches they are generally built of stone, but in the large cathedrals and abbeys they were sometimes of wood. The four arches on the epistle side of the sanctuary of Westminster Abbey, commonly called King Sebert's Tomb, are in fact the sedilia of that church. It is not at all unusual to find a fourth stall, for the assistant priest, in great churches.

Among the most beautiful examples of sedilia, remaining in England, we may mention those at Exeter Cathedral, Southwell Minster, Ripon Cathedral, Tewkesbury Abbey, Adderbury and Dorchester Church, Oxfordshire; Bishopston, Wilts; St. Mary's, Oxford; and Stockport Church, near Manchester. These arched recesses have been frequently termed confessionals, by persons unacquainted with ecclesiastical antiquities, but we need hardly observe, without the slightest foundation. The misrepresentations made on this subject, by persons who shew cathedral and other churches, is most extraordinary. Any perforation in a wall, whether it be to admit light or air, or to command a view of the high altar from some chapel, is invariably called a confessional; even the chantry chapel of the Beauchamp family, at Warwick, is so designated.

* The priest anciently sat during the Epistle in solemn masses.

It is established even beyond a doubt, that there were no confessionals in our ancient churches answering in form to those we see generally used on the Continent: confessions were heard in the church by priests, seated in chairs, whilst the penitent knelt beside them; this may be seen figured in many ancient illuminations. Even on the Continent no confessional can be found older than the last century, and this is alone sufficient to prove the extreme absurdity of the stories circulated by vergers and others, respecting confessionals in the ancient churches.

OF THE SACRARIUM.

Between the sedilia and the eastern wall of the chancel, a small niche was built, in the bottom of which a basin was hollowed out of the stone, with a pipe leading into the ground; over this was a small projecting stone shelf for the altar cruets. The most ancient sacrariums had two basins, as may be seen by those at Salisbury and Lincoln Cathedrals; one for the ablutions of the hands at the *Lavabo,* and the other for the ablutions of the chalice, which were not received by the priest, as at present, but poured down the sacrarium.

The old rubric respecting the Lavabo is as follows: " Eat ad Piscinam dicens Lavabo: reversus dicit In spiritu humilitatis, &c." This is found in many ancient Missals. When the rubric for receiving the ablutions of the chalice became generally observed, the second basin was disused, and the late sacrariums have one basin only.

OF THE ARCH ON THE GOSPEL SIDE OF THE CHANCEL.

On the gospel side of the chancel, and nearly opposite the sedilia, we generally find an arch forming a recess and canopy to an altar tomb: this was used as a sepulchre for the reservation of the blessed sacrament, from Maunday Thursday till Easter Sunday morning, which was anciently practised in the Sarum rite.* There is frequent allusion to this in the wills of pious persons, who desired to have their tombs so built that

* This ceremony is quite distinct from the reservation of the blessed sacrament from Maundy Thursday for the mass of Good Friday, on which day the Church does not allow of any consecration. The blessed sacrament, so reserved, is watched all night, and hence the name of sepulchre has been most improperly given to the chapel in which it is solemnly kept; but there is not the slightest correspondence as to time in the present watching, which takes place on Maundy Thursday night, when our Lord did not suffer till Friday. The watching, according to the Sarum rite, commenced on Good Friday, and continued till Easter-day, early in the morning, when the blessed sacrament was brought forth from the sepulchre with solemn procession. This ceremony was also practised in France and some of the Northern Countries, but there is no trace of it in the Roman rite.

they might serve for the sepulchre; that when men came to pay their devotions to our Lord's body, at that holy time, they might be moved to pray for the repose of their souls. At Long Melford Church, Suffolk, the tomb of one of the Clopton family served for this purpose. Some of the finest examples of stone sepulchres are at Eckington Church, Lincolnshire, and Hawton Church, Nottinghamshire; these are richly decorated in the style of Edward III, with representations of the Roman soldiers asleep, and other appropriate imagery.

OF THE REVESTRY OR SACRISTRY.

It is a remarkable fact, that while sacristies in most cathedral churches were placed on the south side, in parish churches they were generally built on a contrary one. We are quite at a loss to assign any reason for this; as a southern aspect would be most suitable to prevent damp or injury to the vestments. Although most of the ancient fittings of church vestries have been destroyed, we may occasionally find a few old almeries remaining,* but not one vestige of the rich furniture and sacred vessels with which they were filled.†

OF THE ALTAR.

During the first seven centuries of the Church, altars were made indifferently of wood, stone, and metal.‡

Doubtless, during the early persecutions of the Christians,

---

* At Adderbury Church, Oxon; Long Melford, Suffolk; Wells Cathedral; York Minster; in a side Chapel at Carlisle Cathedral·

† In *Lyndwood's Provinciale* we find the following inventory of ornaments required in every parish church:—"Legendam, Antiphonarium, Graduale, Psalterium, Troperium Ordinale, Missale, Manuale, Calicem, Vestimentum Principale cum casula, Dalmatica, Tunica, et cum capa in Choro, cum omnibus suis appendiciis; Frontale ad Magnum altare cum tribus Tuellis, tria supepellicia, unum Rochetum, Crucem Processionalem, Crucem pro Mortuis, Thuribulum, Lucernam, Tintinabulum ad deferendum coram corpore Christi in visitatione infirmorum, Pyxidem pro corpore Christi, honestum Velum Quadragesimale, Campanis cum chordis, Feretrum pro defunctis, Vas pro Aqua Benedicta, Osculatorium Candelabrum pro cereo paschali, Fontem cum serura, Imagines in ecclesia, Imaginem principalem in cancello."

To these may be added a lettern, or brass eagle, to stand in the chancel or choir, for the antiphonarium and graduals. A most beautiful brass lettern of this description was lying, only two years since, in a corner of the tower of St. Martin's Church, Salisbury, utterly neglected, and most probably considered a piece of old Popish lumber.

‡ The Emperor Constantine made seven altars of silver in the Church called after his name, and that of St. John Lateran, which weighed 260lbs. Sixtus III. gave an altar of pure silver, which weighed 300lbs., to the Church of St. Mary Major. St. Athanasius speaks of an altar of wood which the Arians burnt. St. Sylvester I. is said to have forbidden all wooden altars, except that in St. John Lateran's (yet existing), because St. Peter had used it.

altars were generally of wood, as being more portable, and better adapted to the necessities of the time.

Since the seventh century, the use of stone altars in the Church has not only been universal, but obligatory, insomuch that no priest would be allowed to celebrate without, at least, a portable altar stone.

The use of portable altar stones is very ancient; Jonas, monk of St. Wandrille, is the first writer by whom they are mentioned, in the Life of St. Wulfran, where it is recorded that this holy man carried a consecrated stone with him to celebrate on it in his travels, and afterwards gave it to the Abbey of St. Wandrille. "Altare consecratum in quatuor angulorum locis et in medio; reliquias continens sanctorum in modum clypie etc." Portable altars are also mentioned by the venerable Bede, when speaking of the two Ewalds: "Cotidie Sacrificium Deo victimæ salutaris offerebant, habentes secum vascula ad *tabulam altaris* vice dedicatam."

The use of portable altars was however confined to journeys and cases of *great necessity; they were neither meant nor suffered to replace or supersede the stone altars which are required by the Church, and which should be erected in every permanent religious edifice.*

The most ancient altars were open underneath, and supported by pillars: every altar should be sufficiently detached from the wall to admit of passing behind it. The ceremonies of the consecration of an altar, in the Roman pontificial, require the bishop to pass round the altar various times. "*Pontifex circuit septies tabulam altaris aspergens eam et stipitem de aqua ultimo per eum benedicta, &c.*" That the most ancient altars were all detached from the wall is evident by the language of the early ecclesiastical writers.

Excepting during the celebration of the holy sacrifice, neither cross nor candlesticks were formerly left on the altar, but were removed immediately after mass. The book of the holy gospels was alone kept on the altar.*

---

* It does not appear that any cross was placed *on* the altar before the tenth century. The crosses were fixed *over* the altars, and on the ciboriums or canopies, by which they were surmounted: neither was the image of our Lord crucified attached to these crosses. The crucifix was, however, set up on the rood as early as the eighth century; and it was probably on account of the blessed sacrament lying on the altar that the ancient Churchmen would not suffer an image in the presence of the reality; even the present rubric speaks only of a cross on the altar, *crux in medio.* No lights were placed on the altar before the tenth century, and even down to the French revolution, many of the most ancient and illustrious Churches of that country did not admit of any

Before the twelfth century flowers were not suffered on altars, although the custom of hanging garlands and branches, on great feasts, to decorate the church, is of the highest antiquity: even the whole pavement was not unfrequently sprinkled with flowers and aromatic herbs.

It does not appear that even the relics of saints were allowed *on* the ancient altars, especially in presence of the blessed sacrament. Shrines, with relics, were placed under the altars, and on a beam over the altar.*

The blessed srcrament was never reserved at the high altar of a church excepting in a golden dove, or pyx, suspended over the altar.† Mass was never celebrated formerly in presence of the blessed sacrament, even when enclosed in a tower or tabernacle.

---

lights *on the high* altars, but placed round them. Wax tapers were lit in large candlesticks on each side of the altar, hung on prickets in basins before it, and in coronas, or large circles of lights, in the choir, on the *jubé* or rood loft, before images, and near shrines, but not on the altars.

* This was the case at Canterbury cathedral.

+ The custom of reserving the blessed sacrament in gold and silver doves is very ancient. Perpetuus VI., archbishop of Tours, left a silver dove to a priest, Amalarius, for this purpose, " Peristerium et columbam argenteam ad reposito- rium." In the customs of the monastery of Cluny, a dove of gold is mentioned suspended over the altar in which the blessed Eucharist was reserved. This custom was retained till the revolution at the Church of St. Julien d'Angers, St. Maur des Fosses, near Paris, at St. Paul, Sens, at St. Lierche, near Chartres.

" The blessed sacrament was suspended in a pyx, over the high altar at Dur- ham abbey. Within the quire, over the high altar, hung a rich and most sump- tuous canopy for the blessed sacrament to hang within it, which had two irons fastened in the French trieme very finely gilt; which held the canopy over the midst of the said high altar that the pyx hung in, that it could neither move nor stir; whereon stood a pelican all of silver, upon the height of the said canopy, very finely gilt, giving her blood to her young ones, in token that Christ gave his blood for the sins of the world; and it was goodly to behold for the blessed sacrament to hang in. And the pyx wherein the blessed sacrament hung was of most pure gold, curiously wrought of goldsmith's work; and the white cloth that hung over the pyx was of very fine lawn, all embroidered and wrought about with gold and red silk, and four great round knobs of gold curiously wrought, with great tassels of gold and red silk hung at them; and the crook that hung within the cloth that the pyx hung upon was of gold, and the cord which drew it up and down was made of fine strong silk."—*Rites of Durham.*

" French Churches in which the blessed sacrament was suspended in a pyx, before the revolution : St. Maurile d'Angers, Cathedrale de Tours, St. Martin de Tours, St. Siran en Brenne, St. Etienne de Dijon, St. Sieur de Dijon, St. Etienne de Sens, Cathedrale de St. Julien, Mons, Nôtre Dame de Chartres, Nôtre Dame de Paris, St. Ouen de Rouen."—*De Moleon, Voyage Liturgique.*

Matthew Paris speaks of the blessed sacrament being suspended over the high altar of the cathedral Church of Lincoln.—Ad an. 1140. *In Stephano.*

It was doubtless in allusion to these doves that St. John Chrysostom says, the sacred body of our Lord in the Churches is not enveloped in linen, as in the cradle, but in the form of the *Holy Spirit.*

The present tabernacles are by no means ancient, nor did they exist in the old English churches.

The blessed sacrament was either reserved as above-mentioned, in a dove, or a small metal tabernacle in the form of a tower. These towers* are frequently mentioned by old ecclesiastical writers.

St. Renis, archbishop of Rheims, ordered by his will that his successor should make a tabernacle in the form of a tower, weighing ten marks of gold.

Fortunat, bishop of Poitiers, eulogised St. Felix, archbishop of Bruges, for causing a precious tower of gold to be made for the sacred body of our Lord.

Frodoard, priest of Rheims, relates that Landon, archbishop of that see, placed a tower of gold on an altar of the cathedral, for the reservation of the blessed Eucharist.

The fronts of altars were ornamented by antependiums of rich stuffs, of various colours, richly embroidered on panels of silver, parcel gilt and enamelled, and even occasionally set with precious stones. In the inventory of the ornaments of Lincoln Minster, given in Dugdale's *Monasticon*, we find above thirty frontals of velvet and silk, some exceedingly costly. "Imprimis, a costly cloth of gold for the high altar, for principal feasts, having in the midst images of the Holy Trinity, of our Lady, four evangelists, four angels about the Trinity, with patriarchs, prophets, apostles, virgins, with many other images; having a frontlet of cloth of gold, with Scriptures, and a linen cloth infixed to the same, *ex dono Ducis Lancastriæ.*"

There were frontals of precious metals at Rheims Cathedral,

---

* The new Churches of St. Ann's, Keighley; St. Mary's, Uttoxeter; St Wilfred's, Manchester; St. Alban's, Macclesfield; St. Chad's, Birmingham; St. Mary's, Dudley, are all furnished with these towers, instead of modern tabernacles. There is but little doubt that in many of our small parish Churches the blessed Eucharist was reserved in a strong almery, on the gospel side of the chancel. In Germany and Belgium several magnificent tabernacles of stone, carried up to a prodigious height, and equisitely wrought, remain on the gospel side of the choir. Those at St. Lawrence's Church, Nuremberg, and the Cathedral at Ulm, executed by Adam Kraft, are the most beautiful. A tabernacle of this description is still used for its original sacred purpose in the Cathedral of Louvain; but how long this remnant of ancient practice may remain is most uncertain, for the destroying spirit of novelty has already run riot in this once glorious church. The beautiful triptic, over the high altar, has been pulled down and sold, and a wretched marble mass of columns and cornices erected in its stead; the sedilia *demolished;* the unrivalled brass lectorium sold out of the choir; the altars of the choir screen taken away, and the choir thrown open to the nave; and the glorious tabernacle itself menaced with destruction, on account, forsooth, of its being placed on one side of the Church.

the Abbey of St. Ouen, Rouen; St. Germain des Prés, Paris, St. Mark's, Venice; Bayeux Cathedral, and many other churches.

Round the most ancient altars curtains were hung, and closely drawn from the consecration till the communion; this usage was common to both the eastern and western Churches. St. John Chrysostom bears ample testimony to the former, when he says, " that the sacred host is on the altar, and the victim immolated, and these words are pronounced (*Sancta Sanctis*). When the *curtain and veils* are drawn, it seems as if the heavens themselves were opened and the angels descended." (*Hom.* iii. *in Epist. ad Ephes.*) As for the western Church, we read in the lives of many popes,* that they caused curtains of precious stuffs to be hung round the altars of various churches in Rome.

It does not appear that curtains were ever hung *entirely round* the altars in *England*, but *invariably at the sides*, and sometimes at the back. These were called dossels, and are mentioned in the inventory of St. Osmund's Church, at Old Sarum. A curtain or veil was also hung over the imagery, at back of the altars, during Lent. The side curtains remained in use in England till the destruction of the altars, under Edward VI; and in France, in many of the large churches, till the great revolution.

We have already mentioned that previous to the tenth century candles were not placed upon the altar, and from that period down to the sixteenth century the number was generally restricted to two.† The usual number of six is a comparatively modern usage, even at Rome, and the rubric of the Roman missal only requires two lights during the celebration of the Holy Eucharist: " Super altare collocetur crux in medio et candelabra saltem duo cum candelis accensis hinc et inde in utroque ejus latere."

Every altar should be built of stone: the top slab of one piece with five crosses cut on it—one at each angle and in the

* Sergius I, Gregory III, Adrian I, Leo III, Pascal I, Gregory IV, Sergius II, Leo IV, and Nicholas I. "In circuitu altaris tetravela octo; per altaris circuitum vela de rhodino quatuor quæ sacrum altare circumdant. Contulit in basilica apostolorum cortinam lineam unam, velotyra, serica tria, in circuitu altaris."

† Although only two candlesticks were placed on the altar, these were occasionally made to hold several candles, which were doubtless lit on great festivals. In the inventory of the ornaments of Lincoln: " Item, two condlesticks of silver parcel gilt, standing on great feet, with *six towers* gilded, having one great knob in the midst, and in the height six towers about the bowls, with one pike of silver *on either of them*."

centre; the whole of this stone should be consecrated by the bishop, instead of a portable altar being inserted in it, which should only be tolerated in a case of the greatest necessity. The front of the altar, if solid, should he furnished with, at least, an antependium with appropriate ornaments, and a purple frontal for Lent; but, if means would permit, a complete set of frontals of the five colours should be provided. Three linen cloths are required for covering the altar stone: the first is the cere cloth, waxed all over, and made to fit over the stone exactly; this is never removed. The second of fine linen, plain, the length and width of the stone, to lie over the cere cloth. The third should be sufficiently long to hang down at each end of the altar to the pavement; this should be marked with five crosses, and may be ornamented at the ends with needle-work.

A pair of curtains should be hung on each side of the altar, nearly of the same projection from the wall; these should be varied in colour to that of the festival; but, as means will not generally permit of so doing, crimson for ordinary use, with purple for Lent, will be sufficient.

These curtains should be hung sufficiently high to protect the candles from wind, and reach nearly to the ground.

Nothing but the candlesticks, cross, and a small tower for the reservation of the blessed sacrament, should be placed on the altar.

The screen, or dossell, is the proper position for the images of the saints; their relics may repose beneath the sacrificial stone, the walls may be hung with flowers and wreaths, but the altar should be free and unincumbered for the holy sacrifice. All the ancient discipline that we have quoted tended to this point.

The form and ornaments of altars are not matters of mere whim and caprice, but of antiquity and authority; their purpose is far too sacred to admit of their being made the vehicles of paltry display and meretricious ornament.* Yet every reflecting mind must be both struck and pained with the incongruous decorations of most of the modern altars; the chief

---

* It should always be remembered that the ceremonies of the Church are *realities*, not *representations;* that they are instituted not to *dazzle the eye* but *to honour God.* Altars are not meant to be merely seen by man, but should be erected to meet the all-searching eye of God. The holy of holies, under the old law, in which no man except the high-priest entered, was overlaid with gold;—and should our sanctuary for the reality be less splendid than that of the figure? Surely not. Hence gilding and ornament should not be always *turned towards the people,* nor a showy antependium conceal dirt and neglect.

aim of those who arrange them appears to be merely a great show. All mystical reasons, all ancient discipline,* all dignity and solemnity are utterly lost sight of; everything is over-done. Candlesticks are piled on candlesticks as if arranged for sale; whole rows of flower pots mingled with reliquaries, images, and not unfrequently profane ornaments; festoons of upholsterers' drapery : even distorting and distracting looking-glasses are introduced in this medley display ; the effect of which upon persons who are conversant with ancient discipline and practice it is not easy to describe.

Of all decoration, that of ecclesiastical buildings is the most difficult; to unite *richness* with *severity*, to produce *splendour* without *gaudiness*, and to erect a temple somewhat worthy of the holy sacrifice, is a wonderful effort for the human mind: but when decoration is attempted in honour of the victim there offered—the blessed Sacrament itself—art droops unequal, and genius fails. Who is there that can set forth the glory of God, or add lustre to His majesty? The attempt is almost profane. Hence the ancient churchmen veiled the sacred host in mystery, and, like Moses before the burning bush, bowed themselves to the ground. If the faithful are required to adore in silence, during the elevation of the host, as being too solemn a moment for even the psalmody of praise, " Sileat omnis caro a facie Domini quia consurrexit de habitaculo Sancto suo," what forms can be embodied to honour so great a mystery?

The arrangements sometimes made for this purpose are more calculated to throw ridicule on the solemnity than to raise feelings of inward reverence, and however well meant are not the less objectionable. Lights alone can be considered appro-

---

* The greatest innovation of later times is placing altars *all over a church;* formerly they were strictly confined to the eastern ends, and *all protected by screens* in regular chapels. *The mass is not less holy, adorable, and deserving of respect because it is celebrated at an altar which is not the principal one of the church:* the same reasons which require *that* to be screened off from the people, *apply equally to the others.* Now we not only find many altars without screens in modern churches, but *erected against pillars of the nave,* where a great portion of the people must turn their backs on the sacrifice there offered. The nave is erected *for the faithful,* and not as a place wherein to *celebrate the holy mysteries;* the very fact of altars having been erected in such a position, shews how completely the mystical reasons which regulated the architecture and arrangement of ancient catholic Churches, have been lost sight of; and hence arises the gross irreverence to be witnessed on the Continent during the celebration of masses at these altars, and is another proof of the intimate connexion between the externals of religion and internal effect on the mind.

priate emblems near the blessed Eucharist, for they have ever been used by the Church as marks of honour, and figures of the brightness and glory of God: and even these require much judgment in their distribution, inclining more on the side of humble simplicity than of pretension towards an unattainable end; and (like the painter, who, unable to represent the intense grief of the human mind, covered the visage of his figure), confess our inability to *embody* our veneration for the adorable mystery, and substitute for ornament a veil.

It is proper to remark, that all the altars in the churches of which we have given engravings have been erected and decorated with scrupulous regard to the ancient tradition.

We fear we cannot assert, from the examples which we have brought forward, that the English Catholics, as *a body*, are reviving Catholic architecture, for such is unhappily far from the case at present; but we have brought forward sufficient examples to shew that it is *quite possible for them, in the nineteenth century, to revive the ecclesiastical glories of the days of faith*, and it is merely owing to their energies not being sufficiently directed to this important object, that much greater restorations are not achieved. If the piety, faith, and zeal of bygone times are revived, then equal results will soon be attained. There is, at the present time, a great and increasing feeling of admiration for old Catholic art; and among those who have greatly contributed to revive this love of Catholic antiquity, are certain learned members of the Establishment, resident at Oxford; whose endeavours, in this cause, entitle them to the respect and gratitude of all who are anxious to behold a restoration of our ancient solemn churches. Some papers which have appeared in the *British Critic* on this subject, have been written by one who truly feels the principles which actuated the ancient builders in their designs. So much respect indeed do we entertain for the writer in question, that we are pained in being compelled to act as his opponent, although it be only for a time: still the *exclusive* tone he has assumed is so fallacious, that it becomes a duty to point out the inconsistency of it. We repeat we are truly grateful for all the Oxford men have done, and are doing, towards the revival of Catholic art and antiquity: still, hampered as they are by parliamentary restrictions, and their Protestant associates, they can accomplish but little in these respects, compared with what a handful of English Catholics have done who work on the ancient foundation.

We both descend from ancestors who professed one faith

as members of the old Catholic Church of England. The Establishment are the many who, converted by political intriguers, avaricious and ambitious men, abandoned the faith of their fathers, and received parliamentary enactments for the decrees of the Church. The English Catholics are the few who remained witnesses of the truth, under the severest trials of persecution.

The Establishment, although she started strong and mighty, is now miserably fallen; she has existed long enough to suffer the most bitter degradations at the hands of her own nominal children: and having lost the hearts and control of the people—distracted by dissensions—betrayed by false brethren —the learned and pious of her communion look back with longing regret on the happy state of England's Church, ere political intriguers had forced it into schism, and separated it from the communion of the Christian world. Under these circumstances we should have hoped, and expected, that the feeling of deep humility (so beautifully expressed in an article on the Church service in the *British Critic*) would have influenced the tone of the writer on church architecture; but this, we are sorry to perceive, is far from the case. We cannot understand how a church in the old English style, erected by the descendants of those who retained the practice of the old rites, can be a *painful* object* to one *professing Catholic principles;* nor why he should be *edified* (even supposing such were the case) that the new Catholic church and dissenting meeting-house were built in the same manner: unless he were influenced by party feelings, such a falling off should cause his sincere grief. Far be it from us to exult at the abortions raised by the Establishment for her worship; it is on the contrary a subject of deep lamentation, that any persons whose ancestors were members of the Catholic Church should have so wofully deserted from the spirit of antiquity. And on the other hand, when we behold even the intention of restoring Catholic architecture and practices, we are both edified and thankful that such feelings should exist.

We are willing to admit that the modern externals of Catholicism in this country are but little calculated to impress a casual observer with feelings of religious veneration, but as the English Catholics have been driven from every ancient church, and cut off from old associations, their present condition, in these respects, is less astonishing than that of the

---

* " This is indeed a *painfully* beautiful structure."

members of the Establishment, who, with the glories of the old edifices continually before them, have not only departed from every ancient practice, but have defaced and destroyed, in a great measure, the most beautiful portions of these venerable edifices.

It is true that the feelings of many of her children are Catholic, but the Establishment is decidedly Protestant. How would the parochial churches, in their present state, bear the test of an old English episcopal visitation? A solitary surplice and tattered prayer book would but ill answer to the long catalogue of sacred vessels and ornaments extracted from *Lyndwood's Provinciale.* The unoccupied sedilia; the broken sacrarium; the defaced screen, denuded of its emblem of redemption; the dismounted altar stone, trampled under foot; the damp and mouldering chancel; the broken window and uptorn brass, would but ill exhibit that love of Anglican rites, which the writer would fain usurp as the exclusive feeling of the Establishment: and yet this is the state of almost every church in the country, which is not fortunate enough to have an Oxford man for its incumbent: and then, however good may be his intentions, he is so restricted and controlled, that he can do little more than remove some coats of whitewash, and open a blocked-up arch or window. It is a fact, and we say it in sorrow—not exultation, that there is not a single church, in the possession of the Establishment, where *any* of the old Anglican rites are preserved. There is a great deal written respecting them, it is true, but where are the actual results? Do the clergy celebrate in the ancient vestments? Do they burn lights on the altars and near the tombs of the martyrs? Do they venerate the remains of the saints? Do they place hallowed water in the porches of the churches? Are the roods rested over the screens? Are the sedilia occupied by the clergy? For these are all practices of remote antiquity. It is a striking fact, that *Anglican* rites were in use in the Church of England only so *long as she retained her canonical obedience to the holy see, and ceased with her schism.*

A paper has recently appeared, on the Anglo-Catholic use of two lights at the altar, the object of which is excellent; but it is well known that this disuse of the Anglo-Catholic practice is *exactly coeval* with the *formation of the present Establishment,* as they were utterly disused after the short-lived reign of the first book of common prayer. We had in England, from Saxon times downwards, our own missals, rituals, benedictionals, offices, litanies, which included among the most ancient Catholic rites, *some exclusively English*, with vast privileges; and yet all these Anglican rites were abolished to introduce *Lutheran and Genevan discipline, when England's Church was brought under the yoke of foreign sectaries*, by the so-called reformers of the sixteenth century. And if these Anglican rites have in some respects been suspended amongst us, who are the remnant of the whole faith, is it not owing to our having been so deserted and persecuted by our Protestant countrymen that we have been too depressed and divided to keep up the externals and practice of a Church? But, however we may fall short in these respects when compared with the glories of ancient days, we are still wonderfully in advance of the members of the Establishment, who, still writhing under the evil influence of a Peter Martyr and John a Lasco, are unable to revive a single practice of Anglo-catholic antiquity. It ill becomes them to speak in a taunting manner of our deficiencies in these respects, and to make extravagant deductions from accidental contingencies; we allude particularly to the observations made on the position of the church at Derby.*

---

* There is not the slightest foundation for the *significant relation*, asserted by the reviewer, between the church at Derby and the Roman basilicas; there is not, in fact, the smallest similarity between the two. In the basilica, the altar and the celebrant *face the east and the people*, of which we are not aware of any other instance. At Derby, the building was unfortunately forced into a south and north position. The church at Moorfields was erected by a Protestant, who was totally ignorant of any canonical regulation, and was far more influenced by the city commissioners, in not *spoiling the uniformity of the crescent*, than any notions of introducing Roman discipline into London. As for Mr. Fletcher's meeting-house, the mention of which is rather insultingly introduced, the reviewer must be aware that it has no *bearing at all*, there being neither end nor side, but one great galleried preaching house, with benches all round; a vile conventicle, which, we should have thought, any one *professing Catholic feelings* would not have named in conjunction with a church, built on the same site and position, and over the same sacred tombs, as one of the oldest edifices devoted to Christian worship.

There is one observation of the reviewer in which we most heartily concur—the absence of altars at the extremities of the aisles is a *great* defect, although not an *irremediable* one; and we shall hope, before long, to see these, as well as a regular chancel screen, and other arrangements which are absolutely required to be completed, in order to perfect the interior of this edifice.

We cannot conclude these observations without expressing our perfect concurrence in the views of the writer, respecting the propriety and necessity of adhering to the ancient traditional position of churches, from west to east; and we hold, that nothing short of absolute necessity could palliate, even in these times, any departure from this practice. But few persons are acquainted with the difficulties to be encountered in procuring land for the erection of Catholic churches. No sooner does the intention of commencing such a structure become known, than every engine of prejudice and interest is brought to bear in opposition, and sites are sometimes purchased, through necessity, which will not possibly admit of canonical arrangements in the position of the edifice.

Had the writer examined the dimensions of the site, he must at once have perceived that the uncanonical position of the building was occasioned, not through disrespect for the ancient tradition of Christendom—which we revere most highly; not from any idea of introducing Roman peculiarities in England, but from unavoidable necessity, occasioned by want of space, from west to east. Had the church been properly placed, even supposing the whole width of the land occupied, not only would the light of both eastern and western windows have been at the mercy of the adjacent proprietors, but the edifice itself would have been much too short for its required purposes. Every expedient, by placing the tower on the side, &c., was tried, but was reluctantly and of necessity abandoned.

The annexed plan will shew these difficulties; and it will also be seen that the church was brought forward to its present

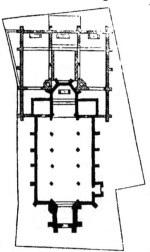

DERBY.*

position to admit of enlarging the chancel, and adding chapels towards the altar end.

---

* As the exterior and interior of this church have been already etched in two plates, published by Dolman, and also illustrated in the "British Critic," it has not been considered necessary to introduce them in this article.

It was certainly a lamentable necessity which compelled the architect to turn the church at Derby towards the north; but yet this is a light defect, when compared with the pewing of St. Alkmund's, where, in a canonically-built church, the congregation not only face the north, but sit in hollow squares and galleries, and *face each other*. The writer could not have selected a more unfortunate example for illustrating the love of Catholic antiquity in the Establishment, than this ancient but desecrated edifice: it is an old Catholic shell, cut up, galleried, defaced, and transformed by every description of Protestant monstrosity, from the Genevan reading-desk, down to the *glazed* and cushioned pew of the last century. But mistaken indeed are the ideas of the reviewer, in imagining that the new church of St. Mary's was erected as if in *hostile opposition* to the venerable fabric of St. Alkmund's; for, desecrated and desolated as it stands, the pious Catholic can gaze with feelings of deep veneration on an edifice from whose tower the bells have oft called the people to early sacrifice, and beneath whose ancient pavement repose the remains of many a faithful soul departed. How little can the writer estimate the feelings of a true English Catholic, if he thinks every stone of the ancient churches is not inestimably dear to him; for, independent of the art and science of their construction, their antiquity alone will awaken associations more holy and consoling, than the most splendid revivals of Catholic art in the present day can produce. It is a strange inconsistency in such men as the reviewer, to misrepresent and disparage the intentions and works of the only body who are capable of carrying out the very ideas he so beautifully expresses. We are quite willing to throw overboard such of the modern Catholic erections as are built without reference to canonical arrangement or the traditions of the Church, to be dealt with as unmercifully as the conventicles which they much resemble. But we protest against charging the whole body with the ignorance of some of its members; and we equally object to the writer claiming Catholic feelings for the Establishment, as a *body*, because such good sentiments have revived among a few of its members. By how small a proportion would the sentiments of the reviewer be *even understood,* and by a how much smaller proportion *appreciated as they deserve.* The very truth contained in his article refutes the position he would attempt to claim. Everything Catholic in England is at so low an ebb at present, that it is folly to boast. All we contend for is, that Catholicism in this country possesses sufficient internal strength to revive its ancient glory; while the Establishment, however willing some of its members may be to produce such a result, cannot, under its present system, achieve it. And why is this? It is not from any want of piety, zeal, learning, disinterestedness, or holiness of life,—for all these requisites are possessed in a high degree by many among them; it is simply for want of a really Catholic foundation. If reunited in communion with the rest of the Christian world, and absolved from the censures which their forefathers incurred, how rapidly would they achieve the greatest works! The spirit of the ancient churchmen breathes in their writings, and in their deeds,—but, like the green shoots from a prostrate trunk, wanting a source, fail in producing fruit; and the men who, in better days, would have raised a Lincoln or founded a Winchester, are scarcely able to preserve common decency of worship, or arrest increasing decay, in the churches which they serve.

Pl. 1.

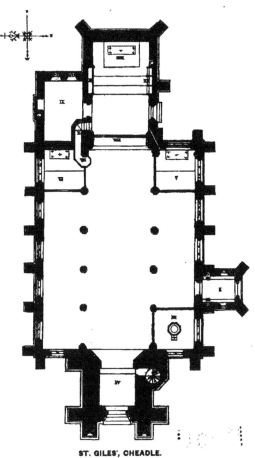

ST. GILES', CHEADLE.

I. Porch	VIII. Screen and Rood
II. Holy water stoups	IX. Sacristy
III. Font and Baptistery	X. Staircase to Rood
IV. Tower	XI. Sepulchre
V. St. Mary's Chapel	XII. Sedilia
VI. St. John's Chapel	XIII. High altar
VII. Pulpit	

Pl. II.

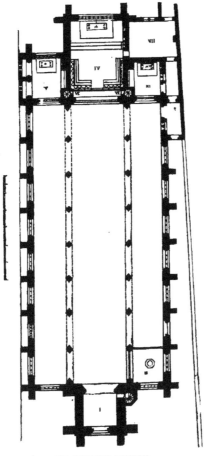

ST. GEORGE'S, LONDON.

ɪ. Tower	v. Chapel of the holy Trinity
ɪɪ. Baptistery and Font	vɪ. Staircases to Rood
ɪɪɪ. St. Mary's Chapel .	vɪɪ. Sacristy
ɪv. Chancel	

Pl. III.

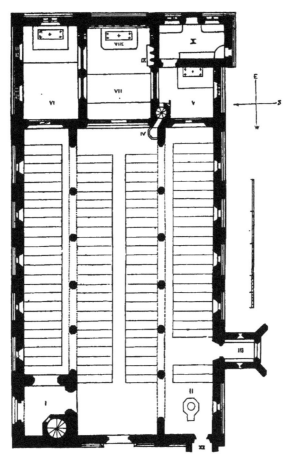

ST. WILFRID'S, MANCHESTER.

I. Tower	VI. St. Mary's Chapel
II. Font	VII. Chancel
III. Porch	VIII. High altar
IV. Pulpit	IX. Sedilia
V. St. Thomas's Chapel	X. Sacristy

Pl. IV.

ST. GILES', CHEADLE.

Pl. V.

ST. GEORGE'S, LONDON.

Pl. VI.

ST. OSWALD'S, LIVERPOOL.

Pl. VII.

ST. WILFRID'S, MANCHESTER.

ST. MARY'S, DUDLEY.

Pl. VIII.

STOCKTON-ON-TEES.

Pl. IX.

ST. ANNE'S, KEIGHLEY.

ST. MARY'S, SOUTHPORT.

Pl. **X.**

ST. MARY'S-ON-THE-SANDS, SOUTHPORT.

Pl. XI.

ST. ALBAN'S, MACCLESFIELD.

Pl. XII.

ST. GEORGE'S FIELDS, LONDON.

Pl. XIII.

ST. GILES', CHEADLE.

Pl. XIV.

CHANCEL OF ST. WILFRID'S, MANCHESTER.

Pl. XV.

ST. MARY'S, UTTOXETER.

Pl. XVI.

CHANCEL OF ST. GILES', CHEADLE.

ON THE PRESENT STATE OF

ECCLESIASTICAL ARCHITECTURE
IN ENGLAND.

———

ARTICLE THE SECOND.
From the DUBLIN REVIEW, No. XXIII.
February 1842.

ECCLESIASTICAL ARCHITECTURE
IN ENGLAND.

Art. III.—1. *A Few Words to Churchwardens, Nos.* 1 *and* 2. *A Few Words to Churchbuilders. A Few Hints on the Practical Study of Ecclesiastical Antiquities. The Ecclesiologist, Nos.* 1 *and* 2 ; *being all publications of the Cambridge Camden Society.*

2. *Two Lectures on the Structure and Decorations of Churches.* By the Rev. G. A. Poole, M.A.

THE increase of public attention to the subject of ecclesiastical antiquities, is one of the most consoling signs of the present times; not that the mere study of pointed architecture is any novelty, but the present views on this important subject are far more satisfactory than those which prevailed but a short time since.

Most elaborate works on the antiquities and topography of this country, faithful delineations, and correct historical accounts of its most interesting monuments, are indeed abundant, and as works of practical utility and useful reference cannot be too strongly commended. But still these partook but little of the ancient spirit, nor did they materially conduce in imparting it to others; they treated upon Stonehenge, and Lincoln minster, a Roman encampment, and a parochial church, in the same tone; they were written, for the most part, more with a view of preserving the remembrance of past glories than reviving their execution, and seemed to treat the productions of our Catholic forefathers as belonging to a state of things utterly gone by, and never to return. Frequently, indeed, the grossest discrepancies are to be found between the text and the subject treated upon. How often the most glorious monuments of ancient piety are mentioned only for the purpose of defaming the religion and intentions of their holy founders! How exceedingly painful in this respect are the otherwise meritorious works of Mr. Britton and many others, of which those portions of the text not devoted to mere architectural descriptions, are one tissue of calumnies against the ancient churchmen of this country, and the faith which they so zealously and worthily maintained.

A far better spirit has at length arisen; and we may truly say, that the Cambridge Camden Society have already done, and are actually doing, immense service in the good cause by the admirable publications they are issuing on this subject, some of which we have selected at the head of this article. They do not treat the ecclesiastical antiquities of this country as mere architectural curiosities; or pointed architecture as a matter of arbitrary taste; neither do they hold learned comparisons on the relative beauties of a Corinthian column and a clustered pillar; but they set forth the construction and decoration of the temples dedicated to God in the true light, as matters of Catholic tradition, and propose the ancient Catholic structures as the only models for imitation. Now we do not hesitate in saying, that they have already achieved more practical good by their unpretending publications, than has been accomplished by the united exertions of the antiquaries of the last half century; for they have brought long-forgotten facts before the parties who ought to be especially reminded of them, but who hitherto have known and cared the least about those matters; and it is well known, while Gough was publishing his great work on monumental antiquities, the sextons were ripping up the brasses for sale; and not unfrequently, while an elaborate plate of some interesting portion of a church was preparing for publication, the clergymen or churchwardens of the place were occupied in demolishing it. Although these works are of course addressed to the members of the Anglican Church, yet they cannot be too strongly recommended to the study and attention of the English Catholics, who, owing to their long exclusion from the sacred buildings raised by their ancestors in faith, have wofully departed from the principles which influenced them in the erection of their religious buildings. Before proceeding to examine the works in detail, we must give one extract to show the high Catholic view in which these writers regard the material structure of the ancient churches.

"We enter the Church militant by Holy Baptism: therefore the font is placed by the entrance of the west end: a church built upon the foundation of the apostles and prophets, just as the earthly building is supported by the massive pillars of the nave : we pass along this, keeping our eyes on the passion of Christ depicted at the eastern end, and trusting to the merits of his sacrifice as represented by the altar, till we arrive at the close of life, imaged by the chancel arch and dome ; this we pass through faith, some typical representation of which is usually to be traced in this arch, as the blessed saints and martyrs have gone before us, whose forms are depicted in the roodscreen ; and thus enter the Church triumphant, represented by the chancel."

What can be more consoling than to find the edifying symbolism of our ancient churches thus beautifully recognized and set forth by those who, but a few years since, were foremost in their destruction ? Our joy would indeed be far greater, if all amongst us were able and willing to join in these ideas, and practically revive them. But to proceed. The first tract is addressed to the churchwardens of rural parishes, and is written in a plain, clear style, so that the instructions may be readily understood by those for whom they are intended. It commences with some excellent admonitions relative to the positive duty of preserving and restoring all that is connected with the service of God ; and then proceeds to point out the many causes of that lamentable decay so generally observable in ancient churches, and with advice as to the means of remedying those defects, and preventing further destruction. We then have some very proper censures on those who venture to remove fonts from their ancient position near the western end, to suit their own convenience and caprice, and the gross inconsistency of administering the sacrament of Baptism in the chancel or holy place. The remarks respecting roofs are so very true, and so important, that we have given the extract in full. A high pitched roof is in itself a great ornament to a building, and adds prodigiously to its grandeur ; it prevailed till the decline of pointed architecture, when it fell like the curve of the arches, and with it half the dignity of our ecclesiastical buildings. Let any one compare the effect of such buildings as Lincoln, Westminster, Amiens, and others which retain their original high-pointed roofs, with the latter buildings, where the roofs are flat in pitch, and consequently invisible from below, and they will soon perceive that the former are twice as majestic as the latter. There cannot be a more striking example of this than the nave of Westminster and Henry the Seventh's chapel, where the parapet and pinnacles detaching on the sky look painfully meagre, while the parapet of the Abbey nave, owing

to the high roof rising behind it, produces an excellent effect.
Nine-tenths of our finest churches have lost half their beauty
owing to the destruction of the high roofs with which they
were once surmounted, and which have been replaced by low
pitched coverings. We now give the words of the tract
on this subject.

"It may not be amiss now to say something about the roof.
There are few churches which have not lost much of their beauty
from their roofs being of a much lower pitch than they used to be.
If you look at the east side of your tower, you may see what is
called the *weather moulding* of the old roof remaining; and from
thence you will be able to judge how much lower the roof is than
it was once. Now the reason is very plain. In this figure, *ABC*
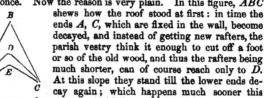 shews how the roof stood at first: in time the
ends *A*, *C*, which are fixed in the wall, become
decayed, and instead of getting new rafters, the
parish vestry think it enough to cut off a foot
or so of the old wood, and thus the rafters being
much shorter, can of course reach only to *D*.
At this slope they stand till the lower ends decay again; which happens much sooner this
time, because they were most likely not very sound at first: and
then another piece is cut off, and the roof sinks down to *E*. Now,
besides the ugliness of a flat ceiling, there is more harm done here.
Suppose that in this church there was a window which reached
nearly as far as *B*. What is to be done with it when the roof gets
down to *D* and to *E*? Why of course it must be blocked up:
and many of the finest windows in the country have been spoilt in
this very way. The best roofing is of lead: in former times
nothing else was ever used; but it is apt to crack with the heat. I
hope you will never think of that shameful way of raising money,
when you want it for the church, to sell the lead, and put tiles in
its place."

It must be in justice remarked, that many of the high roofs
were removed and lowered long before the change of religion;
and this is an additional proof, that with the introduction of the
four-centered arch, and consequent departure from the verticle
principle, the spirit of pointed architecture was on the wane.

The second tract refers to the state of parochial churches
in large and populous towns. After noticing, in the first
place, that the destruction of the ancient fabrics in such situations has not arisen from want of funds, but from the injudicious expenditure of large sums, the writer proceeds to
denounce the common enormities of high pews, galleries,
blocked up arches, huge stoves and pipes, plastered ceilings

under oak roofs, &c. On all these matters the observations
are most judicious, but as they chiefly refer to Protestant
monstrosities, they are not extracted into these pages; but
the following remarks on modern sepulchral monuments are
quite applicable to the vile tablets and memorials for the
dead, which are adopted by many modern Catholics in place
of those appropriate and truly Catholic tombs, slabs, and
brasses, which are to be found in almost every ancient church.*

"I have spoken before at much length about burials in churchyards: but I wish to say a word upon monuments. Nothing can
be more unsightly than most of these, not to say irreverent and
profane. You may often persuade your fellow-parishioners to give

---

* As it is very probable that many persons erect these Pagan and Protestant-
looking tablets and emblems, to the memory of their departed friends, in consequence of their ignorance of ancient design, and inability to procure correct
models, it may be useful to insert the following list of the various sorts of
monuments anciently employed, and the average cost of executing them at the
present time.

	£	£
A high tomb under a canopied arch, crotched and pinnacled, with effigy of deceased vested of natural size, angels and weepers in niches round the high tomb, with scriptures, emblems, &c. from	150 to	500
A high tomb with the effigy natural size, with weepers or tracery and shields round the sides	50 ...	100
A plain arch in a chancel, with effigy natural size	30 ...	100
Ditto, with a slab and monumental cross and inscription	25 ...	50
A plain high tomb with inscription round edge and monumental cross on top	20 ...	30
A whole length brass, under a canopy, with the evangelists in the corners, and inscription	100 ...	200
A whole length brass without canopy or evangelists	50 ...	—
A half brass with inscription and evangelists	25 ...	50
A ditto small	10 ...	20
A quarter-size whole length effigy and inscription	10 ...	20
A chalice with hand over in benediction, a very simple but ancient emblem of a priest's tomb	3 ...	5
A brass of a cross fleury, with inscription on stem and effigy in the centre	25 ...	50
A stone slab with a cross fleury, engraved in lines and inscription, shields, &c.	10 ...	15
A ditto raised in Dos D'Ane, and cross fleury carved in relief on it; these are well calculated for external monuments in church-yards	10 ...	15
Stone crosses with inscriptions, to set up at the heads and feet of graves	5 ...	10
Plain oak crosses with painted inscriptions for the same purpose	1 ...	3

Of course the exact cost of all these different monuments will vary in proportion to quantity of detail and enrichment about them, and the materials in
which they are executed; alabaster will be more costly than stone, and Purbeck
marble than Yorkshire slabs, and so on; but the above lists of monuments,
which are strictly in accordance with Catholic traditions, has been drawn out to
show that the pious memorials used by our forefathers may be revived at the
present time by all classes.

up the ugly headstones, with their vulgar doggrel rhymes, and make them choose proper emblems instead of those which are now most common. What can be worse than poppies and broken columns, which typify everlasting sleep and thwarted hopes, instead of the peaceful and hopeful rest of the Christian? But of all things shun urns: they are heathen and silly emblems, though more used perhaps than anything else. Nor are they put on monuments only: I know of more than one east end stuck about with urns and pots of different sizes and colours; of a beautiful porch groaning under the weight of a shapeless modern urn; and even of a chancel-arch removed altogether to make way for an urn on the top of each pier. At any rate you can hinder the mutilation of the church itself for urns and monuments. It is a shame to cut away piers and carvings and mouldings, and to block up arches and windows for such things as these. It is a shame also to use monumental stones over again, and thus destroy the record of one man's life to make room for that of another. And again, it is worse than dishonest to take gravestones for one's own purposes, and even to give them away to others for doorsteps and lintels, or the like uses.

"Nothing is more strange than the modern taste in monuments: the same people who would gladly get rid of the few statues of saints and martyrs of old which have been saved for us, will themselves put up images to modern preachers, and perhaps even to wicked men, and this over the very altar itself!"

The latter part of this extract does not, of course, refer to any Catholic churches, but it is most gratifying to perceive that the members of the Establishment are at length awakened to the glaring inconsistency of permitting images of pagan divinities to be erected within their churches, while those of saints, and of our blessed Redeemer himself, are rigidly excluded.

The remarks of the writer respecting the churchyard cross, are also quite in the true spirit. He says you should care for this old cross and keep it clean, for none but wicked men would have broken the emblem of all our hopes. His conclusion is so Catholic, that it would seem to have been written ere England's unhappy schism; indeed, such sentiments, and feelings only can belong, consistently, to the old time. May God grant that they are at least the harbingers of better days.

"And now I have done. And though I know how feebly I have raised my voice, yet it has been raised with the one view of trying to recall some of my brethren of the laity of England to a sense of what God claims from those who are entrusted here with the overcharge of His House; and of giving what little aid to them a life devoted to Church-antiquities may have enabled me to give. If I have had much fault to find, it is not from a love of finding fault; far from that, but from a hope of amending. And if many have been persuaded by my former words to do something for God's Church, although with such scanty means, it is not much to hope that some of those to whom I now write, who mostly are so much better able to afford such cost, will also do their part. You to whom I have now been speaking are often men of wealth and influence: you have fair houses and costly furniture, and all comforts you wish for. I earnestly call upon you to think of the claims which the church, which you are allowed to watch and guard, has upon your aid: the church, within which you were by holy baptism made members of the spiritual Church; in which it may be you knelt before the bishop in confirmation, and in holy matrimony plighted your troth in the dearest earthly tie; the church which you have perhaps daily entered for prayer and praise, and how often for holy communion! around which your fathers and brethren who have departed in faith are resting in the sleep of peace; in which lastly the solemn funeral service will ere long be heard over your bier. It is no slight band which ties you to your parish-church; it is no far-off call which is rousing you to do your duty. Your oaths, your honour, your manliness, must force you, one would think, to fill the office which you have taken as a good man should: a happy office surely, to watch that church round which all your hopes are or ought to be centered; and a high office, (it cannot be too often said) to care for the holy house where God himself deigns to dwell.

"Join then for your Church's sake the zealous band who are now on all sides working each in his way for God's glory. I cannot promise you fame: but you will not desire that. I can promise you the love of all who are working in the same good cause; and, what is more, a lasting record of your labours by Him in Whose name and for Whose sake you labour."

We now come to the tract entitled *A Few Words to Church Builders*, which contains much important matter, and is certainly the first distinct publication which has issued from the present Establishment, in which ecclesiastical architecture is viewed in its true light. In the introduction, the writer remarks, that the observations "are intended for the use of those to whom God has given, not only the means, but the will, to undertake a work, *the noblest perhaps in which man can engage*, the building of a house in some degree worthy of His majesty. He farther states, that "it is his intention to dwell rather on the *Catholic* than on the *architectural* principles which ought to influence the building of a church;" and this intention constitutes the great merit, value, and, we may add, in the present day, the novelty of this publication.

The greater portion of the remarks are so excellent, and so fully illustrate the principles of church architecture, that we cannot refrain from giving copious extracts. Speaking of the dedication, the writer observes:

" 5. In a cold and faithless age like this, to attach any importance to the selection of a patron saint will probably provoke a smile in some, and in others may cause a more serious feeling of displeasure at the superstition of those who do it. We are well content, if it be so, to lie under the same charge, and for the same cause, as Andrewes, Hooker, and Whitgift. Let us give an example or two of the motives which lead to the choice of a patron saint now. In a large town in the south of England a meeting-house was built by a dissenter, who called it, out of compliment to his wife, Margaret chapel. This being afterwards bought for a church, is now named *Saint* Margaret's. In the same town is another chapel called All Souls, 'because all souls may there hear the word of God.' Other dedications are now given, which were rarely, if ever, in use among our ancestors. Such are—St. Paul, instead of SS. Peter and Paul ; Christ Church, and St. Saviour's, for a small building ; Emmanuel church, and the like. But who would found a church in England— once the 'England of Saints'—without some attention to the local memory of those holy men whose names still live in the appellations of many of our towns ? Who, in the diocese of Lichfield, would forget St. Chad ? in that of Durham, St. Cuthbert ? in those of Canterbury and Ely, St. Alphege, and St. Etheldreda ? Surely, near St. Edmund's Bury, a church-founder would naturally think of St. Edmund, or in the west of Wales, of St. David ?"

The next remark is very important, and cannot be too strongly urged to those among the English Catholics, who, having been so long confined to mere chapels, have conceived a dislike, and a most Protestant dislike it is, to chancels.

"6. There are two parts, and only two parts, which are absolutely essential to a church—chancel and nave. If it have not the latter, it is at best only a chapel ; if it have not the former, it is little better than a meeting-house. The twelve thousand ancient churches in this land, in whatever else they may differ, agree in this, that every one has or had a well-defined chancel. On the least symbolical grounds, it has always been felt right to separate off from the rest of the church a portion which should be expressly appropriated to the more solemn rites of our religion ; and this portion is the chancel. In this division our ancient architects recognised an emblem of the holy Catholic Church ; as this consists of two parts, the Church militant and the Church triumphant, so does the earthly structure also consist of two parts, the chancel and nave ; the Church militant being typified by the latter, and the

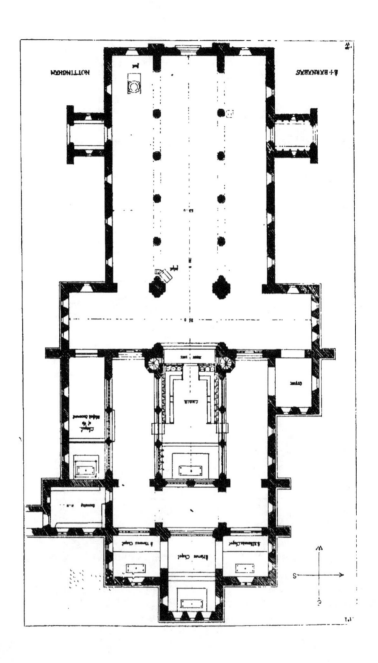

S.t. BARNABAS

NOTTINGHAM

✝ ⛪ BARNABAS NOT

Church triumphant by the former. But in nine-tenths of 'new churches,' we shall find no attempt whatever at having a distinct chancel, or it is at best confined to a small apsidal projection of the altar. And this, one of the most glaring faults of modern buildings, has not met with the reprobation which it so well deserves; nay, has even been connived at by those who knew better. To illustrate the respective sizes of ancient and modern chancels, I subjoin [Plate 2] two ground plans, one of a church built about 1250, the other of one within a mile of it, erected in 1835. And surely, if we had no other reason for the prominence we attach to a chancel than that without one exception our ancestors attached such prominence to it, it ought to be enough for us who profess to admire their wisdom, and as far as we may, to tread in their steps."

In the new Catholic churches of Southport, Keighley, Kenilworth, St. Oswald's, near Liverpool, Macclesfield, Dudley, Pomfret, Masborough, St. George's, London, &c., the chancels are built precisely after the ancient models, and bear a good relative proportion to the length of the church; they are also duly provided with screens, sedilia, sepulchres, reredoses, &c.

"7. This division, essential in the interior, is not always to be traced in the exterior. It is far better indeed, generally speaking, that it should be marked in both; and to this end the breadth of the chancel should be a little less than that of the nave; a difference of four or five feet will be quite sufficient. The height of the chancel is usually less, in the same proportion. Sometimes this latter is the only mark of division, as in the churches of Chailey and Southease, Sussex. In a cross church, it will be sufficiently marked by the transepts. The only kind of church in which it cannot be externally shewn, is where there are chancel and nave, with two aisles to both; but this is rarely the case, except in city churches, or where the builders were cramped for room."

This is frequently to be remarked in those churches built in crowded cities, and in some of the larger parish churches, such as Newark, &c. where most probably this arrangement was adopted for the purpose of obtaining a Lady chapel beyond the high altar. The annexed plate, No. 1, will show the ground-plan of the Catholic church of St. Barnabas, now erecting at Nottingham, where the chancel is entirely surrounded by aisles and eastern chapels.* In the church of St.

---

* We introduce three engravings (Nos. 1, 2, 3) to illustrate the design of this church, which when complete will be the most perfect revival of a large parochial church that has been yet accomplished. Beneath the choir is a crypt, with vaulting springing from two rows of low pillars; at the eastern end of this undercroft is an altar dedicated in honour of St. Peter, as being the foundation or rock of the church. The same staircases which lead up to the rood loft, at the entrance of the choir, are continued down to the crypt, which is lit by the

Andrew, about to be erected at Cambridge, the space being exceedingly limited, the chancel is taken out of the east compartment enclosed by open screen work, with an aisle on each side. The writer then states, respecting cruciform churches:

"9. A cross is of course the most beautiful form in which a church can be built. Yet those persons who think it necessary to a perfect building, are in great error; not one-tenth of the churches in the country having been erected in that shape. From this mistaken idea transepts have been attempted with funds hardly sufficient for chancel and nave, often to the destruction of the fair proportion of the chancel. The symbol conveyed by the cross is certainly better adapted than any other for a Christian place of worship; yet that of a ship, which the other form sets forth, is by no means unsuitable, and was a very favourite one with the early Church, as St. Chrysostom and St. Hilary (writing concerning the Saviour's walking on the sea) testify. A very general fault of modern cross churches is the excessive breadth of each of the four arms; whence the arches to the lantern, or central part of the

---

side openings in the walls of the choir, which being elevated several feet above the pavement of the aisles, afford sufficient space for their introduction. The various chapels, as well as the choir, will be enclosed by oak screens of open tracery and panel work, relieved in colours. That portion of the church eastward of the transept, will be divided off from the rest of the building by open screens and gates on a line with the great roodscreen. The roodloft will extend the whole width between the great east pillars supporting the tower, and raised about fourteen feet from the level of the choir; in breadth it will be about seven feet, and in the centre a great rood will be erected, with appropriate images, standards for lights, &c.

The choir will be furnished with eighteen carved oak stalls and desks, precisely on the old model; and at the back of the stalls are oak screens, which will extend along both sides of the choir between the pillars. The pavement of the choir and sanctuary, as well as that of the eastern chapels, will consist of incrusted tiles of various colours, similar in design and composition to those used in ancient churches. On the epistle side of the altar will be fixed the sedilia, framed and carved in wood, similar in design to those still remaining in the choir of Westminster, and vulgarly called King Sebert's tomb. The high altar will consist of a single slab of stone, supported on eight shafts of Petworth marble, with gilt cap and bases. Immediately behind the altar a rich perforated oak screen will extend across the eastern extremity of the choir, enriched with gold and colours, and surmounted by standards for wax tapers. Through this screen the arched entrance and stained windows of the Lady chapel will be distinctly seen. In a chapel on the epistle or south side of the choir, the blessed sacrament will be reserved, on a rich altar surmounted by a ciborium, or canopy, supported on four gilt pillars, between which curtains will run on brass rods, extending from cap to cap. The windows of this church are all intended to be glazed with stained glass, of various devices and subjects, in the rich early style; and it is proposed eventually to cover all the spandrils of the arches, walls, &c., with painted enrichments. The organ will be placed in the north transept. All the altars will be furnished with candlesticks, sacred vessels, hangings, and other ornaments in the same character as the building; and to the minutest details this church will be a strict revival of Catholic antiquity.

cross, are made obtuse to an almost absurd degre ; and sometimes are omitted altogether, as unnecessary. But if they are unnecessary to the safety of a church, they suggest (according to the great authority on such points, Durandus) an important symbolical meaning ; namely, that by the writings of the four Evangelists the doctrine of the cross has been preached through the whole world. And this is the reason that we so often find the Evangelistic symbols on, or over them."

We most heartily concur with these remarks; cruciform churches should not be attempted, unless the transepts are well prolonged, and they should always be accompanied by a central tower, or four solid stone arches prepared to receive one, and the chancel should be *at least* the depth of one of the transepts. A transept church built in the form of a T, without a chancel, is quite irregular. The evangelistic symbols are found on the extremities of crosses at a very early period, and may be considered indispensable to a rood cross. They are found on the earliest known examples of processional crosses, and were also engraven on, or affixed to, the silver covers of the holy Gospels. The abbey barn at Glastonbury is cruciform, and a most noble structure; in each gable is a quatrefoil with an emblem of an Evangelist, and the same is to be occasionally observed on cross-built churches.

The following remark shows that the writer is fully imbued with the feelings and spirit of the ancient architects.

" 11. There is not the slightest objection, whatever the fastidious taste of modern times may think of it, against building at first one aisle, if the funds are not sufficient for the erection of two. And it is far more in accordance with Catholic principles to build one aisle as it ought to be, than to ' run up ' two cheaply ; always supposing it in this, as in other cases of imperfect design, to be the intention of the builder, that the church shall, at some future time, though perhaps not by himself, be completed. And this leads to an important remark. It is not of consequence that the opposite sides of a church should correspond with each other. Churches with one aisle, or one transept, constantly occur. I will prove this by some examples, taken at random :—Llanfwrog, Denbighshire, has N. aisle ; Tal-y-Llyn, Merion, S. transept ; Brandon, Suffolk, S. aisle ; Avening, Gloucestershire, N. aisle ; Rodborough, Gloucestershire, N. aisle to chancel and nave, and S. transept ; Hunsdon, Herts, S. transept ; Stanford, Berks, N. aisle ; Erith, Kent, S. aisle to chancel and nave.

" But now, in most people's opinion, the great beauty of a church, if it have two aisles, consists in having both sides the same in details ; whereas nothing can be more opposite to the true principles

E

of ecclesiastical architecture than this idea, so cramping to boldness of design and variety of ornament.

"12. This remark applies particularly to the position of the tower. Now-a-days, it is almost universally placed at the west end of the church, that it may 'stand in the middle;' whereas the following positions are equally good : the intersection of a cross church, or between the chancel and nave, where the church is not cross ; these are very common. Other positions are :— Middle of north aisle, Vaucelles, near Caen ; middle of nave, Caen, S. Sauveur ; North of chancel, Berneval, Normandy ; South of chancel, Standon, Hertfordshire ; North end of the north transept, Montgomery ; South end of the south transept, East Lavant, Sussex ; North side of the nave, Goustranville, near Caen ; South side of the nave, Midhurst, Sussex ; East end of the north aisle, Patching, Sussex ; West end of the north aisle, Clapham, Sussex ; East end of the south aisle, West Grinstead, Sussex ; West end of the south aisle, Amiens, S. Loup ; Holyrood, Southampton ; North-west angle of nave, York, St. Crux ; South-west angle of nave, Sacombe, Herts ; Western part of the chancel, Yainville, Normandy. It shows the perverseness of modern times, that the only position in which a tower never ought to be built, namely over the altar, is almost the only one which in modern churches ever takes place of that at the west end ; and it is adopted for the same reason,—it is 'just in the middle,' too."

Now we could embrace the man who wrote this; for the senseless uniformity of modern design is one of its greatest defects. The idea of everything being exactly alike on both sides, has created an unreal style of building which was quite unknown to our ancestors, and it is most delightful to see the very soul of modern deformities thus ably attacked. When once the trammels and bondage of this regularity system are broken through, and people are taught not to consider a portico and two uniform wings the perfection of design, we may expect vast improvements ; and we hail with the greatest satisfaction this champion of true principles, who at once proclaims defiance to the pagan and mock-regularity men, and sets forth a speedy return to the real and consistent manner of building practised in the days of faith.

We pass over in this place the writer's remarks respecting altars and sedilia, as they contain serious errors and mistatements, which will be noticed in full hereafter, and proceed to the subject of fonts, of which he observes:

"28. The subject of Fonts is highly interesting ; a list of models will be given in the Appendix. The reader cannot do better than consult Mr. Poole's before-mentioned little work, where he will find much valuable information on the subject. To his remarks there we may add a few more.

" The shape of the bason may be either square, circular, or octagonal ; the greater number of examples in each style are octagonal ; an octagon being a very ancient symbol of regeneration. Where there is a central, and four corner shafts, the latter have capital and base ; the former has neither. Hexagonal fonts, though they do occur, are not to be imitated ; yet they are not always late ; that at Ramsey, which is Norman, is of this shape. A pentagonal font, of which Mr. Poole has not an example, occurs at Hollington, Sussex ; a heptagonal one at Chaddesden, Derbyshire. I quite agree with Mr. Poole, that coats of arms are to be avoided in ornamenting the instrument of our initiation into Him, who 'was despised and rejected of men.' Yet shields do occur in early fonts : for example, at West Deeping, Lincolnshire, which is early English. And shields, with the instruments of crucifixion, and the like, would be no less beautiful than appropriate ornaments.

" A kneeling-stone at the west side appears desirable ; it may be panelled to any degree of richness. It need hardly be observed that the cover should be richly carved in oak ; there is a magnificent specimen in Castle Acre, Norfolk, about sixteen feet in height. The pulley, by which it is elevated, is sometimes, as in Stamford S. George, curiously carved ; the Fall of Man, the Baptism of our Saviour, and His victory over the devil, are here frequently represented.

" The position of the font *must be in the nave, and near a door ;* this cannot be too much insisted on : it thus typifies the admission of a child into the Church by Holy Baptism. The Canon orders that it shall stand in the ancient usual place ; and I quote the following passages from the Visitation Articles of some of the prelates before-mentioned."

The Rev. G. A. Poole's remarks, to which the writer alludes, are as follows:

" Having well entered the church, the first object that claims our attention is the font, which always is or ought to be placed at the west end, near the principal entrance, to symbolize the great truth, that holy baptism, of which the font is the instrument, is the sacrament of admission into the Christian church. Great varieties of form and arrangement are found in fonts, all appropriate, and many of them exquisite both in design and in execution : for the earlier ecclesiastics of this kingdom, like those who truly represent the Anglican Church at the present day, held holy baptism as the great sacrament of a high mystery and privilege, and accordingly lavished on the font the greatest possible care and art. Nor is there any part of the church, or of its furniture, which has been so often preserved through all the successive changes which have taken place in the

surrounding buildings, as the font. Hence we have many more
Norman fonts than Norman churches; and it is probable that
several fonts now existing in buildings of comparatively recent
date are among the very oldest relics of ancient ecclesiastic architecture.

"One thing is to be observed in all those fonts which deserve
the slightest notice, and it is one which ought on no account whatever to be forgotten at the present day :—that they are all sufficiently large to baptize children by immersion. This is the rule,
however many may be the exceptions, and however accounted for,
of the Church of England : and it is equally irreverent, absurd,
and inconsistent, to substitute a small basin, as is now too often
done, for a deep and broad font.

"But to proceed to some of the forms and ornaments of fonts,—
and to arrange them, nearly at least, in a chronological order :—

"If rudeness be taken as an indication of antiquity, the first
place must be given to some which are little more than large stones,
scarcely reduced to any definite shape, except near the top, and
then hollowed sufficiently for the purpose for which they are designed. Among these may be mentioned the font of Little Maple-
stead, one of the round churches already mentioned,* and that at
Heron Gate, in Essex.†

"The first well-defined shape which the font assumes, seems to
be that of a circular tub-shaped vessel, with little grace of form,
except that which arises from the base being somewhat smaller
than the rim. At St. Martin's church, Canterbury,‡ is a font in
which this proportion is inverted, and the effect is certainly less
pleasing. Some of these round, tub-shaped fonts may be of Saxon,
many of them are certainly of Norman date. Simple as this form
is, it is frequently very graceful; and when adorned with a series
of arches and pillars in relief, with§ or without figures under each
arch, and elevated on a step, or it may be three steps, a font of this
figure is no unworthy occupant of the west end of a Norman church.

"Somewhat later came the square stone, hollowed in the centre,
and supported by a single massive column,‖ to which it forms a
capital; or on one large central, and four smaller columns.¶ This
arrangement obviously affords greater room for the symbolical figures
of the ecclesiastical designer, on the four large flat sides; and,
accordingly, they were often adorned in this way profusely and
most ingeniously. Perhaps the most frequent decorations of such
fonts as these are emblematical representations of the fall of man;
which is the part of scripture history best adapted to the entrance

---

* Britton's Architectural Antiq., vol. i.   † Antiquarian Itinerary, vol. vii·
‡ Britton's Architectural Antiq., vol. v.   § As at Avington, ibid.
‖ As at Castle Rising, Norfolk, ibid.
¶ As at East Meon and Winchester (ibid.); and at Iffley, Oxfordshire (Glos-
sary of Architecture), and several other places.

of our churches, and admirably placed on the font, in which is
washed away the stain which thence descends upon all the descendants of Adam. By way of specimen, I will enumerate the
figures which occupy the two carved sides of the font of East Meon
church, Hampshire.*

" The first group represents the creation of Adam, and the
formation of Eve from his side. Then we have Adam and Eve
standing on either side of the tree of the knowledge of good and
evil, near which is the serpent speaking to them. Eve appears
eating, and Adam just gathering the fruit. These occupy the first
side ; and opposite we have the expulsion of the guilty pair from
paradise, which is represented by the angel with a drawn sword
driving them from a magnificent palace. Afterwards another angel
appears with a spade, from whom Adam is anxiously receiving
instruction in husbandry ; while Eve, who like her husband now
appears in the garment provided for them by the goodness of God,
is diligently occupied with her distaff. The whole design and execution of these several figures is extremely rude, and even gro-
tesque ; but nothing can be more transparent than the meaning of
the whole, which is the principal object : and the appropriateness
of the design in that place is obvious. The font of Winchester
cathedral † is extremely like that just described in general character ;
but the design of the sculpture is different, and instead of being
easily understood, is so obscure as not yet to have been certainly
deciphered. We have, however, a symbol which we should, *a
priori*, expect on a Christian font, and which was, indeed, one of
the first which in the primitive churches was introduced into the
baptistery,—I mean the dove, an emblem of the third person in
the ever blessed and glorious Trinity, by whom we are regenerated
in the water of baptism. A salamander also appears on this font,
in allusion to the words which St. John spake of our blessed Lord,
' He shall baptize you with the Holy Ghost and with fire.'‡

The font of Burnham Deepdale,§ in Norfolk, affords a series of
designs, of which the subject is very clear, but the appropriateness
to the place where they appear not so obvious. Twelve compartments are filled with as many representations of the different
labours of the husbandman. Is not this a translation, so to speak,
into the vernacular tongue, of the processes of the vineyard, by
which the good works of Christians were symbolized in Italy and
other vine countries ? Their vintage and our harvest may symbolize the same moral precepts and religious truths ; and this font
of Burnham Deepdal reads the same lesson with the baptistery of

* Archæologia, x.
† Winkle's Cathedrals. Britton's Arch. Antiq., vol. v.
‡ Matthew, iii. 2. The salamander also appears over a representation of our
blessed Lord's baptism, in the very rude square font at Bridekirk.
§ Archæologia, x. 189.

Constantine, near St. Agnese, in Rome, on the ceiling of which are represented in mosaic the processes of the vintage.[*]

Many other variations of square fonts might be mentioned, and many remarkable decorations might be adduced; but I pass on to more important changes in the form of the font. A font of five sides I do not know to occur any where; and hexagonal fonts, though not rare, are less common than either round, square, or octagonal ones. That at Carlisle Cathedral is hexagonal; and so is that at Farringdon, in Berkshire. Bredon font, Worcestershire, is also hexagonal, and adorned on each face with an escutcheon, charged with arms;[†] and I especially note this ornament in connexion with an hexagonal font, because I think the form and the ornament equally unecclesiastical and barbarous. I can imagine no reason either of symbolical meaning, or of beauty to the eye,[‡] which can plead for a six-sided figure, in preference to a circle, a square, or an octagon: and as for the ensigns of worldly pomp, and of human pride, on the instruments of initiation into the Church of Christ, into the mystical body of Him who was 'despised and rejected of men,' I cannot see any congruity in it at all. And it is worthy of remark, that this inapposite decoration for the font, if decoration it can be called, came into use just when heraldry had lost whatever religion it once had. So long as it was in any sense religious, it was too humble to appear in such a place; but after the conclusion of the Crusades, and with the mock chivalry of the Tudors, with hexagon fonts and debased architecture, first appeared the custom of decorating fonts with armorial bearings.[§]

The custom, however, thus introduced, did not cease until it had deformed many much later fonts; for instance, the somewhat in-

---

[*] Hope's Essay on Architecture.

[†] Which are as follows:—1. A chevron between three garbs. 2. A chevron between three spread eagles. 3 and 5. Seven mascles conjoined, 3, 3, 1. 6. A bend. See Archæologia, x. p. 194.

[‡] The hexagon is, perhaps, the least beautiful of all regular figures when seen singly, but the most beautiful in combination. Indeed, it is, as if by mathematical skill, adapted for close compact: for it is the figure which in composition will enclose the largest space within the smallest circumference, without any intervening spaces. The arrangement of the cells in a honeycomb will exemplify what I mean. Had the cells been triangular or quadrangular, the quantity of wax employed in their walls would have been greater in proportion to their size; had they been any other figures except hexagons, there would have been spaces between them.

[§] I mean that the escutcheon was not introduced till then as the mere receptacle of armorial bearings: when the shield was introduced as a part of the costume of the figures with which the font was adorned, it was probably enough charged with arms. Such figures with shields appear on the font of Wansford, Northamptonshire, figured in the Archæologia, xvi. plate xxxvii., and referred by Mr. Repton (see p. 195) to the eleventh and twelfth century. Even angels are represented in this way bearing blazoned shields, as in one of the bosses in the south transept of York Minster.

elegant octagonal font at Sefton,* (Lancashire,) and the decidedly inelegant font, also octagonal, at South Kilvington, Yorkshire. The latter is figured in the sixteenth volume of the Archæologia, and affords the materials, from its eight escutcheons, of a pedigree of the Scropes.

"I know of but one font whose basin has seven sides. It is at Elmeswell, in Suffolk,† that also is cumbered with armorial bearings.

"And now we arrive at the octagon, the most appropriate form for the font, and the most beautiful as well as the most ecclesiastical; for the octagon is not only a very graceful form, and very favourable to the reception of sculpture on its several faces, but it is also in itself symbolical, according to the ancient method of spiritualising numbers, of the new birth in Baptism: for the seven days' creation of the natural world are symbolised by the number seven; and the new creation by Christ Jesus, by the number eight, in allusion to the eighth day, on which he rose again from the dead. And this reason St. Ambrose, more than fourteen centuries ago, assigned for the octagonal form of the Baptistery:

> 'Octachorum sanctos templum surrexit in usus,
> Octagonus fons est, munere dignus eo.
> Hoc numero decuit sacri baptismatis aulam
> Surgere, quo populis vera salus rediit
> Luce resurgentis Christi, qui claustra resolvit
> Mortis, et a tumulis, suscitet examines.'‡

"A few of the more remarkable fonts of this figure may be noted.

"That at Ware, in Hertfordshire, is charged with whole length figures, in very bold relief, of the salutation of St. John the Baptist, of St. James the less, of St. Catherine, of St. George, of St. Christopher, and of St. Margaret, and the dragon. Between the compartments, busts of angels hold musical instruments, and the instruments of the Passion.§ The font at St. Martin's, Oxford, is figured in the glossary of architecture; it is richly adorned with quatrefoils, niches, and statues. The fonts of St. Mary Magdalen's, and of St. Aldate's, Oxford, are given in the same work: the former of these has the merit of being an example of the decorated style, in which but few fonts are remaining. The last is much later, about A.D. 1520.‖

"But by far the most graceful and splendid form of the font is the octagonal basin elevated on a shaft or column, rising out of

---

* Figured in the antiquities of Sefton church, by R. Bridgens.
† Archæologia, x. 194. I am now able to add that of Bowden Magna Leicestershire.
‡ These lines were formerly inscribed over the font of S. Tecla.
§ Figured in the Antiquarian Itinerary, vol. i.
‖ These three fonts are also figured in the memorials of Oxford.

several steps ; the shaft and basin (and sometimes even the steps), being richly adorned with panels or niches, with statues or groups of figures, and in short, with all the decorations which their style of architecture admits. Fonts of this character may interest us the more, because they are such as ought to be erected in the greater number of new churches, being adapted to the style of architecture, (or to whatever there is of architectural style), now generally affected. An extremely graceful font of this character is that of Worsted, in Norfolk ;* it is without statues, (though there may have been small figures once in the niches of the shaft) but is richly decorated with quatrefoils and flowing tracery. It is not too elaborate to be easily imitated, nor too rich for an ordinary parish church.

" The grace and elegance of this form rises to magnificence, when the niches and compartments are occupied with statues and groups, as in the font of East Dereham, in Norfolk ; which was erected in 1468. The several items of expenditure in its erection, with the manner in which the sum was collected, still remain as a subject of curiosity. The account is too long to repeat. The last font that I shall mention is also the most beautiful. It is that at Walsingham in Norfolk, and is thus described by Britton, who gives also a beautiful plate of it in his Ecclesiastical Antiquities.† 'It is decorated,' he says, ' with all the charms of art ; with all the blandishments of sculpture and architecture.‡ When first raised it must have excited admiration, bordering on enthusiastic devotion. The whole consists of three portions, or divisions in height ; a base or steps, a shaft, and a capital or basin. In the first are two tiers, or series of steps, raised above the pavement, each of which is ornamented on the exterior face with various panels and tracery. Each is also subdivided into two steps : the upper step, or surface, is formed by two divisions in its elevation, and eight in its horizontal plane. From the centre of this rises the shaft, which is surrounded by canopied niches, pinnacles, buttresses, pediments, and statues. At the angles are eight smaller statues standing on pedestals, and a series of trefoil lees extends round the upper member of this shaft, which is surmounted by the basin or font. This consists, like all other parts, of eight faces, each of which displays a canopied recess filled with a group of figures in basso relievo, representing the seven sacraments, with the crucifixion :

---

* Archæologia, xvi. 336.　　　　† Vol. iv. p. 108.

‡ He adds, " and Catholic superstition :" but as I am at a loss to discover any superstition in the representation of certain ceremonies which are surely religious, and which not the sculptor but the person who describes his work calls sacraments, and which in a lower sense than that in which we polemically use the word might safely be called sacraments, I have omitted the word *superstition* in this quotation.

I. Baptism. II. Confirmation. III. Penance. IV. The Eucharist.
V. Ordination. VI. Marriage. VII. Extreme Unction."

We have given these observations at full length, as they
are decidedly the best remarks on the form and decoration of
this *most important* and, we may add, *now most neglected* piece
of church furniture, that have yet appeared. Indeed, the lectures themselves are well deserving the most attentive perusal,
and were it not for certain most inconsistent expressions, they
would be worthy of a Catholic ecclesiastic.

But to return to the Camdenians. In the twenty-ninth
division, the restoration of ancient glazed and figured tile
pavement is advocated; and truly, unless these be revived, our
churches will never produce the rich and harmonious effect
of the ancient ones. The specimens now remaining of these
ornamented tile floors are in general so worn and mutilated,
that they convey but a very imperfect idea of their pristine
beauty to a general observer; but their effect on a grand
scale, as in the chapter-houses of Salisbury, Westminster, or
York, must have been truly splendid; their manufacture has
been lately most successfully revived in the Potteries. The
chancel of the conventual chapel at Birmingham, and that of
St. John's Hospital, Alton, have already been laid after the
ancient manner with great effect; and it is proposed to
lay the whole floor of St. Giles's church, now erecting at
Cheadle, and all the chapels and choirs of St. Barnabas, Nottingham, in a similar manner. The present cost of these
pavements, exclusive of the original moulds and the laying
down, is sixpence per tile, or eighteen shillings the square
yard, and an increased demand would of course have the effect of reducing the expense in proportion. In churches where
much gilding and colour is introduced, these incrusted tiles
of various hues are indispensable to produce harmony of effect;
for if so large a surface as the pavement is left of a dull
uniform tint, whilst the rest of the building is covered with
diaper and ornament, the contrast will be painfully striking.
To remedy this defect, most modern sanctuaries are covered
with drugget or carpeting, but these always produce a cham-
berlike appearance, and soon become faded and shabby, while
enameled tiles far exceed them in richness of appearance, do
not suffer any deterioration from damp, and impart a distinctive ecclesiastical character; of course their introduction does
not preclude carpeting from being laid on the altar steps, &c.
during the celebration of mass. Coopertoria are frequently

mentioned in old church inventories,* but these should be wove in appropriate designs, and as dissimilar as possible to those in ordinary domestic use.

The next important remark is relative to roodscreens.

"35. We have seen that the chancel and nave are to be kept entirely separate. This is done by the roodscreen, that most beautiful and Catholic appendage to a church. We have also seen that the prelates of the seventeenth century required it as a necessary ornament ; and that they who were most inveterate against roodlofts always held the roodscreen sacred. Why is it that *not one* modern church has it ? It constitutes one of the peculiar beauties of English buildings ; for abroad it is very rare. There can be no objection to the erection of a perpendicular screen in a church of earlier style ; because such was the constant practice, and because that style is better adapted for woodwork than any other. The whole may, and indeed ought to be, richly painted and gilded. The lower part, which is not pierced, may be painted with figures of saints, as in Castle Acre, Norfolk ; Therfield, Hertfordshire ; Guilden Morden, Cambridgeshire ; Bradninch, Devonshire ; why S. Edmund the King so often occurs is not known. In the appendix, nothing will be given but what might well serve as a model, though some instances may be much mutilated."

As many English Catholics of the present time, through ignorance of the antiquity and use of these divisions between the clergy and people, entertain most extraordinary, and, we may add, uncatholic prejudices and objections against their revival, it seems proper to enter upon this important subject at some length.

Roodscreens and lofts are not to be regarded as mere architectural enrichments raised for effect, nor as enclosures for the sole purpose of protecting the chancel from improper intrusion ; for although they contribute to both these ends, yet their real intention must be sought for on profound mystical reasons. Father Thiers has divided his learned treatise on

---

* " Cathedral Church of York. Coopertoria.
" Item, one large carpet to lay before the high altar on festivals.
" Item, a small carpet.
" Item, two large carpets to lay on the steps of the high altar, one of which has garbs, the other the arms of the Lord Scrope, lined with canvass.
" Item, a white carpet with double roses.
" Item, three blue carpets, with the arms of N. John Pakenham, late treasurer."—*Dugdale's Monasticon.*
" Item, ten cloths, called pede cloths, to lye before the high altar in the Ladye's chapel.
" Item, four pede cloaths, called tapets."—*Gunton's Hist. of the Church of Peterburgh.*

roodlofts into thirty-four chapters, containing a most elaborate account of their origin and purpose. As this treatise is a good-sized volume in itself, it is only possible to glance at the leading portions of the work, but these will be amply sufficient to set forth their real use and importance. The great intention of these screens and lofts is twofold.

1. To mark the separation between the faithful and the sacrifice, the nave and chancel, emblematic of the Church militant and the Church triumphant, into which latter we can alone enter by the merits of Christ's passion on the cross, whose image, as crucified for our sins, is affixed on high above the centre of the screen.

2. To enable the deacon to chaunt the holy Gospel to the faithful from a high place, in accordance with the practice and tradition of the Church in all ages. This custom is attested by most of the ecclesiastical writers of antiquity, and it was preserved in many of the French cathedrals down to the time of the great revolution of 1790. So that the roodlofts might have been called with propriety, the throne of the Word of God.*

---

* "Cathedral de St. Jean de Lyon.—Le diacre demande la bénédiction au célébrant; et ils vont au jubé en cet ordre. Le portemasse, les deux porte-chandeliers, le soudiacre d'office tenant un coussin devant sa poitrine, un des diacres assistans tenant l'encensoir, puis le diacre tenant les livres des évangiles que personne lorsqu'il passe ne salue, *ils montent au jubé;* là le soudiacre regarde le diacre en face, puis après ces mots, 'sequentia sancti evangelii secundum,' le diacre se tourne avec tout le chœur vers l'autel et fait comme le célébrant un triple signe de croix. On n'encense point le livre ni avant ni après, *mais seulement le grand crucifix du jubé* est encensé de trois coups avant l'évangile et trois coups après.

"St. Maurice D'Angers.—Le grand diacre ayant commencé l'ante évangelium, l'orgue la continue, et cependant on va au jubé en cet ordre. En allant deux thuriféraires parfument d'encens le chemin de chaque côté, suivis de deux porte-chandeliers, puis un petit diacre portant le texte des épîtres, et le grand diacre celui des évangiles, vont tous trois par le côté de l'épître et *montent au jubé,* &c.

"St. Etienne D'Auxerre.—Le diacre va au jubé lire l'évangile, étant précédé d'un enfant de chœur qui porte une voile environ de deux pieds et demi pour couvrir le pupître, sur lequel l'évangile doit être chanté, des deux portechandeliers et du portecroix; puis marchent le thuriféraire, le soudiacre, et le diacre portant le livre des évangiles fort haut: *ils montent en cet ordre au jubé,*" etc.

De Moleon, Voyage Liturgique.

These are only a few of the many instances cited in the above work, to prove that the original use of the roodlofts continued in many of the French Churches till the great revolution.

The "Voyage Liturgique" is a most edifying work, and gives an impressive account of the great solemnity with which the Church celebrated her sacred offices; one page of this book should be quite sufficient to silence the boastings of certain writers of these days, who, with only a bason and a pair of *unlighted candles,* talk about Catholic rites and ceremonies, and that with an authoritative tone which is as unseemly as it is ridiculous.

3. The roodlofts were generally used for preaching, both in the Eastern and Western Churches, previous to the introduction of pulpits, which are not older than the 13th century.

4. The martyrology and lessons were read from the roodlofts.

5. The festivals and fasts were announced to the faithful from the roodlofts.

6. According to a homily of St. John of Chrysostom, the deacon stood in the roodloft to pronounce those awful words *Sancta Sanctis*, to the people, before the communion.

7. The emperors were crowned in the jubé or roodloft of the great church at Constantinople, and the French kings, down to Charles the Tenth, were always enthroned in the roodloft at Rheims cathedral.

8. Antiphons, responds, versicles, and certain prayers, were chaunted from the roodlofts, as also the gradual, Alleluia, and tract.

9. The prophecies preceding the epistles on the Christmas masses, at midnight, break of day, and morning, were chanted from the rood, also the passion of our Lord on Palm Sunday and Good Friday.

These screens were to be found anciently in the greater part of the continental churches, or at least a beam, with the rood and an elevated ambo for the lecture of the Gospel.

In England, every church, previous to the great schism, was provided with a screen and roodloft. It is impossible to say the precise period when these were introduced; many of the Norman and early chancels communicating only by a small archway with the nave, the wall itself became a sort of screen, but there is little doubt that the archway was provided with gates and a rood-beam. Those in the cathedral, conventual, and collegiate churches, were generally built solid of stone, enameled with canopied niches and images, and provided with two staircases for the gospeller and epistler to ascend different ways,* on their proper sides of the choir.

---

* In the noble but shamefully neglected church of Tattershall, Lincolnshire, formerly collegiate, is a splendid roodloft of stone, with recesses for an altar on either side of the choir door; the parapet on the eastern side is corbelled out like a pulpit, for the lector, and provided with desks or ledges for books, excellently devised in the stone work. It is quite lamentable to behold this noble fabric falling to utter ruin; it must have been a sumptuous building in its glory, filled with admirable glass, elaborate carvings, and exquisite monumental brasses, now torn up and lying about, many large fragments and plates being totally lost. To this church was annexed fair collegiate buildings, with cloisters, gardens, orchards, &c.; and the establishment consisted of a master, six

In parochial churches, the screens and lofts were generally constructed of timber, and, with few exceptions, had only one staircase, usually built in a small turret outside the walls,* or in the substance of a large pillar. In this country, owing to the Protestant plan of converting the cathedral choirs into preaching places and pewing them, most of the ancient roodlofts have escaped destruction,† and in this respect our cathedrals are far more perfect than the continental churches, where the partial decay of the ancient solemn discipline, combined with pagan ideas of taste and the ravages of the great revolution, have left but few of the sumptuous roodlofts which were formerly to be found in every great church.‡

The roodlofts in ancient days were splendidly adorned on great festivals with lights and branches: that of All Hallow's,

chaplains, six clerks, six choristers, and fourteen poor brethren, till the suppression, by that sacrilegious tyrant Henry, who granted it to the then Duke of Suffolk.

* Fine examples at Lavenham church, Suffolk; St. Martin's church, Stamford, Lincolnshire; Wells church, Norfolk; Long Melford church, Suffolk; and many others.

† York, Lincoln, Exeter, (Norwich, till the late repairs,) Wells, Canterbury, Bristol, Southwell minster, Ripon minster, Christchurch, Hampshire, have all most splendid stone roodlofts, well preserved, but now used as mere organ lofts, nor have any of the ancient rites been performed in them since the schism of the English Church.

‡ The ancient roodloft of the splendid abbey of St. Ouen, Rouen, engraved in Dom Pomeraye's history of that great house, must have been truly glorious. It was provided with two circular stone staircases on either side; towards the nave it was subdivided into three grand arches, like a cloister; in the centre bay was the choir door, with brass gates of intricate design; in the other bays were two altars with reredoses, enriched with niches, canopies, and images; over the centre bay was the great rood, upwards of sixty feet high from the pavement, with images of our blessed Lady and St. John; and immediately below the base of the cross, on a corbel pedestal, an image of our blessed Lady, called of pity, with the body of our Lord. This splendid monument of Catholic piety and art, sumptuously adorned with painting, gilding, and rich furniture, was greatly injured and defaced by the French Calvinists in 1562, and finally destroyed in the revolution of 1791.

The cathedral of Alby yet possesses a splendid roodloft, of the same style as that formerly at St. Ouen.

At Louvain is a fine roodloft, with a most elaborate cross, painted and gilt in the original colours. A few years since, however, the wretched innovators removed the altars, which stood in arched recesses on each side of the choir door, and thus destroyed the lower part of this splendid screen, which now appears naked and unfinished: the same destructives would have demolished the stone tabernacle for the reservation of the blessed sacrament, because it *stood on one side of the choir,* but in this project they were happily defeated.

Although it is now exceeding rare to find roodscreens in the country parish churches on the continent, they are frequently mentioned in old documents, and there can be no doubt that they were as common as in England. It is quite a mistake to suppose that roods and roodlofts were confined to this country, —they were universal during the good time.

Bread-street, in London, was sometimes lit up with twenty-two tapers, weighing 67 lbs.* The rood and beam lights are frequently mentioned in old church accounts, and pious souls left both lands and houses to maintain these bright emblems of our Lord's glory. Coronas, or circles of light, were often suspended in the roodlofts, as at St. Jean of Lyon, where three crowns with tapers were lit on all doubles. The crosses standing in the loft were richly floreated, and ornamented with emblems of the evangelists at the extremities; and *these in very early times*, Father Thiers says, " Codin temoigne qu'il y avoit une croix d'or qui prezoit cent livres, et qui *toute eclairée de flambeaux*, et toute parseméc de pierreries au dessus du jubé de Sainte Sophie."

The great rood was certainly one of the most impressive features of a Catholic Church; and a screen surmounted with its lights and images, covered with gold and paintings of holy men, forms indeed a glorious entrance to the holy place set apart for sacrifice. We have here introduced an etching of the great screen and rood lately erected in the Cathedral Church of St. Chad, Birmingham (plate IV), and which will afford a tolerable idea of the sublime effect of the ancient roodscreens, before their mutilation under Edward the Sixth. The images are all ancient and were procured from some of the suppressed continental abbeys; the crucifix itself is of the natural size, and carved with wonderful art and expression; the images of our blessed Lady and St. John are less in proportion, which is quite correct. Immediately under tracery panels in front of the loft, are a series of ancient sculptures; the centre of which represents the consecration of St. Chad, patron of the church, the other refers to the life and glories of St. John the Baptist. On the mullions between the open panels, on foliated corbels, are eight images of prophets. The rood is richly gilt and painted, and it is proposed to continue the same decoration over the screen itself. At St. Alban's, Macclesfield, is a perpendicular screen, also surmounted by an ancient rood with images and lights. St. Mary's, Dudley, St. Oswald's, near Liverpool, St. Wilfred's, Manchester, are all furnished with roods and screens, revived faithfully from ancient authorities, enriched with paintings and gilding, ascended by a turret staircase, and in all respects similar to those which existed in the old English Churches previous to their desecration under Protestant ascendency. St. George's-

* Nicholl's Londinum Redivivum, vol. i. p. 21.

in-the-Fields, London, and St. Barnabas, Nottingham, both now erecting, will have spacious roodlofts ascended by double staircases; and at St. Giles's, Cheadle, a screen is in preparation with a ribbed and overhanging canopy, supporting a loft with a splendid rood; the whole of this screen will be enriched with gold and lively colours, and on the lower panels images of apostles and martyrs, painted in the severe style of Christian art. On referring to the engravings accompanying this article, it will be seen that a correct screen and roodloft, with its rood and images, has been erected in every church there figured, and that the English Catholics have revived this mystical and impressive feature of the ancient churches in all its integrity. The sacrilegious destruction of the roods under Edward the Sixth, their subsequent restoration in the reign of Queen Mary, and final demolition on the establishment of Protestant principles by Elizabeth, will be set forth at large hereafter.

Of embroidery and needlework, the writer most justly remarks:

" We may be allowed to ask, would not the time and ingenuity spent on worsted-work, satin-stitch, bead-work, and the like frivolities, be better employed if it were occupied in preparing an offering to God, for the adornment of His holy dwelling places ? Hour after hour is cheerfully sacrificed in the preparation of useless trifles for those charity bazaars, which would fain teach us that we *can* serve God and mammon : no time is then thought too much, no labour spared. But when an altar-cloth or carpet is to be provided, then the commonest materials and commonest work are thought good enough. Better examples were set in former times : as here and there a tattered piece of church embroidery still remains to tell us."

It is most gratifying to perceive that true ideas on these matters are fast spreading themselves,* and it is fervently to be hoped that they will eventually cause a better style of work to be introduced amongst those ladies who profess to embroider for the Church : at present, the generality of their productions, covered as they are with hearts, rosebuds, and doves, stand forth in all their *prettiness*, like valentine letters on a large scale; and truly it would seem as if they derived

---

* We most earnestly recommend the perusal of a work by the Rev. E. Paget, entitled "St. Antholin's or Old Churches and New," which is an admirable production, and enlarges considerably on some of the topics alluded to in the above extract.

80

all their ideas and authorities from such sources. It must,
however, be observed in justice, that although the majority
as yet most obdurately refuse to adopt true ideas when offered
to them, still there are many glorious exceptions, of which
the hangings in St. Chad's are ample testimony; and fresh
converts are being continually made, even among those who
seemed hopelessly entangled in modern trumpery.

From the few examples of ancient vestments that have
escaped destruction, the generality of persons are but little
acquainted with the extreme beauty of the embroidery worked
for ecclesiastical purposes during the Middle Ages. The
countenances of the images were executed with perfect expression, like miniatures in illuminated manuscripts.* Every
parochial church, previous to the change of religion, was
furnished with complete sets of frontals and hangings for the
altars. What then must' have been the overpowering splendour and glory of the cathedral and abbatial churches when
decorated for the great festivals; the canopies, the needlework hangings, the monumental palls covered with heraldic
devices, the altar-cloths, and, above all, the suits of sacred
vestments,† when our bishops celebrated with the whole choir

* In the collection of ecclesiastical antiquities preserved at St. Mary's College, Oscott, are several specimens of copes and vestments of the fifteenth century, the orphreys of which are wonderful examples of ancient skill, the minutest details being perfectly expressed with the richest colouring.

† We read in the inventory of Lincoln, "twenty fair copes of the same suit,
with three wheels of silver in the hoods.

"Item, five red copes of red velvet, with Katharine wheels of gold and orphreys, with images in tabernacles.

"Item, a cope of the root of Jesse.

"Item, thirteen copes of the same suit of blue velvet.

"Item, six copes of one suit broidered with angels, having this scripture,
Da Gloriam Deo, with orphreys of needlework, of which four have the four
evangelists in the morses, and the fifth a lamb in the morse.

"Item, eighteen copes of red satin of one suit, with orphreys of gold, and
images."

There were upwards of two hundred and fifty copes, all of most costly material and elaborate embroidery, belonging to the cathedral church of Lincoln,
till the latter part of Henry the Eighth's reign.

There were one hundred and twenty-eight copes, many exceedingly costly,
belonging to the choir service of the cathedral church of St. Paul, London, besides those which were used for the church of St. Faith's, and various chapels
attached to the mother church.

In the inventory of the ornaments belonging to the church at Peterborough,
one hundred and seventeen copes are mentioned.

"York Minster.—Item, twenty-one copes of white velvet, of one suit, with
gold orphreys.

"Item, eighteen blue copes with orphreys of red cloth of gold."

In all, three hundred and two copes belonging to the revestry of York Minster.

These are only a few examples, to show how splendidly our churches were
furnished with vestments previous to their plunder by that sacrilegious monster
Henry the Eighth.

filled with clergy, in copes, chasubles, and dalmatics, all of most costly material and exquisite detail? In some churches there were twenty or thirty copes in one suit, with a succession of subjects from the life of our Lord in the hoods and orphreys to correspond.

One of the great beauties of the ancient embroidery was its appropriate design; each flower, each leaf, each device had a significant meaning with reference to the festival to which the frontal or vestment belonged. This principle is completely overlooked at present; any design, so long as it is considered to look pretty, is introduced indiscriminately for all seasons, and in all situations. There is no distinction between the pattern of a drawing-room paper and that of a cope, or any perceptible difference in the figure of the stuff sold for dresses and that used in vestments; hence the ecclesiastical costume of the present day looks showy but not rich, and certainly fails in imparting dignity to the ministers of religion. On the contrary, the effect of the ancient vestments, which were exclusively ecclesiastical in their design, and conveyed a symbolic meaning by every ornament about them,* must have been so imposing and edifying, as to fill the beholder with reverence. England was famous for the production of embroidered vestments, insomuch that they were eagerly sought for all over Christendom, and known by the name of English work;† even in the Saxon times we read of nine albs‡ being sent as a present to Rome from this country,

* In the third volume of " Gerbert de Veturi Liturgia Alemannica," three copes of about the tenth century are accurately figured. They are divided into compartments, each containing a subject from the Old or New Testament, the images being so disposed on the half-circle as to appear upright when the cope was worn, and there are certainly not less than one hundred figures on each cope. The Earl of Shrewsbury has at present in his possession a cope of the twelfth century, formerly belonging to the nuns of Sion, divided all over in quatrefoils, each containing a saint or angel, and on the upper part the crucifixion of our Lord, all most exquisitely worked in silk.

A great number of crosses for chasubles, in needlework of the fifteenth century, are yet preserved in Catholic families; in the centre of these is usually the crucifixion of our Lord, while angels in the arms of the cross are raising the sacred blood in chalices; the mere inspection of these must convince every unprejudiced mind of the vast superiority and fitness of the sacred subjects selected for the orphreys of vestments in ancient days, over the mere scroll patterns and unmeaning ornaments that have been substituted in these latter times.

+ Such was the extreme beauty of the English vestments in the reign of Henry the Third, that Innocent the Fourth forwarded bulls to many English bishops, enjoining them to send a certain quantity of embroidered vestments to Rome, for the use of the clergy there.

‡ It must not be supposed that these embroidered albs were composed of lace flounces, in the ball dress style. Such monstrosities were not imagined for eight centuries after the period referred to. The embroidery of these albs

F

and offerings of the same kind were constantly being forwarded to the holy see, till the English schism. These facts are sufficient to show the high state of perfection to which the art of embroidery had arrived in this country during the *dark ages*, and are a complete refutation to those who are so desirous of proving that we were compelled to seek foreign aid in the production of our more costly and finished works. England, while Catholic, was a flower-garden of art; her Church was glorious indeed, and there was more real skill and Christian design exhibited in the erection of any one of her Cathedrals, than is now to be found in the united academies of Europe under the blasting influence of Protestantism and Paganism combined. Not only were all these splendid monuments of her ancient skill mutilated or destroyed, but the spirit which produced them was for a time entirely hid, we

---

consisted of sacred images wrought in the apparels; these apparels were compartments, of about two feet in length and one in width; they were attached to the alb nearly as low as the feet, before and behind, while lesser compartments of the same design and material were affixed to the lower extremity of the sleeve, above the wrist; the mystical signification of these apparels most probably referred to the wounds of our Lord; their use was universal in Christendom, and the ornaments on them were both costly and exceedingly beautiful. Albs with their apparels, are frequently mentioned in inventories of church vestments; they are to be perfectly distinguished on the effigy of every priest or bishop where any vestige of the original painting remains; and they are exceedingly conspicuous on all engraved monumental brasses of ecclesiastics, and in images painted on glass. In 1605, the tomb of Pope Boniface the Eighth, who died in 1305, was opened; the body was found entire, in full vestments, pontifically attired. The two apparels of the albs were filled with scripture histories, in gold and silk; on the front apparel, the history of our Lord, from the annunciation to the finding in the temple; on the back, the passion, resurrection, &c. Each apparel was three-and-a-half palms long and a palm wide. A minute description of the vestments is given in John Rubens (Ross), an English Benedictine, in his "Bonifacius VIII;" Rome, 1651; p. 346. On all the effigies of ecclesiastical persons prior to the sixteenth century, which are remaining in the churches at Rome, the apparels of the albs are most perfectly delineated: in the celebrated picture of the conversion of St. Jerome, the deacon, who is kneeling on the foreground, is habited in an apparelled alb; and in Raphael's "Transfiguration," on the alb of a deacon who is kneeling in the upper corner of the picture, on the left hand, the apparels are shown on the sleeves. De Moleon, in his "Voyage Liturgique," calls these albs "albæ paratæ;" and mentions several churches where they were used in France, when he wrote, as at St. Agnan d'Orleans, St. Maurice d'Angers, &c. His words are as follows: "L'aube a des paremens en bas conformes aux ornemens: ce qui s'appelle dans les brefs, Alba parata: on *s'en sert encore aujourdhui dans les églises cathédrales, et dans les anciennes abbayes.*" As De Moleon wrote only in the last century, the lace flounces must be of very recent introduction in France. Apparels precisely similar in pattern to those engraved on the monumental brasses of ancient churchmen, have been lately wove in gold and coloured silks, and are worn with the albs on festivals; their cost is less than one-half of a modern bordering, and in them are revived, at one time, a striking emblem of our Lord's passion and the universal practice of the Church in the days of her glory.

will not say extinguished,—for now the spirit of the thirteenth century seems to animate many of her children in the nineteenth, and what may we not reasonably hope to see restored? The manufacture of precious stuffs has been lately revived,* and why should not many of the looms which have so long laboured to supply the changing demand of worldly fashion, be again employed in clothing the spouse of Christ—the Church—in her ancient glorious garb?

But we must most earnestly impress on the minds of all those who work in any way for the decoration of the altar, that the only hope of reviving the perfect style is by *strictly adhering to ancient authorities*; illuminated MSS., stained glass, and *especially brasses* (which can easily be copied by rubbing), will furnish excellent examples, and many of them easy of imitation. We cannot yet hope to revive the expression and finish of the old work, but we may readily restore its general character, for many instances could be cited where this has been already most successfully accomplished in buildings engraved in this work; and with a little practice, it is easier and much sooner produced than the trifling no-meaning patterns of the modern style. Is it not reasonable to suppose, that when the whole country was Catholic, and when the decoration of the Church formed the grand object on which the most ingenious efforts were bestowed, that the subject was far better understood than at present? We may have made great improvements in steam-engines, but certainly not in frontals and orphreys; and York and Canterbury will furnish far better patterns than either Paris or Protestant Berlin. The following works might be consulted with great advantage: *Shaw's Illuminated Ornaments*; *Shaw's Decorations of the Middle Ages*; *Waller's Brasses;* and to facilitate the object as much as possible, it is proposed to publish very shortly a series of ornaments, full size, as working-patterns. It is proper to observe, that the heraldic law, of colour being always laid on metal, or metal on colour, should be strictly observed in embroidering; and one of the five canonical colours should be selected as a field for the whole work. Velvet is the best material that can be used, after cloth of gold, for the ground.

The writer is not altogether correct in the observations he makes respecting stained glass. The colours are now most perfectly restored to all their original brilliancy;† the soul

* The cloth of gold for the best suit of vestments offered to St. Chad's Church by the Earl of Shrewsbury, was manufactured at Spitalfields, London, and at a less cost than it could have been imported from Lyons.

† Another great point which has been lately attained is the thickness of the

and feeling of the old glass-painters is alone wanting; and even in this department, some surprising advances have recently been made; though closely following the style, touch, and manner of ancient artists, who were, for the most part, men of extraordinary talent; they expressed so much with simple means, almost all their effect is produced by mere lines or scraping out. The great mistake of modern glass-painters has been, in treating the panes of windows like pictures or transparencies with forcing lights and shadows. The old artists worked in a conventional manner, not through ignorance, but from science: they worked, in fact, *to suit their material.* The beautiful outline of the stone tracery is the better defined, by their manner of filling up the vacant spaces. They did not aim at a picture cut up with mullions, but they enriched the openings left by those mullions; and this principle was rigidly adhered to, till the decline of the pointed style. Those who climb up by means of ladders, and examine these windows in detail, can alone appreciate the wonderful merits of the execution: the grace displayed in the ramifications of foliage, and the tendrils of plants (especially in those windows executed immediately preceding and during the decorated period), is most admirable. Again, nothing can be conceived more elegant than the outline of the crockets, *merely perhaps scraped out.** And as for expression, the countenances are, in many cases, perfectly heavenly; full of devotion, and yet produced by mere lines. How do modern virtuosos and collectors boast in the possession of bacchanalian groups, painted by some *celebrated* pagan artist of the latter times! and what immense sums are paid for a Cupid or Venus, which are trumpeted forth as national acquisitions, while the most exquisite specimens of English art are utterly neglected, scarcely held from ruin by the mouldering bands to which they cling!† We shall probably incur the accusation of wild enthusiasm for the assertion we are about to make;

---

old glass: thin glass will never produce either the richness or the solemn tint of the ancient windows.

* Most of the minute work in the old glass is produced by scraping out; it is a very simple method, but requires the greatest skill in the artist.

† The parochial Churches of York contain many finer executed windows than the cathedral itself, and yet these are utterly neglected. Within the memory of persons yet living, whole windows have been suffered to fall out, and to be replaced *with white panes*; and at the present time some of the most interesting windows, especially at All Saints, North Street, and St. John's and St. Martin's, Micklegate, if *not speedily and effectually repaired will be irrecoverably ruined.* This, although distant from the scene of action, is yet a case for the "Camden;" for the windows alluded to are marvellously fine, and their loss would be irretrievable.

but we will say, that there are yet remaining in obscure churches—almost miraculously preserved from Protestant violence—specimens of native art, executed in the thirteenth century, which for sublimity of expression, simplicity of outline, dignity of position, and devotional effect, very far surpass anything yet introduced in the National Gallery of Painting; and the day will come, sooner or later, that tardy justice will be done to the wonderful talents of Catholic Englishmen in the days of faith; and the brutal stupidity of these who, utterly blinded to the merits of their native country, have filled every museum and institute with pagan casts, will be generally perceived and heartily execrated.*

The following remarks on bells are conceived in a most Catholic spirit:

"55. It may not be out of place to say a few words on the subject of bells. You surely would not wish that instruments, consecrated like these to the praise of God, should be profaned by the foolish, profane, or self-laudatory inscriptions so often found on them. They, as all other parts of church furniture, are holy. The following are examples of ancient inscriptions on bells :

Defunctos ploro, vivos voco, fulgura frango.

Nos jungat thronis vere thronus Salomonis.

Agnus Sancte Dei, duc ad loca me requiei.

Nomen Sancte Jesu, me serva mortis ab esu.

Sanguis Xpi, salva me ! Passio Xpi, conforta me !

Te laudamus, et rogamus	First bell,
Nomen Jesu Christi	Second bell.
Ut attendas et defendas	Third bell,
Nos a morte tristi.	Fourth bell.

To these, we add the inscription on the only bell of the Cathedral of Rouen that escaped the melting-pot at the great Revolution:

"Laudo Deum verum, Plebem voco, congrego clerum,
Defunctos ploro, Pestem fugo, Festa decoro."

The conclusion of this excellent tract is as follows:

"58. Thus then imperfectly, but not, I hope, quite uselessly, have we completed our survey of a church and its ornaments. If

---

* What extraordinary infatuation is exhibited by those who dwell in cathedral towns, in the immediate vicinity of some glorious Church, capable in itself of furnishing ample instruction to every student that might present himself within its walls, when they pretend to found some school of art, and must needs import a shattered bull's head, and a volute as the beau-ideal of sculpture, whereby to pervert the minds and understandings of all the unfortuate youths who attend their institution.

everything else is forgotten, and two points only remembered, THE ABSOLUTE NECESSITY OF A DISTINCT AND SPACIOUS CHANCEL, and THE ABSOLUTE INADMISSIBILITY OF PEWS AND GALLERIES, in any shape whatever, I shall be more than rewarded. I have been writing in the name of a society; physically it may be weak in numbers and pecuniary resources, but morally strong in the zeal of its members and the goodness of its cause. It may, indeed, be years before the great truth is learnt, which that society hopes to be one of the instruments of teaching—the intrinsic holiness of a church, and the duty of building temples to God in some sort worthy of His presence. But learnt sooner or later it will be ; and to be allowed in any way to help forward so good a work, is a high privilege."

We can only observe, that the writer has accomplished his task in a manner quite worthy of the principles he here expresses, with the exception of some painful expressions; but where we find so much that is admirable and praiseworthy, we would fain, in charity, attribute them rather to the inconsistency of his present position, than to any graver cause.

As from the sublime to the ridiculous there is only one step, we may at once descend from the publications of the Camdenians, with their porches, fonts, aisles, screens and chancels, to notice a small book that has recently appeared, of the very opposite character, and entitled, *An Essay on Architectural Practice*. Although the title itself, implying the practice of architecture at the present time, would naturally lead us to expect something exceedingly bad, still the contents of the work exhibit church-building as fallen to a lower state of degradation than could possibly have been anticipated. The history of this production is briefly as follows: the architect having obtained the job of erecting one of the church commissioners' conventicles at the eastern end of the metropolis, instead of being content to pocket his commission and the disgrace of the production quietly, was resolved to set forth this genuine specimen of a London preaching-house of the nineteenth century, in the form of a distinct publication, under the above-mentioned title : having thus dragged forth this unsightly building from its local obscurity, and that at a time when a fine spirit is arising for real ecclesiastical architecture, he must not complain if he get as unmercifully treated as the enormity of his case deserves. Most architects, indeed, are content to build bad things; but to engrave, describe, and publish them afterwards, is something new, even in these pretending days. The illustrations consist of every possible dissection of the building, horizontal, vertical, lateral, transverse longitudinal—east, west, north, south—above, below, and all around; so that the edifice is perfectly set forth in all its poverty and ugliness. We have plans of concrete,—plans of footings,—plans of walls,—plans of pews,—plans of windows,—plans under galleries,—plans over galleries,—plans of slates,—plans of chimneys,—plans of gutters. As the funds allowed by church commissioners are too scanty to admit of much detail, there is not much set forth under this head; but the architect has atoned for the absence of bosses, capitals, niches, and tracery, by representing bricks, most ingeniously disposed in the form of barrel-drains, of varied diameters, and sections, of sewers and stink traps, with all the complicated principles of conveying dirty water from the gutter down a pipe, through a barrel-drain, into the common-sewer, thence to old Father Thames, and so on till lost in the expanse of ocean. In following the architect into these minutiæ, we have been hurried away by the muddy stream from the arrangement and appearance of the structure itself. The interior is a large room, covered with a low-pitched tie-beam roof; and if cleared out, would answer well for a *manège* or riding-school. The whole space is completely filled with pews, seats, and, of course, galleries, which are approached by staircases* at the west, and

---

* While thus noticing gallery staircases in churches, it may not be amiss to draw public attention to the atrocities that have lately been perpetrated in the venerable church of St. Saviour's, Southwark. But a few years since it was one of the most perfect second-class cruciform churches in England, and an edifice full of the most interesting associations connected with the ancient history of this metropolis. The roof was first stripped of its massive and solemn nave; in this state it was left a considerable time exposed to all the injuries of wet and weather; at length it was condemned to be pulled down, and in place of one of the finest specimens of ecclesiastical architecture left in London—with massive walls and pillars, deeply moulded arches, a most interesting south porch, and a splendid western doorway—we have as vile a preaching-place (with crowded galleries, gas-lights, &c.) as ever disgraced the nineteenth century. It is bad enough to see such an erection spring up at all; but when a venerable building is demolished to make room for it, the case is quite intolerable. Will it be believed, that under the centre tower in the transept of this once most beauteous church, *staircases on stilts* have been set up, exactly resembling those by which the company ascend to a booth on a race-course? We entreat every admirer of ancient architecture, every one who cherishes the least love for the ancient glory of his country's church, to visit this desecrated and mutilated fabric, and weep over its wretched condition, and then join in loud and lasting execrations against all concerned in this sacrilegious and barbarous destruction—ecclesiastical, parochial, or civil authorities, architect, builder, and every one in the least implicated in this business. Nothing but Protestantism and the preaching-house system could have brought such utter desolation on a stately church; in fact the abomination is so great that it must be seen to be credited.

carried up in two clumsy erections, intended to look like towers, but of an elevation and scale which at once betray their real purpose. *The style* of the building is what, in the classification of competition drawings, would be termed *Norman*—that is to say, the arches are not pointed; but in other respects, it bears no greater resemblance to the architecture of the tenth century, than it has in common with ordinary cellars, the Greenwich railway, or any round arched buildings. The illustrations are not, however, the most absurd portion of the publication; for the gravity and solemnity with which the most ordinary operations of building are described, are truly ridiculous: we have a full description of the different spots where holes were dug to ascertain the nature of the soil, of which remarkable excavations an accurate plan is inserted in the text. As the spade-handle was not, however, long enough to reach a sound bottom, the ingenious and novel experiment of boring was tried with complete success; by which it was ascertained, that for several feet the site was composed of accumulated rubbish (typical, perhaps, of the intended structure); this leads to a dissertation on concrete; then we have an account of the carting and stacking of bricks, mixing mortar, building the walls, and the whole method of erecting a church on the cheap and nasty principle, winding up, like the address of an actor on a benefit night, with thanks to every body, for their unparalleled efforts and exertions. We are, however, obliged to the author for this publication, for it must do good by its very absurdity; and combining as it does, at one view, so many abominations which are common to the modern practice of church building, it must convince every unprejudiced person of the absolute necessity of strictly adhering to ancient models and authorities in these matters, if we would erect churches at all worthy of their sacred purpose.

We now turn the work in question over to the tender mercies of the Camden Society, where it will not find more favourable treatment than it has met with from us, if we may judge by the tone of the following most admirable critique, which appeared in the first number of the *Ecclesiologist*, a monthly publication that has long been a desideratum, devoted exclusively to ecclesiastical researches and intelligence.

"A church has recently been erected in a very populous part of Cambridge, called New Town, and is now nearly completed, the whole of the exterior being finished, and the internal arrangements in a state of rapid progress. The church is intended to hold an indefinite number of people, that is, as many as can be packed in a small area by means of most extensive galleries, which are ingeniously contrived so as to run round and fill up every part of the interior ; insomuch that upon entering the church, it appears, at first sight, to be *all gallery*, and nothing else.

"The church is of no particular style or shape ; but it may be described as a conspicuous red brick building, of something between Elizabethan and debased perpendicular architecture. A low tower is added at the west end, in order that the rather doubtful ecclesiastical character of the edifice may not be mistaken, and for the purpose of containing, or rather displaying to advantage, three immense clock faces, which will doubtless be useful as well as ornamental appurtenances to the building. The general design of this edifice is marked by the fearless introduction of several remarkable varieties and peculiarities of arrangement, which are strictly original conceptions.

"The tower is low, and of rather plain design than otherwise; superfluity of ornament having been carefully avoided, lest it should be out of character with the rest of the building. The chief features of the tower are four heavy brick walls, having large four-centred belfry windows in the upper part, without cusping or mouldings, but filled up to the top with louvre slates. There are also four octagonal turrets, which rise a few feet above the battlements, and look very humble and unaspiring, as becomes a modest cheap church in these days of refined architectural taste. The most remarkable, and one which is likely soon to prove the most striking peculiarity of this tower, is a vast circular aperture in each of the three sides, for the reception of the clock or clocks already alluded to. These apertures, or rather chasms, are circular holes cut in huge square stones, the four spandrils or corners of which are beautifully ornamented with the figures 1, 1, 4 and 8, which give scope to ingenious combinations, and which may be read in such an order as to make the date of the year, 1841. The hole is large enough for a full-grown bullock to leap through, were he desirous to try the experiment, as the tumbler does through a hoop ; and we should say the sooner each of them is stopped up by a good large clock (that of St. Paul's Cathedral, if procurable second-hand, would answer pretty well,) the better, since the upper part of the tower has at present the novel and rather unpleasant appearance from a distance of standing upon four legs.

" The church is constructed of very red brick indeed, agreeably relieved at the corners by nice little white quoins of dressed ashlar, imparting a very picturesque appearance to the whole edifice. There are patterns, too, representing visionary trellis-work, playfully displayed in the construction in black bricks, which really have a delightful effect, though we fear that this is a plagiarism from the beautiful new brick church recently erected in Barnwell. It is intended, we presume, for a pied variety of Great St. Mary's in this town ; though others suppose it rather to be a travesty of the chapel of Magdalene College, Oxford.

"The windows of the aisles (for there are two real aisles, and a well developed clerestory lighted by rows of neat square cottage windows) are perhaps just a thought too large ; but if the mullions had not stood *quite* on the same plane with the wall, and the heads had been pointed instead of square, and the jambs had had something of a moulding, and the lights been cinquefoiled in the head and under the transom, they would not have looked altogether unlike church windows. But here we cannot sufficiently admire the ingenuity which has completely obviated any objection to their size by intercepting the upper half with galleries, which appear indeed to be supported on the transoms, though this is only an ingenious deception, since the mullions would most infallibly give way under the weight of such extensive structures when filled with people. There are real arches and piers inside ; none of your cheap cast-iron pillars, but sturdy brick columns, without capitals, covered over with plaster that looks at a reasonable distance very like stone, and supporting four-centered arches with neat discontinuous mouldings cast in the plaister. The roof is a kind of flat deal ceiling, with thin pieces of wood here and there to look like purlins, principals, &c. &c. ; and the whole, being varnished very brightly, looks as gay as the roof of the saloon in a first-rate steam ship. As the altar is not yet put up, and probably not yet thought of, we cannot say where it will be placed ; but we have been unable, upon the closest inspection, to discover any place adapted for its reception : indeed, we are inclined to fear that it has been forgotten altogether. The elevation of the east end is rather peculiar. There is *no chancel whatever;* not even the smallest recess as an apology for one. But there is a beautiful vestry ; a low square building, lighted with square windows, and having an embattled parapet reaching as high as the sill of the east window. The interior is fitted up very snugly with a fire-place and other conveniences, and is indeed by far the most respectable part of the whole building. The gable of the nave is ornamented with a graduated parapet, which looks like a flight of perilous steps to a small cross which surmounts the highest point. As the architect perhaps intended to be symbolical herein, we shall say nothing of its appearance, nor of the great sprawling east window, if we may be allowed such a harsh expression, with consumptive-looking mullions and transom, and destitute of tracery. Both this and the west window in the tower are rather unsuccessful specimens of modern Gothic ; or perhaps we should have said, very good examples of modern, but very bad ones of ancient Gothic.

"We have thus briefly detailed the general features of this extremely interesting building, because we feel certain that those who have not seen it, cannot form a thoroughly correct and comprehensive idea of a CHEAP CHURCH OF THE NINETEENTH CENTURY."

We have seen and examined the building which has called forth these severe remarks, and we most willingly bear full testimony to their justice: indeed it is scarcely possible to speak in adequate terms of this wretched edifice; erected as if in mockery, under the very shadow of so many beautiful specimens of ancient skill, which still remain in this venerable university. It is only by depicting modern deformities in forcible language that we can hope for their being remedied. Milk-and-water men never effect anything; they deserve drowning in their own insipid compositions.

We have been induced to give this extract at full length, first on account of its being the very best description of a Protestant church that has yet appeared; and secondly, as we perceived with much regret that owing to the sensitive feelings of some black sheep in the society, who protested against it on very absurd grounds, the committee, after some sensible observations in defence of the remarks, have consented, for the sake of peace, to withdraw them, and reprint the number in which they were contained. Now if the feelings of individuals are to be consulted instead of truth, no correct observations will ever be published; for in the present state of ecclesiastical architecture, if you allude to imitation stone, meagre tracery, gallery fronts, and the like, the observations can be so generally applied, that, as the poet says,

"If you mention vice or bribe, you so point to all the tribe,
    Each one cries that was levelled at me,"

and the incumbents of five hundred new churches will take fire at once. We do hope, therefore, that in future the society will not compromise truth in any shape; and they can well afford to spare those who are not prepared to take a high ground in these matters, for such individuals are mere drags on the grand revival. At all events the admirable remarks which drew forth this protestation will not be consigned to oblivion; they are here reproduced in full, and we hope they will be printed on a fly-sheet and circulated at architectural societies, competition committees, and church-building meetings, as Methodist sabbath-breaking denunciations are distributed in tea-gardens and steam-boats; they should be headed "*Beware of the Camden,*" and hung up *in terrorem* in every church-competing architect's office, to deter those gentlemen from proceeding in the present wretched system, and lead them, if possible, into the old track.

We proceed to notice several ecclesiastical structures, either lately erected or now in progress, which will show that some of the English Catholics, fully inheriting the zeal and feelings of their forefathers, are reviving Christian architecture in all its original spirit; and it is indeed gratifying to perceive, that those who work on the ancient foundation of faith, although slender in means and few in number, are enabled, by the blessing of God, to achieve far greater practical results than those of their countrymen who, possessing equal ardour in the good cause and vast temporal resources, are precluded by their present unfortuuate position from carrying out in practice their excellent intentions.

THE HOSPITAL OF ST. JOHN. PLATE V.

This hospital, of which the annexed plate represents a bird's-eye view, is now erecting in the village of Alton, Staffordshire, within half a mile of the seat of the Earl of Shrewsbury, by whose pious munificence it is being raised; and when completed it is intended for the following foundation: a warden and confrater, both in priest's orders; six chaplains or decayed priests, a sacrist, twelve poor brethren, a schoolmaster, and an unlimited number of poor scholars. To accommodate these various persons, the building will consist of a chapel, school, lodging for the warden, common hall, kitchen, chambers and library for the six chaplains, lodgings for the poor brethren, and a residence for the schoolmaster, all connected by a cloister. Of these buildings the chapel, school, warden's lodgings, part of the cloister, and schoolmaster's house are already completed, and a few years will suffice to finish the remaining portions of the edifice as shown in the view. The whole is constructed of hewn stone in the most solid and durable manner, and the principal roofs, as well as flooring joists, and beams, are worked in English oak. Immediately facing the western end of the school is a stone cross raised on steps; the base is quadrangular, with an Evangelist within a quatrefoil on each face; the upper part of the shaft terminates in a foliated cap supporting a quadrangular niche containing an angel bearing emblems of our Lord's passion on every side; at the summit of which is a floreated cross of stone. Over the porch, or entrance to the cloister and warden's lodgings, is a niche containing an image of St. John the Baptist with the lamb; and another image of St. Nicholas with the three boys is placed in a canopied niche in the west window of the school. The side windows of this

UorM

ST JOHNS CHURCH ALTON STAFFS

school are filled with painted glass, consisting of armorial bearings, figured quarries and borders; and round the lower lights of the seven windows is the following inscription: "Of your charity pray for the good estate of John the sixteenth Earl of Shrewsbury, who founded this hospital in honour of St. John the Baptist, Anno Domini 1840. St. John pray for us. Amen."

To the eastward of the school is the chapel, an interior view of which is here given, Plate VI. This portion of the building has been most carefully finished, and contains much decoration. The whole floor is laid with figured tiles, charged with the Talbot arms and other devices. The benches are precisely similar to those remaining in some ancient parish churches in Norfolk, with low backs filled with perforated tracery of various patterns; the poppy-heads are all carved, representing oak and vine leaves, lilies, roses, lions, angels, and other emblems. The chancel is divided off by a rich screen, surmounted with a rood and images. The shields in the brestsummer are all charged with sacred emblems in gold and colours. The rood is also richly gilt. Each principal of the roof springs from an angel corbel, bearing each a shield or a scripture; the braces, tiebeams, rafters, and purloins of this roof are moulded, and the spandrils filled with open tracery. On each side of the east window is a niche with images of St. Katharine and St. Barbara. The reredos and altar are both worked in alabaster;* the former consists of a series of richly canopied niches surmounted by an open brattishing; images of the apostles holding the emblems of their martyrdom, with our blessed Lord in the centre, occupy these niches. The altar itself consists of three large and three lesser compartments, with the images of our blessed Lady, St. John the Baptist, and St. Alban, with two angels seated on thrones

---

* It is to be hoped that the use of this beautiful material, which was constantly used by the Catholic artists in their more elaborate works, will be generally revived. It is admirably adapted for the finest style of carving, easily worked, exceedingly durable, and capable of receiving a high polish. The best quarries are at Tutbury, in Staffordshire; but at present they remain quite neglected, being only casually worked, when materials for plaister are required. Blocks of a sufficient size for sepulchral effigies might be easily procured, and at a moderate cost. Many of the most beautiful ancient monuments were worked in alabaster; also reredoses of altars, and generally images. In the churchwardens' accounts in the time of Edward VI. (when the spoliation and destruction of the English parochial churches was commenced), we frequently find entries of sums received for *alabaster work sold by weight as material for making plaster !!!* And at that fatal period many of the most exquisite productions in this material perished in the kiln.

bearing the lamb and cross. The sunk work is picked out in azure; the raised mouldings and carved ornaments gilt, and the remainder polished alabaster, similar to some of the costly tombs yet remaining in Westminster. and other churches. On each side of this altar silk curtains are suspended on rods. The cross is an exquisite specimen of ancient silver work of the fifteenth century, made, as the inscription round the foot relates, by one Peter, for a German bishop, who bore the charge for the love of Christ crucified. This precious relic of Christian art is parcel-gilt, and covered with ornaments and images of wonderful execution. A pair of parcel-gilt silver candlesticks have been made to correspond in style with this cross; they are richly chased, engraven, and ornamented with enamels.

On the gospel side of the chancel is a small chapel, containing an altar for the reservation of the most holy sacrament, which is placed within a gilt tower. surmounted by a cross. This chapel communicates with the chancel by a richly moulded and paneled doorway, and also by an arched opening of the same description, containing a high tomb with tracery and emblems, to serve for the sepulchre at Easter.

On the north side of the chapel is a three-light window, and in every light an angel bearing the cross, the pillar, and the holy name, with this scripture, "By thy cross and passion, O Lord, deliver us." In the east window are also three lights, with an image of our blessed Lady with our Lord in the centre, St. John the Baptist with the lamb on the right, and St. Nicholas, vested as he used to say mass, with the three children, on the left, all under rich canopies; and in the upper part of the window, angels with labels and scriptures. The side windows are filled with ornamental quarries and rich bordures and quatrefoils, containing the emblems of the four Evangelists, the annunciation of our blessed Lady, the pot of lilies with the angelical salutation entwined, and the holy name of our Lord.

The sacristy is fitted with oak almeries for vestments, and furnished with such sacred vessels and ornaments as are required in the solemn celebration of the divine office. The cloister is paved with figured tiles, and the windows contain many arms and emblems in stained glass; while the walls are enriched with niches containing sculptured representations of our Lord's passion, and other edifying mysteries of the Christian faith.

The site that has been selected for this hospital is one of

the most beautiful and suitable for such an edifice that can well be imagined. From the north wing, which stands on the verge of a steep rock some hundred feet in height, a most extensive view of the rich valleys and surrounding country is obtained; while to the south a well-sheltered slope is admirably calculated for gardens. From its immediate vicinity to the ruins of the ancient castle,* with its overshadowed moat and winding paths, it offers easy access to the most retired and sheltered walks, well suited to the meditation of its aged inmates; and being only a few paces distant from the village, it will afford all the consolations of the regular divine office, that will be celebrated daily within its walls to the Catholic inhabitants. When viewed from the opposite hills, its turrets and crosses seem to form but one group with the more venerable tower of the parochial church and the varied outline of the castle buildings. As no reasonable cost has been spared by the noble founder in the erection of this building, when completed it will present, both in its exterior and internal arrangements, a perfect revival of a Catholic hospital of the old time, of which so many were seized, demolished, and perverted by the sacrilegious tyrant Henry and his successors in church plunder; and in lieu of these most Christian and pious foundations for our poorer brethren, prisons are now substituted for those convicted of poverty,— a state voluntarily embraced by thousands in days of faith, as one of great perfection and most pleasing to Almighty God, but in these modern and enlightened times accounted a heinous offence.

---

* Of this castle Buck the antiquary gives the following account: "It is a castle more ancient than the Norman conquest. In the 22d of Henry II, Bertram de Verdun was lord of it, whose residence it was, and that of the family, till the 3d of Edward II. During the minority of Thomas de Verdun, William Fitz Richard had the care of his estates; the manor had not less than ten (some say fourteen) villages belonging to it. Male issue failing, it came by marriage to the Furnivals, who held it in two successions; when by the same means it came to Thomas Nevil, brother to the Earl of Westmoreland; but he also leaving an only daughter, it passed by her to the famous Sir John Talbot (with her other estates), who by right of his wife was lord of this castle, and Lord Furnival, but afterwards created Earl of Shrewsbury, in which family it still remains." The ruins of this castle, as engraved in Buck's work, appear to have been very considerable in his time, but they have been sadly demolished during the last century, huge masses being frequently hurled down for the purpose of mending the roads. The ravages were stopped by the late earl; and these interesting remains are now preserved with the greatest care. The exact situation of the original gateway, with its circular towers, was ascertained by excavation on clearing away the rubbish in 1840. At that time a most interesting thurible of the twelfth century was discovered buried in the moat, and close to the site of the castle chapel.

It is now 744 years since the monastery of Citeaux was founded in a wild and desert place near Chalon-sur-Saone, by blessed Robert abbot of Molesme, and a few holy monks who were his companions, that they might the better serve God in austerities, silence, mortifications, and prayer, according to the primitive rule of St. Benedict of glorious memory.

From this edifying example devout men arose in all the countries of Christendom, eager to follow in the path they had so wisely chosen; and through the fervour and zeal of this new and rigid order, England soon beheld some of the noblest churches that ever graced this glorious land arising in the solitude of her forests and uncultivated valleys. Even yet, how famous are the names of Fountains, Furness, Tintern, Joreval, Kirkstall, and a host of others,* although the glory of their sanctuaries is departed, and little more than prostrate pillars and crumbling walls remain to attest their ancient dignity, so desolate indeed do they seem, and so passed away is the generation of men by whom they were raised and inhabited; so changed is the spirit of mortification, solitude, and prayer, which instigated their erection; that when we behold the chilling spectacle of their sad decay, we might indeed mourn the ancient faith as utterly departed. But so unsearchable are the decrees and ways of God, that monastic institutions have revived in this land by the means of a convulsion that would have seemed as the annihilation of their very existence.

Whilst Protestant tyranny and fanaticism ruled in this country with an iron rod, many of the scattered religious found refuge in foreign lands; and when the continent in its turn became the scene of revolution, anarchy, and infidelity, England gladly received and sheltered the communities that by unjust laws had been so long separated from her. Amongst others, the English Cistercians from the monastery of La Trappe† returned to their native soil; and to these the com-

---

* "The first English monastery of Cistercians was founded at Waverley, in Surrey, A. D. 1129; and in the reign of king Edward the First, there were sixty-two houses of this order in England."—Stevens' Continuation to Dugdale.

† It is erroneously imagined by many persons that the monks of La Trappe are a new order, whose rule is framed with unexampled and unnatural severity. But, in fact, they are only a reform of the Cistercians, established by the famous Abbé Rancy, in the monastery of La Trappe, in France, from whence the

munity of Mount St. Bernard owes its existence. It is not necessary to enter at length into the various vicissitudes they encountered, or the circumstances that led them eventually to establish a monastery in Leicestershire, as these will be detailed at length in a separate publication on the subject by Ambrose Lisle Phillipps, Esq, that will shortly appear; but it must be no small consolation to every Catholic mind, that in the nineteenth century, a community of men flourish in the very heart of England, bound by the same rules, practising the same austerities, devotions, and charity, wearing the same habit, and in all respects like to the devout men of old, whose works and lives are yet the theme of admiration and respect among men of true piety and antiquarian research.

The prospect of the monastery, which is taken from the south-west, represents the edifice as complete, and gives a general idea of the locality in which it is placed. The country immediately surrounding the monastery is exceedingly wild and romantic, more, indeed, resembling Sicilian than English scenery. Irregular masses of granite rocks of most picturesque outline surround the land cultivated by the monks; and as the situation is exceedingly elevated, the extensive prospects which open out beyond these from different points of view, are truly glorious to behold. The monastery is sheltered on the north side by a huge rock, on the summit of which it is purposed to erect a calvary, as shown in the view, which will be visible from an immense extent of the surrounding country. Although, from its exposed position, the land is far from desirable in an agricultural point of view, the unceasing toil of the religious has so far overcome natural difficulties, that a considerable portion of the ground is already brought into excellent cultivation. The whole of the regular buildings, cloister, chapter-house, refectory, dormitory, calefactory, guest-house, prior's lodgings, lavatory, kitchen offices, &c., are now actually finished; and arrangements are in progress for completing as soon as possible a

---

appellation of Trappists has been applied most improperly to those religious who returned to the strict observance of the primitive rule of the order, which although it may seem unsupportably austere in these days of decayed zeal and fervour, was only the ordinary state of religious life observed by the ancient monks. The extraordinary piety and fervour of the Abbé de Rancy naturally excited the animosity of those lax members of the religious orders, of which there were but too many instances in the corrupt age in which he commenced his reform; and many infamous calumnies were published against him. The best refutation of these is to be found in a small work entitled " Défence de la Trappe," of which the celebrated Father Thiers was the supposed author.

sufficient portion of the church to enable the monks to celebrate the divine office with becoming solemnity; when this
is achieved, the community will leave their present temporary
edifice, and enter on the occupation of this new monastery.

The whole of the buildings are erected in the greatest
severity of the lancet style, with massive walls and buttresses, long and narrow windows, high gables and roofs,
with deeply arched doorways. Solemnity and simplicity are
the characteristics of the monastery, and every portion of the
architecture and fittings corresponds to the austerity of the
order for whom it has been raised. The space inclosed by
the cloisters is appointed for the cemetery; a stone cross,
similar to those which were formerly erected in every churchyard, will be set up in the centre, and the memorials of departed brethren will be inserted on plain wooden crosses at
the head of the graves. The view from this inclosure is
particularly striking. From the nature of the material used (a
sort of rubble granite) and the massiveness of the architecture,
the building already possesses the appearance of antiquity;
and this being combined with the stillness of the place and
the presence of the religious, clad in the venerable habits of
the order, the mind is most forcibly carried back to the days
of England's faith.

The second plate, VIII. represents the interior of the conventual church as designed, taken from the western end of the
nave. The arches are shewn as springing from pillars of
nine feet in circumference, ornamented with foliated caps.
The framing of the roof, which will be decorated with painting,
is open to the church, and springs from stone corbels, level
with the base of clerestory windows; the high altar is at the
eastern end, against a reredos of arched panels, below the
triple lights of the end gable; four massive pillars support
the arches of the centre tower, which is shewn in the external
prospect. On the eastern walls of the transepts are two
altars, that on the south dedicated in honour of our blessed
Ladye, and the northern one in honour of St. Joseph. As the
chapter-house joins close to the southern wall of the transept,
a rose window will be erected in the gable, and three large
lancet lights on the opposite end; the sacristy is on the
south side, and forms in the plan a continuation of the transept gable wall nearly as far eastward as the termination of
the church. The whole choir is surrounded by spacious aisles
for solemn processions. The stalls for the religious extend

S BERNARDE ABBEY CHVRCH

'down a considerable portion of the nave,* as far as the large stone rood loft, shewn in the engraving, which will be ascended by two stone staircases immediately behind the prior's and subprior's stalls. This roodloft is supported by three open arches, the two side ones containing stone altars, surmounted by paintings and other enrichments. The custom of placing altars in the rood screens, which is exceedingly ancient, originated in the monastic churches: we are not aware of existing instances where they occur in any other. The reason is obvious: as the people were entirely excluded from the eastern portion of the church, and confined to that part of the nave which remained between the rood loft and the western end, the monks naturally resorted to this expedient for administering the consolation of the holy sacrifice to such of the faithful as might visit their churches through devotion. It may be further remarked, in support of this reason, that these altars are found only in such of the churches and cathedrals as were either originally monasteries, as Peterborough, Gloucester, St. Alban's; or were served by monks, as Durham and Norwich. The rood screen and altars of Durham have perished; but the annexed note† will

---

* Examples of these are yet to be found at Westminster, Glòucester, Winchester, Tewkesbury, St. Alban's, and Norwich.

† " In the body of the church, between two of the highest pillars supporting the west side of the lantern, opposite the choir door, was Jesus' altar, where Jesus' mass was sung every Friday in the year, and on the back-side of the said altar was a high stone wall, at each end whereof was a door, which was locked every night, and called the two rood doors, for the procession to go forth and return at; betwixt the two doors was Jesus' altar, placed as aforesaid, and each end of the altar was closed up with fine wainscot, like to a porch, adjoining to each rood door, finely varnished with red varnish. In the wainscot, at the south end of the altar, were four great almeries, to preserve the chalices and silver cruets, and two or three suits of vestments, and other ornaments belonging to the said altar, for holy and principal days; and at the north end of the altar, in the wainscot, was a door to come into the said porch, which was always locked. There was also standing against the wall a most curious fine table, with two leaves to open and shut; comprehending the passion of our Lord Jesus Christ, richly set in fine lively colours, all like burnished gold, as he was tormented on the cross; a most lamentable sight to behold; which table was always locked but on principal days. Also the fore part of the said porch, from the utmost corner of the porch to the other was a door, with two broad leaves to open from side to side, all of fine thorough carved work; the height was somewhat above a man's breast, and the upper part stricken full of iron spikes, so that none should climb over; which door hung all on gimmers, and had clasps on the inside to fasten them. And on principal days, when any of the monks said mass at the said altar, then the table standing thereon was opened, and the door with two leaves that composed the fore-part of the said porch was set open also, that every man might come in and see the table in the manner aforesaid.

enable the reader to understand their ancient position in that noble church. We believe that at Norwich Cathedral, since the *improvements* in the choirs, all traces of the altars which stood on either side of the choir door have disappeared; but a few years since the outline of the altars and the reredoses themselves were most distinctly marked. At St. Alban's the screen across the nave is called St. Cuthbert's: the altar, as at Durham, stood in the centre, with a doorway at each side, leading into the choir; and there is every reason to suppose a similar screen formerly existed at Romney Abbey. The arrangement of the rood screen, as shewn in the plate, is therefore quite correct for a monastic church; the depth of the arches under which the altars are placed, is considerable; and, with the staircases, this loft will occupy one bay of the nave in width; above the screen, the rood* will be fixed with the

---

" There was also in the height of the wall, from pillar to pillar, the whole story and passion of our Lord, wrought in stone, and curiously gilt; and also above the said story and passion, there was the whole story and picture of the twelve apostles, very artificially set forth, and finely gilt, extending from one pillar to the other; and on the top, above all the aforesaid stories, was set up a border artificially wrought in stone, with marvellous fine colours, and gilt with branches and flowers; insomuch that the more a man looked on it the more was his desire to behold it; and, though in stone, it could not have been finer in any kind *of* metal. And likewise on the top of all stood the most famous rood that was in all the land, with the picture of St. Mary on one side, of our Saviour and St. John on the other; with two glittering archangels, one on the one side of St. Mary and the other on the other side of St. John. So that for the beauty of the wall, stateliness of the picture, and the liveliness of the painting, it was thought to be one of the grandest monuments in the church."

Antiquities of Durham Abbey, pp. 35–6.

The altar, rood, and images, were all demolished and defaced in the reign of Edward the Sixth, and the screen itself was destroyed soon after.

* A very curious account is given in Peck's " Stamford," chap. iv. p. 3, illustrative of the antiquity of roods. It refers to the sacking and plunder of the monastery at Burg, A. D. 1069; and it appears that on the robbers effecting an entrance into the church, *they got up to the rood,* and took away a crown from our Lord's head, a crown made entirely of gold. From this description we not only gather the existence of a rood set up in a high place in the church, but also that the image on the same was one of those mystical representations of our Lord, as a king vested in royal robes, fastened to a rich cross, which were frequent in early times; and the miraculous crucifix still preserved in the second chapel on the gospel side of the nave in Amiens cathedral, is of this style. This conventional manner of treating the sublime and overpowering mystery of our Lord's sacrifice on the cross, is truly beautiful; and it will probably be revived ere long, with many other long-forgotten but profound and admirable conceptions of the Middle Ages. The cross itself was treated from the earliest times as an emblem of glory. Hence, whether it was carved on sepulchral slabs, erected on churches, set up on roods, embroidered on altar cloths or vestments, it was invariably more or less floreated with enriched terminations branching out, as the fruitful and never-fading source of the Christian's brightest hopes. Many of the crosses erected in England, were, in themselves, most beautiful structures, and of the richest design. A large

Church of the Sacred Heart of Jesus.

Church of the Sacred Heart of Jesus.

appropriate images, all richly painted and gilt. The upper extremity of the cross will be upwards of fifty feet in height from the level of the pavement, and the width across the arms about twelve feet. By the rules of the Cistercian order, the rood loft is used for all its ancient purposes, and will be provided with letterns, standards for lights, and other necessary. furniture.

JESUS CHAPEL, NEAR POMFRET, PLATES IX AND X.

This edifice has been erected by Mrs. Tempest, who resides at the Grange, near Pomfret, to serve as a private chapel to the mansion with which it communicates, by means of a cloister on the north side. It consists of a nave, chancel, chantry, chapel containing a family vault, and a sacristry: the accompanying plate will afford a correct idea of its style and appearance. The architecture is that of the decorated period, and to the smallest details has been carefully and faithfully revived from original authorities. The niches on each side of the chancel window contain images of our Blessed Lady and the angel Gabriel, and the Holy Trinity in the centre niche of the gable. A belfry for the Sanctus is erected on the eastern end of the nave, and a floreated cross on the centre of the west gable. A massive and deeply moulded stone arch leads from the nave to the chancel, across which an oak screen of open panels, surmounted by a rood, has been erected. The roof of the nave is waggon-headed, divided by and divided into compartments by the principals of the roof, which are again subdivided by moulded ribs into panels, diapered in colours. The ceiling of the chancel is arched, also divided into compartments by ribs, but of a richer character than that of the nave; at each intersection is a boss, carved with emblems of the passion and

---

plain cross seems to be the extent to which the imagination of those who design these things at the present day on the continent will reach, and these are not unfrequently painted a bright green. In England the case is in some respects worse, for, the original intention of these holy emblems being disregarded, they have been prostituted to the vilest party purposes; and the design of one of those truly beautiful and appropriate Eleanor crosses has been degraded to serve for the memorial of three of those miserable ecclesiastics who betrayed the church of which they were such unworthy members, and were mainly instrumental in the overthrow not only of the material crosses which had been raised by the piety of our forefathers, but that true and ancient faith which had shone so conspicuous in the English Church for so many succeeding generations, and which, down to that fatal period, which severed this country from the unity of Christ's Church, had covered the face of the land with the most glorious monuments that the skill and energy of man ever raised in honour of Almighty God.

other devices; and from each of these spring four foliage
cusps, corresponding to the angles of the panels. The relieved
portions of this ceiling are pricked out in gold and colour;
the field is painted azure, powdered with stars and suns. All
the windows are filled with stained glass; those of the nave
contained figured quarries, rich borders, and quatrefoils filled
with sacred emblems; in the east window of the chantry, the
centre light is filled with an image of our Ladye with our
Lord, under a canopy, and a serpent crushed beneath her
feet: the two other lights contain the emblems of the four
Evangelists, and the holy name in bordered quatrefoils. The
upper part of the window is filled with angels, holding labels
and scriptures.

The east window of the chancel contains the crucifixion of
our Lord, the adoration of the wise men, and the resurrection,
with appropriate scriptures. The side window of the chantry
chapel is filled with armorial bearings of the Tempest family.
On the Gospel side of the chancel is a richly ornamented
niche, which is also open towards the chantry, and within it
a high tomb to serve for the sepulchre at Easter. Immediately opposite to this are the sedilia, with crocketed canopies and pinnacles, and a sacrarium of the same ornamental
character. The front of the principal altar is divided into
five compartments or niches, with crocketed gablets, and each
containing an image. The altar of the chantry is plain, and
hung with a frontal of velvet, relieved with gold embroidery.
Each altar is furnished with a pair of candlesticks and a crucifix on standing crosses. Curtains of silk are suspended on
projecting rods on each side of the chancel altar, and on the
upper steps are placed two high standards for the elevation
candles. There is also a suspended lamp to burn before
the blessed sacrament. The floors of the chancel and chantry
chapel are laid with incrusted tiles of various patterns, similar
to those with which the ancient churches were originally
paved; and in all respects this chapel presents a very faithful
revival of a small religious edifice of the fine period of Edward
the Third.

BISHOP'S HOUSE, BIRMINGHAM. PLATE XI.

Next in importance to the erection of the church itself, is
that of a suitable edifice for the habitation of those ecclesiastics who are appointed to serve its altars, and minister
spiritual and temporal consolation to the faithful who flock
within its walls. Hence we hail with no small gratification

N° II + Bishops House Birmingham NW view

+ THE BISHOPS CHAPEL

+ THE COMMON HALL

the erection of the present building, which is a consoling
proof of the great revival of ancient principles in this most·
neglected branch of ecclesiastical architecture.   We say *most
neglected,* for even those who admitted the principle of imitating
in some respects the ideas and style of our Catholic ancestors
in their churches, rejected with ridicule all suggestions of
following them in other matters; and, on the pleas of economy
and convenience, have descended to the erection of the vilest
sash-window and street-door residences that ever were raised.*
Now, with respect to economy, it is impossible to build sub-
stantially in any style so cheap as the pointed or Christian;
and, as to convenience, our ancestors were by no means such
fools, or such comfortless barbarians as is generally imagined

---

* When this error has been avoided, the residences for the clergy have been
made to look extremely like portions of the church ; and what at a short distance might appear as a transept, or a chancel, is discovered on a nearer
approach to be nothing more than an ill-constructed house, whose several floors,
by dint of blackened glass and other contrivances, are disguised into long-looking
lancet windows ; while the clerestory serves the domestics for an attic, and the
supposed crypt contains the cooking department, with even meaner offices ; and
the building which had passed for a cruciform church, from a casual external
survey, presents, on entering, a mere nave, which must naturally appear much
smaller than it really is from the disappointment of the spectator.—We know
of one case, where parlour, dining room, and bed chamber are all lighted
from what appears externally to be the east window of the chancel, while
the maid servant receives air from two huge quatrefoils in the tracery of
the said window, the smoke from all these rooms being carried up a *flue turret*
and perforated pinnacle.   It is impossible to describe half the indecencies that
must and do arise from men presuming to make their habitations under the
roof of a building that should be solemnly consecrated to God alone ; and it is
almost difficult to reconcile the existence of such an abuse with the extreme
reverence and veneration with which all members of the Catholic Church are
necessarily bound to regard all that is connected with the worship of Almighty
God, and the sacred character which is imparted even to the material walls of
a church.   Besides, a church which forms part of a house will never be viewed
or entered with the peculiar respect that it should command; it sinks to the
level of an ordinary place : servants cleanse the sanctuary as they do an entry;
the thuribles and candlesticks are carried for convenience to the kitchen, vestments are kept in bedrooms.   The exclusive character of all these things is soon
lost, and irreverence succeeds.   Then, instead of solemn-sounding bells, preparing the mind for prayer and sacrifice, we have rapping of knockers, closing
of doors, shrill calls of domestics, and in some instances the savoury odours of
kitchens overpowering the incense itself.   Now all these things have originated
in straightened necessity, but they should not continue through indifference; and
very lately new buildings have been erected on a plan which must necessarily
entail all these wretched consequences.   How utterly dead must a man be, we
will not say to mystical reasons alone, but to natural ones also, who builds a
chimney-stack in place of the east window, turns an aisle into an entry, and
lights his kitchen from the sanctuary !   Yet such and worse exist—nor shall we
be readily delivered from them except by conflagration, which catastrophe is
not by any means improbable, considering the ordinary risk which is attached
to dwelling-houses.

by the moderns, who seem to derive all their ideas on these
matters from delapidated buildings, unfurnished and unin-
habited perhaps for centuries; a modern empty house looks
miserable enough in all conscience after it has been vacated
for only a few weeks; but only let us conceive its appearance
after fifty years' neglect, which is the longest period which can
be assigned for *its existence in any shape;* surely an old specimen of six times that age would then appear to no small
advantage by its side. Under the name of modern convenience, people have been cheated into thin walls and plaster,
in place of solid construction and oak beams. Of course there
are sundry practical improvements made from time to time,
which could and should be engrafted on old principles; but we
have cast off in too many instances strength and real convenience, for empty display and cheap magnificence; and a
modern house, with its cracking plaster and compo, peeling
paper, rubbed off graining, marble veneers, dirty paint, and
faded finery, is an erection that could not have arisen in any
less fictitious age than the present.

But to return to our object. Ecclesiastical residences were
always erected in harmony of design with the sacred structures to which they formed necessary appendages, that is to
say, they *exhibited a solid, solemn, and scholastic character,
that bespoke them at once to be the habitations of men who were
removed far beyond the ordinary pursuits of life.* If we turn
to the Vicar's Close at Wells, the hospital of St. Cross, or
any of the collegiate or conventual buildings which remain,
defaced and modernized as they are, they inspire reverence
and respect; and what must have been their effect as originally left by their pious founders? This impression on the
mind is not produced by richness of detail, for they are re-
markably plain for the most part; but it is owing to the *absence
of all artificial resources, and the severity and simplicity in which
they have been raised;* there is no attempt at concealment, no
trick, no deception, no false show, no mock materials; they
appear as true and solid as the faith itself. Who does not
feel some instinctive respect as he passes under the vaulting
of an old gate-house and finds himself in a cloistered quadrangle? In such a place the mind is predisposed to reverence
the ministers of religion; they seem as if occupying a position exclusively their own, and where they hold undisturbed
right to teach and command; and as regards the ecclesiastics
themselves, do not these arches, these mullioned windows, these
cloistered alleys, tend to cherish and preserve within their

breasts that gravity and religious composure. so essential to
the high state to which they belong. How violent is the
contrast between the choir of a cathedral and the drawing-
room of an Anglo-Protestant Prebendary, with its piano,
nick-knacs, mirrors, and ottomans! surely the church was not
intended to be the only place where the thoughts of God were
to be imparted and cherished,—else why those long cloisters,
that solemn chapter-room, that vast refectory, that common
hall, those oratories, those crosses, those saintly images and
emblems, those studious chambers and solemn buildings which
our Catholic ancestors erected around every sacred pile? they
knew that devotion *in* the sanctuary was only to be obtained
by gravity and solemnity *without*. The ancient ecclesiastics
did not perform parts in churches for a brief hour, and then
put off the cleric with the surplice,* but carried their reverend
garb and demeanour throughout every ordinary action in
which they were engaged; and this it would not have been
possible for them to have performed had they not resided in
the solemn and retired structures provided for them. But if
such edifices were found necessary for the promotion of regularity and discipline in the days of faith, and in times when
the clergy had such vast resources in mutual support, how
much more are they required amongst us at the present time,
when our ecclesiastics are scattered in populous towns, frequently alone and unsupported, and where almost every spot,
except their own domain, is poisoned with heresy, infidelity,
and licentiousness! The only resource left in such a situation
is to create an ecclesiastical atmosphere, a green spot in the
desert, where both the architecture and fittings of the edifice
breathe the reverend spirit of ancient days, and where the
man of God, consecrated to the all-important work of leading
his countrymen back to the true paths, with cassock and
crucifix, may hold secret communion of soul with those glorious churchmen of old, whose fervent and mortified spirit he
strives to imitate. Nor will such a residence, so different
from the worldly habitations (filled with cheap and vulgar
show) which surround it, fail in producing the most salutary
effect on those souls who, filled with vague impressions of
ancient Catholic solemnity, are seeking where they may find

* A striking instance of the great reverence with which the ancient churchmen regarded the celebration of the divine office, is to be found in the construction of several sacristies at Rouen cathedral, and other places, which are provided with a chamber where the hebdomadarius who sung the chapter-mass
remained during the week, in silence and meditation.

a realization of the ideas they have imbibed in the study of past ages, and finding it not at the neat family parsonage, nor at the modernised canonry,* come with trembling hopes to the once despised priests of the old faith.

Such are some of the ideas which suggested the absolute necessity of erecting a residence for the bishops and clergy of St. Chad's cathedral, corresponding in style and arrangements with the old ecclesiastical houses. The ground selected for this purpose is situated immediately opposite to the church, and being nearly ten feet lower on the north side, admits of increased accommodation in the base story of that wing; by

---

* The horrible mutilations of the ancient ecclesiastical residences attached to cathedrals, in order to render them at all suitable to the altered style of living, as practised by the present race of bishops, deans, canons, &c., afford the most striking examples of modern degeneracy; and are in themselves convincing proofs that the married worldly clergy of the day, are utterly unsuited for the venerable habitations which they occupy, and the glorious churches that they profess to serve. The great hall has been generally floored in the height, and subdivided into bed-chambers; while the chesnut roof, with its massive timbers and moulded braces, has become a mere dark attic, used as a depository for lumber, or for drying linen. It is almost superfluous to observe, that the domestic chapel has in every instance been degraded to some secular purpose, or totally destroyed. In one case it serves the canon's lady, or Mrs. Archdeacon, as a boudoir, where she deposits her nick-knacs and albums; in another it is used for a wash and brew-house, a huge copper occupying the place of ancient sacrifice; in a third it has become the canon's dressing-room; indeed so changed are the destination of the rooms, so altered the characteristics and features of these residences, that were it not for a few feet of moulded stringcourse appearing occasionally on the cemented walls, an ornamented chimney stack, and a high pitched gable, they could scarcely be recognised as having once belonged to the ancient churchmen. What painful intrusions meet the eye at every turn in a cathedral close of the present time! one venerable building is converted into a finishing school for young ladies; another, with the blinds drawn down, is the residence of a dissenting minister; this vicar's house is a music shop, that a baker's; one canonry is let to some sporting gents; the deanery is shut up, and so are all the houses of those who are not on residence; or if unlet to lay intruders, these buildings exhibit only signs of habitation at long and distant periods, between which they remain as if hermetically closed: only when *the* canon is about leaving residence and *another* canon's time draws near, the shutters of a house suddenly are unclosed, windows are thrown open, and bedding hung out in the sun to air; sundry old women are seen either entering with pails and brooms, or in the act of cleaning; curtains are delivered from brown holland confinement, and looking-glass frames from gauze and paper coverings; fire-irons and polished grates are freed from grease, and brass ornaments affixed to the register fronts; stacks of chairs, sofas, and ottomans, are unpiled from the centre of the drawing-room, and disposed in tasteful variety round its confines; chimney ornaments and cut lustres resume their wonted station on the marble shelves. All is now ready, and in due time the whole party arrive; the canon and the canon's lady, the governess and the young canonesses, house-maids, kitchen-maids, lady's-maid, nursery-maids, and the complete modern ecclesiastical establishment; to remain three long months in this horribly dull old place, with the odious bell of the cathedral dismally sounding; and no relief except a few evening card parties and a juvenile ball.

means of a court left in the centre of the building, the whole is well lighted and ventilated. The entrance is from an arched doorway in Bath-street, communicating directly with a small cloister leading on the right towards the kitchen and offices, and on the left to the living and other rooms. On the ground floor are four chambers for priests, a chancery for the business of the district, and a strong room for muniments; and as by a distinct approach, housekeeper's and servants' rooms. In the basement are a waiting room, servants' hall, kitchen, scullery, cellars, larder and other offices. On the upper or principal floor, are, a common hall or dining room, communicating by a separate staircase with the kitchen, a private chapel, a library and two audience and sleeping chambers for the lord bishop and his right reverend coadjutor. Over these are four principal bed rooms, and eight cells for strangers. The annexed plate represents a view of the building taken from Bath-street; it will be seen that convenience has dictated the design, and that the elevation has been left in that natural irregularity produced by the internal arrangements, to which we owe the picturesque effect of the ancient buildings. The walls are built entirely of brick with stone dressings; and some ornamental devices are occasionally worked on the walls with vitrified bricks. At the corner of Weaman-street is an angle niche, containing an image of St. Chad standing on an angel corbel; the arms and initials of the Right Rev. Dr. Walsh are also introduced in tracery panels. The interior of both chapel and common hall are given in the same plate as the exterior view; in the former is a stained glass window with an image of St. Chad vested as he used to say mass, standing under a canopy, together with shields charged with his cross, and in the upper part of the window, many angels. The reredos of the altar is worked in stone gilt and paneled; it represents the Annunciation of our blessed Lady, in three niches and two compartments, as shown in the etching; the lower part of the altar is hung with a rich frontal of velvet and gold. On the Gospel side of the sanctuary is an almery for vestments; the altar is furnished with silk curtains, cross, candlesticks, and sacred vessels; and two exceedingly curious early German paintings, presented by the Earl of Shrewsbury, are fixed on each side of the altar window. The hall is capable of dining about sixty persons, and has a bay window and high dais at the upper end, and is protected from draughts by a glazed screen at the bottom. The fire place is of carved stone divided over the arch into three quatrefoils, with the arms of St. Chad, Bishop Walsh, and

Bishop Wiseman, surmounted by gilt mitres. The side windows are also filled with ornamented quarries, rich borders and arms, with the scriptures, *vigilandum*, and *omnia pro Christo*, running bendy. In the bay window, are the arms of the four new vicars-apostolic; and in the window, at the upper end, the arms of the present Queen, the Earl of Shrewsbury, and the late C. R. Blundell, of Ince, great benefactors to these buildings. Immediately over the screen at the bottom of the hall, and affixed to the wall, is a stone canopy, under which are three angels, bearing the arms of St. Chad, surmounted by a mitre, all richly painted and gilt, and very similar in arrangement to the arms formerly in the dining hall of the archiepiscopal palace at Croydon, Surrey; the tables, benches and other furniture of this hall are solidly framed and in perfect character with the style of the building. The library is a lofty room entirely surmounted with bookcases; the three windows are over these, and contain six shields of arms;— Bishop Walsh, Bishop Wiseman, the Earl of Shrewsbury, Mr. J. Hardman, St. Chad's, and St. Mary's, Oscott. The audience chambers are each provided with carved fireplaces, and oriel windows with emblems in stained glass, representing the holy name of our Lord illuminated, the emblems of the Passion, and a device illustrative of the most Holy Trinity, with appropriate scriptures. The remainder of the rooms contain nothing worthy of particular notice, and the rest of the building is fitted up with the most rigid simplicity. The cost of this edifice, including every expense, does not exceed £4,000, the stained glass and other decorations being contributed by benefactors; thus a residence which both in its ecclesiastical character and extent of accommodations, is in all respects suited for the occupation of the bishops and clergy, and also for transacting the increasing business of the district, has been erected for a sum which does not involve a greater annual outlay than would have been required for two large modern houses which must have been destitute of every requisite for this important purpose.

CONVENTS OF THE SISTERS OF MERCY AT BIRMINGHAM AND LIVERPOOL. (PLATE XII.)

Among the many important objects that have been lately accomplished by the English Catholics, the establishment of these charitable sisters is one which must prove most beneficial to the poorer classes and to the progress of religion in general. At London, Birmingham, and Liverpool, regu-

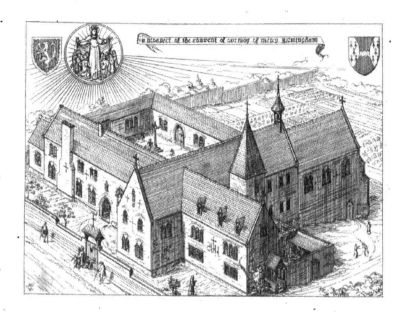

A Prospect of the Convent of Carmony of Mercy, Birmingham

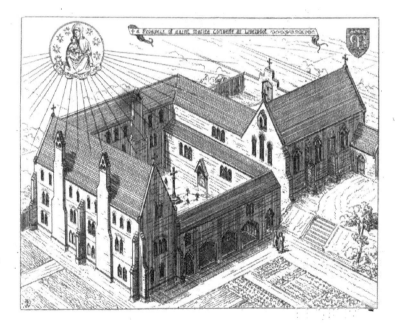

A Prospect of Saint Maries Convent at Liverpool

lar communities are now formed, living in conventual buildings, and fulfilling all the sacred duties of the order with scrupulous exactitude. It is not our purpose to enlarge on the rule of these exemplary sisters, or the blessings and consolations that they are the means of imparting to the suffering population, these being matters which are generally understood. We will therefore turn at once to the consideration of the edifices that have been raised for the habitation of these sisterhoods, and which are the first regular conventual buildings erected in this country since the change of religion. The upper engraving represents the convent at Birmingham, lately completed; and the lower that about to be built at Liverpool. As the internal arrangement of both these houses will be essentially the same, it will be sufficient to describe that of Birmingham. This foundation owes its existence to the piety and munificence of Mr. John Hardman, sen., aided by a large grant from the Earl of Shrewsbury,—both great benefactors to the religious edifices lately erected in this town. The conventual buildings are constructed of bricks with stone doorways, windows, gables and dressings; and, as may be perceived by the engraving, the whole are extremely simple in design but yet of strictly ecclesiastical character; and from the unity of style which pervades the whole of this edifice, and which extends to the furniture and other fittings, it produces a striking illustration of the old religious houses, as they existed in all their regularity and order. The following is a list of the various chambers, &c. contained in this building;—chapel, cloisters, oratory, cemetery, sacristy, refectory, noviciate parlour, community room, work room for religious, twenty cells, school-room, dining room for poor children, dormitory and playing-room for ditto, kitchen and other offices. Within the chapel is a regular choir, containing twenty stalls, divided off by an open screen and rood from the ante-chapel. To the eastward of this is the sanctuary; the altar is of plain stone, with a frontal of silk, embroidered and ornamented with the Lamb, and emblems of the four evangelists; the reredos is of oak, with rich diapered panels, of various patterns; a pair of curtains are suspended on each side; and on the altar is a gilt tower for the reservation of the blessed Sacrament, and a pair of candlesticks. On either side of the east window, is an angel standing on a carved corbel and bearing a shield, charged with the five wounds of our Lord, and the emblems of the Passion. The roof is covered with inscriptions and ornaments in rich colours, the pattern consisting of quatrefoils, with the holy

name connected by bands inscribed "mercy;" and round the
upper parts of the walls "the angelical salutation" in illuminated letters. The floors of both choir and sanctuary are laid
with figured tiles, charged with the armorial bearings of Lord
Shrewsbury, and other appropriate devices: the east window,
of three lights, is filled with stained glass, presented by the noble earl: in the middle day is an image of our blessed Lady,
under a rich canopy; and on either side are effigies of the Earl
of Shrewsbury and Mr. Hardman, as co-founders, in a kneeling attitude, attended by their patron saints. St. John the
Baptist and St. John the Evangelist. The side windows of
the choir are also filled with stained glass, of varied design and
rich effect. This chapel is well furnished with sacred vessels
and vestments, of a style corresponding to that of the building, and facsimiles to those used in England previous to the
spoliation of the churches. A doorway on the north side of
the lower end of the chapel leads into the cloisters, which are
decorated by a succession of ancient images in niches, all richly
diapered and painted according to their original colours; among
these is the crucifixion of our Lord, with SS. Mary and John
on a Calvary, St. Ann and our blessed Lady, St. Etheldreda,
the wise men's offering, and the Annunciation of our blessed
Lady. At the end of the north alley is an oratory with a stained
window, and a large niche, containing the crucifixion of our
Lord beautifully set forth in gold and colours, with a stone
lantern for a lamp, by its side, similar to those remaining in
the cloisters of Augsburg Cathedral; the space inclosed by
these cloisters is consecrated for a cemetery with a floreated
stone cross, raised on steps in the centre. This may be distinctly perceived by referring to the engraving, which will
fully illustrate the external appearance and arrangement of
the building. As the community rooms and cells have been
finished in the simplest possible style, there is nothing farther
to merit particular notice, except the absence of all those
trifling ornaments and unworthy devotional emblems that
sometimes disgrace the walls and shelves of modern convents,
and which must have the effect of lessening in the minds of
casual observers the respect that they would otherwise feel
for their devout and exemplary inmates.

BENEDICTINE PRIORY OF ST. GREGORY'S, DOWNSIDE, NEAR
BATH. (PLATE XIII.)

The next conventual building which we proceed to notice
is one of a far more extended description, and of which a

tolerably correct idea may be formed from the accompanying view, which represents the whole edifice as complete. It is intended to erect so much of this design at present as the increasing wants of the community absolutely require, and to proceed with the remaining portions of the plan as means may admit. The building is an exact revival of one of the larger English monasteries: consisting of a church, great cloisters, with carrols for study, lavatory, and chapter-house, a refectory, with buttery, cellars and kitchens, calefactory, noviciate, library, dormitory, prior's lodgings, infirmary, and a chapel for the sick, with spacious offices and almonries, a strangers' court, with guest-rooms and hall, and a separate quadrangle for scholars, with class and lecture-rooms.

It is not many years since this community expended a considerable sum in the erection of a church, and other buildings; but these they found wholly inadequate to the present increasing wants; and being, moreover, deficient in solidity and convenience, it has been wisely determined to erect the new buildings so as to form part of a grand and perfect plan; in order that an edifice may be eventually completed in some degree worthy of this most venerable and famous order, to whom England is indebted for many of the most glorious monuments of ancient skill,—among which we can yet reckon the names of Westminster, Peterborough, Durham, and Gloucester, that have not been demolished for the repair of roads, or to satisfy the sacrilegious rapacity of court favourites.* The style adopted for this structure is early lancet,

---

* If Gloucester and Peterborough had not been converted into cathedral churches, they would doubtless have perished, like Glastonbury, Reading, Croyland, and many others, which were by no means inferior to them, either in extent, grandeur, or sacred associations. Westminster Abbey itself had a narrow escape from being levelled by the sacrilegious hands of the Protector Somerset, under Edward VI. Heylin says, " But the lord protector thinking it altogether unnecessary that two Cathedrals should be founded so near to one another, and thinking the church of Westminster (as being of a later foundation) might best be spared, had cast a longing eye on the goodly patrimony which remained unto it, and, being then unfurnished of a house or palace proportionable to his greatness, he *doubted not to find room upon the dissolution and destruction of so large a fabrick* to raise a *palace equal to his vast design*, and he was only turned from the execution of this detestable project by the Dean, Benson, surrendering to him more than half the estates belonging to it. For this last act, coupled with his original surrender of the abbey, this wretched ecclesiastic was so tortured with remorse, that he died miserably a few months after. Tewkesbury abbey church, all glorious as it is with tombs and chapels of most surpassing interest and beauty, was also condemned to destruction, and only saved from immediate demolition by being purchased for a parochial church by the townsmen." The following entry respecting Tewkesbury abbey occurs in the account of the

as combining simplicity with true ecclesiastical character.
Each alley of the cloister will measure above one hundred
and fifty feet in length, the refectory eighty by thirty, the
wall three and four feet thick; which may afford some data
by which the extent and solidity of the buildings can be
imagined. They will be constructed on the ancient principle
of convenience and strength combined. without affectation of
forced regularity and unnecessary features. Each portion of
the edifice will bespeak its purpose, from the chapter-house to
the kitchen. Roofs and chimney shafts stand forth undis-
guised in all the unadorned grandeur produced by their
extent and solidity; and, when completed, this building will
furnish an admirable proof of the vast superiority of effect
that is produced by the *natural architecture of our Catholic
ancestors mock-regularity system of modern builders.*

ST. BEDE'S MASBRO. (PLATE XIV).

We have great pleasure in introducing the accompanying
views and plan of a small church, lately erected at Masbro,
near Rotherham, under the superintendence of Mr. Matthew
Hatfield. This may be regarded as an earnest of this gentleman's future intention of reviving true Catholic principles
in such ecclesiastical buildings as he may be engaged to erect.
It is indeed truly gratifying to see the rapid extension of
correct ideas on these matters; for many earlier edifices
raised by this architect were serious departures from the true
Christian style, and we feel assured he will now be willing to
admit the truth of this remark: but whatever errors of judgment he may formerly have committed, he now comes forward
as a reviver of the true old school, and as such we hail him
with unmingled satisfaction. On referring to the engraving,
it will be perceived that all the essentials of a Catholic
Church are included in the arrangement of this building.

---

suppression, and is truly characteristic of the spirit which introduced *what are
now termed Anglo-Catholic principles.*
    " Houses and buildings remaining undefaced.—The lodgings called the Newark,
leading from the gate to the late abbot's lodgings, with *buttery, pantry, cellar,
kitchen, larder,* and *pastry.* The abbot's lodgings, *stable, bakehouse, brewhouse*
and *slaughterhouse, almery, barn, dairyhouse, maltinghouse, the oxhouse,* &c.
    " Buildings deemed to be superfluous.—The *church, with chapels, cloister,
chapterhouse, misericord;* the two *dormitories, infirmary, with chapels,* and lodging
within the same, &c.
    Thus, only a few cooking offices were thought worthy of being preserved of
all this stupendous monastery, which, even its present delapidated and neglected state, fills every observer with admiration.

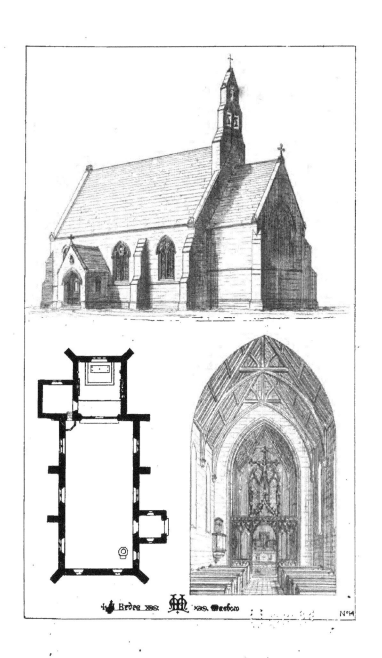

N°14

Nave, southern porch, font, chancel, rood screen, altar, sedilia, sepulchre, belfry, &c.; and all those various features are designed in a correct style and in accordance with ancient models; and we trust that they will be fully carried out in execution, without curtailment · or modification. As some persons have imagined that this building, from its striking resemblance to others lately erected under the superintendence of Mr. Pugin, must have been copied from them, it is only right, in justice to the architect, to say a few words on the subject. When buildings are derived from a common source, it it very natural that they should greatly resemble each other; hence, in the present revival of the Catholic architecture, the authorities for which can only be found in the ancient edifices of the country, it is very possible and even probable that two architects may erect precisely the same edifice; and this circumstance, *so far from being injurious to the reputation of either, is creditable to both.** We seek for *authority*, not *originality*, in these matters; for the establishment of *a principle, not individual celebrity;* and any man who possesses the true spirit of Christian art, so far from desiring to occupy an unrivalled position, is delighted when he is equalled, and overjoyed to be surpassed. It is far more gratifying to see a principle understood and practised by a number of persons, than for one man to enjoy an exclusive celebrity; and these are precisely the points which distinguish the Catholic from the Pagan artist. The former seek the glory of God and the Church; the latter the applause and admiration of men: the one is content to labour in accordance with the ancient traditions, from which he does not venture to deviate; the latter is perpetually seeking novelties, whereby he may attract attention and gain notoriety; hence all the horrible innovations introduced in the 16th century by the semi-pagan artists, who despised and rejected the

---

* Mr. Pugin, we believe, never claimed the least merit on the score of originality : nor does he profess to invent new combinations, but simply to revive, as far as circumstances and means will admit, the glorious but till lately despised works of the Middle Ages ; and no man can be more sensible of the great inferiority of the buildings he erects when compared with the original types from which they are derived ; for although in the debased and degenerate age in which we live, the most trifling revival of better times seems a gigantic achievement, yet how insignificant do our greatest efforts appear, when compared with the works of Catholic antiquity ; and although we may exult in the enthusiasm of the moment over the meagre imitations of ancient excellence which are being produced, yet, on mature consideration, and reference to the original types, we shall find them rather occasions for humiliation than for glory.

H

Catholic wisdom of centuries, that they might astonish for a
season by their extravagances. These men, who sacrificed
everything for a worldly triumph, were filled with envyings,
jealousies, and detractions; but such vile passions, although
natural to the Pagan courts of the Medici, found no place
among the Catholic architects of the cloister, who, after
raising the most glorious piles that ever emanated from the
genius of man, wholly devoted to the *object* for which they
laboured, have not even transmitted their names to posterity:
and may we not hope that many artists will arise, as in days
of old, to carry on the great work in the true spirit;—not in
strife and contentions, not in prostitution of their art for the
mere sake of gain;—not in pandering to the ignorance and
whimsical fancies of those by whom they may chance to be
employed;—but in a firm and uncompromising spirit revive
Catholic art and architecture in all its integrity. If Mr.
Pugin has been a somewhat successful restorer of ancient
glory, he has attained the necessary knowledge by means
which are open to all. He does not profess to hold any patent
for the exercise of his art, nor to be in possession of hidden
secrets, nor of any peculiar information that may not be
obtained by patient study and research. Those who wish to
attain excellence, *must distrust themselves, and become humble
disciples of the old Catholic architects, whose silent teaching may
be learnt from every venerable pile, from the humblest parish
church to the vast and lofty cathedral;* and then, indeed,
correct ideas and satisfactory buildings would soon become
general, as in former times.

NEW CATHOLIC CHURCH AT ISLINGTON.

This church, so far from exhibiting the adoption of true
Catholic principles, which we have had so much pleasure in
describing at Masbro, is certainly the most original combination of modern deformity that has been erected for some time
past for the sacred purpose of a Catholic church. It has been
a fine opportunity thrown away; and the only consolation
we can derive from its erection, is the hope that its palpable
defects, by serving as an additional evidence of the absolute
necessity of adhering to ancient Catholic examples in the
churches we erect, may induce those in ecclesiastical authority
to adopt this system in all cases, and to refuse their sanction
to any modern experiments in ecclesiastical architecture.

What renders the present case the more deplorable, is the
fact that an ancient Catholic parochial church, dedicated in

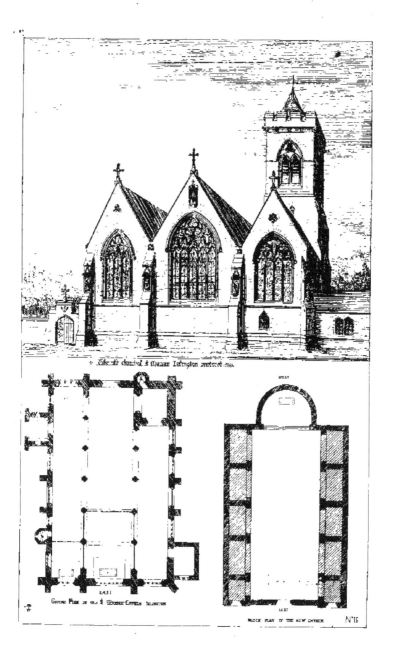

+ After the chancel & Nauses Islington restored 1584.

Ground Plan of old S. Georges Church Islington

Block Plan of the New Church

N° 16

honour of the Blessed Virgin, and in all respects suited to the present site and wants of the congregation, formerly existed at Islington, and was demolished only a few years since, to make room for the pewed and galleried assembly room which is at present used for the parochial Protestant service.

In the annexed plate (xv) we have given a view of this church as it would have appeared if erected on the site of the present building; in which case it would have stood in correct canonical position, due east and west, the high altar and side chapels facing the New River; while the tower, at the extremity of the north aisle, would have imparted the true character of a parochial church to the building, without encroaching on lateral space. By the plan, which is also given in the plate, it will be perceived that the high altar could be perfectly seen from all parts of the old church; which, strangely enough, was the reason advanced for departing from ancient arrangements, and confining the congregation to the mere nave of the present design, and blocking up the space which should have been occupied by the aisles, with cross walls.* See block plan of new church.

We are unwilling to attribute all the defects of this building to the architect, who has on former occasions shown himself capable of doing very much better, and who would be a valuable ally in the good cause, if he would seek to do what is positively right and correct, rather than what may please for the moment; and we fear he has been induced to arrange this building on the same principle that artists occasionally paint family portraits, out of all harmony and proportion,— so much pain, so much money. Yet surely this is quite unworthy of an ecclesiastical architect; these are not times for compromise; the English Catholics are no longer an obscure body, but stand as a light and a beacon to others who are on

---

* Some persons have pretended to justify this extraordinary arrangement of cross walls, by alleging that glorious example of ancient art, King's College Chapel at Cambridge; but independently of the manifest absurdity of selecting an example of the latter pointed architecture as any authority for an edifice which by its round-headed arches is evidently intended as an imitation of the Norman style, every one acquainted with the chapel of King's must be aware that the lateral chapels were suggested by the enormous projection of the buttresses, which were *absolutely necessary* to *resist the lateral thrust of the flattened groined ceiling of massive masonry.* But at Islington, so far from any thing like groining, there is an open truss roof without any thrust at all; and instead of the cross walls being required as buttresses, they are not carried up higher than the bottom of the clerestory, so that in fact they answer no other end than to block up the space which should be open for aisles, and to reduce the accommodation of the church by nearly one-half.

H 2

all sides seeking the truth; they are at the present time in a fearful state of responsibility, and sad it is indeed that by the erection of this, or similar departures from true Catholic architecture, they should afford a temporary triumph to the infidels. The Church at Islington is built on the *all front principle* of Dissenters, and is by no means equal to the Puritan edition of York Minster at the Scotch Kirk, Regent-square, though it likewise apes two diminutive towers at the west end of a church which is neither collegiate, conventual, nor cathedral. The united cost of these would have erected a good massive parochial tower at the western end. Indeed this building is in all respects so painful a subject, that it would not have been introduced at all, if the exposure of error did not contribute greatly to the advancement of truth; and in the present case it seems absolutely necessary to demonstrate the fallacy of the principle which instigated its extraordinary arrangement, and to set forth the great superiority which aisled Churches possess, in every respect, over large rooms, which some persons in these days advocate strongly as the best form for religious structures.

The annexed plate (xvi) represents the section and plan of one compartment of a large assembly room, quite square, with a flat ceiling, shown by the walls lightly tinted; and a Catholic Church, with nave and aisles, indicated by the dark plan and walls.

By this engraving it will be seen, that a mere room of fifty feet in width, if it possess requisite strength of walls and timber of sufficient scantling to bear a flat truss for such a span, will require considerably more material, both for walling and roof, than a church with aisles of sixty or even seventy feet wide in the clear, on account of the subdivision of the roof into three parts. Few persons are aware of the vast expense attendant on the erection of large rooms; the mere cost of hoisting principals of fifty feet wide into their places would cover that of fixing the roofs on an aisled Church complete, while the *ornamental plaster ceiling* that is required to hide the flat-framed roofs of these modern rooms would literally furnish an ordinary Church with altars, stained glass, and fittings. Hence, by adhering to the old Catholic method of Church building, we have an increased width of ten to twenty feet, a great saving of materials and expense, and a most solemn and impressive effect produced upon the mind. Aisle roofs act as buttresses without obstruction. Islington Church is *only a nave after all;* if it had aisles, all the people who

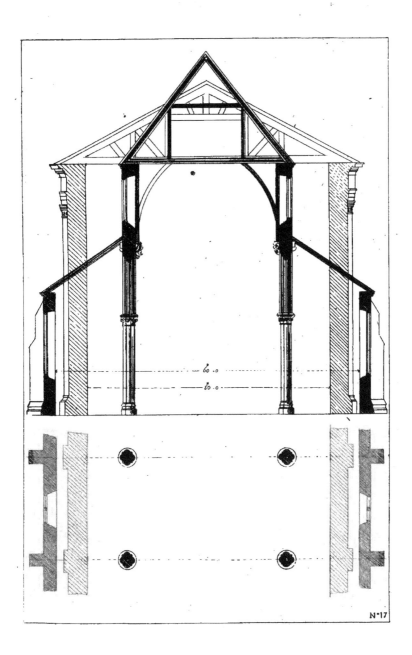

60 . 0

50 . 0

N°17

are at present accommodated would not be inconvenienced, and half as many more would be nearly as well located even on the score of seeing the altar; for the pillars in the naves of the old parochial churches are but very slight obstructions.

But increase of space, coupled with economy, is not the only reason for the superiority of the aisle arrangement. *A large square room is the worst possible form for the conveyance of sound;* and the voice of the same individual that can be distinctly heard in a large church subdivided by pillars, would be utterly lost in an unbroken space of considerably less extent. It will now be seen that the superiority of the Catholic over the modern or Pagan form of a church, can be demonstrated for the soundest practical reasons: as for mystical ones, they are so evident as scarcely to need any notice. All the associations of aisles are Catholic; the very word itself conjures up to our minds solemn processions, long and tapering perspectives, monastic grandeur, and heavenly chants; they form, in fact, after the chancel, the most striking external characteristic which distinguishes the temple of God from a common assembly room, the church from the conventicle; and most earnestly do we hope, that these most essential portions of a true Catholic church will never again be omitted, for the sake of substituting a set of unsightly recesses, not very dissimilar from those lately erected under the Greenwich and Blackwall railways, or the divisions technically termed wing-rooms, which serve as depositories for scenery on the stages of the metropolitan theatres.

In a former part of this article we have endeavoured to render all possible justice to the able advocacy of Catholic architecture and antiquities by certain learned writers of the Anglican Church. While doing this we felt it necessary to allude occasionally to certain inconsistencies and erroneous statements which are found in these publications.* We now

---

* In the "Christian Remembrancer" of a few months since, we noticed some remarks on an article treating on ecclesiastical architecture (that had appeared in this Review), which were conceived in the most anti-catholic spirit, although the writer at the same time appeared very anxious to be considered as one of the faithful. He evidently belongs to that class of persons who assume the title of Catholic as a *nom de guerre*, the better to forward certain heretical designs in which they are engaged, and while professing to revive truth and antiquity, are proved by their very writings to be the promulgators of dangerous errors and foolish conceits. The assertions of the writer in question are made with so much confidence, and have at the same time so little foundation in truth, that it becomes a duty to expose the errors and inconsistencies into which he has fallen. In the first place, he attributes to *mere inadvertence* the passages which refer to the lingering love of ancient architecture that partially existed

purpose to show wherein these consist, and to prove that, excellent as are the principles advanced in these writings, they are

---

in England after the change of religion. Now, so far from these accounts being unguarded admissions, they were sober testimonies, made with much satisfaction, and referred to authorities; and there is not one passage of the article in question that can possibly deserve the accusation of disingenuousness. The writer in the "Christian Remembrancer" does not appear to possess much candour or sincerity; he states a few isolated facts, and makes general deductions from them, and not unfrequently perverts the true meaning of the statements themselves. He first attempts to prove the continuance of Catholic rites in the present Anglican church, from the fact of some old candlesticks being occasionally mentioned in church inventories, which he is obliged to confess are not used for lights; and then farther on he argues against the use of lights at all, by perverting the obvious meaning of a passage in the "Review." Respecting the communion plate, which he speaks of in the better sort of parish churches, the reviewer has had ample opportunity of inspecting the same, and a viler collection of misshapen vessels are not to be found in Christendom; goblet-shaped chalices, huge flagons, somewhat resembling black jacks, spreading salvers, without one vestige or type of Catholic antiquity about them; and as for candlesticks, they may be occasionally found, but void of tapers or lights; for, as the Anglo-German father, Bucer, says of candles,

> " Their use for ornament
> On God's board may be innocent,
> *But do not light them as on stages,*
> *So may two candles last for ages,*
> *Yet better 'twere you used none*
> *For shunning superstition."*

And this latter advice is generally observed; for, notwithstanding the boastings of this writer, it would be scarcely possible for him to point out one church in the occupation of the Establishment, where lights are used during the celebration of the communion service, unless the impenetrable obscurity of a London fog might haply serve as reasonable excuse for reviving this Anglo-Catholic practice on a solitary occasion. The only instance where lights were attempted to be used on the old mystical principles in these latter times, was speedily followed by an injunction from the bishop for the immediate removal of candlesticks and all Popish ornaments out of the chancel. While we are on this subject, it may be proper to mention the egregious mistake into which the writer has fallen respecting the antiquity of the mystical use of lights in the church: it was mentioned in the review, that lights were not placed *on the altar* previous to the 10th century; but in the concluding part of the passage it stated *where they were disposed, round the altar, in coronas, on the rood beams in suspended lamps,* &c.; but this latter portion, not suiting his object, he leaves unnoticed, and exclaims in exultation, " So, if we have no lights at all, we are following the primitive usage; for it is admitted there were no candles on the altar in the early church;" and he adds, in a note, that Durandus, who wrote in the beginning of the 13th century, speaks only of one candelabrum, and which he does not describe, as on the altar; and that in the church of St. Clement, at Rome, this candelabrum was in *the choir adjoining one of the pulpits.* Now it is by no means surprising that a man, who has been both educated a Protestant, and remains a member of a Protestant communion, possessing but meagre sources for information on these matters, should fall into great mistakes; but it is astonishing that any one so utterly deficient in the ordinary knowledge of ecclesiastical antiquities, can so boldly advance such untenable positions. Durandus, so far from confining his account of lights to one candelabrum, has devoted a whole chapter to the subject, divided under five heads; the first of

frequently advocated on *false and untenable grounds.* In doing
this we shall probably offend many whose goodwill we should

---

which is as follows: " Candelabrorum et lucernarum *usus antiquissimus.*" In
every liturgical writer of any note, this subject is explained and illustrated at
great length, and in a most satisfactory and conclusive manner.

Respecting the one candelabrum at St. Clement's church, it is neither more
nor less than the pascal candlestick for the great candle lighted at Easter ;
which in many of the Roman churches is a *fixture on the gospel side of the choir,
which is its correct position;* and it was placed adjacent to one of the pulpits, not
for the purpose of affording light to a reader, as the italics of the writer would
seem to imply, but for the greater convenience of the deacon, who during the
chanting of the hymn " Exultat," has to infix five grains of incense in the
candle, and also attach the pascal table, or list of moveable feasts, and other
ecclesiastical matters, to it. As the candle is in itself generally of a considerable
size, with a corresponding pedestal, the deacon is necessarily obliged to ascend
a fixed or moveable pulpit for these purposes'; hence the position of the candelabrum at St. Clement's. In D'Agincourt's great work on art, there are three
representations of such pascal candlesticks, by pulpits or ambones, with the
deacon ; and in " Gerberti de Cantu et Musica Sacra a prima Ecclesiæ ætate
usque ad præsens tempus," a very curious representation of the tenth century is
given, of a pascal candlestick rich in ornament, close to an ambo or pulpit, in
which the deacon is figured in the act of affixing the pascal table to the candle.
It is impossible to have more conclusive proof of the real intention of these
candelabra, and the absurdity of the deductions which the writer in the
" Remembrancer" has attempted to draw from them. His observations respecting vestments betray equal ignorance ; he evidently confounds the alb with the
surplice, and the cope with the chasuble. The English surplice is, in fact, the
Roman one ; it may be seen figured in every plate of the Roman pontifical, is
still used in that city, and worn by a great portion of the English Catholic clergy,
at the present day ; and the crimped surplices were only partially introduced in
this country in consequence of the English Catholics being driven by the severity of penal laws to seek education in France; as this Anglo-*Catholic* state
at that time obliged every man to swear himself a *Protestant, or lose his lands,
liberty, and even life:* but these, like other temporary innovations consequent on
Protestant ascendency, are rapidly disappearing with the revival of ancient
solemnity.

Albs are not crimped or curtailed, but, several of the modern ones are flounced,
and are vastly similar in style to ladies' dresses. Albs of the ancient form, and
*apparelled in precisely the same manner as those which belonged to the old English
churches previous to the reign of Edward the Sixth,* have been revived in many
places; while they are utterly disused by the members of the Establishment,
who certainly have little room for reproaching others with any neglect or departures in these respects, since of all the ancient vestments they have retained
nothing but the surplice—*which is not by any means a distinguishing habit for the
priestly office:* and this, open in front, and hastily adjusted over a fashionably
cut coat, tight pantaloons, and a modern cravat, fails to convey the least resemblance of an ecclesiastic of the olden time. As regarding copes, which this
writer strangely confounds with vestments or chasubles, they have never experienced any alteration whatever in form, and those used by the English
Catholic clergy at the present time are precisely similar in shape and make to
those used before the change of religion; while the copes cited by the writer as
worn at the coronations, are for the most part strange departures from ancient
authority.

The chasuble has been terribly clipped in modern times of its original ample
form, but it has lately regained much of its former dignity ; indeed no one
would attempt to deny that poverty and bad taste combined have curtailed the

be anxious to retain, but the cause of Catholic truth is too
sacred to admit of our acquiescing in false views on the score
of expediency, or from the hope of obtaining certain ends which
would seem to be better advanced by following such a course.
We purpose, therefore, to set forth from the most authentic
sources the real history of the disasters that have fallen on
our sacred edifices since the sixteenth century; and this has

---

sacred vestments of half their ancient splendour, but still *the principle has never been abandoned by the English Catholics even under the most trying circumstances.* The clergy were compelled at one time to carry the vestments rolled into as small a compass as possible, from house to house, where they administered the consolations of religion to the scattered faithful: they were mean, they were ugly, *but there were the things; no priest ventured to celebrate without them, or without repeating the solemn prayers ordered by the Church while vesting.* Thus the traditions of England have been preserved by a few proscribed and persecuted Catholics, while the Anglicans have lost every vestige of ancient dignity; and at this moment the former are restoring the rites of the old religion in all their solemnity, while the latter *dare not even adhere to the trifling ornament allowed by the rubric;* but vestments, altars, and lights, are at complete variance with the *spirit of the present system.* Its founders abolished them altogether; they were partially revived through the whim of the tyrant Elizabeth, and the terrified puritans and irreverent dissenters, whom she introduced into the English bishoprics, consented to disguise themselves awhile in copes and surplices, the readier to infuse their pestilent doctrines among the people; for such are the reasons urged for their compliance by the foreign Protestants whom they consulted. (See Strype.) These relics of the old Church were rapidly dying away, when Laud attempted to stem the tide of Protestantism, but in vain; and copes, bishops, and king, fell victims to the Protestant principles that had so long been fostered among the people. Whatever might have been the efforts of a few Catholic-minded men at the restoration, the *glorious revolution* utterly extinguished all hopes of better things; and since that time Anglo-Protestantism has appeared as bare, meagre, and irreverent as its first concoctors and Genevan fathers could possibly desire.

We have gone at length into these remarks, because the writer in the "Christian Remembrancer" represents a most subtle and dangerous section existing in the Anglican Church; who by pushing forward the opinions of certain isolated writers, exceptions to the rule, and condemned by their cotemporaries as favourers of popery, are endeavouring to claim for the transactions of the Anglican Church for the last three centuries, a character which it is impossible on true grounds to substantiate. These men would affect Catholic rites, without possessing one particle of Catholic feeling or principle; they would fain enjoy the estate without fulfilling the tenure by which it must be held, and would assume the externals of antiquity the better to delude the people. But copes and two candlesticks are not the test of Catholicism; and if these persons did even figure for a while in the lion's skin they would soon betray the ass underneath, and only succeed in disgusting the Protestants with whom they associate, without either gaining grace, or advancing one step towards extricating themselves from the tangles of heresy which enthral them. These men of proud and obdurate hearts must not be confounded with those devout souls yet in the communion of the Anglican Church, who in austerities, mortifications, and humble piety, are seriously seeking the truth, and whose works and lives breathe the spirit of holiness and the feelings of ancient and better times. Humility, combined with an earnest desire of unity and truth, must be rewarded with the Divine blessing; but insolent and unfounded pretensions can only tend to promote the anger of the Almighty, and the ridicule and indignation of men.

become the more necessary, as doubtless there are many sincere men who write on these subjects *rather as they hope and wish than from actual research*, and are but little acquainted with the real state of the case, or the direful sacrilege that has been perpetrated under the system they extol. Far be it from us to charge the present race of Anglican clergy with any participation, by approval or otherwise, in the guilt of these enormities, or to hold them as answerable for sins of which our common fathers were guilty; indeed their works and writings for the most part prove them to possess a far different and better spirit: but our present object is to show the great inconsistency, or rather (to speak more properly) the impossibility of maintaining the principles which they now advocate on any but the ancient grounds; and the absurdity of claiming Catholic practices as belonging to the present system, which have in fact been abolished from its very commencement, and the very idea of which is a perfect novelty among the Anglicans themselves. That learned and reflecting men should be utterly disgusted with the meagre worship and Protestantism of the establishment, is natural, and at the same time gratifying; but they should endeavour to draw reasonable and legitimate conclusions from their convictions, and not put forth an imaginary Catholic system, and endeavour to throw the whole odium of Church plunder and desecration on the Puritan faction during the civil wars, who, after all, had but a comparatively small share in the execrable work. It does also seem most inconsistent, that those who have fallen to the lowest ebb in ecclesiastical rites and observances, and who have been as yet unable to extricate themselves from their degraded position, should assail in no very measured terms of reproach and insult, the English Catholic body; who, although far from exhibiting a standard of Catholic perfection, have retained the light of the old faith through a long series of bitter trials; and, with all the disadvantages under which they labour, are practically restoring at the present hour the very glories which their defamers can advocate only in theory.

With respect to the Puritans under Cromwell, so far from their being the great instrument for the destruction of England's glorious churches, these were defaced, plundered, and desecrated from the commencement of the so-called Reformation; and the ravages of the Cromwellian faction, execrable as they were, can by no means be compared to the sacrilegious outrages which preceded them, under the *direct sanction of the leading schismatics during the reigns of Henry the Eighth, Ed-*

ward the Sixth, and Elizabeth. It is now become a habit with Anglican writers to talk very largely about the demolitions of the seventeenth century; but when these accounts are tested by historical documents, we shall find the second Cromwell bleaches by the side of his more ancient namesake;—he certainly demolished many curious castellated mansions; and some ecclesiastical buildings suffered no little damage by shot and outrage; but it would be difficult to prove that he consigned one noble church to wilful destruction; while, during the reign of Henry, many of the *very finest* churches in Christendom were barbarously destroyed for the mere material, and scarcely a stone of them left standing: and how can the tossing over of a few communion tables, of mean material and vile design, be compared to the entire plunder and demolition of the ancient altars, consecrated by our most holy prelates, and on many of which the eucharistic sacrifice had been offered up, almost from the planting of the faith itself in the land?—altars sparkling with jewels, rich with gold, marbles, and enamels, exquisite in design, and whose precious frontals were but types of the more precious relics of God's holy saints that lay enshrined beneath them; and those gems and rich offerings were plundered, and those sacred relics scattered, and those consecrated stones, on which the holy bishops of old had poured out the sacred oil, split, and laid as paving for the infidels to trample on. And this, not by Puritans of the seventeenth, but of the sixteenth century, by that *arch apostate, the father of Puritans and modern Anglicans, Cranmer and his Zuinglian associates, whom he introduced and fostered to blaspheme and profane the saintly ecclesiastics and churches of our land.* Roundhead troopers had found nought to steal but a few mean copes and surplices; royal commissioners had long before cleared out the oaken almeries that lined the vaulted sacristies of old,—they were plundered of their costly contents by kingly robbers of an older date. Jewelled mitres, copes and vestments of golden tissue, orphreys of pearls, and curious silken imagery, were considered as Popish superstitions by Anglican fathers, and very *meet for regal use.* When were the shrines of Bede the venerable, the saintly Hugh of Lincoln, St. Cuthbert of Durham, St. Guthlae of Croyland, St. Chad of Lichfield, St. Swithun of Winchester, St. Thomas of Canterbury, and St. Alban, England's protomartyr, with hosts of others, seized and destroyed?—not by Puritans, but by English schismatics, who, having basely sold their birthright to a tyrant, denied their faith, renounced their spiritual allegiance to Christ's vicar, and became by the punishment of God the witnesses and instruments of their own shame. When did Canterbury's vaulted crypt, where holy prelates lie entombed, first echo with Huguenot preachers? *—when were those solemn piles, that faithful Englishmen had reared to God, desecrated by Walloon and Dutch ministers.† The Catholic structures were never more defiled in *Barebones'* days than this, —yet such were the motley crews welcomed by the innovators to assist in poisoning the minds and faith of the people.

The Puritans of Cromwell's time did but work out the principles of what is termed England's Reformation; there is not, in fact, one act of horrible sacrilege, contempt of ecclesiastical authority, or desecration of holy things and places, of which the Puritans were guilty, that had not been perpetrated ten times over, and under far more aggravated circumstances, by those who first reduced the English Church to her wretched state of schism and temporal bondage. Let our holy and just indignation fall on the truly guilty. Let us go at once to the *source of the evil, and assail the root, and condemn the betrayers rather than the betrayed.* We can even feel compassion and sorrow for the poor, ignorant, and misled fanatic of the latter times; but we will contend, with loud and lasting denunciations against the *authors of the lamentable evil,—those apostate bishops who betrayed the Church of which they were the unworthy pastors; who first abolished sacrifice, destroyed the altars of God, violated the sanctuaries, and instilled those principles of irreverence and infidelity into the minds of the people,* which, from that fatal period, have always lain smouldering and unextinguished, and from time to time break forth in open outrages;—of which the Cromwellian rebellion is but a fearful example. We will now proceed to bring forward historical documents in support of our positions.

OF THE DESTRUCTION OF ALTARS.

The destruction and desecration of altars during the reign of Henry must have been very extensive, owing to the vast

---

* A portion of the crypt at Canterbury was assigned for a French Protestant church, shortly after the establishment of Protestantism. See Hasted's "Canterbury Cathedral."

† The Austin Friars, in London, was given to the Dutch Protestants as a preaching place; it was once a most glorious church. Stow, who remembered it in its glory, describes it thus: "A large church, having a most fine spired steeple, small, high, and straight, *so that I have not seen the like.* But that goodly steeple, and all the eastern end, hath been lately taken down for one man's commodity," &c.

number of the most spacious and splendid churches belonging
to religious houses, which were demolished immediately after
the suppression of the monastic establishments; and among
these were probably some of the richest in the country: but
it does not appear that any altars in parochial, collegiate or
cathedral churches, were either destroyed or plundered to any
great extent till the succeeding reign of Edward the Sixth,
when the Protestantism of the so-called reformers was fully
developed; and Cranmer, who during the life of Henry had
outwardly conformed to the old rites, ceased to dissemble his
real opinions, and, urged by the instigations of the Calvinist
and Zuinglian faction, soon stripped the English Church of
her ancient solemnity, and rendered her, both in externals
and ritual, as bare and meager as the Genevan heretics of the
day could possibly desire.

In the account of the coronation of King Edward the
Sixth, given in *Strype's Memorials of Cranmer*, p. 142, the
high altar of Westminster is described as richly garnished
with divers and costly jewels and ornaments, of much esti-
mation and value; and also the tombs on each side of the high
altar, richly hanged with fine gold arras. Cranmer himself
also appeared on this occasion in the ancient archiepiscopal
vestments; for we read in the same account, that at nine of
the clock all Westminster choir was in their copes, and three
goodly crosses before them: and after them other three goodly
rich crosses, and the king's chapel, with his children following,
all in scarlet, with surplices and copes on their backs; and
after them ten bishops in scarlet, with their rochets and rich
copes on their backs, and their mitres on their heads, did set
forth at the west door of Westminster, towards the king's
palace, there to receive his grace; *and my Lord of Canterbury,
with his cross before him, alone, and his mitre on his head.*
Such were the solemnities retained in the English Church in
1546, after the reign of such a destructive tyrant as Henry;
but the Genevan emissaries had not yet arrived to extinguish
the fading light of England's ancient glory; for, after their
ever-to-be-detested presence, under the protection of Cranmer,—(who having betrayed the Church to the merciless tyranny of the state, introduced these wretched foreigners to
complete the havoc, and annihilate the faith), so rapid were
the strides of sacrilege and irreverence, that within four years
of the event just described at Westminster, *scarcely one altar
was left standing or unpillaged throughout the whole land ;* and
soon after, the very ornaments which decorated the altar on

the solemnity of the coronation, were conveyed away from the church by the authorized robbers of the day.*

1550 was the eventful year in which the destruction of those altars, on which the English clergy had offered up the holy sacrifice for so many centuries, were defaced and over-thrown. Heylin's account of the proceedings is so very important, that it is here given at length.

"But the great business of this year was the taking down of altars, in many places by the public authority; which in some few had formerly been pulled down by the irregular forwardness of the common people. The principal motive whereunto was, *in the first place, the opinion of some dislikes, which had been taken by Calvin against the Liturgy; and the desire of those of the Zuinglian faction to reduce this church unto the nakedness and simplicity of those transmarine churches which followed the Helvetian or Calvinian forms.* For the advancement of which work, it had been preached by Hooper, above-mentioned, before the king about the beginning of this year,—that it would be very well, that it might please the magistrates to turn the altars into tables, according to the first institution of Christ; and thereby to take away the false persuasion of the people, which they have of sacrifices to be done upon the altars. Because (saith he) as long as altars remain, both the ignorant people and the ignorant and evil persuaded priest, will dream always of sacrifice. This was enough to put the thoughts of the alteration into the heads of some great men about the Court, who thereby promised themselves no small hopes of profit by the disfurnishing of the altars, of the hangings, pales, plate and other rich utensils, which every parish, more or less, had provided for them. And that this consideration might prevail upon them as much as any other, if perhaps not more, may be collected from an inquiry made about two years after, in which it was to be interrogated, what jewels of gold and silver, or silver crosses, candlesticks, censors, chalices, copes, and other vestments, were then remaining in any of the cathedral or parochial churches; or otherwise had been embezzled or taken away; the leaving of one chalice to

* Heylin, p. 133. "That in pursuance of the faculties and instructions wherewith the king's commissioners were empowered…on May the 9th, 1553, Sir Roger Chomley, knight, lord chief justice, and Sir Robert Bowes, knight, master of the rolls, the king's commissioners for gathering ecclesiastical goods, held their session at Westminster, and called before them the dean of that cathedral, and certain others of the same house, and commanded them by virtue of the commission, to bring to them a true inventory of all the plate, cups, vestments, and other ecclesiastical goods which belonged to the church; which goods, the 12th day of the same month, were delivered to the said collectors; *who left no more unto the Church than two cups with the covers gilt, and one white silver pot, with a few carpets, cushions, and hearse-cloths!!*"

every church, with a cloth or covering for the communion table, being thought sufficient.

"The matter being thus resolved on, a letter comes to bishop Ridley, in the name of the king, *signed with his royal signet, but subscribed by Somerset, and other of the Lords of the Council*, concerning the taking down of altars and setting up tables in the stead thereof : which letter, because it relates to somewhat which was done before, in some of the churches, and seems only to pretend to an uniformity in all the rest, I shall here subjoin, that being the chief ground on which so great an alteration must be supposed to have been raised. Now the tenour of the said letter is as followeth :

"Right Reverend Father in God, right trusty and well beloved, we greet you well : whereas it is come to our knowledge, that, being the altars within the more part of the churches of the realm, upon good and godly considerations, are taken down, there doth yet remain altars standing in divers other churches ; by occasion whereof much variance and contention ariseth among sundry of our subjects, which, if good foresight we had not, might perhaps engender great hurt and inconvenience. We let you wit, that minding to have all occasions of contentions taken away, which many times groweth by those and such like diversities ; and considering, that amongst other things belonging to our royal office and care, we do account the greatest to be to maintain the common quiet of our realm ; we have thought good, by the advice of our council, to require you, and nevertheless especially to charge and command you, for the avoiding of all matters of further contention and strife about the standing or taking away of the said altars, to give substantial order through all your diocese ; that with all diligence, all the altars in every church or chapel, as well in places exempted as not exempted, within your said diocese, be taken down, and instead of them a table to be set up in some convenient part of the chancel within every such church or chapel, to serve for the ministration of the blessed communion. And, to the intent the same may be done without the offence of such of our loving subjects as be not yet so well persuaded in that behalf as we could wish, we send unto you herewith certain considerations, gathered and collected, that make for the purpose. The which and such others as you shall think meet, to be set forth to persuade the weak to embrace our proceedings in this part, we pray you cause to be declared to the people by some discreet preachers in such places as you shall think meet, before the taking down of the said altars, so as both the weak consciences of others may be instructed and satisfied as much as may be ; and this our pleasure the more quietly executed. For the better doing whereof we require you to open the foresaid considerations, in that our cathedral church, in your own person if you conveniently may, or otherwise by your chancellor or other grave preacher, both there and in such other market towns and most notable places of your diocese, as you may think most requisite.

" Which letter, bearing date on the 24th of November, in the fourth year of the king, was subscribed by the Duke of Somerset, the Archbishop of Canterbury, the lord Admiral Clinton, the Earls of Warwick, Bedford, and Wiltshire ; the Bishop of Ely, the Lords Wentworth and North.

" Now the effect of the said reasons mentioned in the last part of this letter, were, first, to move the people from the superstitious opinions of the people of the Popish mass unto the right use of the Lord's Supper ; *the use of an altar being to sacrifice upon, and the use of a table to eat upon* ; and therefore a table to be far more fit for our feeding on him, who was once only crucified and offered for us. Secondly, that in the *Book of the Common Prayer*, the name of altar, the Lord's board, and table, are used indifferently, without prescribing anything in the form thereof. For as it is called a table, and the Lord's board, in reference to the Lord's Supper, which is there administered, so it is called an altar also, in reference to the sacrifice of praise and thanksgiving, which is there offered unto God. And so the changing the altars into tables not to be any way repugnant to the rules of the Liturgy. The third reason seems to be no other than an illustration of the first, for taking away the superstitious opinion out of the minds of the people touching the sacrifice of the mass, which was not to be celebrated but upon an altar. The fourth, that the altars were erected for the sacrifices of the law, which being now ceased, the form of the altar was to cease together with them. The fifth, that as Christ did institute the sacrament of his body and blood at a table, and not at an altar (as it appeareth by the three Evangelists), so it is not to be found that any of the Apostles did ever use an altar in the ministration. And finally, that it is declared in the preface to the *Book of Common Prayer*, that if any doubt arise in the use and practising of the said book, that then, to appease all such diversity, the matter shall be referred unto the bishop of the diocese, who by his discretion shall take order for the quieting of it.

" The letter, with these reasons, being brought to Ridley, there was no time for him to dispute the commands of the one, or to examine the validity and strength of the other. And thereupon proceeding shortly after to his first visitation, he gave out one injunction, amongst others, to this effect, that those churches in his diocese, where the altars do remain, shall conform themselves unto those other churches which had taken them down ; and that instead of the multitude of their altars they should set up one decent table in every Church. But this being done, a question afterwards did arise about the form of the Lord's board, some using it in the form of a table, and others in the form of an altar : which being referred unto the determination of the bishop, he declared himself in favour of that posture or position of it, which he conceived most likely to procure an uniformity in all his diocese, and to be more agreeably to the king's godly proceedings, in abolishing divers vain and superstitious opinions about the mass out of the hearts of the people. Upon which declaration, or determination, he appointed the form of a right table to be used in his diocese ; and caused the wall standing on the back side of the altar, in the Church of St. Paul's, to be broken down for an example to the rest. And being thus a leading case to all the rest of the kingdom, it was followed, either with a swifter or a slower pace, according as the bishops in their several dioceses, or the clergy in their several parishes, stood affected to it. No universal change of altars into tables, in all parts of the realm, till the repealing of the first liturgy, in which the priest is appointed to stand before the middest of the altar in the celebration ; and the establishing of the second, in which it is required that the priest shall stand on the north side of the table, had put an end to the dispute."

From this account we may gather the following important facts :—

1st. That Calvin and the Zuinglians were the authors of this detestable sacrilege.

2d. That excepting Cranmer and a few apostates of the same class, the English clergy had no part in the foul deed.

3d. That the order proceeded from lay authorities.

4th. That the object of these lay authorities was plunder of church ornaments.

5th. That the reason assigned by Cranmer and the Protestant clergy for the demolition was, in order to *abolish the idea of sacrifice.*

6th. That the destruction of the ancient altars must be referred to this period, and not to the Puritanic rebellion under Cromwell.

Refusal to desecrate the altars of God, was considered a sufficient cause for depriving a bishop of his see : for we are informed by Strype (Cranmer, p. 228), that Bishop Hethe, of Worcester, came before the "council, and being asked *what he said to the letters sent to him from the king's majesty,* he answered, that he could not conform *his conscience to take down altars in the churches,* and in lieu of them to set up tables as the letter appointed ; alleging further, that Scripture and the fathers were in their favour." Cranmer and Ridley both endeavoured to dissuade the bishop from his opinion, but without effect.

Four days after, Bishop Day, of Chichester, was summoned on

the same account, and remanded till the 7th, when he answered plainly he could not comply in conscience with the injunctions of the *king's letter;* for the "altars seemed to him a thing anciently established by the agreement of the holy fathers, and confirmed by the ancient doctors, with the custom also of a number of years, and as he thought according to the Scriptures; wherefore he could not consent to the abolishing of them, and determined rather to lose all that he ever had than to condemn his own conscience." Whereupon, Strype adds, for his contempt, he was committed by order of the council; so we hear no more of him and his fellow the bishop of Worcester, till nine months hence; *so we leave them in the Fleet.* At the expiration of that time they were both deposed, and the Puritan Hooper was introduced into Worcester, to make havoc of that glorious Church, and to deface it, in the same manner as he had previously done at Gloucester; Scory, of Rochester, was nominated to Chichester.[*]

We find in Dugdale's History of St. Paul's, that in the 7th year of king Edward the Sixth, the dean and chapter of that church petitioned for an allowance of £28. 6s. 4d. towards their expenses *in taking down the steps and place of the high altar,* and other alterations. From this item it will be see that *Dowsing's* proceedings in the reign of Cromwell were quite in the true Protestant spirit of the reformed Anglican Church; for he ordered chancel steps to be levelled, which was done by the mother church of London a century previous. Not content with demolishing altars, it was customary to lay down the consecrated slab *as a common paving-stone,* in which position many still remain at Lincoln Minster, and other places.

The parish accounts of this period furnish most interesting particulars respecting the sale of altars, which were made into lots.

"St. Lawrence's Church, Reading, 1551.	s.	d.
Received of Mr. Grey for St John's altar and *the cope chest*	6	8
Received of Mr. Grey, for the Trinitie altar of marble, with the trimming	10	8

---

[*] Thus were the sacrilegious destructions, termed in our days *Anglo-Catholic reforms,* carried on by an apostate archbishop and some plundering courtiers; and if any ecclesiastics dared to resist the usurped power and defend the ancient customs of the Church, they were imprisoned and deposed, to make room for Puritanic intruders, fresh from Frankfort or Geneva, and ready for any work of savage fanaticism.

I

Received of Mr. Buckland for Jesus' altar, and St. Thomas
altar   4   0
Received of Mr. Bell for the high altar *and two gates in the
churchyard*   6   8

Coates' Antiquities of Reading, 162.

Wigtoft Church, Lincolnshire, 1550.

Thes be yᵉ receytt of yᵉ aforesayd Wyllm & Roger for yᵉ year. *s. d.*
Fryst of Gregory Wolmer, gent., for ye altar in our Lady
qwere   3   3
Item of John Wolgat for the altar in Nycholas qwere . 2   0
Item of Gorge Atkynson for the seyd (side) altar . . 10   0
Item of Kyrke of Boston for xxiii Stone of Leten* . . 8   4

The sale and seizure of altar candlesticks was general.
In the articles of visitation to be followed and observed according to *the king's majesty's injunctions and proceedings.*

1. That all parsons, vicars, and curates, omit in the reading
of the injunctions, all such as make mention of the Popish
mass, of chantries, of *candles upon the altar*, or any other such
like thing; also no *minister is to set any light upon God's
board at any time,*†—Art. 2. In Art. 9, " no man to maintain *lights, candles, altars*," ‡ &c.

By these new arrangements, the chancel was rendered useless; for the table was ordered *not to stand altarways, but to
be brought down into the body of the Church.* Thus the whole
mystical arrangements of the ancient buildings were violated
and destroyed, and screen, altar-steps, reredos, sedilia, sacrarium and sanctuary, were deprived at once of their original
intention, and rendered useless; for the new form was
indeed far more suited to the conventicle than to the glorious
fabrics where it was performed, and which were mutilated,
ruined, and defaced, to make them accord in any degree with
the meagre novelties with which they were desecrated. On
the revival of the ancient rites under Queen Mary, the preceding ravages were as far as possible repaired. In the archdeacon's " Visitation for London, 1554," the 5th article is
as follows:—

" Whether there be in the church an high altar of stone, *consecrated and dedicated specially to sing or say mass upon ;* and it is
not meant any grave-stones taken up from the burial or other

---

* Leten, laten, the metal of which the candlesticks and other furniture of the
altars was made.
 † There is no instance recorded in which the commissioners allowed candlesticks to remain in any church.
 ‡ Burnet's History of the Reformation.

unseemly place, and put up for an altar, but a meet and convenient stone as hath been accustomed in times past."—*Collins' Ecclesiastical Hist.* vol. ii. Col. p. 87.

In the Churchwardens' accounts of S. Mary's, Reading, 1558.

	s.	d.
Paide for the hallowing of the altars	13	0
Paide for a pynte of oyle	0	4
Paide for a pound and a half of franckeinsence	0	11
Paide for v yards of cere cloth for the altars	2	8

Coates' Antiquities of Reading, p. 130.

In the parish annals of St. Pancras, Soper Lane, is a charge, anno 1555, Oct. 30, to *make up the altars* by November.

" Allhallows, Bread Street, 1554.

" The great stone which had been the cover of the high altar, was taken up from the body of the church, *where it had formed part of the pavement,* and was replaced for its original use."

These are merely a few random extracts, illustrative of the partial restoration of the English churches under the unfortunate Queen Mary. We shall now proceed to notice the destruction that again befel them after the accession of Elizabeth. This queen appeared in some respects rather favourably inclined towards the external splendour of the ancient faith ; and some of the ornaments that had been disused under Edward the Sixth, were retained in the Protestant service enacted under Elizabeth ; but the new clergy, and especially those she introduced into the sees of the old bishops, were Puritans at heart, and rather connived at these things from dread of the queen's displeasure, than adopted them from any veneration for ancient usages ; and, as we shall have occasion hereafter to show, they were soon abolished in practice, although they were theoretically held to the present day. The altars which the piety of the preceding reign had re-edified and consecrated, were soon ordered to be demolished, and in the act passed for that purpose, *the ordinary of the Church was constituted the overseer of this sacrilegious work.*

The period of Elizabeth is mentioned by some modern writers as the golden days of *Anglo-Catholic practices* ; but the following extracts will prove facts which are certainly incompatible with the existence of much Catholic feeling.

" Aug. 13, 1559, Skory, new Bishop of Hereford, preached at St. Paul's while the *visitation of the Church was in hand,* two days after the rood there, *with the altar, was pulled down.*"—*Strype's Annals,* vol. i. 134.

" St. Andrews, Holborn, 2d of Elizabeth.

" In the 1st and 2d year of her Majestie's reign, *all the altars and superstitious things* set up in Queen Marie's days, were now again (*to God's glory*) *pulled down.*"—*Nicholl, Lond. Red.* vol. ii. 187.

" 2d of Elizabeth, St. Giles's Church, Reading.   *s. d.*

For pulling down the awlters and rydding away of the rubbis   2   3

" St. Lawrence's Church, Reading, 1559.

For taking down the awlters and *layinge the stones*   .   .   5   0
Coates' Antiquities of Reading.

" 1559.   St. Margaret's Westminster.

Paid for taking down the table* over the high altars and
     taking down the holy water stock   1   0

1563.   Received for the altar table which was revived in the
     late Court of Augmentation, *defaced*   .   .   . 5   0

The altar itself escaped till 1570: for in that year we find
the following item,—

For altering and *defacing* of the aulter stone and *laying down
     of the same*   1   4

Churchwardens' accounts of St. Helen's, Abingdon, A.D. 1559,

For taking down the altere   1   8

Payde for tymber and making the communion table   .   . 6   0

For mending and paving the place where the alterre stoode .   2   8
Nichol's Illustration of Ancient Times.

Innumerable documents can be brought forward of the same kind as those now set forth, which prove the destruction of altars on the re-establishment of Protestantism under Elizabeth. Indeed the acts of parliament are themselves sufficient evidence of the fact; but as many persons are now endeavouring to affix the odium of this sacrilege on the Puritans during the great rebellion, we have selected corroborative testimony from parochial accounts, &c.

Strype, in his *Annals,* relates the queen was at first inclined to have such altars as had been demolished by the Protestant party in an irregular manner restored; but Cox, Sandys, Grindall, and others, drew up six reasons for the demolition, and eventually prevailed. These reasons are very similar to those urged in King Edward's days, and fully prove that the Anglican Church had abandoned all idea of the Eucharistic sacrifice. For in the fifth reason: " Furthermore, *an altar*

---

* The word table, as here used, signifies a tryptic, or folding picture of a centre and two leaves; these were frequently richly carved as well as painted.

hath *relation* to *sacrifice ; so that of necessity, if we allow an altar, we must grant a sacrifice,*" &c.,—seeing the one was ordained for the other. No language can be clearer on this point, and it is evident that even the use of the word altar is scarcely allowable according to true Anglican principles.

The sixth reason is very important, as it shows that the modern recesses of the preaching houses of the day are in accordance with the spirit of Anglicanism. " Moreover, if the communion be ministered at an altar, the *godly prayers spoken by the minister cannot be heard of the people ;*" and for this reason the table was brought down for the communion service, *where the clergyman might best be heard.* All the mystical reasons which instigated the erection of the ancient churches are here at once abolished ; and this is one of the many evident facts, which should convince the good men who are so earnestly labouring for the revival of Catholic church architecture, that we must have the Catholic service revived, in the first place, before any real good can posssibly be accomplished,—unless this be done, difficulties arise at every step. The present communion is, after all, a sort of preaching service ; it is not a solemn act of sacrifice, where the priest, in silence, within *the holy place,* is ministering for the people, according to the custom of even primitive antiquity ;* but they are to assist, as at a sermon, by *listening* to the *clergyman.* This is pointedly assigned as a reason for demolishing the altars ; because, if admitted at an altar, *the prayers spoken by the minister cannot be heard by the people.* Now it is very certain that the construction of the ancient deep chancels was entirely owing to the respect paid by our ancestors to the august mysteries celebrated within them. A deep chancel, under the present system is an absurdity ; the very principles on which the Book of Common Prayer was framed are against it. In fact, all idea of reverence ceased with its introduction, and chancels were filled with seats as early as 1578 (see parish accounts) ; and the reason assigned for enclosing the communion table with rails, was no other than *irreverent*

---

* The learned father Le Brun, in his " Liturgies de toutes les Eglises," 4 vols. 8vo., Paris, 1726, has gone at great length into the very important subject of the ancient manner of celebrating the sacred mysteries, and fully proves that from the earliest times the *communion was recited by the priest in silence.* This portion of the work is entitled " L'usage de réciter en silence une partie des prières de la messe, *dans toutes les Eglises* et *dans toutes les siècles.*" He cites the fathers, councils, and liturgies, in proof of this most important fact, which is an irresistible argument for the ancient construction of the churches, and also for the celebration of the sacred mysteries in the ancient language.

*people sitting upon it during service time.** The old churches are utterly unsuited for the present form of worship; and wherever we go, we find that immense sums have been expended on the ancient buildings, to ruin them and destroy all their beauty and propriety of arrangement; *abolish altars and sacrifice, and what can possibly become of a Christian church?* All the partitions, and dividing off of naves, filling up chancels with pews, cutting away screens, erection of galleries, are but consequences of the established system. These monstrosities followed as naturally in the wake of the Common Prayer Book, as chancels and crosses rose at the teaching of the ancient churchmen; and this will be perceived ere long by those who are making such strenuous exertions for the revival of ancient architecture. It may be urged, that the chancels were ordered to remain as in times past; true, but in this same order will be found a clause which deprived them at once of the very spirit of their existence: and we will ask, how long did the chancels remain as in time past? certainly not after a table was set at the lower end, and they were denuded of all their former glory. The walls and roofs might remain,—in some cases they remain now,—but *not as in times past:* and indeed it would be extremely difficult, if not impossible, to point out one instance where the chancel has been preserved with even decent respect; it is generally blocked up with pews, with backs to the east end, so as to face the pulpit; frequently it is one of the *common entrances into the church:* at Yarmouth the place of the table was occupied by *benches* on *evening lectures;* and along the Norfolk coast the *chancels of their truly glorious churches are, with very few exceptions, in ruins.* Again, the usual plan of converting the conventual churches into parochial ones, was to wall up the end of the nave, leave a few feet for the table, and either demolish the transepts and choir for materials, or leave them to decay. In cathedral churches the mob sit with their backs to the east, right up to the rails; and certainly, from the preceding note they did not pay greater respect to sanctuaries in Elizabeth's time, when Anglicanism was green and new, than they do at the present day.

---

* In the MS. visitation, preserved at St. Paul's, the following remark occurs, which shows the utter loss of all reverence for sacred places among the people of London in Elizabeth's reign, 1598: "In the upper quier where the common [communion] table dothe stande, there is met unreverente people *walking with their hatts on their heddes* commonly *all service tyme,* no man reproving them for yt."

But how could it be possible to preserve feelings of veneration among the people, when the altars were demolished, and the blessed sacrament itself, the soul of sanctity and veneration, expelled from the desecrated sanctuaries,—the relics of the ancient bishops and confessors turned out on a dunghill or consumed with fire,—and the portraiture of our blessed Redeemer and his saints hacked and mutilated? These fearful enormities have wrought such a debasement of feeling among the people of this land, that nothing but the almighty power of God can restore the blessing of reverence among them; and this cannot possibly be accomplished in any other manner than by the revival of the ancient faith; and the only misgiving we feel, respecting the labours of the present learned societies for the revival of church architecture, is the fact of their beginning at the wrong end, for unless the old faith and rites be restored, the deep chancels of antiquity would be no better than the other architectural masquerades of the day. An ancient chancel requires a consecrated altar, and a solemn sacrifice offered thereupon; it requires an assembly of the faithful, who do not come to *see and hear,* but to *assist in humble prayer at the celebration of the sacred mysteries,* and these require to be instructed in *the faith of the English Church, before her altars were overthrown, and her mysteries abolished, by Puritan bishops, and authorised blasphemers of sacred things;* truly there are other matters which require moulding to the good old fashion, besides blocks of stone and baulks of timber; and this must be evident to those who are labouring to preserve the departed glory of the sanctuary: not that we would by any means discourage their praiseworthy attempts, on the contrary, we hail them with thankfulness as the means of bringing men to reflect on glories they have abandoned and lost, and of comparing the wonderful achievements of our Catholic ancestors under the ennobling influence of the ancient faith, and the dismal results of the Protestant system of their latter times. A Catholic cathedral is no bad atmosphere wherein to imbibe a thorough detestation of Protestantism; for the contrast between the majesty of the building and the meagreness of the modern rites, appeal at once to the evidence of the senses:* and the study of ancient church architecture

---

* On the same principle a French cathedral of the present time is an excellent preventive against the revival of paganism; for here the abominations of modern design and trumpery stand forth in all their hideous inconsistency, by the side of the old Catholic work, which they dishonour by the intrusion.

is an admirable preparation for the old faith. One thing is certain, either the revival of true Christian churches, or the present service, must give way; for it is quite impossible for any man who abides in the Anglican Church, as she is at present constituted, to *build a Catholic Church and use it afterwards.* All that we have as yet seen attempted are wretched failures; every now and then we hear that a *real Catholic* church is going to be erected, and when completed, it has something of the shell of an old building, but no kernel; *it lacketh the one thing needful:* and there are certain inseparable arrangements which stamp Protestant on it at first sight: but if it were the very facsimile of Howden in all its glory,—when the consecration day arrived, and instead of the acolytes, and thurifer, and processional cross, and tapers, and copes, and mitres, and the holy chrism, and the pontifical with solemn antiphon, and the rich ferettum, with its saintly relics; the churchwardens are dressed in their best coats, and the charity children are drawn out, and a few Genevan gownmen appear as black as crows, and the bishop drives up with his lady;—the most resolute champion of Anglican rites, would relinquish his hopeless pretensions in despair.

But to return to communion tables. By the act of the first year of Elizabeth above-mentioned, which ordered the demolition of altars, the table was commanded to stand in the place where the altar stood, *except during the time of communion,* when it was to be brought down where the minister might be the more readily heard by the people; and after the communion, done from time to time, the table to be placed where it stood before;—so that, inconsistently enough, by this arrangement, it was to occupy the proper position of an altar, *unless it was wanted for the purposes of communion.* But owing to the death of many of the old clergy, and the deprivation of many of the most learned and pious;—owing to their refusal to receive the new order that was attempted to be thrust upon them, there was not a sufficient number of learned men to supply the cures, and, to use Heylin's own words, the church was filled with an ignorant and illiterate clergy, hastily procured among *mechanics and others of the same class;*

* John Rastel, in his answer to Jewel's challenge, thus addresses him, in p. 162: "Whereas the Church of God, so well ordered with excellent men of living and godliness, is constrained to suffer coblers, weavers, tinkers, tanners, cordmakers, tapsters, fidlers, juglers, and others of the like profession, *not only to enter into disputes with her, but also to climb up* into pulpits, and to keep the place of priests and ministers; or that any bagpipers, horsecoursers, gaolers,

while many were raised to great preferments, who, strongly attached *Genevan discipline*, had returned to England *much disaffected to episcopal government, and rites and ceremonies*. Accordingly, the *altar steps* were too Catholic for these new churchmen; and by 1561, we find that Parker was obliged to issue an injunction *against taking down altar steps*, and bringing the table into *the middle of the church*: by this new order, the communion table is commanded to stand in the place where the steps then were, or *had formerly stood*, which seemed to imply that it was not to be moved in time of communion. These injunctions could not have produced much effect, for, by the reign of Charles I, those clergy who attempted to administer the communion from the table so placed, were loudly denounced as favourers of Popery,—consequently the attempt must have been viewed as a restoration of an obsolete practice at that time.

The revival of this position of the table was undoubtedly owing to the celebrated and unfortunate Archbishop Laud; for, in the 19th of Charles I, we read in Rushworth's *Historical Collections*, that, in these times, the communion table *began to be placed altarwise in parochial churches*, after the manner of cathedrals.

And in vol. ii. p. 207, he gives some exceedingly curious particulars relative to a dispute between the parishioners of St. Gregory's Church, near St. Paul's, London, and the dean and chapter of that cathedral, who were the ordinaries therefore, and who had ordered the table to be removed up to the eastern end of the chancel, which gave great offence. A

---

aletasters, were admitted of old time into the clergy, without good and long trials of their conversations." The same author says in another place, " In the primitive Church, altars were allowed amongst Christians, upon which they offered the unbloody sacrifice of Christ's body ; yet your company [speaking to Jewel], to declare what followers they are of antiquity, do account it even one of the kinds of idolatry *if one keep an altar standing;* and indeed you follow a certain antiquity, not of the Catholics, but of desperate heretics—the Donatists, who did break, rase, and remove the altar of God."

From the other charges urged by this writer against the Anglican Church, and which Peter Heylin says (in his " History," p. 347), " are too many *sad truths faithfully delivered*," we may gather that the following practices were by no means uncommon;—ministers using only their ordinary apparel while officiating in the church;—the processions in Rogation week retained merely for the purpose of keeping up the memory of the parish bounds, and not to move Almighty God by supplication for mercy;—the remains of the consecrated elements, after communion being taken by the clergyman, or parish-clerk, for their *own domestic use;*—that many of the new bishops refused to wear a white rochet, or to be distinguished from the laity by honest priests' apparel, and many other matters of a similar description.

similar case occurred about the same time between the parishioners and vicar of Grantham.

The history of the Anglican Church, in this eventful
period, must show the utter hopelessness of accomplishing
any restoration of ancient rites and reverence, excepting
through the *legitimate channel of real ecclesiastical authority.*
Of all Protestant churchmen,* Laud ventured the farthest in
his endeavours towards a partial restoration of ancient solemnity; yet never was there a more signal failure, and never
did a great man appear in a more pitiable and degrading
position than when he attempted a Protestant defence of
these proceedings, on his trial before the parliament. The
particulars of the charges brought against him are so curious,
and bear so strongly on passing events, that we have thought
it right to take some notice of them. One of the chief
articles was the ceremonies he used in the consecration of St.
Katharine, creed-church, London: the term consecration is
used by all the writers who have described the event, but as
St. Katharine was an old church, and had been only desecrated
by repairs, a reconciliation would have been a more correct
expression; but at all events, the ceremonies used by the
archbishop, if it be not using too irreverent a term, were a
mere burlesque of the ancient rites, and serve as a farther
proof of the necessity of adhering to authority and tradition
in these matters.

"First, as the bishop approached the west door of the church,
some that were prepared for it, cried with a loud voice, 'Open, open,
ye everlasting gates, that the King of Glory may come in;' and
presently the doors were opened; and the bishop, with some
doctors, and many principal men, went in, and immediately falling
upon his knees, with his eyes lifted up and his arms spread out, he
exclaimed, 'This place is holy! this ground is holy! in the name
of the Father, Son, and Holy Ghost, I pronounce it holy!' then he
took up some of the dust, and threw it up in the air several times
in his going up to the chancel. When the bishop approached near
the rail and communion table, he bowed several times, and retiring,
went round the church in procession, &c. After this the bishop
pronounced curses on those who should profane the holy place, and
blessings on those who should contribute to its support. Then
followed the sermon. This ended, as the bishop approached the
communion table, he made several lowly bowings, and coming up
to the side of the table where the bread and wine were covered, *he*

* When on the very scaffold, Laud declared he died as *good a Protestant as
any man in England.*

bowed seven times, and after the reading of many prayers, he came near the bread, and gently lifted up the corner of the napkin wherein the bread was laid, and when he beheld the bread, he laid it down again, stepped back, bowed three times towards it, then drew near again, and opened the napkin, and bowed as before. Then he laid his hand on the cup, which was full of wine, with a cover upon it, which he let go again, went back, bowed thrice towards it, then he came near again, and lifting up the cover of the cup, looked into it, and seeing the wine, retired back and bowed as before. Then he received the sacrament, and gave it to some principal men ; after which, with many prayers, the consecration ended."

Now throughout the whole of this ceremony, we cannot discover one act which was performed in accordance with any ancient ritual or pontifical ; the whole was an invention of the archbishop's, and filled with inconsistencies ; the antiphon, "Be ye opened," &c., said at doors, should only be used at the consecration of a new church ; for a reconciliation the bishop should commence the more appropriate antiphon, "Asperges me Domine," &c.

2. The bishop, immediately on entering, declared the place holy, pronouncing the supplicatory prayers to that effect after the benediction.

3. The matter of dust was a perfect novelty, blessed water being the matter used by the Church in benedictions ; moreover, all matter used for such a purpose, requires to be first purified by prayer and exorcism, whereas the dust used by the archbishop was common dust from the pavement.

4. The altar of a church which is to be reconciled, should be utterly denuded of ornaments, while the communion table at St. Katharine's was prepared with the elements, cloths, &c.

5. The reverences made by the bishop to the mere elements previous to consecration, were utterly irregular, and even superstitious. But the defence made by the bishop when accused of these proceedings, was far poorer than the ceremonies themselves; he could not devise better arguments wherewith to defend the consecration of the church, than appeals to *Jewish practices* and *examples* of the *Mosaic Law*, which were very properly objected to by his adversaries as belonging to a dispensation which had passed away : he afterwards referred to the testimony of Eusebius, touching the consecration of the churches under Constantine, which was certainly more to the point. But when men are without the existing authority of the Church to appeal to, into what miser-

able evasions are they not driven! here was Laud, standing in
the place of the lord primate of all England, appearing as
successor to a race of prelates who had consecrated a long succession of churches and kings ; and yet cut off from them by
his protestations : he does not venture an appeal to the *ancient
usages of the English Church*, but changes from Levitical ceremonies to Constantine, and then to the authority of Bishop
Andrewes, an inferior ecclesiastic of course to the archbishop ; and when pressed on the subject of images and
sacred representations, appeals even to the heresiarch *Calvin*,
to the no small exultation and triumph of his opponents, who at
length overpowered and silenced the archbishop by quoting the
homilies and common practices of the modern Anglican Church
against him. This is indeed a most forcible example of the
utter impossibility of any, but those who build on the rock of
Peter, effecting any permanent good in the revival of ancient
solemnity. Had the lot of Laud fallen in Catholic and better
times, he would in all probability have proved himself a
worthy successor of St. Austin ; but influenced by his Protestant position, all that he accomplished in Church reform,
was attained more after the manner of a temporal magistrate
than with archiepiscopal authority. Accused afterwards of
these very revivals, he endeavours to shelter himself under
mean and evasive excuses; and when condemned (most un-
justly) to die, he declares himself a *good Protestant*, and by
that miserable admission forfeits all claim to martyrdom, and
his decollation sinks at once to a mere state execution.

The other charges, which are detailed at length in Rushworth's *Historical Collections*, and other works, were sub-
stantially as follows :—

Setting up of pictures (stained glass) in the windows of his
chapels at Lambeth and Croydon, bowing towards the table
or altar, and using of copes at the sacrament. Now from
the very fact of such charges being gravely preferred in the
English Parliament against the archbishop, we may certainly
infer, that the good practices complained of, *could not be
very general* in the established Church at that period, 1643,

* We have, however, authorities to show that some copes were retained till
the Rebellion, at the cathedral churches of old St. Paul's, Durham, Norwich,
Peterborough, the abbey church of Westminster, the archiepiscopal chapels of
Lambeth, Croydon, and the royal chapel of St. James's. At the three latter places
they appear to have been introduced by the archbishop himself; and from the
evidence of Laud, his predecessors must have allowed both the chapels at Lambeth and Croydon to fall into disgraceful decay ; for he says, " that they lay so

10 Charles I; and we must moreover remember, that these charges were brought forward not on *professedly Puritan grounds*, but as *contrary to the religion as by law established;* and during the whole enquiry, the arguments made use of by the adversaries of the archbishop, were taken from the authorised rubrics, acts, &c., of the *modern Anglican Church:* but one of the most important facts to be gathered from these interesting proceedings, is the usual position occupied by the communion table, from the reign of Elizabeth to Charles the First. It was alleged, that the communion tables were *generally placed throughout the realm in the midst of the choir or chancel*, with the ENDS *east and west*, in which posture they generally *stood in all churches and chapels*, and in *Lambeth chapel itself for one;* since the *injunctions were published, till this innovating archbishop altered this their ancient position.*

It was therefore declared an innovation, and a Popish one too, tending to *remove the Lord's table as far as possible* from the *audience of the common people*, when the sacrament is celebrated at it.*

It does not appear that Laud ventured to set up any stone altar, or such an act would certainly not have been omitted in the charges alleged against him; his great offence seems to have consisted in placing the *communion table altarwise;* and the only authentic account of any attempt at the erection of a stone altar at this period, is to be found in the Grantham Controversy, under the title of *the holy table, name and thing.* It appears that the vicar had moved the communion table up to the eastern end of the church; and one Wheatly, an alderman of the place, commanded his officers to bring it *down again to its accustomed place in the church*, which was accomplished after some altercation, and even striking; upon this the vicar declared that he cared not what they did with their *old tressel*, for he would make him *an altar of stone at his own charge*, and fix it in the old altar place; the parishioners reply that he should set up *no dresser* of stone in the church; nor does it appear that he was ever able to accomplish his intention. All existing documents tend to prove, that *no altars*

---

nastily that he was ashamed to behold them." The period of Charles the First gave many indications of a reviving Catholic spirit; amongst other instances the parish church of St. Giles's, London, was glazed with stained glass, the parishioners combining and giving lights as in olden times.

* From this and other documents previously produced, it will be seen that *deep and reverend* chancels are utterly opposed to the principles and rubrics of the present Establishment.

whatever, *old or new*, were standing in the English churches
at the commencement of the great Rebellion; and the Puritan
faction must be entirely exonerated from the charge of altar
demolishing, which has been preferred against them by those
who are anxious to revive altars under the present system,
and who would fain make it appear that dissenters, and not
the establishment, were the altar-destroying party; but it
will be seen from the evidence here adduced, that their position
is quite untenable, and that those who are desirous of restoring
altars, must first revive the rites and worship to which they
belong.

On the ascendancy of the Puritan faction, most of those
altar steps which *had not been previously demolished*, were
ordered to be levelled, and the communion tables themselves
in many instances were broken up and burnt. The principles of the Protestant Reformation were now fully developed,
and all legal restraint being removed, the fanatics of the new
opinions blazed forth in all their original fury, and scenes of
Cranmerian violence were again enacted on those remains
which had survived the first attack. These Reformers
had, however, but little left whereon to expend their fury,
except shattered windows, mutilated tombs, and bare walls;
all the rich and costly decorations having perished in times of
former outrage; and with the exception of some brass inscriptions, organ-pipes, and bells, they found little to satisfy their
sacrilegious avarice. After the Restoration, the communion
tables appear to have been generally set altarwise, as we now
see them; and in order to accommodate this arrangement to
the principles of the congregation *hearing the communion service*, in all churches built since that period we find the table
is placed in a *mere recess*, a few feet deep, and railed off; and
this is the correct arrangement for the present Anglican service;—it is certainly the antipodes of a *Catholic arrangement
of a church;*—but the present service is not a Catholic service, nor was it composed by Catholics: it is of most Protestant origin, very Protestant in its character, and requires
Protestant structures for its celebration; and it is as utterly
impossible to square a Catholic building with the present
rites, as to mingle oil and water. It is most delightful to see
the feeling reviving in the Anglican Church for the sanctity
and depth of chancels; and as a preliminary step to better
things, it should receive all possible encouragement; but
those who think merely to build chancels, without reviving
the ancient faith, will be miserably deceived in their expecta-

tions; in these days there is certainly no fear of being hung or beheaded for such matters; but if the present revival of Catholic antiquity is suffered to proceed much farther, it will be seen that *either the Common Prayer or the ancient models must be abandoned.*

In tracing down the history of communion tables from the Restoration, we find them treated with little respect in any place, and usually with much indignity; in some churches they serve for the transaction of parish business, in others as the depository for the caps, cloaks, and wallets of the school children, who were *taught in the chancels as a spare portion of the church.* In those churches where communion service is celebrated only once a year, we not unfrequently find them moved altogether on one side, and generally rotten and disjointed, neglected and perishing;—perhaps a decayed and moth-eaten cover, whitened with the dung of birds, hangs in tattered fragments about it,—perhaps it is utterly bare.

A communion table serves a multitude of purposes: sometimes it forms a scaffold for the mason who is affixing a marble blister against the chancel arch; sometimes for the baptismal bason; sometimes for the parish register; occasionally as a rostrum for some vestry orator; and often as a seat for the cleaning functionaries to rest both themselves and implements upon. It would be tedious to lengthen this sad list of desecrations, which are common *even at the present time*, and universal but a few years since. A better spirit has at length arisen, and in many places the tables have been not only decently but well adorned, and what is far more important, the essential doctrine of the Eucharistic sacrifice is again put forth; but with what hope of ultimate success, at the present eventful crisis of events, it is impossible for human penetration to foresee.

SUMMARY OF THE ABOVE ACCOUNT.

1. All stone altars ordered to be demolished (as favouring the ancient idea of sacrifice) by Cranmer and his Protestant adherents, in 1550.

2. Stone altars revived under Queen Mary.

3. Demolished again by act of parliament under Elizabeth, 1559.

4. Communion tables, in lieu of altars, to stand in their place when not used; but during communion service to be moved down, for the purpose of enabling the minister to be better heard.

5. Ordered subsequently to remain at all times at the upper end of the chancel.

6. This order not observed. Communion tables left in the middle of the chancel, with the ends *east* and *west*, till partially changed in the time of Archbishop Laud.

7. These changes made by the archbishop condemned as contrary to the spirit and ritual of the Anglican Church.

8. Tables after the Restoration placed altarwise.

9. Consequent shallow recesses, in lieu of chancels, introduced in all churches erected subsequent to that period.

10. Great irreverence exercised in general towards communion tables.

11. Partial revival of ancient reverence at the present time.

OF THE DESTRUCTION OF ROODS.

In every English Church, previous to the reign of Edward the Sixth, over the chancel screen stood a rood with the image of our blessed Redeemer crucified; and on either side, an image of his blessed mother and beloved disciple St. John. Of the propriety of such an edifying image in a Christian church, there can exist but little variety of opinion among men of Catholic mind; and the character of the reverence due from the faithful to so sacred a representation is admirably conveyed by the following lines, frequently inscribed over similar images on the continent:

> " Effigiem Christi dum transis pronus honora
> Sed non effigiem sed quem designat adora."

The antiquity of these roods is undoubtedly very great, and there is ample authority to prove that the image of our crucified Lord was sculptured on the rood previous to its introduction on the altar cross. Our present purpose is not however to enter on the history of the introduction of these sacred representations, but to describe their demolition. The first notice that we meet with in the annals of the Reformation respecting roods, is the account of the rood at Boxley, which was made to move with wires, and after being exposed to the people, was publicly burnt at Paul's Cross, on Sunday the 24th of February, 1538. If this was really meant as an imposture, the authors and abettors of it deserved burning far more than the image. But it seems very doubtful if it was, after all, any thing more than a figure used in the sacred plays, or mysteries as they were termed, and which were frequently represented even in churches. Of the propriety of these exhibitions it is not our purpose to treat; they would be highly objectionable at the present time, but they might have been productive of good at the time they were in vogue, and it is difficult for us to judge accurately of the simplicity of those days. They can, however, be no longer a subject of difference; as such representations have, since the Council of Trent, been generally discontinued. But to return to the rood of Boxley. What seems more confirmatory of the opinion that its machinery was not used for the purpose of deception, is the fact that Henry was seeking everywhere for occasions to justify in appearance the sacrilegious projects he meditated; it does also seem almost impossible that such a standing deception could be suffered to exist in the diocese of an English bishop, and it is quite unaccountable, that in the case of such a gross and blasphemous imposture being discovered, the agents would escape unnoticed and unpunished; we have not, however, the least account of who they were, nor of their being even suspended for the offence; and, taking all circumstances into consideration, there seems every reasonable probability of this far-famed illustration of popish craft being nothing more than a piece of ingenious but injudicious mechanism.

On the 17th of November, 1547, Heylin says: "the image of Christ, best known by the name of the rood, together with the images of Mary and John, and all other images in the church of St. Paul, London, were taken down, as also in all the other churches in London."

The parish accounts are exceedingly curious as details of these devastations. The roodloft of All Hallows' Staining, was pulled down in 1550, and the roodloft hangings fetched twelve shillings. On the revival of the ancient faith under Queen Mary, the parish churches were required to repair these demolitions as speedily as possible. In the archdeacon's visitation for the diocese of London, printed by Collier in his records for the Church History, p. 87, in the sixth article is enquired, if there be a roodloft crucifix, as in times past has been accustomed. The rood hangings of All Hallows' Staining, that were sold for twelve shillings, were repurchased in 1554 by the churchwardens at an advance of two shillings; the new crucifix or rood cost 6l. 3s. The parishioners of St. Pancras, Soper-lane, were enjoined in October 1555 to make up the roodloft, with the rood, Mary and John, of five feet long, by Candlemas.

K

St. Helen's Church, Abingdon, 1555.   *s. d.*
Payde for making the roode and peynting the same   .   5 4
For making the roode lyghtes 10 6
Payed for peynting the roode, of Mary and John and the
  patron of the church* 6 0
To fasten the tabernacle where the patron of the church
  standeth 0 8

Among other expenses of St. Mary Hill, London, 1555, on the rood, Mary and John, the patroness, the *tabernacle of the patroness*, painting the patroness, and refreshing the tabernacle.

St. Giles, Reading, 1558.
Paid for making of a rode, with Mary and John, and for
  the making of the patron of our church   .   .   40 0

In 1560, being under Elizabeth, we find,
For pulling down these same images   .   .   .   0 4
For *white liming the roode* 0 1

This was probably for the purpose of obliterating the painting on the loft; it shews that the whitewash bucket was very soon in vogue after the establishment of Anglicanism. Official injunctions were issued about this time for the total destruction of the roods with the images.

Strype relates in his *Annals*, that many crucifixes were brought by the people into Smithfield, and there broke to pieces and burnt; and he adds, "and this *was no more than were ordered by the Queen's visitors and her injunctions*, which were executed about Bartholomew tide, when in Paul's church-yard, as well as Smithfield, the roods (as they called the crosses) were burnt to ashes, and together with these in some places, *copes*, also *vestments, altar-cloaths, &c.*" Strype, at p. 135, gives an account of a sermon preached Nov. 5, 1559, at St. Botolph, Bishopsgate, at the *wedding of a priest to a priest's widow at Ware!!!* when one *West, a new doctor*, took occasion to speak freely and earnestly *against roodlofts*.

St. Margaret's, Westminster, 1559.
Item, paid to John Rial for his three days' work to take
  down the rood, Mary and John   :   .   .   2 8
Item, for *cleaving* and *sawing* of the rood, Mary and John   1 0

This last item is another fearful illustration of the barbarous sacrilege of these times,—the image of our Saviour hacked and sawn to pieces!!

* The image of the saint in whose honour the church was dedicated, was usually placed in the roodlofts, and probably about the base of the cross.

Same year, St. Mary Hill, London.

For bringing down the images and other things to be burnt   1   0

St. Helen's, Abingdon, 1561. This parish, by the accounts, appears to have adhered to the ancient rites for some time; for there is an entry for candles for the Christmas morning at the mass under the above date, being the fourth of Elizabeth, and it was only this year the roodloft was destroyed.

To the somner for bringing the order for the roodloft   .   0   8

To the carpenters and others taking down the roodloft and
   stopping the holes in the wall where the joices stood .   15   8

To the peynter for writing the scripture where the roodloft stood   3   4

St. Andrew's, Holborn, first of Elizabeth: the rood, Mary and John, were this year burnt to ashes, by command of the commissioners. It is useless to pursue this sad catalogue of destruction any farther; sufficient testimony has been produced to shew that these *truly Anglo-Catholic* and edifying ornaments were not only removed and abolished owing to the establishment of Protestantism, but treated with the most barbarous indignity. The first rood set up in England, since the revival of Catholicism, was at the chapel of that zealous champion of the ancient faith of his country, Ambrose Lisle Phillipps, Esq.; and they are now commonly erected in the English Catholic Churches, with precisely the same ornaments and furniture as in times past.

SOME ACCOUNT OF OTHER DESTRUCTIONS THAT BEFEL THE ENGLISH CHURCHES, PRIOR TO THE GREAT REBELLION.

We do not pretend even to glance at the demolition of the great abbatial and conventual buildings, wherein perished many of the very finest monuments of ancient piety, but we purpose to confine our remarks to such cathedrals and parochial churches as were allowed to remain for religious worship. The inventory of plate, jewels, shrines, vestments, &c. which belonged to the church of St. Paul, London, prior to Henry VIII, occupies thirty folio pages of Dugdale's elaborate work on that cathedral. In the seventh year of Edward the Sixth, all the plate and ornaments suffered to remain in the church were as follows:

" Imp. chalices.

Item, 2 pair of basyns to bring the communion bread and offerings of the poor.

Item, a sylver pot to put the wine in for the communion table, weighing 40 oz.

Item, the written text of the Gospels and Epistles.

Item, a large canopie of tissew for the king's majesty when he cometh hither.

Item, a pall of black velvet to lay on the herse.

Item, a border of black sarcenet, with a fringe of black silk mixed with gold for the burial of noble persons.

Item, baudkins of divers sorts and colours, for garnishing the quire for the *king's coming*, and for the bishop's seat; as also at other times when the quire shall be apparelled *for the honour of the realm.*

Item, 8 cusheons.

Item, 30 albes to make surplices for the ministers and choristers.

Item, 24 old cusheons to kneel on.

Item, 7 cloaths of lynnen plain and diaper for the communion table.

Item, 5 towells.

Item, 2 hangings of tapestrie for the quire.

Item, a Turkey carpet for the communion table.

Item, a pastoral staff for the bishop."

And even these scanty ornaments were afterwards still farther reduced.

The inventory of the jewels and ornaments which anciently belonged to Lincoln minster, is given at length in Dugdale's *Monasticon Anglicanum.*

" Some idea of the surpassing beauty and richness of the ornaments may be formed from the fact of 2621 oz. of pure gold, 4285 oz. of silver, besides a great quantity of pearls and precious stones of immense value, being seized by the commissioners empowered by Henry VIII, for that purpose, June 11, 1540. Previous to that time, there were two shrines in the cathedral church : the one of pure gold, called St. Hugh's shrine, standing behind the high altar, near unto Dalison's tomb. The place is easily to be known by the irons yet fastened in paving stones there. The other, St. John of Dalderby : his shrine was of pure silver, standing in the south end of the great cross aisle, not far from the door where the gallery court is said to be kept."—*Dugdale.*

" In the seventh year of king Edward the Sixth, of all the ancient plate, there remained but three chalices, one pix, and an ampul."—*Ibid.*

" The church of St. Martin's, Ludgate, London, was richly furnished with plate, vestments, hangings, &c. Amongst other things, were seven chalices, which weighed 100 oz. ; a silver cross and

* The honour of festival days is not alluded to.

crucifix, 53 oz.; a thurible, silver, 31 oz.; the ship for ditto, 9 oz.; a chrismatory, 13 oz.; a berile, garnished with silver, containing the precious relics of saints; a tabernacle of silver, ornamented with the image of St. Martin; there were nine altar frontals of cloth of gold, embroidered, one with the twelve apostles; above the altar of our Lady was the coronation of the blessed Virgin, and in a second compartment the Salutation; before the rood were suspended hangings painted with the Nativity of our Lord, emblems of his passion, &c. with a multitude of other curious and rich ornaments, all sold or destroyed under Edward VI. - In the year 1612, this church had but one chalice."—*Nicholson's Londinum Redivivum,* vol. iv. p. 363.

Dugdale says:—

"In the time of Edward VI, and beginning of Elizabeth, such pretenders were some to zeal for a thorough reformation in religion, that, under colour of pulling down those images here which had been superstitiously worshipped by the people (*as then was said*), the beautiful and costly portraitures of brass, fixed on several marbles in sundry churches of this realm, and so consequently in this escaping not the sacrilegious hands, were *torn away, and for a small matter sold to coppersmiths and tinkers.* Amongst the many that were at that time destroyed, those whose names I have here expressed, had their monumental stones and memorials here. Henry de Sandwich, Richard de Gravesend, Ralph de Baldok, Richard de Newport, Michael de Northburgh, Richard Clifford, Richard Hill, and Richard Fitzjames, as afterwards John Elmore, Richard Fletcher, and Richard Vaughan, all bishops of London; and many others."

Churchwarden's Accounts, St. Mary's, Reading, 1555.

" Item, Receyvid of John Saunders for 3 cwt. lacking 9 lb. of metal, that *was taken up of the greaves* and of old candlesticks, at 16*s.* the hundred . . . 46 2
" St. Andrew's, Holborn.
" 1st, Edward the Sixth. 36*s.* were received from brass taken from the tombs.
" The tombs which formerly stood in the Grey Friars' church, Newgate-street (now Christ Church), and many of which were equal to the royal monuments at Westminster, were destroyed in 1545, by Sir Martin Bowes, mayor, who sold ten high tombs, and one hundred and forty grave stones, with brasses, for 50*l.*"—*Stowe's Survey of London.*

To show the exact conformity of Protestant proceedings at different periods, we subjoin the following extracts from the churchwarden's accounts of Walberswick Church, 1644, about one century later.

April 8. Paid for taking up the brasses of gravestones
before the *officer* Dowson (William Dowsing) came .   1   0
Received for 40lbs. weight of brasses at 3½*d.* a lb.   .   11 8
" This system of plundering brasses was forbidden by proclama-
tion, in the second year of Elizabeth's reign ; but the prohibition
was little regarded."—*Weever's Funeral Monuments.*

It was by no means an uncommon practice for sextons to
sell brasses in Gough's time ; and it is most surprising that
any of these beautiful memorials of the departed faithful
have been found in the present time.

Church ornaments sold in the reign of Edward VI.

" St. Mary Hill, London.

1547. Received of Jasper, the basket-maker, for 7½ lbs.
of alabaster* 0 17 6
For taking down the tabernacle over the vestry door,
and other work 0 13 4
1549. Silver ornaments, sold at 5*s.* 8*d.* and 5*s.* 11*d.* per
ounce, to the sum of   .   .   .   18 5 8
Charge for taking down the high altar .   .   .   1 2 6

" Allhallow's, Staining.

1550. Two copes, 3 vestments, the cross banners, were
sold by the churchwardens, for   .   .   .   6 13 4
Two copes and 7 vestments   .   .   .   4 0 0
Formerly belonging to the high altar of the said church. .

A silver gilt cross with images of the Blessed Virgin and St.
John, weighing 81 oz.

Another cross of wood, plated with silver and gilt, with silver
images of our Lord, the B. Virgin, and St. John ; the five wounds of
our Lord were five rubies ; in the base a crystal, with the holy
name ; a pax of mother-of-pearl, set in silver, another of silver gilt,
with the crucifixion, two thuribles, 63½ oz., 4 chalices from 12 to
8 oz.

In 1551, three of these chalices were sold at 6*s.* an ounce.
1609. The church possessed but one chalice and patin.

" Allhallow's, London-wall.

The high altar was adorned with the following rich ornaments :
a cross of silver, parcel gilt, weighing 93 oz. ; two chalices, 12 oz.
each, and a third, 9½ oz. ; a chrismatory, 20½ oz. ; a cross to bear the
blessed sacrament ; a pax, 6 oz. ; a do. with three images of sylver ;
a pontifical of St. Thomas of Canterbury, clossed in silver ; a bone
of St. Davy, clossed in silver ; a chalice, 8 oz.

In 1572, this church did not possess a single article of silver ;
the sacramental *vessels were all pewter.*

* This was evidently alabaster carving and imagery.

" St. Mary's, Reading.

1551. Sold to Sir Thomas Wynsore, knight, two altar cloaths of Tyshewe, and two white vestments for deken and subdeken.

Item, sold to two men of London the sute of crymsyn velvett, with eleven copes of the same, a cope of blewe velvet; with a vestyment and one dekyng, the best canopy, four corporis cases (burses) with four old copes, and an old vestyment, 14*l.* 13*s.* 4*d.*

Item, the church plate sold as followeth; that ys to saye, the whyte and the parcel gylte, for 5*s.* 4*d.* the unnce, the gilt 6*s.* the unnce

Item, two belles sold weighing 38 cwt. 4 lb. at 30*s.* the cwt.

Item, ten foder of lead* sold at 6*l.* 16*s.* 8*d.* the foder.

" St. Lawrence, Reading, 1546.

1546. Received for certain plate sold, that is to witt a bason weying 23 oz.; a censer weying 30 oz.; a pomannder,† 3½ oz.; a shippe weying 9½ oz.; a chrismatorie, weying 22 oz.; the silver uppon ye boks (probably the holy gospels), weyhing 13 oz.; an old crosse, weying 3¼ oz.—at 4*s.* 9*d.* the once.

" Ditto, 1549.

Received for the remaining church plate, 48*l.* 18*s.*

Paid to the carpenters for taking down the images and taber-nacles, xii*d.*

Paid to N. Bell, mayor (*of that was made of a chalice*), for paving in the streets, 54*s.* 4*d.*

Paid and delivered by N. Bell, by N. Nicholas, upon the *two chalices sold by him, towards the pavinge of the strets*, 53*s.*

---

* The following letter, from Richard Bellycys to Cromwell, time of Henry the Eighth, is a curious illustration of the lead-stripping period: " Pleasyth your good lordshipp to be advertysed I have taken down all the lead of *Jervase*, and made itt in pecys of half foders, which lead amounteth to the numbre of eighteen score and five foders, with thirty-four foders which were there before. And the said lead cannot be conveit nor carryed until the next sombre, for the wayes in that contre are so foule and deepe that no carrage can passe in wynter. *And as concerning the raising and taking doune the house,* if it be your lordship's pleasure ·I am minded to let itt stand to the spring of the yere, by reason of the days are now so short it would be double charge to do it now. And as *concerning the selling of the bells,* I cannot sell them above fifteen shillings the hundredth, wherein I would gladly know your lordship's pleasure, whether I should sell them after that price or send them up to London; and if they be sent up surely the carriage wolbe costly frome that place to the water: and as for Byrdlington I have done nothing there as yet, but sparethe it to Marche next, because the days are now so shorte; and *from such tyme as I begyn I trust shortly to dispatche it in such fashion that when all is finished I trust that your lord-shipp shall think I have bene no evyll howsbound in all such things as your lordshipp had appointed me to doo.* And thus the *Holy Ghost* ever preserve your lordshipp in honour [blasphemous scoundrel]; at York, the 14th day of November, by your most bounden beadsman, RICHARD BELLYCYS.—*Hist. of Bridlington, Rev. M. Pricket.*

† A silver vessel like an apple, filled with warm water, for the priest to warm his fingers during excessive cold, to prevent accidents in handling the chalice.

"St. Giles, Reading, 1549.

For stones of the crosse sold, 2*s.* (this was probably the cross in the churchyard.)

1560, 2d of Elizabeth.

Paid for pulling down of images, 4*d.*

"St. Margaret's, Westminster.

1552. Paid for a *a recreation for the quest,* on the 12th of July, when they came to view the inventory of the church goods 6 8

Paid to Mr. Curat and Nicholas Poole, for making the book of the church goods to be *presented to the king's commissioners,* and the pains they took about it . . 10 0

The result of this quest was the sale and destruction of the ornaments.

The hideous boarding, with the writing, at the back of the communion table, in place of the ancient reredos, is mentioned as early as 1547.

Paid for 2 waynscotte boards, for the high altar . . 1 0

Paid for wryghtyng of the scriptures upon the same boards* 5 0

1547. The churchwardens sold images and altar curtains to the amount of 3*l.* 6*s.* 8*d.*

1549. There appears to have been a tumultuous assembly to hear Lattymer deliver one of his irreverent discourses; for we find, "paid to William Curlewe, for *mending of diverse pews,*† when Dr. Lattymer did preach." The congregation must have been very disorderly, for the seats at that time were not ¾-deal, but 3-inch oak.

In *Neale's Parish Churches,* a most curious inventory is given of the plate, vestments, and ornaments, which belonged to Long Melford church, Suffolk; the whole of which were removed, sold, plundered, or destroyed, in the reign of Edward VI. Geneva psalm books are frequently mentioned.

"Abingdon, 1573. Payde for a quire of paper to make 4 bokes of Geneva Salmes, 4*d.*"

Whitewashing was introduced very early, probably for the purpose of effacing the ancient paintings and ornaments on the walls.

---

* "Walberswick church, 1596. Payd unto the paynter for writing of the ten commandments and *making of the queen's arms,* 14*s.* 4*d.*

† The open seats were called pews, but regular Protestant pews, lined with baize, &c., were erected in this church as early as 1611. "Item, paid to Goodwyfe Wells, for salt to *destroy the fleas in the churchwarden's pew,* 6*d.*

"Great Wigston, Leicestershire, 1591.
Paid John West, for whitewashing the church . 1 18 10
"St. Mary's Reading, 1551.
Paid for the whyte liming of the church . . 0 14 8

The following letter, sent by the commissioners under Queen Elizabeth to the Dean and Chapter of Bristol, will fully account for the horrible mutilation of the altar screens in that church, and many reredoses of exquisite beauty that were defaced at the same time.

"After our hartie commendacyons. Whereas we are credibly informed, that there are divers tabernacles for images, as well in the fronture of the roodloft of the cathedral church of Bristol, as also in the frontures, back, and ends of the wall where the communion table standeth ; forasmuch as the same church should be a light and good example to th-ole city and dioc. we have thought good to direct these our desires unto you, and to require you to *cause the sade tabernacles to be defaced and hewn down*, and afterwards a *playne wall* with *mortar, plaster, or otherwise*, and some scriptures to be written in the places, and namely, that upon the wall where the communion table doth usually stand, the *table of the commandments painted in large characters* with convenient speed ; and further according to the orders lately set forthe by virtue of the queene's majesty's commission for causes ecclesiastical, at the cost and charges of the said church, whereof we require you not to faile, and so we bid you farewell. From London, the 21st of December, 1561."

Here then is an injunction issued by the glorious Queen Bess and her *Anglo-Catholic* officers, which cannot be distinguished, either in terms or intentions, from the orders issued by William Dowsing or any other Puritan of Cromwell's time. It is certain that we owe the preservation of such glorious monuments as have yet escaped, more to inadvertency, or sheer weariness of destruction, than to any better cause : such injunctions as these, if carried out, would have demolished the screens of Winchester and St. Alban's, equally with those of Bristol ; for *niches* and *tabernacles* are things here described : the images had been defaced or removed under Edward the Sixth, but even the screens themselves were far too popish for the new system. At that period all the dignitaries of the Church *were confirmed Puritans ;* there was no other class of ecclesiastics to be found who would con-

---

* Amongst these we cannot omit to notice Dean Wittingham, who was appointed by Elizabeth to that noble church of Durham : where holy Cuthbert and venerable Bede once lay gloriously enshrined ; and this wretched Puritan soon completed the havoc and destruction commenced under Henry, and carried on by Edward's commissioners. Heylin says that this man had been at

sent to the innovations, and after the deprivation of the old Catholic ecclesiastics, their offices must have been supplied by the Genevan men, or left altogether vacant. Afterwards a better spirit sprang up, of which Laud, Andrewes, Hooker and others are instances; but they could effect little: and Protestantism, combined with the universal decay of Catholic art and feelings throughout the world, has so altered the English churches, that the very best are but lamentable wrecks of their former glory.*

---

the head of the Francfort schismatics; and, while dean of Durham, actually advised and aided the infamous John Knox, in setting up Presbyterianism in Scotland. Certain is it that this noble abbey, which but few years previous to his time was inferior to none either in richness or solemnity, became a perfect wreck under his control; and he scrupled not to deface the tombs of the bishops, and even to apply the sacred ornaments to profane uses.

" The priors buried in the centry garth had each one a tombstone, either of marble or freestone, which *Dean Wittingham caused to be pulled down and taken away; and broke and defaced all such stones as had any pictures of brass, or other imagery work, or chalices,* wrought upon them; and *the rest he took away and employed them to his own use, in making a wash-house at the end of the centry garth for his laundresses!!!*

" Within the abbey church were two marble holy-water stones, bossed with hollow bosses, on the outsides thereof curiously wrought. These were taken away by *Dean Wittingham, and removed into his kitchen, and employed to profane uses:* they stood there during his life; his servants steeped their beef and salt-fish in them. Moreover, *Mrs. Wittingham,* after her husband's, the dean's death, took away the lesser holy-water stone, and had it set in the kitchen in her own house. She likewise carried from the centry garth several gravestones *of blue marble, and other tombstones that lay upon priors and monks, which she built in her own house,* in the Bailey."—*Sanderson's Antiquities of Durham Abbey.*

The same destructions were carrying on, at the same time, in other cathedrals, by Puritan deans and bishops, with the aid of their wives and servants. The immense body of evidence that can be collected on these matters, would prove the Puritans of latter times to be only faint imitators of their originals. Every bishop of the Establishment was *de facto* an altar demolisher and Iconoclast; even stained glass was quite contrary to the real spirit of Anglicanism. In a word, under the system as established the cathedrals were useless, the parochial churches inconvenient, and the ancient ornaments incongruous.

* No doubt England deserved this scourge; she had become unworthy of the blessings she enjoyed; and this dreadful chastisement may have been given in mercy; but whatever ulterior good may be eventually brought about by this awful convulsion, surely it is most inconsistent for any man to *defend the instruments of this searching visitation,* and to glory in their humiliation and decay. As well might they extol the cruel Jews who nailed our Lord upon the cross, or the traitor Judas who betrayed him, because such things were suffered by God to be. Let sounder views of persons and events arise, and party altercations cease; there is but little cause to boast. The Catholics lacked faith and zeal, betrayed their trust, renounced their spiritual obedience, and even participated in Church plunder; Protestants were sacrilegious, fanatical, and filled with blasphemous heresies; they were the firebrands of God's wrath, to lay waste the vineyard; and those who defend either them or the system, or who would palliate their offences, are guilty of defending sin, and participate in their guilt. And, on the other hand, let no Catholic suppose that the *cause* of this tribulation came from *without.* Here, in England, in Catholic England,

From these lamentable chronicles some correct idea may be formed of the desecrated state of England's churches 'after the great schism of the sixteenth century. Truly does it seem that the words of Jeremiah in his Lamentations had come to pass in this unhappy land: "Viæ Sion lugent eo *quod non sint qui veniant ad solemnitatem*, omnes portæ ejus destructæ, *sacerdotes ejus gementes, virgines ejus squalidæ*, et ipsa oppressa amaritudine." Again, "Quomodo obscuratum est aurum, mutatus est color optimus, *dispersi sunt lapides Sanctuarii* in capite omnium platearum;" and yet this dark and dismal period of sacrilege, of infidelity, and irreverence, is strangely distinguished as *Anglo-Catholic*, by men who are professionally engaged in building up the walls of Sion. The misapplication of the term *Anglo-Catholic* at the present time is truly surprising, and by gross inconsistency it is used *exclusively* to signify times and events *essentially Protestant*. While the almost Puritan service of the last three centuries, composed under the immediate superintendence of *foreign heretics*, with all its meagreness, departure from antiquity, and inconsistency, is denominated Anglo-Catholic, the ancient rites of the *English Church, which she held in common with the rest of Christendom*, are termed Romish, and not unfrequently this expression is actually applied to the very liturgies and ceremonies compiled by the old English bishops, and which were in a manner peculiar to this country. The modern English service is *very Genevan*, but the ancient English liturgy, although approved and sanctioned by the holy see, was *not Roman*. Gregory of ever-blessed memory, commanded St. Austin to adopt such rites and customs as he found practised in the churches of those countries through which he passed on his journey to England, as might tend to the increase of edification; and to introduce them in the English Church: and we may reason-

was a stronghold preparing for that monster heresy, in the hearts of those who should have stood like bulwarks against his approach. The spirit of luxury, the spirit of indifference, the spirit of the world, were extending among all ranks. Sacraments were neglected, apparel was extravagant, mortifications were rare, humility had fled,—pride and paganism were spreading fast. And when novelties and infidelities arose, they found a soil prepared to nurture them, in a land where in better days they would have been withered in a moment: for Protestantism *cannot plant itself, much less take root, in a truly Catholic atmosphere.* England's Church had degenerated, and it fell; and when Protestants can be brought to view the things in which they now glory, as so many vials of God's wrath, and when Catholics discern the true causes of this sad decay, and, burning with zeal and faith, stand forth with ancient devotion and fervour, despising the world and all things but God and His holy Church, and shine as lights before their fellow-men, then may we hope indeed for the blessings of unity and peace.

ably conclude, that ours was a very perfect ritual. At the time' when Calvin undertook to revise and alter the English Liturgy, was it not filled with commemorations of those saintly prelates and kings, who had shone as lights of faith in this once truly glorious land? and had not a canonised bishop of England composed so holy and approved an office, that in the missals and rituals it is termed "ad usum *insignis et præclare* ecclesiæ Sarum?" was not God worshipped with marvellous solemnity in the old English Church? and indeed, was there any portion of Christendom to be compared with it, for the multitude and glory of its pious monuments and religious buildings? and while many of them were erecting, Rome was a perfect desert. Yet in face of all these facts, we continually hear of "Romish altars," "Romish roods," "Romish ceremonies," "built by the old Romans," "a Roman priest" (probably a rector with a chasuble and chalice, who never was out of England in his life), "Romish bishops," "Romish superstitions," and the like; and men have been so deluded with these ideas, that they have brought themselves to hate the Church of their country and of their fathers as *foreign*, and to embrace and cherish *really foreign novelties* as English. But it is to be remembered, that although these ancient glories were by God's blessing brought to the highest perfection in this land, we did not possess or hold them as *Englishmen*, but as *Catholics;* our country was as indeed a bright gem, but it was only one jewel in the crown of the Catholic Church. And although in the days of Faith we were permitted to excel most other nations in the majesty of our rites, it was by virtue of our communion and holy obedience to Christ's vicar, the Bishop of Rome, successor to the Prince of Apostles. Once severed from his authority, cathedrals, abbeys, cloisters, altars, shrines, bishops, priests, lands, and privileges, availed nothing, —they passed away at a breath. Their glory was as a dream, and their place knew them no more: the source of life was severed, and they were dried up and withered away. And let those who think by mere arch or pinnacle to revive solemnities and retrieve the past, read the awful lesson of England's punishment written with iron hand on every glorious pile. When courtier bishops and trembling priests first signed the fatal act of schism, that separated England from the mother church of Rome, their possessions were ample, their pastures were green, their buildings were spacious, lofty, and beauteous, the furniture of the altars was all-glorious, the majesty of the temples was unimpaired, and the Church of England seemed like a fabric, so strong, so venerable, and so mighty, that it could not be shaken. And for a few days' length it looked the same, and the matins were sung, the mass was solemnized, the procession winded through the aisles, and tapers burnt round the shrines, and in the foolishness of their hearts the people said, what need have we of any pope? but a dark speck soon appeared on the horizon, and a whirlwind of destruction arose, and the foundations of this vast fabric were undermined, and the choirs ceased to echo with the sound of praise, and soon they were roofless; and the lights of the sanctuary were extinguished, and costly jewels and gold were no longer to be seen; and the relics of saints were scattered, and the treasures of the Church were pillaged, and her authority became a name, and the altars of God were overthrown, and the image of Christ was defaced, and strange ministers stood in the temple of God and mocked the olden solemnity. And although three hundred years have passed away, and men have somewhat of a *taste* for the things that their *fathers revered*, and axes and hammers are laid by, and restorations are in hand, yet when we stand beneath the vaulted roof of Catholic antiquity, and view the motley group that sit in old churchmen's stalls to hear some anthem sung, while the stripped and mutilated sanctuary is abandoned and forlorn, filled up with benches of the meanest sort, we must in sorrow feel that the anger of God is not withdrawn, that His hand is still heavy on us; and we may in truth exclaim—"Patres nostri peccaverunt et non sunt; et nos iniquitates eorum portavimus:" nor can we hope to see England freed from the curse that has fallen on her for her ancient offences, till the cause which provoked it is removed. Let those, then, who would build up the sanctuary of God, first prostrate themselves in humility before the tribunal of Christ upon earth, and then, under holy obedience, and in the true spirit of England's ancient Churchmen, turn to the re-edification of those material temples which heresy has defaced and destroyed; but the present system is too rotten and decayed to work upon; and patching up Protestantism with copes and candles, would be no better than whitening a sepulchre: for choirs, chancels, altars, and roods, have no part with modern Liturgies and Calvinised rubrics; either the things or the system must be abandoned: the glories of pointed architecture, if viewed *distinct from their Catholic origin, and as symbols of the true and ancient faith,* lose at once their greatest claim on our veneration; and far better would it be to see the churches left ruined as they are than revived as a mere disguise for Protestantism. We hail th present feelings of admiration for Anglo-Catholic antiquity only as a probable means of eventually restoring the faith, and not as an abstract question of art or taste; but let us hope that God in his mercy has stirred up these sentiments in the breasts of our separated countrymen, for the accomplishment of some great end; for if they fail in working them out to a right conclusion, the cause is hopeless indeed; the English Catholics are too reduced and degenerated to accomplish any revival on the great scale of antiquity; moreover, the fervour of their ancestors does not shine by any means conspicuous among them; and what has been already accomplished under these unfavourable circumstances is little short of miraculous; and by showing what a *few* out of a *remnant* who work on the old foundation can achieve, should serve as an encouragement to others, who have greater means and equal desire, but want the authority. In a word, the will is on one side, the power on the other; once united, a few years would restore centuries of decay. One thing, however, seems certain, that we must shortly prepare for some wonderful change to be worked, either on the side of God or of Satan; for those who are really animated with Catholic feeling will never remain satisfied with the mere shadow of antiquity; and Protestants and infidels clamour loudly against the trifling return to mere decorum that has already been accomplished in certain places.

The *via media* is rapidly narrowing on those who tread that dangerous and deceptive road; it will soon be utterly impracticable. Two paths will then present themselves for choice: *this* returns to England's Church, with her priests, her altars, her sanctuaries, and her ancient solemnity, communion with Christendom, and part with her glorious saints and martyrs of old; *that*, on to the conventicle, with its preaching throne and galleries, the divisions of dissent, and portion with heresiarchs and blasphemers. The hour is at hand when ambiguous expressions and subtle evasions will no longer shelter or conceal. Men must stand forth the avowed champions of Catholic truth or Protestant error; and blessed indeed will they be who, at the hour of trial, fail not, but, counting all loss as gain in the cause of Christ, apply themselves to the holy work of England's conversion, like blessed Austin of old, strengthened and supported by that rock of Peter which cannot be moved, and against whom the world and Satan shall never prevail.

FINIS.

A CATALOGUE

OF

ENGLISH CATHOLIC WORKS,

KEPT ON SALE,

AND FOR THE MOST PART PUBLISHED

BY

CHARLES DOLMAN,

No. 61, NEW BOND STREET, LONDON.

Contents.

A Catalogue

OF

ENGLISH CATHOLIC WORKS.

History and Biography.

THE CHURCH HISTORY OF ENGLAND,

FROM THE YEAR 1500 TO 1688,

CHIEFLY WITH REGARD TO CATHOLICS,

BY CHARLES DODD.

With Notes, and a Continuation to the Beginning of the Present Century,

BY THE REV. M. A. TIERNEY, F.R.S. F.S.A.

Vols I. to IV. are published, price 12s. each in cloth.

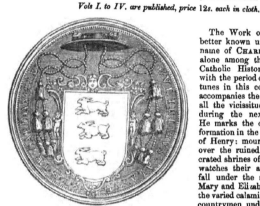

SEAL OF CARDINAL ALLEN.

The Work of HUGH TOOTLE, better known under the assumed name of CHARLES DODD, stands alone among the compilations of Catholic History. Commencing with the period of her first misfortunes in this country, the writer accompanies the ancient Church in all the vicissitudes of her course, during the next two centuries. He marks the origin of the Reformation in the wayward passions of Henry: mourns, with religion, over the ruined altars and desecrated shrines of Edward's reign: watches their alternate rise and fall under the sister sovereigns, Mary and Elizabeth; and, tracing the varied calamities of his Catholic countrymen under the dynasty of the Stuarts, closes his work with the closing fortunes of that unhappy family. The readers of Dodd are aware that his history is divided into eight parts, corresponding with the eight reigns over which it extends. Of these parts, each is again divided into the three other parts of History, Biography, and Records; and these are still farther subdivided into an indefinite number of articles, according to the variety of the subjects to be treated, or to the rank of the several persons whose lives are to be recorded. It is needless to point out the inconvenience of this complex and disjointed arrangement. To remedy this defect, it is proposed, in the present edition, to place the work under the two grand divisions of History and Biography; to print the History in the earlier, the Biography in the latter, volumes; to subjoin to each volume an Appendix, containing its own records properly arranged: and to insert a reference in the notes to each article of that appendix, according as its subject arises in the course of the narrative. It is only requisite to add, that the lives, in the biographical part, will be methodically disposed; that the authorities, both of Dodd and of the Editor, will be carefully stated in the notes; and that a General Index to the contents of the whole work will be given at the end of the Continuation.

TO BE COMPLETED IN FOURTEEN VOLUMES.

FIFTY Copies printed on LARGE PAPER in royal 8vo. price 21s. each volume, cloth.

N.B. Subscribers' Names may be transmitted to the Publisher through any Bookseller in the Country.

THE HISTORY OF THE CHURCH, translated from the German of the Rev. J. J. IG. DÖLLINGER, D.D. Professor of Theology in the Royal University of Munich, by the Rev. EDWARD COX, D.D. President of St. Edmund's College. To be completed in seven or eight volumes. Vols. 1 to 4 are published, price 9s. each, in cloth.

We may safely state, that the appearance of any work of the learned Professor DÖLLINGER, in the English language, would be most acceptable to our country. But the universally acknowledged want of an Ecclesiastical History in our Language, will, it is trusted, render the appearance of the present work the more acceptable to all who desire to become acquainted with the first institution, and the many interesting events which have accompanied the progress, of the Church of Christ.

BRENAN (Rev. M. J. O.S.F.) An Ecclesiastical History of Ireland, from the Introduction of Christianity into that Country to the year 1829, *Dublin*, 1840, 2 vols. 8vo. cloth, 15s.

CAREW (Rev. P. J.) An Ecclesiastical History of Ireland, from the Introduction of Christianity into that Country to the Commencement of the Thirteenth Century, *Dublin*, 1835, 8vo. boards, 7s.

LANIGAN (Rev. John, D.D.) An Ecclesiastical History of Ireland, from the first Introduction of Christianity among the Irish, to the beginning of the Thirteenth Century, *Dublin*, 1829, in 4 vols. 8vo. boards

LINGARD (Rev. John, D.D.) A History of England, from the First Invasion by the Romans, 3rd edition, 14 vols. 8vo. 6l. 6s.

—— Ditto, 4th edition, corrected and considerably enlarged, in 13 vols. foolscap 8vo. cloth lettered, 3l. 5s.

—— A Vindication of Certain Passages in the Fourth and Fifth Volumes of the History of England, 8vo. 2s. 6d.

—— Documents to ascertain the Sentiments of British Catholics in former Ages respecting the power of the Popes, 8vo. 2s.

THE HISTORY and Survey of the Antiquities of Winchester, by the late Right Rev. JOHN MILNER, D.D. F.S.A., with Supplementary Notes. Also a Biographical Memoir by the Rev. F.C. HUSENBETH. A new edition, in imperial 8vo. cloth lettered, price 1l. 4s.

THE HISTORY and Antiquities of the Castle and Town of Arundel, including the Biography of its Earls, from the Conquest to the Present Time. By the Rev. M. A. TIERNEY, F.R.S. F.S.A. Chaplain to his Grace the Duke of Norfolk. In 2 vols. royal 8vo. illustrated with numerous Engravings, Etchings, and Pedigrees, price 1l. 12s. cloth boards.

"When we say that more than one-half of this work is Biography, and that Biography immediately connected with the general history of England, it will be perceived that this is a work of a more attractive character than can generally be assigned to topography."—*Gent. Magazine.*

BOSSUET'S Universal History, from the Creation of the World to the Time of Charlemagne, 8vo. 7s.

—— History of the Variations of the Protestant Churches, 2 vols. 8vo. reduced to 7s.

CARRUTHER'S (Rev. James) The History of Scotland during the Life of Queen Mary, and until the Accession of her Son James to the Crown of England, 8vo. 12s.

CAREY (M.) Vindiciæ Hibernicæ; or, Ireland vindicated from the Errors and Misrepresentations respecting Ireland, in the Histories of May, Temple, Whitelock, Borlase, Rushworth, Clarendon, Cox, Carte, Leland, Warner, Macauley, Hume, and others. Third edition, enlarged, 8vo. 12s. 6d.

A General HISTORY OF EUROPE, from the Beginning of the Sixteenth Century to the Peace of Paris, 1815; with Addenda, bringing the History down to 1840, 12mo. cloth, 6s. 6d.

MOORE (Thomas) The History of Ireland, in 4 volumes, small 8vo. 6s. each.

MURPHY (John) Concise History of Great Britain and Ireland, abridged from Hume, Smollett, and others, 4 vols. 12mo. 10s. cloth.

MYLIUS (W.) An Abridged History of England, for the Use of Schools, 12mo. 6s. 6d.

PLOWDEN (Francis) History of Ireland, from its Invasion under Henry the Second to its Union with Great Britain, 2 vols. 12mo. 9s.

REEVE (Rev. Joseph) A Short View of the History of the Christian Church, from its Establishment to the Present Century, 8vo. bds. *Dublin,* 1837, 8s.

ST. GEORGE (Mrs.) Civil and Ecclesiastical History of England, from the first invasion of Britain to 1829, 2 vols. 12mo. boards, 14s.

A SHORT HISTORY OF THE PROTESTANT REFORMA-TION, principally as to its Rise and Progress in England, in a Series of Conferences held by the most eminent Protestant Historians of the Present and Former Times. Edited by the Rev. H. SMITH. In Numbers, price 3d. each.

SHORT HISTORY OF THE FIRST BEGINNING AND PRO-GRESS OF THE PROTESTANT RELIGION, gathered out of the best Protestant Writers, by way of question and answer. By the Right Rev. Dr. Challoner 18mo. 6d.

WATERWORTH (REV. J.) SIX HISTORICAL LECTURES on the Origin and Progress in this Country of the change of Religion called THE REFORMATION. 12mo. cloth, 8s.

—— Digest of the Penal Laws passed against Catholics, with Historical Notes and Illustrations. 8vo. 10d.

ONTRASTS; or, a PARALLEL between the Noble Edifices of the Middle Ages, and Corresponding Buildings of the Present Day. Setting forth the present decay of pure taste. Accompanied by appropriate text, by A. WELBY PUGIN, Architect. In 1 vol. 4to. price 1l. 10s. cloth lettered. The Second Edition, much enlarged.

This Edition, which contains several new and additional illustrations both on copper and wood, has been carefully purged of all the original errors, and many seeming inconsistencies explained. The text has also been considerably enlarged; and the rise, progress, and effects of the revived Pagan, or debased style, which commenced in the sixteenth century, and replaced Christian art in Catholic Continental countries, is fully set forth, and its influence on true Catholic Architecture illustrated; with the comparative destructive results produced by it, and Protestant principles, on the ancient Ecclesiastical buildings of Europe; deduced from the actual state of the English and Continental churches.

MORES CATHOLICI, or, AGES OF FAITH, in 11 Books.
*** The first five volumes being totally *out of print,* the fortunate possessors of these volumes should lose no time in completing their sets.

MORUS, by K. H. DIGBY, ESQ. Original Edition, 8vo. boards, reduced to 6s.
*** This volume was reprinted verbatim as the third book of the "Broadstone of Honour, or the True Sense and Practice of Chivalry,"—now entirely out of print, and very rare.

A THIRD LETTER TO AMBROSE LISLE PHILLIPPS, ESQ. of Grace Dieu Manor, from JOHN, EARL OF SHREWSBURY, chiefly in reference to his former Letter "On the Present Posture of Affairs." Large 8vo. price 7s. 6d.

THE DUBLIN REVIEW.—Published Quarterly, Price Six Shillings.
*** Any Number may be had separately.—A few Sets, second-hand, at low prices.
N.B. This Review (from its peculiar circulation) will be found an excellent medium for Advertisements connected with Literature and the Fine Arts;—the scale of charges being calculated on the most moderate terms.

BELL (REV. JOHN) NEW DICTIONARY OF ALL RELI-GIONS, with an Account of the Original Tenets of each, 8vo. boards, 8s.

BUTLER (REV. ALBAN) THE LIVES OF THE FATHERS, MARTYRS, AND OTHER PRINCIPAL SAINTS. With a Preface by the Right Rev. Dr. DOYLE, and containing all the Chronological Centenary Tables and General Indexes formerly attached to the twelve volume edition, in 2 large volumes, imperial 8vo. price 2l. 2s. cloth lettered.

N.B. Copies may be had on common paper, price 1l. 10s. cloth lettered.

This edition was undertaken at the request of all the Archbishops and Bishops of Ireland, in accordance with their desire of affording it at such a cheap rate, as to ensure its extensive use in all Catholic Colleges and Schools; and also, that every private family should be possessed of this invaluable treasure of religion, learning, and piety.

—— Appendix to Ditto, containing the Life by C. Butler, Chronological and Centenary Tables, with General Index, 1 vol. 8vo. 4s.

—— Select Lives of Saints, from the Work of the Rev. Alban Butler, 1 vol. 8vo. 5s.

—— The Moveable Feasts, Fasts, and other Annual Observances of the Catholic Church, 8vo. 7s.

—— Continuation of the Rev. Alban Butler's Lives of the Saints to the Present Time; with Bibliographical Accounts of the Holy Family, Pope Pius VI, Cardinal Ximenes, Cardinal Bellarmine, Bartholomew de Martyribus, and St. Vincent de Paul, with Historical Minutes of the Society of Jesus, by Charles Butler, 8vo. bds. 5s.

BUTLER'S (CHARLES) BIOGRAPHICAL AND PHILOSOPHICAL WORKS; 5 vols. 8vo. boards, 1l. 10s.

Containing: The Horæ Biblicæ—History of the Germanic Empire—Horæ Juridicæ—Life of Michael l'Hopital—Lives of Fenelon, Bossuet—Boudon—De Rance—Thomas a Kempis, and Alban Butler—Confessions of Faith, and History of the Church of France.

MEMOIRS OF MISSIONARY PRIESTS, and other Catholics of both Sexes, who suffered Death in England on Religious Accounts from 1577 to 1684, by the Right Rev. RICHARD CHALLONER, D.D. with Appendices, containing State and other valuable Papers, &c. 8vo. cloth lettered, 9s. 6d.

MEMORIAL OF ANCIENT BRITISH PIETY, or, a BRITISH MARTYROLOGY; giving a Short Account of such Britons as have been honoured of old amongst the Saints. To which is annexed a Translation of two Saxon Manuscripts relating to the Burying-Places of the English Saints. By the Right Rev. RICHARD CHALLONER, 12mo. 3s.

LIFE of Our Lord and Saviour Jesus Christ, from the Latin of St. Bonaventure, 12mo. 3s. 6d.

BARNARD'S (REV. JAMES) LIFE OF THE RIGHT REV. RICHARD CHALLONER, BISHOP OF DEBRA, collected from his Writings, and from Authentic Records, 12mo. 2s. 6d.

HISTORY of the Life, Writings, and Doctrines of Martin Luther, by J. M. V. AUDIN, translated from the French, 8vo. 12s. 6d.

LIFE of St. Anselm, Archbishop of Canterbury. A Contribution to a Knowledge of the Moral, Ecclesiastical, and Literary Life of the Eleventh and Twelfth Centuries. Translated from the German of the late J. A. Möhler, D.D. Professor of Theology in the University of Munich, author of "The Symbolik," &c. &c. By HENRY RYMER, Student of St. Edmund's College, Old Hall Green. 12mo. price 3s. 6d.

LIFE OF ST. FRANCIS DE SALES, Founder of the Order of the Visitation, translated from the French of Marsollier, by the Rev. W. H. COOMBES, D.D. 2 vols. 8vo. 16s.

HISTORY OF THE LIFE OF ST. JANE FRANCES DE CHANTAL, Foundress of the Order of the Visitation, collected from Original Documents and Records, by the Rev. W. H. COOMBES, D.D. 2 vols. 8vo. reduced to 12s.

THE HISTORY OF ST. ELIZABETH OF HUNGARY, Duchess of Thuringia (1207-1231); by the COUNT DE MONTALEMBERT, Peer of France. Translated by AMBROSE LISLE PHILLIPS, Esq. of Grace Dieu Manor, Leicestershire. Dedicated to the Queen. With a Title, illuminated in the style of the Ancient Missals. Volume the First, price 1l. 1s. in royal 4to. boards. Or illustrated with beautiful plates, by the celebrated Painter Octave Hauser of Germany, price 1l. 12s.

HISTORY of the Order of St. Ursula, containing the Life of St. Angela de Merici, the Origin of the Order, and her different Establishments in Italy, 18mo. 1s.

LIFE of St. Francis Xavier, Apostle of the Indies and of Japan, translated from the French of Father D. Bouhours, by J. Dryden, 12mo. bd. 3s. 6d.

LIFE of Sir Thomas More, by his Son-in-law William Roper, Esq., with Notes and an Appendix of Letters by S. W. Singer, small 8vo. boards, 5s.

LIFE and Times of Sir Thomas More, illustrated from his own Writings and Contemporary Documents, by W. J. Walter. With a Portrait. Small 8vo. 5s.

LIFE of Sir Thomas More, by T. Roper, and of John Fisher, Bishop of Rochester, by Bailey, 12mo. bound, 3s. 6d.

LIFE AND VIRTUES OF THE VENERABLE MOTHER MARY OF THE HOLY CROSS, Abbess of the Poor Clares at Rouen, who died there in the sweet odour of sanctity, March 21, Anno 1735, by A. B. 12mo. 2s. 6d.

LIFE of St. Teresa, to which is added the Novena, 18mo. 6d.

THE LIVES OF ST. ALPHONSUS LIGUORI, ST. FRANCIS DE GIROLAMO, ST. JOHN JOSEPH OF THE CROSS, ST. PACIFICUS OF SAN SEVERINO, AND ST. VERONICA GIULIANI, whose Canonization took place on Trinity Sunday, 26th of May, 1839. 1 vol. 12mo. bds. 4s. 6d.

THE MODEL OF YOUNG MEN; or, Edifying Life of Claude le Peletier de Sousi, translated from the French of Abbé Proyart, by the Rev. E. Peach, 18mo. cloth lettered, 1s. 6d.

PIOUS BIOGRAPHY for Young Men; or, The Virtuous Scholars. From the French of Abbé Carron. Consisting of the Lives of St. Stanislaus Kostka, St. Aloysius Gonzaga, Alexander Bercius, John Berchmans, Antony Mary Ubaldini, Charles Clarentin, William Rufin, Francis Bline, John James Daumond, the young Duke of Burgundy, Peter de Martineau, John Baptist Baily, and Raphael Emmerson. In 18mo. 2s.

SELECTION OF SAINTS' LIVES, with Reflections on the Moral and Practical Duties of Christians in all the stations of Life, and designed for Religious Entertainments on the evenings of Sundays and Holidays throughout the Year, plates, 12mo. 5s. 6d.

Controversial.

AN AMICABLE DISCUSSION ON THE CHURCH OF ENGLAND, and on the Reformation in general: translated from the French of the "DISCUSSION AMICALE," by the Right Rev. Dr. Treverne, Bishop of Strasbourg; by the Rev. W. Richmond, in 2 vols. 8vo. boards, 1l. 1s.

ANDREWS' (W. E.) Catholic Christian's Vade Mecum, or Controversial Companion, 12mo. 1s. 2d.

BADDELEY'S Sure Way to the True Religion, 18mo. 9d.

BAGGS' (Rev. Dr.) Letter to the Rev. R. Burgess on Remarks in his work entitled "Greece and the Levant," 8vo. 1s. 6d.

—— Discourse on the Supremacy of the Roman Pontiffs, 8vo. 2s.

BAINES (Rt. Rev. Dr. Bishop of Siga) Defence of the Christian Religion, 8vo. boards, 4s.

—— Inquiry into the Nature and Object of the Religion of Jesus Christ, 8vo. 3s.

—— Outlines of Christianity, being the substance of Six Lectures delivered at Bath, 8vo. 3s.

BARNARD'S Divinity of Christ demonstrated, 12mo. 2s. 6d.

BOSSUET'S Exposition of the Doctrine of the Catholic Church, 18mo. 1s. 6d.

—— Ditto, with Notes, by the Rev. Dr. Fletcher, 8vo. 5s.

—— Conference with Claude on the Authority of the Church, 8vo. 1s. 6d.

—— History of the Variations of the Protestant Churches, 2 vols. 8vo. boards, reduced to 7s.

BRISTOW (Rev. Charles) The Roman Catholic and Protestant Churches proved to be nearer related to each other than most men imagine, 12mo. 2s.

BROWN (Right Rev. Thomas, Bishop of Apollonia) Letter to Daubeny on Transubstantiation, 8vo. 1s. 6d.

—— Discussion at Cheltenham on the Rule of Faith, 8vo. 2s.

—— Supplement to the Downside Discussion, 8vo. 1s. 6d.

BRUNSWICK'S (Duke of) Fifty Reasons for embracing the Catholic Religion, 18mo. 6d.

BUTLER (REV. THOMAS, D.D.) THE TRUTHS OF THE CATHOLIC RELIGION PROVED FROM SCRIPTURE ALONE, in a Series of Lectures, 2 vols. 12mo. 7s.

THE CATECHISM OF THE COUNCIL OF TRENT, translated into English by the Rev. J. Donovan, Professor at the College of Maynooth, 8vo. boards, 10s. 6d.

Preparing for Press, with the approbation of the Most Rev. John M'Hale, D.D. Archbishop of Tuam, a translation into English of

THE CANONS AND DECREES OF THE COUNCIL OF TRENT, by the Very Rev. Dr. Kirwan.

CATHOLIC INSTITUTE Tracts, Vol. I. Tracts 1 to 38, 8vo. cl. lettered, 5s. 6d.

CHALLONER (Right Rev. Dr.) The Catholic Christian instructed in the Sacrifice, Sacraments, and Ceremonies of the Church, 18mo. good edition, large type, bound, 3s.

—— Ditto, inferior edition, bound, 2s. 6d.

—— Grounds of the Catholic Doctrine contained in the Profession of Faith by Pius IV, 18mo. 6d.

—— Grounds of the Old Religion, or some general Arguments in Favour of the Catholic Apostolic Roman Communion, 18mo. bound, 3s. 6d.

—— Touchstone of the Reformed Gospel, or Sixty Assertions of the Protestants disproved by Scripture alone, 18mo. 3d.

—— Young Gentleman instructed in the Grounds of the Christian Religion, 12mo. 2s. 6d.

COOMBES (Rev. Dr.) Essence of Religious Controversy, contained in a Series of Observations on a Protestant Catechism, 8vo. boards, reduced to 6s. 6d.

CORLESS (Rev. G.) Catholic Doctrine of Transubstantiation, 8vo. 1s.

—— Reply to Townshend on his Review of the Declaration of the Catholic Bishops, 8vo. 3s. 6d.

—— Letter to Faber, 8vo. 1s.

DIALOGUES on the Catholic and Protestant Rules of Faith, 12mo. boards, 6s.

DISCUSSION between the Rev. Thomas Maguire and the Rev. T. Pope, in Dublin in April 1827, 8vo. boards, 3s. 6d.

—— between the Rev. Thomas Maguire and the Rev. T. D. Gregg, in the Rotunda, Dublin, May 1839, 8vo. boards, 9s. 6d.

—— between the Rev. John Cumming and Daniel French, Esq. at Hammersmith, in 1839, 8vo. cloth, 12s.

—— at Downside College, between the Rev. Mr. Tottenham and the Rev. T. J. Brown (now Bishop of Appolonia), in 1836, 8vo. 6s.

ESSAY towards a Proposal for Catholic Communion, 12mo. 2s. 6d.

FLETCHER'S (Rev. Dr.) Campian's Ten Reasons for embracing the Catholic Faith, 8vo. 1s. 6d.

—— Letter of Fenelon to the Bishop of Arras on the Use of the Bible, with Illustrations, cloth, boards, 3s.

—— Letters on the Spanish Inquisition, by the Count Joseph de Maitre, with Notes, cloth boards, 3s. 6d.

—— Prudent Christian, or Considerations on the Importance and Happiness of attending to the Care of our Salvation, 12mo. boards, 2s. 6d.

—— Comparative View of the Grounds of the Catholic and Protestant Churches, 8vo. boards, 12s.

—— Anthony de Dominis' Motives for renouncing the Protestant Religion, 8vo. 1s. 6d.

—— Difficulties of Protestantism, 8vo. boards, 5s.

—— Guide to the True Religion, in Sermons on the Marks and Character of the Church of Christ, 8vo. boards, 10s. 6d.

—— Letters on Transubstantiation, 8vo. boards, 3s. 6d.

—— Second Letter to Lord —— on Transubstantiation, 8vo. 2s. 6d.

Preparing for press, the third edition,

FAITH OF CATHOLICS on Certain Points of Controversy confirmed by Scripture and attested by the Fathers of the first five Centuries of the Church; entirely revised, and every quotation from the Fathers collated with the best editions, by the Rev. J. Waterworth.

GALLITZIN'S Defence of Catholic Principles in opposition to the Vindication of the Doctrine of the Reformation, 18mo. 8d.
—— Letter to a Protestant Friend on the Holy Scriptures, 18mo. 8d.

GILBERT'S Inquiry into the Marks of the True Church, 18mo. 1s. 3d.
—— Vindication of the Catholic Doctrine of the Eucharist, 12mo. 2s. 6d.

GOTHER (Rev. John) A Papist Misrepresented and Represented; or, a Twofold Character of Popery : the one containing a sum of the superstitions, idolatries, cruelties, treacheries, and wicked principles laid to their charge; the other laying open that religion which those termed Papists own and profess, the chief articles of their faith, and the principal grounds and reasons which attach them to it. Selected from the original of the Rev. John Gother, by the late Ven. and Right Rev. Richard Challoner, D.D. 1s.

GREEN'S (Rev. T. L.) Correspondence with the Rector of Tixall, on the Marriage and Funerals of Catholics and Dissenters, 8vo. with Notes, &c. 1s. 6d.
—— Catholic Church Vindicated, in Two Letters to the Rev. G. Hodson, in reply to his pamphlet entitled, " The Church of Rome's Traffic in Pardons," letter first, 1s. letter second, 2s.

HIERURGIA; OR THE HOLY SACRIFICE OF THE MASS :

with Notes and Dissertations, elucidating its Doctrines and Ceremonies. By DANIEL ROCK, D.D. In 2 vols. 8vo. with above Forty Plates, price 1l. 8s. cloth lettered.

In the Second Part are treated at length : TRANSUBSTANTIATION, RELICS, INVOCATION OF SAINTS AND ANGELS, PURGATORY, the USE OF HOLY WATER, LIGHTS, and INCENSE, the DYPTICHS, &c. with Appendices containing " Extracts from Ancient Liturgies," &c.

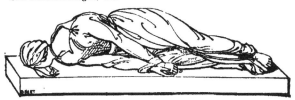

BODY OF ST. CECILIA, AS DISCOVERED UNDER THE HIGH ALTAR OF HER CHURCH IN 1599.

N.B. A few copies taken off with the plates on India Paper, 1l. 14s. cl. lettered

" The Notes on the Rubrics will be found very interesting to the general reader, Catholic as well as Protestant, not merely on account of the lucid explanation which they afford of the different parts of the liturgy and its ceremonies, but also on account of the numerous scriptural and other references with which the notes are enriched."—*Edinb. Cath. Mag.*

Preparing for Press, a translation from the German by the Rev. C. F. Husenbeth, of

THE RESULT OF MY WANDERINGS THROUGH THE TERRITORY OF PROTESTANT LITERATURE; or, the Necessity of Return to the Catholic Church demonstrated, exclusively from the Confessions of Protestant Theologians and Philosophers. By Dr. Julius Hœninghaus. To be completed in 2 volumes.

HORNIHOLD'S (Rev. J.) Works, including the Real Principles of Catholics, 3 vols. 12mo. bound, 12s.

HUSENBETH'S (Rev. F. C.) Defence of the Creed and Discipline of the Church against Blanco White, 12mo. 1s.
—— Difficulties of Faberism, 8vo. 2s. 6d.
—— Reply to Faber's Supplement to his Difficulties of Romanism, 8vo. boards, 10s.
—— Faberism Exposed and Refuted, 8vo. boards, 12s.
—— Further Exposure of Faberism, 8vo. 1s.
—— St. Cyprian Vindicated against certain Misrepresentations of his Doctrine, by the Rev. G. A. Poole, 8vo. 3s.

KENRICK (REV. P. H.) THE VALIDITY OF THE ANGLICAN OR-DINATIONS EXAMINED; or, a Review of Certain Facts regarding the Con-secration of Matthew Parker, first Protestant Archbishop of Canterbury, by the Very Rev. Peter Richard Kenrick, Philadelphia, 12mo. cloth, 5s. 6d.

LANIGAN (Right Rev. Dr.) Catechetical Conferences on the Holy Eucharist, 18mo. 1s.
—— Ditto on Penance, 18mo. 1s.

LINGARD (REV. DR.) REVIEW OF CERTAIN ANTI-CATHOLIC PUBLICATIONS by Dr. Hungerford, Dr. Tomline, Lord Kenyon, &c. 8vo. 2s.
—— COLLECTION OF TRACTS, complete in 1 vol. 8vo. boards, 10s. 6d.
—— CATECHETICAL INSTRUCTIONS ON THE DOCTRINES AND WORSHIP OF THE CATHOLIC CHURCH, 12mo. 2s. 6d.
    Notice.—The above work contains a short exposition of Catholic Doctrine, and Catholic practice, with the chief authorities and principles on which that doctrine and practice are founded. To the well-informed it can offer nothing with which they are not already acquainted; but it is hoped that it may prove useful to two classes of persons; to the young who are preparing themselves for their first communion, and to the more aged who have been suffered to grow up to manhood without a competent knowledge of their religion.

LUCAS (FRED.) REASONS FOR BECOMING A ROMAN CATHOLIC, addressed to the Society of Friends, third edition, 12mo. 1s. 6d.

LUTHER'S Catechism, extracted from his works, 18mo. 2d.

MACDONALD (Alexander) A Summary of the Catholic Religion, including its History, from the Birth of our Saviour until the Present Time, 8vo. cloth, 6s.

M'HALE (THE MOST REV. JOHN, D.D. ARCHBISHOP OF TUAM) EVIDENCES AND DOCTRINES OF THE CATHOLIC CHURCH, second edition, revised, with additional notes.

MASON'S (Rev. J. A.) Account of his Conversion, 12mo. 9d.
—— Safety Lamp, wherewith to explore the richest Vein in the Mine of Ca-tholicism, 1s.
—— Vindication of the Doctrine of the Real Presence of Jesus Christ in the Holy Eucharist, 6d.
—— Strictures on Wesley's Pretended Roman Catechism, 12mo. 1s. 4d.
—— Appeal to the People called Methodists, 12mo. 6d.
—— Value of Sincerity in Religion, 12mo. 4d.
—— Conversion of E. Corser, Esq. with the Address by the Rev. F. Martyn, 4d.
—— Wonderful Discoveries elicited from a Ghost, with a review of the above Pam-phlet, 12mo. 6d.
—— Review of Dr. Hook's Sermon, 12mo. 8d.
—— Touchstone for Methodism, in a Dialogue on the Forgiveness of Sins, 12mo. 10d.
—— The Glory of Methodism, or August will come, 2d.

MANNING'S England's Conversion and Reformation compared, 18mo. bd. 2s. 6d.
—— Shortest Way to end Disputes about Religion, 12mo. bound, 2s. 6d.
—— Celebrated Answer to Lesley's " Case stated between the Church of Rome and the Church of England, 8vo. boards, 9s.

MANZONI'S Vindication of Catholic Morality against Sismondi, from the Italian, 12mo. 2s.

MILNER'S End of Religious Controversy, 18mo. bound, 3s. 6d.
—— Ditto, new edition, with additional letters, edited by W. E. Andrews, and em-bellished with the Apostolic Tree, and other engravings, designed by the Right Rev. Author, 12mo. boards, 4s.
—— Letters to a Prebendary, fine edition, 8vo. with portrait, 6s.
—— Ditto, small edition, 12mo. 3s. 6d.

MUMFORD (Rev. J.) The Catholic Scripturist, or the Plea of Roman Catholics, shewing the Scriptures to hold the Roman Catholic Faith, in Forty-Five Points of Controversy now under debate, 12mo. 2s. 6d.
—— The Question of Questions, which rightly resolved, resolves all our Questions in Religion, 18mo. 3s. 6d.
NET for the Fishers of Men, the same which Christ gave his Apostles, 6d.
PAGANI (Rev. J. B.) The Pillar and Foundation of Truth, 12mo. 2s.
PAX VOBIS, or Gospel and Liberty, 12mo. 10d.
PERPETUITY of the Faith of the Catholic Church on the Eucharist, with the Refutation of the Reply of the Calvinistic Minister, 8vo. boards, 5s. 6d.
POYNTER'S (R. R. Dr.) Christianity; or Evidences and Characters of the Christian Religion, 12mo. cloth, 2s.
PROTESTANT Advocate for Popery, proving it to have been, for all ages, the sure path to Salvation, by the admission of its Adversaries, 18mo. 8d.
PROTESTANT Principle (The) of Appealing to the Holy Scriptures, subversive of Protestant Doctrine, and confirmatory of the Catholic Faith, 12mo. 2s. 6d.
RATHBORNE (Rev. J.) The Church in its Relations with Truth and the State, in reply to the work entitled " The State in its Relations with the Church," by W. E. Gladstone, Esq. 8vo. 2s. 6d.
RULE OF FAITH ; chiefly an Epitome of Milner's End of Controversy, by the Rev. S. Jones, 12mo. 1s. 6d.
RULE OF FAITH, from the French of Veron, by Rev. J. Waterworth, 8vo. 2s. 6d.
SIBTHORP (REV. R. WALDO) SOME ANSWER TO THE ENQUIRY " Why have you become a Catholic," 12mo. 6d.
—— A FURTHER ANSWER TO THE ENQUIRY "WHY HAVE YOU become a Catholic," in a Second Letter to a Friend, containing a Notice of the Strictures of the Rev. Messrs. Palmer and Dodsworth upon a former letter, 8vo. 1s. 6d.
SIDDEN (Rev. John) Remarks on the Rev. C. J. Yorke's Protestant Catechism, 12mo. 1s. 6d.
—— (Rev. Joseph) Manifestation of Christ in the Eucharist, 12mo. 1s.
—— The Church of Peace and Truth, a Discourse delivered before the Guildford Protestant Association, 8vo. 6d.
SILVEIRA, Scriptural and Historical Proofs of the Catholic Doctrine of Purgatory, 18mo. 4d.
SPENCER'S (Hon. and Rev. George) Letters in Defence of Various Points of Catholic Faith, 8vo. 1s. 8d.
STARCK, Philosophical Dialogues on the Reunion of the different Christian Communions, 8vo. 9s.
TERTULLIAN'S Prescriptions, or the Shield of Catholic Faith, 18mo. 1s. 6d.
VERAX, A Reply to the Work of the Rev. Dr. Hook, entitled " Friendly Advice to the Roman Catholics," 8vo.
—— Short Vindication of the Church of Rome, consisting of Letters on the Catholic Church, on the Church of England, on the Eucharist, and the Holy Fathers, &c. 1s.
—— Letters addressed to the Rev. W. F. Hook, D.D. on the Eucharist, the Mass, Communion under one species, with a Reply to the " Novelties of Romanism," 1s.
—— The Triumph of Truth, being a Reply to " A Short Enquiry into the Doctrines of the Churches of England and Rome," 12mo. 1s. 6d.
—— Four Letters to the Rev. W. Palmer, M.A. on the most important Points of Controversy between Catholics and Protestants, 8vo. 2s. 10d.
VOICE of the Church from the remotest Ages of Christianity, compiled by the Rev. W. Young, 18mo. 6d.
WATERWORTH (Rev. J.) Correspondence with the Rev. R. Simpson, Protestant Curate of Newark, on certain Doctrines and Practices ascribed to the Catholic Church, 8vo. 2s. 6d.
—— Examination of the Evidence adduced by Mr. Keary against the Invocation of Saints and Angels, 8vo. 1s. 6d.
—— Examination of the Distinctive Principle of Protestantism, 8vo. 2s. 6d.
—— Historical Lectures on the Origin and Progress, in this Country, of the Change of Religion called the Reformation, 12mo. cloth, 8s.
WHITE'S Confutation of Church of Englandism, and correct Exposition of the Catholic Faith on the Points of Controversy between the Two Churches. Translated from the Original (Latin) by Edmund W. O'Mahoney, Esq. Middle Temple, 8vo. 7s. 6d.

WORKS BY THE

RIGHT REV. NICHOLAS WISEMAN, D.D.

Bishop of Melipotamus.

LECTURES ON THE PRINCIPAL DOCTRINES AND PRACTICES
OF THE CATHOLIC CHURCH, delivered at St. Mary's, Moorfields, during the
Lent of 1836. In 16 numbers, 12mo. price 6d. each, or in 2 vols. price 8s. 6d.
boards or cloth.

LECTURES ON THE REAL PRESENCE OF JESUS CHRIST IN
THE BLESSED EUCHARIST. Delivered in the English College, Rome.
Part I. Scriptural Proofs, 8vo. price 8s. 6d. cloth boards.—Part II. Proofs from
Tradition, preparing for press.

A REPLY TO DR. TURTON.—PHILALETHES CANTABRIGIENSIS,
THE BRITISH CRITIC, THE CHURCH OF ENGLAND QUARTERLY
REVIEW, on the Catholic Doctrine of the Eucharist. In 8vo. price 6s. boards.

FOUR LECTURES ON THE OFFICES AND CEREMONIES

OF HOLY WEEK, as performed in the Papal Chapels, delivered in Rome, in the
Lent of MDCCCXXXVII. Illustrated with nine beautiful engravings, and a plan of the
Papal Chapels. In 8vo. price 8s. 6d. in cloth boards.

LETTERS TO JOHN POYNDER, ESQ. upon his Work entitled " Popery
in Alliance with Heathenism." In 8vo. 2s. sewed.

A LETTER addressed to the Rev. J. H. NEWMAN, upon some Passages in
his Letter to the Rev. Dr. Jelf, 4th edition, 8vo. 1s.

REMARKS on a Letter from the Rev. W. PALMER, M.A. of Worceste
College, Oxford. In 8vo. price 2s. 6d.

A LETTER ON CATHOLIC UNITY, addressed to the Right Hon. the
Earl of Shrewsbury. In 8vo. 1s.

Preparing for Press, a new edition, revised and enlarged.

TWELVE LECTURES ON THE CONNEXION BETWEEN

SCIENCE AND REVEALED RELIGION, with Maps and Plates.

Instruction, Meditation, and Devotion.

ST. ALOYSIUS GONZAGA, Meditations and Pious Exercises for the Devotion of the Six Sundays and for the Novena in his honour, 18mo. 1s. 3d.

ARVISENET, Treatise on Holy Purity, 32mo. 6d.

AUGUSTIN (St.) Confessions; or Praises of God, 18mo. bound, 2s. 6d.

BAKER (Rev. P.) Lenten Monitor, for every Day in Lent, 18mo. sheep, 4s.

BAUDRAND'S Elevation of the Soul to God by Spiritual Considerations and Affections, 12mo. 3s. 6d.

—— Religious Soul elevated to Perfection by the Exercises of an Interior Life, 2s. 6d.

—— The Soul on Calvary, meditating on the Sufferings of Jesus Christ, &c., 12mo. 2s. 6d.

BERTHIER'S God and I, or a Week's Spiritual Retreat, 32mo. 8d.

BLOSIUS, Meditations on the Life and Death of Jesus Christ, 18mo. 1s.

BOUDON, God everywhere present, translated by the Right Rev. Dr. Challoner, 18mo. 4d.

BOURDALOUE'S Spiritual Retreat, for eight successive days, 18mo. bound. 3s.

CHALLONER (Rt. Rev. Dr.) Meditations for every Day in the Year, 1 vol. 12mo. bound, 5s.

—— Ditto, new edition, Revised by the Rev. F. C. Husenbeth, 1 vol. 12mo. cloth, 6s. 6d.

—— Think well on't; or Reflections on the Great Truths of Religion, 24mo. sheep 1s.

CHRISTIAN at the Foot of the Cross, 32mo. 4d.

Christian Instructions for Youth; adapted to every Age and Condition of Life; interspersed with impressive and edifying Examples, from Historical and other authentic Sources, in cloth, neat, reduced to 2s. 6d.

—— Reflections for every Day in the Month, translated by the Rev. J. Birdsall, 18mo. sewed, 4s. 6d.

—— Student, or Duties of a Young Man who desires to sanctify his Studies, 18mo. 1s. 6d.

CLINTON on Frequent Communion, 12mo. large print, sewed 3s. 6d.

—— Ditto, smaller type, bound 3s. 6d.

CONFIDENCE in the Mercy of God, 18mo. 1s. 6d.

CONTRITE and Humble Heart, with motives and considerations, 18mo. 2s. 6d.

COUNSELS of a Christian Mother to her Daughter, 18mo. 1s.

CURR (Rev. J.) Familiar Instructions in the Faith and Morality of the Catholic Church, 18mo. 1s. 3d.

DORRELL (Rev. W.) Moral Reflections on the Epistles and Gospels, for every Sunday throughout the whole Year, 2 vols. 12mo. bound, 8s.

DUQUENE (Abbé) Devout Meditations on the Gospel, for every Day in the Year, abridged from the French, 4 vols. 8vo. boards, 10s.

EXPOSITION of the Lamentations of the Prophet Jeremiah, 32mo. 6d.

FENELON'S Pious Reflections for every Day of the Month, 48mo. 8d.

—— The Education of Daughters, 18mo. 1s. 6d.

FLETCHER (Rev. Dr.) The Prudent Christian; or Considerations on the Importance and Happiness of attending to the Care of our Salvation, 12mo. 2s. 6d.

FLOCK'S Instructions and Meditations for every day in Advent, 24mo. 6d.

FRANCIS DE SALES (St.) Beauties of, selected by Camus, and translated into English, 12mo. boards, 6s.

—— Introduction to a Devout Life, 18mo. sheep, 3s.

—— Ditto, smaller type, 18mo. 2s.

—— Maxims and Religious Counsels, 12mo. 1s.

—— Treatise on the Love of God, 8vo. boards, 5s.

FLOWERS FROM THE HOLY FATHERS (with Frontispiece), fcp. 8vo. cloth, 7s. 6d.

GERBET (ABBÉ) CONSIDERATIONS ON THE EUCHARIST, viewed as the generative Dogma of Catholic Piety, translated from the French by a Catholic Clergyman, 12mo. 4s. 6d. cloth lettered.

GLORIES of Jesus contemplated in the Mirror of Divine Love, translated from the French, 18mo. 1s. 3d.

—— of St. Joseph, translated from the French. 32mo. 1s. 4d.

GLOVER (Rev. E.) Explanation of the Prayers and Ceremonies of the Mass, 18mo. 1s. 6d.
—— Explanation of the Sacraments, and other Practices of the Catholic Church, 18mo. 1s. 6d.
GOBINET'S Instructions of Youth in Christian Piety, 12mo bound, 5s.
GOTHER'S Instructions for Confession and Communion, bound, 1s.
—— on the Epistles and Gospels for every Sunday in the Year, and every Day in Lent, 3 vols. 12mo 6s.
—— Ditto, 1 vol. 12mo. 5s.
—— Instructions and Devotions for Hearing Mass, 12mo. bound, 1s. 6d.
—— Instructions and Prayers for the Afflicted Sick and Dying, 12mo. bound, 2s. 6d.
—— Practical Catechism for the Sundays and Festivals, 18mo. bound, 1s. 6d.
—— Sinner's Complaints to God, being Devout Entertainments of the Soul with God, fitted for all states and conditions of Christians, new ed. 12mo. cloth lett. 4s. 6d.
GRANADA (Lewis of), Memorial of a Christian Life, 12mo. bound, 4s.
—— Exhortation to Alms Deeds, 32mo. 8d.
—— The Sinner's Guide, 12mo. 5s.
GROU, (Abbé) Characters of real Devotion, 18mo. 1s., and 32mo. 6d.
—— Christian Sanctified by the Lord's Prayer, 12mo. bound, 2s. 6d.
—— School of Christ, 12mo. bound, 4s.
HAY'S (R. R. Dr.) Devout Christian Instructed in the Law of Christ, 1 vol. 12mo. bound, 5s.
—— Pious Christian Instructed in the Nature and Practice of the Principal Exercises of Piety used in the Catholic Church, 12mo. bound, 5s.
—— Sincere Christian Instructed in the Faith of Christ, 1 vol. 12mo. bound, 5s.
HERBERT (Mrs.) and the Villagers, or Familiar Conversations on the Duties of Christians, 2 vols. 18mo. cloth, 4s.
HORNIHOLD (Rev. J.) Commandments and Sacraments explained, 12mo. bound, 5s.
—— Works, including the real principles of Catholics, 3 vols. 12mo. bound, 12s.
HUBY'S Meditations on Divine Love, 12mo. bound, 4s. 6d.
IMITATION of Christ, 18mo. bound, 2s.
—— digested into verses, cloth lettered, 1s. 6d.
—— miniature edition, bound, 1s. 6d.
—— with Reflections and a Prayer at the end of each chapter, by the Rev. J. Jones, cloth lettered, 2s. 6d.
—— of the Blessed Virgin, 32mo. (small print) bound, 1s.
JOURNAL of Meditations for every Day in the Year, 12mo. sheep lettered, 5s.
KEMPIS (Thomas) The little Garden of Roses, and Valley of Lillies, 32mo. 1s. 6d.
LAUDATE Pueri Dominum; or, Hymns for my Children, fcp. 8vo. with plates, cloth, 5s. 6d.
LIGUORI'S Glories of Mary, 32mo. sewed 1s.
—— Conformity to the Will of God, 32mo. 3d.
—— Love of Jesus Christ, reduced to Practice, 18mo. cloth, 1s. 6d.
—— True Spouse of Jesus Christ; or, The Nun Sanctified, 12mo. 2s. 6d.
—— Treatise on Prayer, 18mo. 1s. 6d.
—— Visits to the Blessed Sacrament, by Curr, 18mo. 1s. 3d.
—— Way of Salvation; Meditations for every Day of the Year, translated by the Rev. J. Jones.
—— Spirit of, a Selection from his shorter Spiritual Treatises, by the Rev. J. Jones, 24mo. cloth, 1s. 8d.
MANNING (Rev. R.) Moral Entertainments, on the most important Truths of the Christian Religion, 12mo. bound, 5s.
MARTYN (Rev. F.) History of Tobias, in Homilies adapted to the generality of Christians living in the world, 12mo. 2s. 6d.
THE NEW MONTH OF MARY; or, Reflections for each Day of the Month, on the different Titles applied to the Holy Mother of God, in the Litany of Loretto; principally designed for the Month of May. By the Very Rev. P. R. Kenrick, 18mo. 1s. 6d.
NIEREMBERG'S Treatise on the Difference between Temporal and Eternal, 12mo. bound, 5s.
NOUET (Père), Forty-two Meditations on the Passion of Our Blessed Saviour, 12mo. 9d.

PEACH (Rev. E.) Practical Reflections for every Day in the Year, by R. Lane, and enlarged by Rev. E. Peach, 12mo. 4s.
—— Practical Reflections exemplified ; or an Abridged Account of the Life of the Saint, for every Day of the Year ; followed by Reflections, 2 vols. 12mo. cloth lettered, 12s,
PERSONS' (Rev. R.) A Christian Directory guiding Men to their Salvation. New Edition, 12mo. 5s.
PIETY Exemplified, from Historical and other sources, 2 vols. 18mo. 3s.
PINAMONTI'S Meditations on the Four Last Things, 4d.
—— One Thing Necessary, by Rutter, 1s.
—— Hell opened to Christians, 1s.
POWER (Rev. T.) Instructions and curious Epistles from Clergymen of the Society of Jesus, selected from the "Lettres Edifiantes," 12mo. 5s.
PRACTICAL Methods of performing the ordinary actions of a Christian Life with fervour of spirit, 18mo. 1s. 6d.
REFLECTIONS on the Prerogatives and Protection of St. Joseph, 18mo. 1s. 3d.
REGNAULT'S Instructions for First Communicants, 18mo. bound, 1s. 6d.
RODIGUEZ (Alphonsus), The Practice of Christian and Religious perfection, 3 vols. 8vo. 19s. 6d.
RULES OF A CHRISTIAN LIFE; selected from the most Spiritual Writers ; with Letters on Matrimony ; on the Choice of a State of Life ; and on Monastic Institutions, &c., by the Rev. C. Premord, 2 vols. 12mo. boards, 10s.
SALAZAR, The Sinner's Conversion reduced to principles; to which are added the Spiritual Exercises of St. Ignatius, 18mo. bound, 1s. 6d.

Sermons.

ARCHER'S (Rev. James, D.D.) Sermons for Sundays,and some of the Festivals, &c., first series, 2 vols. 8vo. bds. 1l. 1s.
—— Second Series, of Sermons for Sundays and for Festivals, 2 vols. boards, 18s.
—— Four Miscellaneous Sermons, 8vo. boards, 2s. 6d.
CATHOLIC PULPIT, containing Sermons for all the Sundays and Holidays of the year, 2 vols. 8vo. 11s.
GAHAN'S Sermons for the Year, with Preface, &c., by the Rt. Rev. Dr. Doyle, 8vo. boards, 12s.
MURPHY'S (Rev. B.) Sermons for every Sunday, 2 vols. 12mo. boards, 9s.
PEACH (Rev. Edward) A series of Familiar Discourses for every Sunday and Festival of the Year, 2 vols. 8vo. boards, 10s.
REEVE (Rev. Joseph) Practical Discourses on the Perfections and Wonderful Works of God, 2nd ed., 12mo. cloth, 3s.
RIGBY (Rev. Dr.) Catechistical Discourses on Natural and Revealed Religion, 4 vols. 12mo., reduced to 10s.
ULLATHORNE (Rev. W., D.D., O.S.B.) Sermons with Prefaces, 8vo. 4s 6d.
WHEELER (Rev. J.) Sermons on the Gospels for every Sunday in the Year, 2 vols. 8vo. 18s.
—— Sermons on the Festivals, and a Selection of Sermons, 8vo. 9s.
WHITE (Rev. T.) Sermons for every Sunday, and on other occasions, selected by the Rev. Dr. Lingard, 2 vols. 8vo. 18s.

Separate Sermons.

ARCHER (Rev. James, D.D.) Sermon on Universal Benevolence, containing some reflections on Religious Persecution, and the alledged proceedings at Nismes, 8vo. 6d.
—— Sermon at the opening of the Catholic Chapel at Chelsea, for the use of the wounded and disabled soldiers, 8vo. 6d.
—— Sermon on the Love of Our Country, 8vo. 6d.
BAGGS' (Rev. Dr.) Discourse on the Supremacy of the Roman Pontiffs, 8vo. 2s.
—— Funeral Oration of the Lady Gwendaline Talbot, Princess Borghese,8vo.6d.
BAINES (R. R. Dr.) Sermon on Faith, Hope, and Charity, 8vo. 1s. 6d.
—— on the Propagation of the Faith, 6d.
—— Two Sermons at York, 8vo. 6d.
—— on the Dedication of the Cathedral Church of St. Chad, 6d.

GILLIS (R. Rev. Dr.) Account of his Consecration, with Two Sermons by Bishops Murdoch and Baines, 8vo. 1s.

GILL (Rev. T. E.) Sermon on Resignation to the Will of God, 6d.

MURDOCH (Bishop) a Sermon preached at the opening of the Chapel of St. Margaret's Convent, Edinburgh, 8vo. 6d.

RIGBY (Rev. N.) Two Sermons on the Means which Jesus Christ has left for the Propagation of his Gospel in all Ages, 8vo. 1s.

SIBTHORP (Rev. R. W.) Two Sermons preached at St. Chad's, on St. Patrick's Day, 1842, 6d. each.

SPENCER'S (Hon. and Rev. George) Sermon at Leamington, for the benefit of the Mission in that place, 6d.

—— Sermon at the Funeral of the Rev. F. Martyn, Pastor of Walsall, July 25th, 1838, 6d.

—— Sermon at Loughborough (The True Method of making Converts to the Church of Christ), 6d.

—— Sermon on occasion of the Consecration of the Right Rev. Dr. Wareing, Bishop of Ariopolis, 3d.

—— Two Sermons preached in the Catholic Chapel at Hinkley, in Leicestershire, 3d.

—— A Sermon preached in St. Michael's Church, Westbromwich, 3d.

—— Sermon at the Laying of the First Stone of the Catholic Church of St. Mary, Derby (the Politics of Catholics proved Loyal), 6d.

SPOONER (Rev. S.) Sermon on occasion of the Demise of her Royal Highness the Princess Charlotte of Wales, 8vo. 6d.

TEMPEST (Rev. T.) Sermon preached on occasion of laying the first stone of a Catholic Chapel at Melton Mowbray, 6d.

WEEDALL (Rev. Dr.) Discourse on Ecclesiastical Seminaries, 8vo. 6d.

WELD (Cardinal) Sermon on the Passion of our Lord, 8vo. 6d.

WISEMAN (R. R. Dr. Bishop of Melipotamus) Funeral Oration on his Eminence Cardinal Weld, delivered at his Solemn Obsequies in the Church of St. Maria in Aquiro, April 22, 1837. With a Plate of the Cenotaph erected on the occasion, 8vo. 2s. sewed.

—— Sermon at the Solemn Dedication of the Cathedral Church of St. Chad, 6d.

—— at the Consecration of the Church of St. Andrew, Westland-row, 1s.

—— at the Opening of St. Mary's Catholic Church, in Derby, 8vo. 6d.

—— Sermons delivered at St. Patrick's, Huddersfield, September 26th, 1839, on occasion of the Anniversary of the Holy Catholic Guild there established, 4d.

SOUTHWELL (Robert) Marie Magdalen's Funeral Teares for the Death of Our Saviour, 18mo. 1s. 6d.

SPIRITUAL ADVICE, or Instructions to Virtue, 18mo. 2s. 6d.

—— Combat, to which is added the Peace of the Soul, &c., 18mo. bound, 2s.

—— Ditto, 32mo. bound, 2s. 6d.

—— Ditto (small type), 32mo. bound, 1s.

—— Consolation, or Treatise on Interior Peace, from the French of P. Lombez, 12mo. 5s.

—— Director, a Preparation for the Holy Sacraments, 12mo. 6s. 6d.

—— Director of Devout and Religious Souls, from the French of St. Francis de Sales, 18mo. 1s. 6d.

—— Retreat for Religious Persons, 18mo. 3s.

STATIONS, or Devotions on the Passion of Our Lord Crucified, as they are made in Jerusalem, 32mo. 1s.

SUFFERINGS OF OUR LORD JESUS CHRIST, by F. Thomas, 2 vols. 12mo. bound, 8s.

TERESA'S (St.) Meditations before and after Communion, 18mo. 8d.

TREATISE on the Sanctity and on the Duties of the Monastic state, translated from the French of De Rance, Abbot of La Trappe, 2 vols. 12mo. 9s.

—— on the advantages of Frequent Communion, translated from the French of Abbé Faure by a Lady.

VEITH'S Words of the Enemies of Christ during his Sacred Passion, translated from the German by the Rev. Dr. Cox, of St. Edmund's College, 1 vol. 12mo. reduced to 2s.

WALSH (Viscomte) The Christian Festivals, translated by a Lady, Part First, 12mo. 1s. 6d.

WAY TO PARADISE, to which are added Meditations for every Day in the Week, by the Rev. B. Crosbie, 18mo. 10d.

Instructive and Amusing Works.

GERALDINE, A TALE OF CONSCIENCE; by E. C. A. A new edition, 1 vol. fcp. 8vo. uniform with the Standard Novels, 6s.

"'Geraldine' is a work peculiarly calculated for an inquirer after truth—of that numerous class who, though not deeply read, possess the clear and cultivated intelligence which enables them to fix upon the leading points of the controversy, and to decide upon the kind of evidence which their own minds would require for coming to a decision upon them."—*Dublin Review.*

ILLUSTRATIONS OF THE CORPORAL AND SPIRITUAL WORKS OF MERCY, in Sixteen Designs, engraved in outline, with descriptive anecdotes in four languages, and a Sketch of the Order of Mercy, by a Sister of the religious Order of Our Lady of Mercy, 1 vol. oblong 4to. half-bound, 20s.

THE YOUNG COMMUNICANTS. Written for the use of the Poor School, Bermondsey, and respectfully dedicated to the Rev. Peter Butler, by the authoress of "GERALDINE, a Tale of Conscience," with the approbation of the Right Rev. Dr. Griffiths, V.A.L., 18mo. 2s. cloth.

ALTON Park, or Conversations on Moral and Religious Subjects, 12mo., reduced to 4s.

CHRISTIAN STUDENT; or a treatise on the duties of a young man who desires to sanctify his studies, 18mo. 1s. 6d.

THE CONVERTS; a Tale of the Nineteenth Century; or, Romanism and Protestantism brought to bear in their true light against one another, 18mo. 5s.

FATHER ROWLAND; or, the Force of Truth; a Catholic tale of North America, 18mo. 1s. 6d.

GERAMB (MARIE JOSEPH), ABBOT OF LA TRAPPE, Journey from La Trappe to Rome, 8vo. 6s.

—— Pilgrimage to Jerusalem and the Holy Land, plates, 2 vols. 8vo. 1l. 1s.

—— On the Premature Death of Lady Gwendalina Catherine Talbot, Princess Borghese, 12mo. 6d.

GIRAUDEAU (Père B.) Parables, or Religious Tales, 18mo. 1s. 3d.

HERBERT (Mrs) and the Villagers; or, Familiar Conversations on the Duties of Christians, 2 vols. 18mo. 4s.

INNISFOYLE ABBEY; A Tale of Modern Times, by DENNIS IGNATIUS MORIARTY, Esq., author of the "Wife Hunter," "Husband Hunter," &c., 3 vols. 12mo. boards, 18s.

"A racy, vigorous, and entertaining tale."—*Dublin Morning Register.*

"This is one of the best novels of the season."—*Pilot.*

"The work is a rare and valuable combination of sterling patriotism, controversial acumen, and keen observation of character and manners."—*Belfast Vindicator.*

ISIDORE, or the Pious Labourer; a Model for Country People, 18mo. 1s.

LOUISA, or the Virtuous Villager, 18mo. 1s. 3d.

MERRYE ENGLANDE; or, the Golden Daies of Good Queene Besse, 12mo. 4s. 6d.

PARISH PRIEST and his Parishioners; or Answers to Popular Prejudices against Religion, translated from the French by the Rev. E. M'Dawson, 18mo. 2s. 6d.

PIETY Exemplified, in apposite Illustrations from Historical and other sources; interspersed with familiar Reflections for the Improvement of the Mind and Heart, by the Rev. B. Rayment, 2 vols. 18mo. 4s.

CAPTAIN ROCK in Rome, written by himself in the Capital of the Christian World, 2 vols. 12mo. illustrated, 7s.

REMINISCENCES of Rome; or a Religious, Moral, and Literary View of the Eternal City, in a Series of Letters, 2 vols. 12mo. 12s.

STORIES about Alfred the Great, for the Amusement and Instruction of Children, by A. M. S., 18mo. 1s.

—— about some of Alfred the Great's successors, for the Amusement and Instruction of Children, by A. M. S., 18mo. 2s.

VILLAGE EVENINGS, or Conversations on Morality, interspersed with entertaining Histories, 18mo. 1s. 6d.

VIRTUOUS SCHOLAR, or edifying Life of a Student, 18mo. 1s. 6d.

Catechisms, and Works on Education.

ABRIDGMENT of the Christian Doctrine, 1½d.
—— Ditto, large print, 18mo.
AN ABSTRACT of the Douay Catechism, 3d.
BUTLER'S General Catechism, 18mo. 4d.
CATECHISM for Confirmation, 1½d.
—— for First Communicants, 3d.
CATECHETICAL Instructions on the Doctrine and Worship of the Catholic Church, by John Lingard, D.D., 12mo. boards, 2s. 6d.
FLEURY'S Historical Catechism, containing a Summary of the Sacred History and Christian Doctrine, 18mo. sheep, 1s. 6d.
—— Short Historical Catechism 32mo. sewed, 3s.
HELP to Parents in the Instruction of their own Children, by the Rev. H. Rutter, 12mo. 2s.
THE POOR MAN'S Catechism, or Christian Doctrine explained, with Admonitions, 18mo. bound, 2s.
A PRACTICAL Catechism for the Sundays, Feasts, and Fasts of the whole year, by the Rev. J. Gother, 18mo. bound, 1s. 6d.
A CATECHISM OF THE HISTORY OF ENGLAND, by A LADY, 18mo. 1s.
INTRODUCTION to Geography, an Elementary Work, used at the Benedictine Convent at Winchester. (at press.)
THE CATHOLIC School Book, 18mo. sheep, 1s. 4d.
CONCISE VIEWS of Sacred and Ecclesiastical History for Youth, 18mo. 6d.
ENGLAND (Right Rev. Dr.) Rudiments of Spelling and Reading, 18mo. 1s.
—— Reading Book, 18mo. 1s. 6d.
AN INTRODUCTION to the Latin Language, a New Edition, with alterations and additions, 18mo. 6d.
READING LESSONS for the Use of Schools; a New Series, from words of Two Syllables upwards, by a Catholic Clergyman—Fifty-six Lessons, 5s. the set.
—— compiled by the Brothers of the Christian Schools; First Book, 4d., Second Book, 10d., Third Book, 1s. 6d., Literary Class Book, or Fourth Book, 2s. 6d.
THE SUNBEAM of CATHOLICITY—The Catholic Monitor, or Sunday-school Magazine, by P. Whittle, F.S.A., 3 vols. 24mo. cloth, 4s. 6d.

The Holy Scriptures.

THE HOLY BIBLE, translated from the Latin Vulgate, and compared with the Hebrew, Greek, and other editions: the Old Testament, first published by the English College at Douay, A.D. 1609; and the New Testament, first published by the English College at Rheims, A.D. 1582, stereotype edition, in demy 8vo. at various prices, according to the binding.
—— The same, on fine paper, royal 8vo. handsomely bound in calf, 1l. 1s.
—— The same, in 4to. cloth, 1l. 10s.
—— The same, small pocket edition, from 5s. upwards.
THE NEW TESTAMENT, 8vo. boards, 7s. 6d.
—— Ditto, newly revised and corrected, according to the Clementine edition of the Scriptures, royal 12mo. fine paper, calf gilt, 7s.
—— Ditto, edited by M. Sidney, and revised by the Rev. R. Horrabin, good type, 12mo. bound, 4s.
—— Ditto, stereotype edition, Dublin, 12mo. bound, 1s. 6d.
—— Ditto, stereotype edition, 32mo. bound, 1s. 6d.
BUTLER (Charles) Horæ Biblicæ; or Notes on the Text and History of the Bibles, and on the Sacred Books of the Mahometans, Chinese, &c. &c. 5th edition, 8vo. boards, 12s.
THE HISTORY of the Holy Bible, interspersed with moral and instructive Reflections, by the Rev. J. Reeve, 12mo. illustrated, 6s.

A NEW VERSION OF THE FOUR GOSPELS; with Notes, Critical
and Explanatory, by a Catholic, 8vo. boards, 10s. 6d.

Amongst the principal reasons which have led to this *New Version*, are—*first*, to
show, in opposition to the Protestant principle, that the Scriptures are the *sole rule
of faith*,—" The impracticability of drawing from the narratives of the FOUR
EVANGELISTS, without the aid of *oral testimony or tradition*, all their knowledge of
Christian faith, or Christian practice."—*Vide* PREFACE.

2ndly, To present a new translation from the *Original Greek*, with explanatory
and interesting notes; which, in removing the defects that exist in the present
versions, and offering a more elegant translation of these divinely-inspired books,
should render them more intelligible and attractive, and thus create a more general
attention to their perusal.

It is also meant, hereby, to refute the false and unfounded assertions, " that
Catholics are deficient in BIBLICAL CRITICISM, and dare not attempt it;" and,
" that they forbid, or impede the reading the Holy Scriptures;" accusations which
they reject with indignation.

Church Service.

THE MISSAL FOR THE USE OF THE LAITY; with the Masses for
all the Days throughout the Year, according to the Roman Missal; and those for
the English Sain's in their respective places. Newly arranged and in great
measure translated by the Rev. F. C. Husenbeth, 3rd edition, improved, price
6s. 6d. in sheep lettered, and 8s. in calf.

N.B. The Missal may be had either with or without Plates, at the option of the
purchaser. Some copies are kept bound in the Ancient Monastic Style of the
Middle Ages, from designs by A. Welby Pugin, Esq.; adorned with brass corners
and clasps in the same style; and some are splendidly bound in rich velvet, with
metal gilt corners and clasps.

THE VESPERS BOOK, for the use of the Laity, according to the Roman
Breviary; with the offices of the English Saints and those recently inserted in the
Calendar, in their respective places, newly arranged and translated by the Rev. F.
C. Husenbeth, price 4s. 6d. bound in coloured sheep, lettered.

ADDRESS.—This edition of the Vespers Book will be found to possess some
valuable recommendations. It is arranged strictly in accordance with the Roman
Breviary, so that the Proper of Saints follows immediately after the Sundays, and
the Common of Saints has its appropriate place at the end. The Hymns, and the
Antiphons after Complin, are all newly translated, in the same metre as the Latin
originals.

Several offices, which in former Vespers Books were inaccurately given, are
here corrected; others, subsequently raised to a higher rite, are properly noted;
and the offices of saints more recently introduced, inserted in their proper places.

The version of the Prayers is the same as in the Missal by the same editor : the
two works are arranged and printed to correspond with each other : and it is hoped
that the encouraging patronage which the Missal has experienced will be extended
to this much improved edition of the Vespers Book.—COSSEY, June 26th, 1841.

APPROBATIONS.

" We approve of the " Vespers Book for the use of the Laity," newly arranged and
translated by the Rev. F. C. Husenbeth; and permit the publication and use of
it in our respective Districts.

    † WILLIAM, *Bishop of Ariopolis, V.A.E.D.*
    † PETER AUGUSTIN, *Bishop of Siga, V.A.W.D.*
    † THOMAS, *Bishop of Cambysopolis, V.A.C.D.*
    † NICHOLAS, *Bishop of Melipotamus, Coadjutor.*
    † JOHN, *Bishop of Trachis, V.A.Y.D.*
    † THOMAS, *Bishop of Olena, V.A. Lond. D.*
    † GEORGE, *Bishop of Bugia, V.A. Lanc. D.*
    † THOMAS JOSEPH, *Bishop of Appolonia, V.A. Welsh D.*
    † FRANCIS, *Bishop of Abydos, V.A.N.D.*

ORDINARY of the Mass, in Latin and English, 12mo. large print, sewed, 1s. 6d.
SELECTIONS from Merati on the Ceremonies of the Church, translated into English, 12mo. cloth boards, reduced to 1s. 6d.
TENEBRÆ, or Evening Office of Holy Week, 18mo. bound, 1s. 6d.
ORDO Administrandi Sacramenta et alia quædam Officia Ecclesiastica Rite Peragenda in Missione Anglicana, sewed 2s. 6d. in black calf, 5s.
RITUALE Romanum Pauli V. jussu editum, 18mo. 2s. 6d.
MISSALE Romanum, with the "Missæ propriæ pro Anglia," folio, morocco, gilt edges, 5l. 5s.
—— Idem, red and black type, 12mo. sewed, a most beautifully printed work, 10s. 6d.
PONTIFICALE Romanum, Clementis VIII. et Urbani VIII. Auctor, Recog. cum Figuris æri incisis, 3 vols. 8vo. sewed, 15s.
—— Romanum, Clem. VIII. Urbani VIII. inde vero a Benedicto XIV. recog. et castig. 12mo. sewed, 12s.
PROCESSIONALE Romanum pro Ecclesiis Urbanis et Ruralibus, 4to. 9s. 6d.
SUPPEMENTUM novum ad Breviarium et Missale Romanum, 8vo. 4s.
—— novum ad Breviarium Monasticon adjectis officiis Sanctorum Angliæ, 8vo. 9s.
—— ad Breviarium, containing the New Offices appointed in the Ordo Recitandi of 1841, in red and black type, 8vo. and 12mo. price 6d. each.
THE RITE of the Consecration of Bishops in the Catholic Church, 12mo. 6d.

Church Music.

WEBBE'S Collection of Masses, with an accompaniment for the Organ, particularly designed for the use of small choirs, bound, 10s. 6d.
—— Ditto, Motetts, or Antiphons, for 1, 2, 3, 4, voices or chorus, calculated for the more solemn parts of divine worship, bound, 10s. 6d.
—— COLLECTION of Sacred Music, as used at the Sardinian Chapel, 12s.
CANTICA Vespera. The Psalms chaunted at Vespers and Complin, adapted to the Gregorian Tones, by J. Alfred Novello, 8vo. 2s.

N.B. Novello's Church Music procured to order.

Prayer-Books.

ARDENT LOVER of Jesus, or Soul elevated to Jesus in the Adorable Sacrament, 18mo. bd. 1s. 6d.
BONA MORS, or the Art of Dying Happily, 32mo. bd. 8d.
CATHOLIC HOURS, or the Family Prayer Book, 24mo. embossed roan and gilt, 3s.; sheep, 2s.
THE CATHOLIC'S Prayer-book, or the Exercises of a Christian Life, by the Rev. Dr. Fletcher, 18mo. bd. 3s.
CHRISTIAN'S Guide to Heaven, 18mo. bd. 3s. 6d.
DAILY COMPANION, or little Pocket Manual, 32mo. bd. 1s.
—— Exercises for Children, with Woodcuts and the First Catechism, 32mo. bd. 1s.
DEVOUT PRAYER to our Blessed Redeemer, in honour of his bitter Passion, 12mo. sewed, 3d.
DEVOTIONS to the Sacred Heart of Jesus, containing Exercises for Confession, Communion, and the Holy Mass, &c. translated from the French by the Rev. J. Joy Dean, 12mo. bd. 4s. 6d.
—— to the Three Hours' Agony of Christ, 32mo. bd. 10d.
THE DEVOUT COMMUNICANT, or Pious Meditations and Aspirations for three days before and after receiving the HOLY EUCHARIST. To which is added, a method of visiting the Blessed Sacrament with fervent Prayers and Acts of Devótión. By the Rev. P. Baker, O.S.F. A new edition, in good type, 18mo. sheep, 2s.
THE DIAMOND CATHOLIC MANUAL, containing Spiritual Exercises and Devotions, with the Ordinary of the Mass in Latin and English, 48mo. cloth, 1s.; roan tuck, 2s.; roan embossed, 2s. 6d.
FLOWERS OF PIETY, selected from approved sources, and adapted for general use, 48mo. cloth, 1s.; roan, gilt edges, 2s. 6d.
GRIFFETT'S Method of Mass, applied to Holy Communion, 4d.

GARDEN OF THE SOUL, or Manual of Spiritual Exercises and Instructions, new stereotype edition, approved by the Right Rev. Vicar Apostolic in the London District, sheep, 1s. 4d.

    N.B.—To the Clergy for distribution, at only 14s. per dozen.
—— the same on fine paper, bd. calf gilt, 4s.

    N.B.—It is also kept in morocco and other bindings, in great variety.

GOTHER'S Prayers for Sundays and Festivals, adapted to the use of Private Families or Congregations, with an Appendix, containing Prayers before and after Mass, and Evening Devotions, 18mo. bd. 3s. 6d.

HOHENLOHE'S Prayer-Book, or the Christian praying in the spirit of the Catholic Church, new edition, with the Ordinary of the Mass, 18mo. calf gilt, 4s.
—— the same, common edition, 18mo. bd. 1s. 6d.

JAMELIN'S Manual of Prayers, with an Explanation of the Ceremonies of the Mass, &c. 12mo. bd. 4s.

JOURNÉE DU CHRÉTIEN, large print, 12mo. sewed, 3s.
—— the same, by M. De la Hogne, 24mo. sewed, 2s. 6d.
—— the same, fine paper, calf gilt, 4s. 6d.

THE KEY of Paradise, 18mo. bd. 3s.; calf gilt, 5s.

MANUAL of Devout Prayers, and other Christian Devotions, by the Right Rev. Dr. Challoner, 12mo. bd. 4s.
—— of Scriptural Prayer, and Practical Meditation, 12mo. sewed, 4s. 6d.

MANUEL du Chrétien, containing: Imitation de Jésus Christ—Les Pscaumes, Ordinaire de la Messe—Litanies, &c. 18mo. sewed, 3s.

THE MISSAL FOR THE USE OF THE LAITY, with the Masses for all the Days throughout the Year, according to the Roman Missal; and those for the English Saints in their respective places. Newly arranged, and in great measure translated by the Rev. F.C. HUSENBETH. 3rd edition, improved, price 6s. 6d. sheep lettered; in calf gilt, 8s.

    ⁎ This Missal is kept in a great variety of bindings, with or without plates, at various prices.
—— (Pocket) containing the Masses for every Sunday, 32mo. bd. 3s.

MOREL (Rev. F.) The Pious Communicant, or Devotions to Jesus Christ in the most Holy Sacrament of the Altar, 18mo. bd. 3s.

POSEY OF PRAYERS, or KEY OF HEAVEN, 18mo. bd. 2s. 6d.
—— Ditto ditto, fine paper, calf gilt, 4s. 6d.

PRAYERS before and after Mass for Country Congregations, 18mo. sewed, 6d.

PREPARATIONS for Death, 32mo. bd. 8d.

SACRAMENTAL Companion for three days before and after Confession and Communion, 32mo. cloth, 8d.

SOUL united to Jesus in his adorable Sacrament, 18mo. bd. 1s. 6d.

STATIONS and Devotions to the Passion of Christ, 32mo. bd. 1s.

TRUE PIETY, or a Day well spent, by Dr. Coppinger, 18mo. bd. 2s. 6d.

URSULINE MANUAL, a Collection of Prayers, Spiritual Exercises, &c. 12mo. good type, best edition, bd. 6s.; 18mo. Dublin edition, bd. 5s.

VESPERS BOOK, FOR THE USE OF THE LAITY, newly arranged and translated by the Rev. F.C. HUSENBETH, with the approbation of all the Right Rev. the Vicars Apostolic of England, price 4s. 6d. bound.

Prints.

A Selection of Coloured Prints from Paris, at various prices, always on Sale.
The Angel Guardian, 6 inches by 4, Sixpence.
The Crucifixion, engraved in outline, Sixpence.
St. Francis Xavier preaching to the Indians, 1s.

The following Prints, designed and engraved by A. Welby Pugin, Esq. price 6d. each.
The Celebration of High Mass—The Crucifixion, with the B.V.M. and St. John—
The Adoration of the Shepherds—The Annunciation of the B.V.M.—
The Resurrection—The Descent of the Holy Ghost.

Just published, a beautiful Engraving from the design of FREDERIC OVERBECK, of the
DEAD CHRIST AND THE BLESSED VIRGIN, engraved by
LEWIS GRUNER. Proofs on India paper, 4s ; plain prints, 1s. 6d.

Also,
THE GOOD SHEPHERD, by FREDERIC OVERBECK, engraved by
LEWIS GRUNER. Proofs on India paper, 3s.; plain prints, 1s. 6d.

Now in course of publication.
A SELECTION OF PLATES illustrative of the LIFE AND
PASSION OF OUR LORD JESUS CHRIST, engraved on steel, from the
designs of FREDERIC OVERBECK. Plain prints, 6d. each; on India paper, 1s. each.

Already published :
The Nativity—The Saviour seated, bearing the Cross—The Death of St. Joseph—The
Assumption of the B.V.M.—The Communion—Our Saviour at the Tomb—
Jesus stript of his Garments—The Resurrection.
. Four others are in the Engravers' hands.

THE VIRGIN AND CHILD, from Leonardo da Vinci, price 2s. 6d.

Portraits.

Of the Rev Thomas Southworth, engraved by Turner, 5s.
Pope Pius VII. 1s 6d.
the Rev. Dr. Fryer (proofs on India paper) 5s.
the Right Rev Dr. Wiseman (from a bust by Clint) 5s.
the Very Rev. Dr. Kirwan, 2s. 6d.

Views.

Of Ampleforth College, 1s 6d.
Ancient Crosses, Sandbach, Cheshire, 1s, 6d.
Antwerp Cathedral, 1s. 6d.
Of the English Benedictine College at Douay, 1s. 6d.
Exterior and Interior of the Catholic Chapel at Edinburgh, 3s. the pair.
——————— of St. Mary's Church at Derby, engraved by A. W. Pugin,
7s. 6d. the pair.
Exterior of the Old College of St. Mary's, Oscott, 1s. 6d.
Interior of the Chapel of the New College of St. Mary's, Oscott, engraved by
Pugin, 5s.
Pulpit in the Church of St. Gudule, at Brussels, 1s.
Interior and Exterior of the New Church of St. George, London, 2s.
——————————— of the Church of St. Barnabas, Nottingham (India proofs)
1s 6d. each.
——————————— St. Bernard's Abbey Church, Leicestershire (India proofs)
1s. 6d. each.
St. Gregory's College, Downside, near Bath, India proofs, 1s. 6d.
St. John's Chapel, Alton, India proofs, 1s. 6d.
——————— Hospital, India proofs, 1s. 6d.
Interior and Exterior of the Jesus Chapel, Pomfret, India proofs, 1s. 6d. each.

THE

ENGLISH CATHOLIC LIBRARY,

BEING

A REPUBLICATION OF SOME OF THE RARE CONTROVERSIAL
AND DEVOTIONAL WRITINGS OF THE FOLLOWING
AUTHORS:

SIR THOMAS MORE.	BISHOP SMITH.
BISHOP FISHER.	ANTHONY CHAMPNEY.
BISHOP GARDINER.	MATTHEW KELLISON.
BISHOP BONNER.	FRANCIS WALSINGHAM.
CARDINAL ALLEN.	SILVESTER NORRIS.
THOMAS HARDING.	LAURENCE ANDERTON.
THOMAS STAPLETON.	EDWARD KNOTT.
NICHOLAS SANDERS.	ARCHBISHOP TALBOT.
EDWARD BRISTOW.	ABRAHAM WOODHEAD.
GREGORY MARTIN.	THOMAS CARR.
ROBERT PERSONS.	WILLIAM CLIFFORD.
JOHN BRERELY.	EDWARD HAWARDEN.
FATHER BAKER.	

THE Subscribers and the Public are respectfully informed that this work will commence with a reprint of the "SEARCH INTO MATTERS OF RELIGION, BY FRANCIS WALSINGHAM," which is expected to be ready in about three months.

In accordance with a wish expressed by many of the Subscribers, the volumes will be printed uniform, in a smaller size (crown octavo) than was originally intended, in order that they may be sold at the lowest possible price.

Though the Publisher has thus resolved to commence the work, it is right to say that the list of Subscribers hitherto received has not yet reached the number originally considered necessary to secure him against loss. To the merits of his undertaking, however, he is still willing to trust his claims to future patronage; and, in the meantime, he will only add that the names of persons desirous of supporting the present publication on the condition before announced—namely, that of receiving their copies at one-fourth less than the publication price—will continue to be admitted until the 23rd of July.

61, *New Bond Street, May 31st,* 1842.

THE

ENGLISH CATHOLIC LIBRARY.

𝔘𝔫𝔡𝔢𝔯 𝔱𝔥𝔢 𝔓𝔞𝔱𝔯𝔬𝔫𝔞𝔤𝔢 𝔬𝔣

HIS GRACE THE DUKE OF NORFOLK, E.M.

THE RIGHT HON. LORD STOURTON.

THE RIGHT REV. DR. GRIFFITHS, V.A.

THE HONOURABLE EDWARD PETRE.

THE HONOURABLE CHARLES CLIFFORD.

THE extreme rarity of most of the works, written by the defenders of our holy faith, during the sixteenth and seventeenth centuries in this country, added to the intrinsic value of their contents, and the consequent avidity with which they are sought for and purchased, even at the high prices at which they are generally sold, has suggested the idea of supplying a deficiency, which has too long existed in Catholic literature. Whilst the Protestant press has been exercising its reproductive powers on the calumnies of JEWEL and others of our ancient adversaries, no effort has been made to arrest the progress of the evil, by the counteracting influences with which it was originally met. These books have been suffered to go forth to the world, as if they had never been confuted. The answers of STAPLETON have been forgotten: the triumphant replies of HARDING have been thrown aside; and the calm reasoning, the convincing arguments, and the affectionate earnestness of FISHER, SMITH, WALSINGHAM, and a host of others, have been left beyond the reach, and almost beyond the knowledge, of the general reader. Yet it is in the productions of these men, that the strong grounds of our faith, no less than the holy and abiding influences of our religion, are more beautifully set forth than perhaps in any other similar publications. They talk to us of what was passing centuries ago. They familiarize us with the struggles of the past, they remind us of the triumph of the present, and they teach us to look forward with confidence and exultation to the glorious consummation of the future. In them, in a word, we have all that can confute an adversary, or conciliate and convince a friend; and it is time, therefore, that their usefulness were generally known, that their power were made available for the propagation of truth, and that they were taken at length from the cupboard of the student, and the shelf of the collector, to be made accessible to the mass of the community.

It is with these feelings on their minds, and with a view to the formation of a STANDARD CATHOLIC LIBRARY, in which the choicest works of our old polemical and devotional writers may be found, that the projectors of the

3

present undertaking confidently place themselves before the public. Among the authors from whom their selections will be made, are—

SIR THOMAS MORE.	BISHOP SMITH.
BISHOP FISHER.	WILLIAM CRASHAWE.
BISHOP GARDINER.	ANTHONY CHAMPNEY.
BISHOP BONNER.	MATTHEW KELLISON.
CARDINAL ALLEN.	FRANCIS WALSINGHAM.
THOMAS HARDING.	SILVESTER NORRIS.
THOMAS STAPLETON.	LAURENCE ANDERTON.
NICHOLAS SANDERS.	EDWARD KNOTT.
EDWARD BRISTOW.	ARCHBISHOP TALBOT.
GREGORY MARTIN.	ABRAHAM WOODHEAD.
ROBERT PERSONS.	THOMAS CARR.
JOHN BRERELY.	WILLIAM CLIFFORD.
FATHER BAKER.	EDWARD HAWARDEN.

Each Author will be faithfully printed from the best edition, but in modern orthography: a short sketch of his life will be prefixed to the volume : and, where practicable, a portrait and facsimile of his handwriting will be added.

The Rev. M. A. TIERNEY, F.R.S., F.S.A., has consented to connect his name with the undertaking, as guiding the choice of works to be reprinted, and directing the supervision of each book through the press.

It is proposed to publish the works uniform, in octavo ; and it is the resolution of the publisher never to suffer the price to exceed (*it will frequently fall below*) TEN shillings the volume: the type and paper will invariably be of the best quality ; and the printing will commence so soon as

4

the promised support of TWO HUNDRED AND FIFTY subscribers shall have been obtained.

The first TWO HUNDRED AND FIFTY persons on the subscription list, will be entitled to receive their copies of the reprinted works, at one-fourth less than the publication price: while, in order to lighten the subscription as much as possible, it is intended to publish only four volumes within the year. Of these, one will appear every third month.

Persons, desirous of encouraging this undertaking, are respectfully invited to forward their names to MR. CHARLES DOLMAN, 61 NEW BOND STREET, LONDON, before the Feast of ST. GEORGE, THE PATRON OF ENGLAND, on the 23rd of April next.

RICHARDS, PRINTER, ST. MARTIN'S LANE.

THE

Church History of England,

FROM THE YEAR 1500 TO THE YEAR 1688,

CHIEFLY WITH REGARD TO CATHOLICS,

BY CHARLES DODD.

A New Edition,

WITH NOTES, AND A CONTINUATION TO THE BEGINNING OF
THE PRESENT CENTURY,

BY THE REV. M. A. TIERNEY, F.S.A.

THE Work of HUGH TOOTLE, better known under the assumed
name of CHARLES DODD, stands alone among the compilations of
Catholic History.   Commencing with the period of her first misfortunes in this country, the writer accompanies the ancient Church
in all the vicissitudes of her course, during the next two centuries.
He marks the origin of the Reformation in the wayward passions
of Henry : mourns, with religion, over the ruined altars and desecrated shrines of Edward's reign : watches their alternate rise and
fall under the sister sovereigns, Mary and Elizabeth ; and, tracing
the varied calamities of his Catholic countrymen under the dynasty
of the Stuarts, closes his work with the closing fortunes of that
unhappy family.   But it is not in the extensive range of the history,
nor in the interest, thrilling, as it must be, to every Catholic feeling,
that the whole merit of Dodd's performance consists.   To talents
of an eminent order, he added an industry peculiar to himself, a
patience of research seldom equalled, and a liberality of mind and
expression as admirable as, unfortunately, it is uncommon.   " In

the compilation of this work," says Mr. Berington, " he spent almost thirty years. It contains much curious matter, collected with great assiduity, and many original records. His style, when the subject admits expression, is pure and unencumbered,—his narrative easy,—his reflections just and liberal. I have seldom known a writer, and that writer a Churchman, so free from preju- dice, and the degrading impressions of party zeal."* " The attention," says Mr. Butler, speaking of himself, " which the writer has given to Dodd's History, has increased his opinion of the value, the importance, and the impartiality of the work."† " Having had repeated occasions to consult it," says the Protestant Mr. Chalmers, " we are ready to acknowledge our obligations to this History. . . . . . It remained for many years unknown, and we can remem- ber when it was sold almost at the price of waste paper. Its worth is now better ascertained ; and the last copy offered for sale, belong- ing to the Marquis Townshend's library, was sold for ten guineas."‡

The performance of Dodd is the history of the downfall of the Catholic religion in this country. On the one hand, we see the efforts of its enemies to overthrow, on the other, the struggles of its adherents to support and defend, it. The former are more gene- rally known: the latter, which abound with recollections of the most interesting kind, are, with few exceptions, to be found only in the pages of Dodd. Among these, are the foundation and history of the English colleges abroad,—the attempts to restore the hier- richy,—the institution of an arch-priest,—the appointment of the two bishops of Chalcedon,—the establishment and jurisdiction of the chapter,—the introduction of vicars-apostolic,—and the mission of Gregorio Panzani. Nor must we omit the biographical notices, so copiously scattered through the work. In this portion of his task, indeed, the talents and industry of the writer are eminently conspicuous. From sources inaccessible to others, from the diaries of colleges, and the unpublished correspondence of individuals, he has drawn a body of information at once original and important. He has sketched the lives of the most distinguished members of the Catholic community ; has described the works, and traced the

---

* Memoirs of Panzani, Pref. ix.   † Memoirs of Eng. Catholics, iv. 452.
‡ Biog. Dict. xii. 147. Since then, copies have sold as high as £17. 10s.

literary career, of its numerous writers; and, carrying us back to the period of its severest trial, has left the sufferings and the constancy of its martyrs to edify and improve the world. Such are a portion only of the interesting subjects contained in the Church History of England.

It is not, however, pretended that this great and important work is entirely free from imperfection. Dodd was not only a Catholic, but also a clergyman. Living, therefore, in a state of proscription, surrounded by alarms, and shut out from the intercourse of the learned, he was compelled to prosecute his studies in secret, and to send forth their result to the world without that final correction which they might, perhaps, otherwise have received. The sources, moreover, of his information were, in many instances, distant and far apart. A manuscript overlooked, or accidentally laid aside, would not be likely to reclaim attention: a transcript, made in haste, and imperfectly collated, could not afterwards be amended; and an error, though only in the name or date of an instrument, would, not unfrequently, lead to the most inaccurate representations of events. Hence, with all his excellencies, Dodd is sometimes defective, and frequently incorrect. With him, dates and names are too often mistaken, or confounded: transactions of stirring interest, or of lasting importance, are occasionally dispatched with the indifference of a passing allusion; and occurrences, that scarcely merit a casual notice, are swollen into consequence, with the fulness of a circumstantial detail. But the principal fault of the writer lies in the defective arrangement of his materials. This was long since complained of by Mr. Berington: it has been felt and noticed by all who have had occasion to consult the pages of the History; and, united with the want of a proper index, has, no doubt, contributed, in a great degree, to diminish the general usefulness of the work.

From the mention of these defects, the public will readily anticipate the design of the present edition. Where an error shall appear, it will be corrected; where an omission of consequence shall be discovered, it will be supplied. If the mistake extend only to a date, or affect only an immaterial portion of the narrative, it will be rectified, without notice, in the text. In other instances, whether of inaccuracy or of omission, a note will be inserted; and whatever the researches of later historians may have discovered, will invariably be added. It may be farther stated, that, of the MSS. referred to by Dodd, many have been brought to England, and are now, with numerous others, confided to the custody of the Editor. These will all be applied to the purposes of the present edition. The papers already printed will be collated; and many important documents, not hitherto published, will be inserted.

The arrangement of the different parts of the work is a more delicate task. To remodel is more difficult than to construct: alteration is, in general, but a bad apology for weakening an original design. In the present case, however, it has been thought, that, without injury to the author, his plan might, at least, be partially simplified and improved. The readers of Dodd are aware that his history is divided into eight parts, corresponding with the eight reigns over which it extends. Of these parts, each is again divided into the three other parts of History, Biography, and Records; and these are still farther subdivided into an indefinite number of articles, according to the variety of the subjects to be treated, or to the rank of the several persons whose lives are to be recorded. It is needless to point out the inconvenience of this complex and disjointed arrangement. To remedy the defect, it is proposed, in the present edition, to place the work under the two grand divisions of History and Biography; to print the History in the earlier, the Biography in the later, volumes; to subjoin to each volume an Appendix, containing its own records properly arranged; and to insert a reference in the notes to each article of that Appendix, according as its subject arises in the course of the narrative. It is only requisite to add, that the lives, in the biographical part, will be chronologically disposed; that the authorities, both of Dodd and of the Editor, will be carefully stated in the notes; and that a General Index to the contents of the whole work will be given at the end of the Continuation.

Of that Continuation it now becomes necessary to speak. The Revolution of 1688 has been denominated " the triumph of the Protestant over the Catholic Establishment." Yet the Catholics still existed as a body. They had contrived to organize a system of ecclesiastical government : they had preserved their foreign seminaries, for the supply of their missions, and for the education of their youth; and it required only the influence of a milder spirit on their rulers, to secure them in the possession of calmer and more prosperous years. That spirit was already awakened in Europe: it had begun to operate even in this country; and, accordingly, it is from that very event, which might have been expected to extinguish them as a body, that the reviving importance of the English Catholics may, in reality, be dated. It is through this happier period of their history that the continuator of Dodd will have to conduct his readers. It is not, indeed, to be expected, that the voice of intolerance will be instantly silenced, or that the uplifted arm of persecution will be suddenly arrested in its descent. New laws will still be enacted, and fresh attempts to extirpate the ancient religion of the country will still be made. But through the darkness of the time a growing light will be seen to spread: the better feelings of the country will gradually find a voice: the Catholics will continue to increase and consolidate their means of advancement; and the great day of religious toleration will at length burst upon the land. Such will be the general scope, such the happy and interesting conclusion of the proposed work.

Of the materials to be employed in the execution of this task, and of the sources whence those materials are to be derived, a short account may, perhaps, be expected. Following the example of his predecessor, the author has resolved to found his narrative, as far as possible, on original documents; to seek whatever information he can obtain from unpublished records; and, where the importance of a paper seems to require its insertion, to print it entire in the Appendix. Of such documents it fortunately happens that several large collections have been preserved. Some were rescued from the foreign colleges, at the period of the first French Revolution: others were gradually formed, in this country, by the persons to whose successors they now belong. They consist of private and official correspondence, between various members of the clergy themselves, or between the clergy and their agents, in Rome,—of bulls and public despatches,—of diaries and visitations of colleges, —and of various other papers, whose character it is unnecessary to describe more particularly in this place. With a liberality which

6   PROSPECTUS.
```

cannot be too warmly or too gratefully acknowledged, these have all been unreservedly placed in the hands of the author. There are some others, also, to which he still hopes to obtain access; and with them, and with such other documents as he expects will be transcribed for him abroad, he trusts that he shall have collected sufficient for the completion of his present undertaking.

To be Published in successive Octavo Volumes, price 12*s.* each.

*The First Volume to appear in April next, and to be completed in about Twelve or Fourteen Volumes.*

It is intended to print FIFTY COPIES on Large Paper, in *Royal Octavo*, to obtain which it will be necessary to send immediate orders.

**Subscribers' Names already received.**

HIS GRACE THE DUKE OF NORFOLK.
RIGHT REV. DR. BAINES, V.A.W.
RIGHT REV. DR. BRIGGS, V.A.N.
RIGHT REV. DR. GILLIS, V. A.
RIGHT REV. DR. GRIFFITHS, V.A.L.
HON. CHARLES CLIFFORD, *L. P.* 2 *copies.*
HON. EDWARD PETRE, *L. P.*
SIR EDWARD VAVASOUR, BART.

DR. BISSHOPP.
THOMAS BUCKLEY, ESQ. *L. P.*
REV. THOMAS DOYLE.
REV. DR. FLETCHER.
EDWARD FOXHALL, ESQ. *L. P.*
JOHN GAGE, ESQ. F.S.A.
REV. W. HOGARTH.
REV. J. HOLDSTOCK.
REV. E. HUDDLESTON.
REV. F. C. HUSENBETH.
HENRY HOWARD, ESQ.
F. C. HUSENBETH, ESQ.
REV. F. JARRETT, *L. P.*
REV. A. MAGEE
W. CONSTABLE MAXWELL, ESQ. *L. P.*
MARMADUKE MAXWELL, ESQ. *L. P.*
THOMAS MARTIN, ESQ.
THOMAS MOORE, ESQ.
G. R. MORGAN, ESQ.

DANIEL O'CONNELL, ESQ. M.P. 2 *copies.*
REV. JULIUS PICQUOT.
A. WELBY PUGIN, ESQ.
REV. JOSEPH RENDER.
JOHN REES, ESQ.
HENRY ROBINSON, ESQ.
REV. JOHN ROLFE,
    PRESIDENT OF ST. EDMUND'S COLLEGE.
JAMES SCOLES, ESQ.
JOHN SELBY, ESQ.
JOHN STARR, ESQ.
HON. GEORGE TALBOT.
W. VAUGHAN, ESQ.
REV. W. VAUGHAN.
REV. DR. WEEDALL, 2 *copies,*
    PRESIDENT OF ST. MARY'S COLL., OSCOTT.
JOSEPH WELD, ESQ.
REV. J. WHITE.
REV. W. WILDS.
REV. DR. YOUENS.

*N.B. A complete List of Subscribers will be printed in the last volume.*

**London:**
BOOKER AND DOLMAN, 61, NEW BOND STREET.

PRINTED BY C. RICHARDS, ST. MARTIN'S LANE
```

redeem the loss of all their substance, by an exorbitant composition. Not to enter upon the legality of this proceeding, it was an indication of king Henry's temper, and that he was resolved to stretch the laws as far as they would go, to the prejudice of the see of Rome. But of these matters I shall have an occasion to speak more at large hereafter.[a]

Most part of the year 1531 being spent, without any progress in the controversy of the divorce, and the king's late proceedings against the see of Rome rather prognosticating a farther rupture, than an agreement, this induced the French to interpose, and appear as mediators. For, though hitherto they had been great sticklers for the divorce, when they were in hopes thereby to bring about a match between king Henry and a princess of France, yet, when they came to be fully convinced that Anne Boleyn was the person made choice of, their zeal and politics drew them another way; but so, that they would omit nothing towards keeping up a good understanding with the king of England. It had been agreed between the two kings, that they should have an interview. When

[a] [In the Appendix, No. xxvi, will be found a despatch from Dr. Bennet to the king, containing some additional information, on the subject of Henry's proceedings during the present year. In January, Bennet had accompanied the earl of Wiltshire, in his mission to the emperor and the pope, at Bologna. He was afterwards employed to continue the negotiation with Clement, and, when the latter returned to Rome, was ordered to proceed, in quality of envoy, to that city. His instructions were, to act in concert with the bishop of Tarbes, now elevated to the dignity of cardinal; to solicit a commission either for the prelates of Canterbury, London, and Lincoln, or, if that were refused, for the clergy of the archdiocese of Canterbury, empowering them to hear and decide the cause of the divorce, in England; and, supposing this request to have failed, to enquire whether, in the event of Henry's taking the matter into his own hands, and deciding it according to the dictates of his conscience, the pontiff would engage to abstain from all interference, either by inhibition, interdict, or otherwise. If the answer were unfavourable, he was then to seek an extension of time, and to demand that all farther proceedings should be stayed for the present. Clement listened to the application, and replied at once to the demand. To the commission he had no objection, provided the queen's consent could be obtained. But he would enter into no engagement as to the future. The queen had appealed to his tribunal: justice and duty alike required that he should listen to her; and neither king nor emperor should induce him to swerve from the line, which that justice and that duty prescribed. On the subject of delay, he would willingly gratify the king. Still, it was necessary to consult the other side. He had, therefore, already written to the emperor, stating the wishes of the English monarch, and requesting his assent to such

1532 they were met, which was in October, 1532, among other matters, something was proposed, tending towards a reconciliation between king Henry and the see of Rome; and it was agreed, that the two French cardinals, Tournon and Grammont, being soon after to go to Rome on the French king's affairs, should, at the same time, use their endeavours with his holiness, in favour of the king of England. The general method proposed was, that, whereas a meeting and conference was, in a little time, to be appointed between the pope and the king of France, it would be very convenient if the king of England would contrive to be one at that conference, where, face to face, they might talk over what related to that great and tedious contest which had been between them. When the two French cardinals arrived at Rome, they dissembled not the case with his holiness: they told him plainly, that they had observed such dispositions in the king of England, that they believed he would make an entire breach with the see of Rome, if he did not obtain a divorce; wherefore, they earnestly begged of his holiness, that, all politic considerations

---

an arrangement; and, as he should probably receive an answer to his letter within the space of three weeks, he would, to manifest his affection for the king, suspend the progress of the suit for that term. It is needless to add, that this reply failed to satisfy the desires of Henry.

There is another subject, incidentally mentioned in Bennet's despatch, to which I will here briefly advert. The reader will recollect the enquiries formerly proposed by Henry, as to the possibility of obtaining a dispensation to have two wives. These enquiries, as I have already remarked, were addressed, not to the pope, but to the canonists at Rome. The suggestion, however, became known; Clement resolved to turn it to advantage; and, in one of his first conversations with Bennet, casually mentioned the expedient, as a matter not undeserving of consideration. On these facts, bishop Burnet, assisted by the more than doubtful authority of Gregory da Casali, has founded a charge against the pontiff, of a willingness to countenance polygamy (i. 90.) The present despatch, however, satisfactorily disposes of the accusation. It shews that it was to Bennet, not to Casali, that Clement mentioned the subject; that it was proposed for the purpose either of amusing Henry, or of raising an argument against him; and that, instead of admitting, the pope distinctly denied, the validity of any dispensation, which should pretend to authorize a marriage with two women at the same time. Casali's letter, which has supplied Burnet with the grounds of his accusation, is in *Herbert*, 330. From a comparison of dates, it is not improbable that the writer had heard something of the conversation between Clement and Bennet, and, without knowing the details, had hastened to communicate it to Henry, as a proof of his zeal in the service of that monarch.—*T.*]

A CATALOGUE OF BOOKS,

In Various Languages,

COMPRISING MANY

SCARCE & VALUABLE THEOLOGICAL WORKS,

Fathers of the Church, &c.

OFFERED FOR SALE AT THE PRICES ANNEXED,

BY

CHARLES DOLMAN,

No. 61, NEW BOND STREET, LONDON.

☞ *Orders for Articles from this and* C. DOLMAN's *other Catalogues are received at Liverpool by* BOOKER & Co. 37, *Ranelagh Street.*

1565 ACKERMANN (F.) Archæologia Biblica breviter exposita,8vo.10s.6d. *Viennæ*,1826
1566 Actes de l'Assemblée générale du Clergé de France de MDCLXXXV, concernant la Religion, avec Reflexions, 18mo. 1s. 6d.   1685
1567 Adoration perpétuelle du Saint Sacrement de l'Autel érigée dans l'Eglise de St. Germain en Laye, 18mo. 1s.6d.   *Paris*, 1707
1568 Amante (l') du Sauveur honorant le Sacré Cœur de Jésus, zélée pour le salût des Ames, &c. 18mo. 1s.   *ib.* 1798
1569 Ambroise, (S.) Les Offices de, traduit par l'Abbé de Bellegarde,12mo.3s. *ib.*1689
1570 ―― Vie de, par M. Godefroy Hermant, 4to. 8s. 6d.   *ib.* 1678
1571 Ame unie à Jésus Christ dans le très Saint Sacrement de l'Autel, ou preparations pour la Sainte Communion, 2 vols. 12mo. *calf gilt,* 8s.   *ib.* 1833
1572 Annales de la Propagation de la Foi, Receuil périodique, faisant suite à toutes les editions des Lettres Edifiantes, vols. 1 to 9, 8vo. *sewed,* 2l. 5s. *Lyon,* 1837
1573 Antoine Theologia Moralis Universa, 4 vols. 12mo. 6s.   *Leodii,* 1779
1574 Arvisinet, Sapientia Christiana, 2 vols. 12mo. 5s.   *Mechlin,* 1818
1575 Asseline, Œuvres Choisies, par M. l'Abbé Premord, 6 vols.12mo. 15s. *Paris,* 1823
1576 Association à la Dévotion, et l'amour des Sacrés Cœurs de Jésus et de Marie, 32mo. 1s. 6d.   *Besançon,* 1833
1577 Athanase (S. Patriarche d'Alexandre) Vie de, avec l'histoire de St. Eustache, St. Hilaire, St. Eusèbe, des Papes Jules et Libère, avec la naissance et le progrès de l'Arianisme, par M. Godefroy Hermant, 2 vols. 8vo.12s. *Paris,*1672
1578 Avrillon, Esprit de, avec sa Vie, par Oudoul, 18mo. 3s.6d.   *ib.* 1836
1579 - ―― Conduite pour passer saintement le temps de l'Avent,12mo. 3s.6d. *ib.*1827
1580 ―― Conduite pour passer saintement le Carême, 12mo. 3s. 6d.   *ib.* 1811
1581 Augustini (S.) De Civitate Dei, lib. xxii. notis Lud. Vivis, 8vo. 6s.   1622
1582 ―― Six Livres contre Julien, défenseur de l'hérésie Pelagienne, 2 vols. 12mo. 5s.   *Paris,* 1736
1583 ―― Morale tirée de ses Confessions, par l'Abbé Grou, 2 vols.12mo.6s. *ib.*1786
1584 Baronii (C.) Epitome Annalium Ecclesiasticorum Spondani, 3 vols. folio, 1l. 1s.   *Lugduni,* 1660
1585 Barradii, Comment. in Conc. et Hist. in Evangelistas, 4 vols. in 2, folio, 1l.4s.
                                                                    Antwerp, 1613
1586 Basile (S.) Lettres de, traduites du Grec, 8vo. 5s.   *Paris,* 1693

C. RICHARDS, PRINTER, ST. MARTIN'S LANE, CHARING CROSS.

1587 Basile (S.) Les Ascetiques, ou Traitez Spirituels, traduit par G. Hermant, 8vo.
5s. 6d.   *Paris,* 1779
1588 Baudrand, L'Ame affermie dans la Foi, et prémunie contre la séduction de
l'Erreur, 12mo. 3s.   *ib.* 1802
1589 ―― L'Ame sur le Calvaire, considérant les souffrances de Jésus Christ, 12mo.
bound, 4s.   *Valognes,* 1827
1590 ―― L'Ame élevée à Dieu, par les Reflexions et les Sentimens pour chaque
jour du mois, 12mo. *bound, 4s. 6d.*   *Lyon,* 1809
1591 ―― le même, suivie de l'Ame Penitente, 12mo. *bound, 5s.*   *Paris,* 1834
1592 ―― L'Ame Intérieure, ou Conduite Spirituelle dans les voies de Dieu, 12mo.
3s. 6d.   *Lyon,* 1802
1593 ―― Histoires Edifiantes et Curieuses, avec Reflexions Morales, 12mo. 4s.
Tours, 1832
1594 ―― le même, 12mo. 2s. 6d.   *Rouen,* 1815
1595 Beautés de l'Histoire Sainte, ou Epoques intéressantes, belles actions, &c.―
Ouvrage propre à orner le cœur et l'esprit de la Jeunesse, par H. Lemaire,
12mo. 2s. 6d.   *Paris,* 1816
1596 Bellarmini, (Card.) De eterna felicitate Sanctorum, lib. v. 18mo. 3s. *Colon.* 1618
1597 ―― De Officio Principis Christiani, lib. iii. 18mo. 2s. 6d.   *ib.* 1619
1598 Belle Mort (La) exprimée en la personne d'un jeune enfant devôt à Notre
Dame, avec une pratique de bien mourir, 18mo. 1s.   *Paris,* 1666
1599 Bell' Haver, (Th.) Dottrina facile et breve per ridurre l'Hebræo al conoscimento
del vero Messia, et Salvator del Mondo, 4to. 3s. 6d.   *Venezia,* 1608
1600 Bergier, Certitude des Preuves du Christianisme, 2 vols. 12mo. 4s. *Paris,* 1771
1601 Berti (J. L.) Breviarium Historiæ Ecclesiasticæ, 8vo. scarce, 6s. *Bassani,* 1791
1602 Bible Sainte, avec des notes, par M. de Saci, 12 vols. 12mo. 18s. *Paris,* 1713
1603 Biblia Sacra, Vulg. Ed. 8vo. 12s.   *ib.* 1838
1604 Bienfaits de la Religion, ou Histoire des Institutions et des Etablissemens utiles
qu'elle a fondés, &c. par M. Delacroix, 18mo. 2s. 6d.   *ib.* 1833
1605 Biroat (J.) Sermons sur les Mystères de Notre Seigneur, 8vo. 2s. 6d. *ib.* 1671
1606 ―― Sermons de la Penitence, 8vo. 2s. 6d.   *ib.* 1673
1607 Biveri (R. P. Petro) Sacrum Oratorium Piarum Imaginum Immaculatæ Mariæ
et Animæ Creatæ ac Baptismo, Pœnitentia et Eucharistia Innovatæ Ars
Nova Bene Vivendi et Moriendi, Emblematis et Illustrata, 4to. 26 plates,
some wanting, 15s.   *Antwerp,* 1634
1608 Boldetti, Osservazioni sopra i Cimiteri de Santi Martiri ed Antichi Cristiani
di Roma, folio, *vellum, many plates,* 1l. 8s.   *Roma,* 1720
1609 Bonaventuræ (S.) Opuscula, folio, 1l.8s.   *Lugduni,* 1647
1610 Borderies, (M. *Evêque de Versailles*) Œuvres de, précédées d'une notice sur sa
Vie, 4 vols. 12mo. 12s.   *Paris,* 1834
1611 Bossuet. De la Connaissance de Dieu et de Soi-même, 12mo. bd. 3s.6d. *ib.* 1819
1612 ―― Exposition de la Doctrine de l'Eglise Catholique, 12mo. 1s. 6d. *ib.* 1686
1613 ―― Elévations à Dieu sur tous les Mystères de la Religion Chrétienne, 12mo.
3s. 6d.   *ib.* 1727
1614 ―― Explication de l'Apocalypse, 12mo. 4s.   *Louvain,* 1741
1615 ―― Traitez du Libre Arbitre, et de la Concupiscence, 12mo. 3s.   *Paris,* 1742
1616 ―― Opuscules de, 5 vols. 12mo. 15s.   *ib.* 1751
1617 ―― Histoire des Variations des Eglises Protestantes, 5 vols.12mo.12s.6d. *ib.*1770
1618 Boudon, l'Amour de Dieu seul, ou la Vie de la Sœur Marie Angelique de la
Providence, 12mo. *bound, 3s.*   *Lyon,* 1825
1619 Bremont, Abbé, de la Raison dans l'Homme, 5 vols. 10s.   *Paris,* 1785
1620 Breviare Romain, (en Latin) 4 vols. 8vo. red and black type, 1l.4s. *ib.* 1706
1621 Breviarium Monasticum Supplementum Novum, adjectis Officiis Sanctorum
Angliæ, 8vo. *boards,* 6s.   *Liverpool,* 1832
1622 Breviarium Romanum, complete in 1 vol. 12mo. *sewed,* 18s.   *Lugduni,* 1836

1623 Brevini, (J.) Vita Christi abscondita S. R. E. Justitiam defendens, imputativam evertens, 2 vols. in 1, 12mo. 3*s.* 6*d.* *Rome,* 1679
1624 Canisii (Petri, *Soc. Jesu*) Opus Catechisticum, sive de Summa Doctrinæ Christianæ præclaris Divinæ Scripturæ Testimoniis, Sanctorumque Patrum Sententiis sedulo illustratum Opera D. Petri Busæi, fol. *neat,* 1*l.*4*s.* *Colon.*1577
1625 Canonization of St. Ignatius Loyola, St. Francis Xavier, St. Isidore, St. Philip Neri, and St. Theresa, by Gregory XV, on March 12, 1622, illustrated in 25 plates of the Ceremonies, and 5 plates, portraits of the Saints, engraved by M. Gzeuter, folio, 14*s.* *Rome,* 1622
1626 Cantiques de St. Sulpice, avec tous les Airs en Musique, 18mo. *bd.*2*s.* *Paris,*1826
1627 Carron, le Beau Soir de la Vie, ou Traité sur l'Amour Divin, 18mo. *bound,* 2*s.* 6*d.* *Londres,* 1807
1628 —— les Attraits de la Morale, ou la Vertu parée de tous ses Charmes, 12mo. 3*s.* *ib.* 1813
1629 —— de l'Education, ou Tableaux des plus doux Sentimens de la Nature, 2 vols. 18mo. 4*s.* *Paris,* 1819
1630 Carron, Abbé, les Ecoliers Vertueux, 12mo. 3*s.* 6*d.* *Londres,* 1811
1631 —— le même, 2 vols. 18mo. 4*s.* *Paris,* 1817
1632 Castori, (B, *Soc. Jesu*) Institutione Civile e Christiana per uno, che desideri vivere tanto in Corte, come altrove honoratamente, e Christianamente, 4to. 5*s.* *Roma,* 1622
1633 Catéchisme de Montpellier, ou Instructions Générales en forme de Catéchisme, 5 vols. 12mo. 12*s.* 6*d.* *Brusselle,* 1722
1634 —— le même, 3 vols. 12mo. 7*s.* 6*d.* *Paris,* 1739
1635 Caussini (N.) Tragœdiæ Sacræ, 18mo. 2*s.* *Col. Ag.* 1621
1636 Cérémonial du Sacre des Rois de France, 12mo. 3*s.* 6*d.* *Paris,* 1775
1637 Cérémonies des Petites-Messes, représentées en 35 figures, avec leur conformités à la Passion de N. S. J. C. 12mo. 5*s.* *ib.*
1638 Charles Borromée, (St.) Office Propre de, 12mo. 2*s.* *ib.* 1758
1639 Châteaubriand, Génie du Christianisme, ou Beautés de la Religion Chrétienne, 2 vols. 12mo. 5*s.* *ib.* 1809
1640 —— Génie du Christianisme, 2 vols. 12mo. *half-bound,* 4*s.* *ib.* 1808
1641 Chefs-d'Œuvres d'Eloquence Chrétienne, ou Sermons de Bourdaloue, Bossuet, Fénélon, Massillon, sur la Vérité de la Religion, 2 vols. 12mo. 8*s.* *ib.* 1810
1642 Chemin du Ciel, dédié aux Officiers, 32mo. 1*s.* 3*d.* *Avignon,* 1811
1643 Chemin de la Sanctification, ou le Vrai Conducteur des Ames dans la Voie du Saint, 18mo. *bound,* 2*s.* 6*d.* *Beaune,* 1830
1644 Choix des Lettres Edifiantes, écrites des Missions Etrangères, 8 vols. 8vo. *sewed,* 1*l.* 12*s.* *Paris,* 1835
1645 Chrétien Etranger sur la Terre, ou les Sentimens et les Devoirs d'une Ame Fidèle qui se regarde comme étrangère en ce monde, 12mo. 3*s.*6*d.* *ib.*1782
1646 Chrétien Sanctifié par les Pieux Exercises, par M. l'Abbé La Sausse, 12mo. *bound,* 4*s.* *ib.* 1819
1647 Chrétien au pied de la Croix, ou Choix des Méditations sur la Passion, 32mo. *bound,* 2*s.* *ib.* 1830
1648 Chronologie des Saints, ou les Points Principaux de la Vie et de la Mort de ceux que l'Eglise honore d'un culte public, 8vo. 4*s.* 6*d.* *ib.* 1707
1649 Clement, Elévations de l'Ame à Dieu, ou Prières tirées de l'Ecriture Sainte, 18mo. *bound,* 2*s.* 6*d.* *St. Brieux,* 1818
1650 —— Entretiens de l'Ame avec Dieu, tirées des Paroles de St. Augustin, 18mo. 2*s.* *Paris,* 1774
1651 Cœur Chrétien, ou Instructions sur les Indulgences et la Jubilé, en forme de Dialogues, suivies d'Exercises, 24mo. 1*s.* 6*d.* *ib.* 1802
1652 Collet, Méditations pour servir aux Retraites, soit annuelles, soit d'un Jour par Mois, pour les Personnes consacrées à Dieu, 12mo. 3*s.* 6*d.* *ib.* 1769

1653 Collet, l'Ecolier Chrétien, ou Traité des Devoirs d'un Jeune Homme, 18mo.
    1*s.* 6*d.*   *Lyon,* 1783
1654 Collombet, Histoire Civile et Religieuse des Lettres Latines au IVe et au Ve
    Siècle, 8vo. 8*s.* 6*d.*   *Paris,* 1839
1655 Concilii Tridentini Catechismus, ad Ordinandos, 12mo. 3*s.* 6*d.*   *ib.* 1717
1656 Conduite pour conserver la Piété Chrétienne, à l'usage des Enfans, 18mo.
    2*s.*   *Lyon,* 1826
1657 Conduite pour la Première Communion, avec la Vie d'un Enfant après sa
    Première Communion, pour en conserver le Fruit, 18mo. 2*s.*6*d. Paris,* 1802
1658 Consolation du Chrétien, ou Motifs de Confiance en Dieu dans les Diverses
    Circonstances de la Vie, par *Roisard,* 12mo. *bound,* 3*s.* 6*d.*   *ib.* 1824
1659 —— le même, 2 vols. 12mo. *bound,* 6*s.*   *ib.* 1818
1660 Consolations (les) de la Religion dans la perte des Personnes qui nous sont
    chères, 18mo. 2*s.* 6*d.*   *ib.* 1832
1661 Consolations des Divines Ecritures, 2 vols. 18mo. 3*s.*   *ib.* 1798
1662 Conversations sur plusieurs sujets de Morale, propres à former les Jeunes
    Demoiselles à la Piété, 12mo. 3*s.*   *Lyon,* 1814
1663 Costeri Enchiridion Controversiarum præcipuum nostri temporis de Religione,
    in gratiam Sodalitatis B. V. Mariæ, 12mo. 4*s.* 6*d.*   *Col. Ag.* 1600
1664 Courbon, les Colloques du Calvaire, ou Méditations sur la Passion de N. S. Jésus
    Christ, 18mo. *bound,* 2*s.* 6*d.*   *Marseille,* 1830
1665 —— Entretiens Spirituels sur les Devoirs des Personnes consacrées à Dieu,
    12mo. 3*s.* 6*d.*   *Paris,* 1752
1666 Crasset, le Chrétien en Solitude, 12mo. *bound,* 5*s.*   *ib.* 1829
1667 Cyprien (S.) consolant les Fidèles persecutés de l'Eglise de France, par l'Abbé
    de la Hogue, 12mo. 2*s.*   *Londres,* 1797
1668 Cyrilli (S.) Apologi Morales, ex antiquæ MS. codicæ, in lucem editi per B.
    Corderium, 18mo. 3*s.* 6*d.*   *Vien.* 1630
1669 Daniel, (G.) Traité Théologique touchant l'efficacité de la Grâce, 12mo.
    2*s.*   *Paris,* 1705
1670 De la Hogue, Tractatus de Religione, 12mo. 6*s.*   *Dublin,* 1820
1671 De la Rue, Panégyriques des Saints, 3 vols. 12mo. 7*s.* 6*d.*   *Paris,* 1740
1672 —— Sermons pour le Carême, 3 vols. 12mo. 7*s.* 6*d.*   *Lyon,* 1719
1673 Dens Theologia Moralis, 7 vols. 8vo. 1*l.* 11*s.* 6*d.*   *Mechlin,* 1838
1674 —— Idem, 8 vols. 12mo. 1*l.*16*s.*   *Dublin,* 1832
1675 Dévotion au Sacre Cœur de N. S. Jésus Christ, établie parmi les Religieuses de
    la Visitation, 12mo. *bound,* 4*s.*   *Nancy,* 1803
1676 Dévotion aux Souffrances et à la Croix de N. S. Jésus Christ, 12mo. 2*s.*6*d.*
                                                          Paris, 1811
1677 Diario Sacro d'Esercizj di Divizione per onorare Ogni Giorno la Beatissima
    Vergine, tomo primo, January to March, 18mo. 2*s.* 6*d.*   *Venezia,* 1738
1678 Dictionarium Pauperum, vel Cornucopiæ Concionatorum Verbi Dei, A. F. P.
    Rodulphio à Tossignano, 8vo. 3*s.* 6*d.*   *Lugduni,* 1599
1679 Didaci de Beza, (Soc. Jesu) Commentariorum Allegoricorum et Moralium de
    Christo figurato in Veteri Testamento, folio, 7 vols. in 3, 1*l.*1*s.* *ib.* 1641
1680 Dorothée (St.) Père de l'Eglise Grecque, Instructions de, 8vo. 5*s.*6*d. Paris,* 1686
1681 Drach, Deuxième Lettre d'un Rabbin Converti aux Israelites ses Frères sur
    les motifs de sa Conversion, 8vo. 3*s.* 6*d.*   *ib.* 1827
1682 Duquesne, les Grandeurs de Marie, ou Méditations pour chaque Octave des
    Fêtes de la Ste Vierge, 2 vols. 12mo. *bound,* 7*s.*   *Avignon,* 1823
1683 Du Voisin, (J.) De Vera Religione ad usum Theol. Cand. 2 vols. 12mo. 6*s.*
                                                          Paris, 1785
1684 Eclaircissemens touchant l'Usage de toutes les parties du Sacrement de
    Penitence, addressez aux Pasteurs, par M. G. de Choyseul, Evesque de
    Tournay, 12mo. 4*s.*   *Lille,* 1683

1685 Economie de la Providence dans l'Etablissement de la Religion, suite de la Religion defendue contre l'Incrédulité du Siècle, 2 vols. 18mo. 4*s.* *Paris*, 1787

1686 Elévations sur les Mystères de la Vie de N. S. Jésus Christ, 18mo. 2*s.* *ib.* 1834

1687 Elizabethæ (S.) Historia succinta Hospitalis S. Elizabethæ extra muros imperialis monasterii S. Maximini ordinis S. Benedicti prope Treviros, 8vo. 5*s.* *Londini*, 1786

1688 Epîtres et Evangiles, des Dimanches et Fêtes, &c. avec Reflexions, 12mo. 2*s.* 6*d.* *Paris*, 1811

1689 Entretien d'un Chevalier converti, avec une Marquise, touchant la Religion, 12mo. 3*s.* *ib.* 1779

1690 Entretiens d'une Ame Pénitente avec son Créateur, 12mo. 3*s.* *Lille*, 1767

1691 —— le même, augmentée, 3 vols. 12mo. 7*s.* 6*d.* *ib.* 1771

1692 Entretiens Spirituels de la Piété, de la Prière, et de l'Humilité, 12mo. 1*s.* 6*d.* *Paris*, 1700

1693 Esprit Prophétique, Traité dans lequel on examine la Nature de cet Esprit, son Objet, &c. 12mo. 2*s.* 6*d.* *ib.* 1767

1694 Examen et Resolutions des principales difficultés qui se rencontrent dans la Célébration des SS. Mystères, 12mo. 4*s.* *Louvain*, 1757

1695 Exercise de Retraite, 12mo. 3*s.* *Paris*, 1688

1696 Exercises Spirituels de St. Ignace, traduits par Clément, 18mo. *sewed,* 2*s.* *Lyon*, 1834

1697 Exercises de la Vie Intérieure, ou l'Esprit Intérieur dont on doit animer ses actions durant le Jour, surtout pendant la Rétraite, 18mo. 2*s.* *Angers*

1698 Exercises de la Vie Chrétienne, ou l'on donne des Instructions pour remplir tous les Devoirs de la Religion, 12mo. 3*s.* *Lyon*, 1801

1699 Extrait et Abrégé des Reflexions Demonstratives sur la Vérité, et sur la force du Mot de Vérité, selon la decision de la Sorbonne du 21 Avril, 1750. Addressé à Messieurs les Docteurs et Académiciens de l'Université d'Oxford, suivi de Deux Lettres du 4 Octobre, 1751, aux Docteurs de France et l'Académie François, sur le même Sujet, 4to. 4*s.* 6*d.* *Londres*, 1751

1700 Feller, Dictionnaire Historique, ou Histoire abrégée des Hommes qui se sont fait un nom par le génie, les talens, les vertus, les erreurs, depuis le commencement du Monde jusqu'à nos Jours, 12 vols. 8vo. *sewed,* 2*l.* 8*s.* *Paris*, 1818

1701 —— Dictionnaire Historique, ou Biographie Universelle des Hommes qui se sont fait un nom par leur génie, leur talents, leur vertus, leur erreurs, ou leur crimes, 8me edition, 20 vols. 8vo. 4*l.* *ib.* 1836

1702 —— Catechisme Philosophique, ou Recueil d'Observations propres à défendre la Religion Chrétienne contre ses ennemis, 3 vols. 12mo. *sewed,* 7*s.* 6*d.* *Clermont*, 1825.

1703 Fénélon, Sentimens de Piété, où il est traité de la nécessité d'aimer Dieu, &c. 12mo. 4*s.* *Paris*, 1734

1704 —— Livre de Prière, avec ses Reflexions pour tous les Jours du Mois, 18mo. 2*s.* 6*d.* *Besançon*, 1824

1705 —— Œuvres Complètes, 10 vols. 8vo. *Paris*, 1810

1706 Flechier, Oraisons Funèbres, 12mo. 2*s.* *ib.* 1682

1707 Fin des Temps, ou l'Accomplissement de l'Apocalypse et des Anciennes Propheties, 8vo. 7*s.* *ib.* 1840

1708 Fleury, Catéchisme Historique, 12mo. 3*s.* 6*d.* *ib.* 1823

1709 —— le même abrégé, 18mo. 9*d.* *Tours*, 1825

1710 —— Discours sur l'Histoire Ecclésiastique, 12mo. 3*s.* *Paris*, 1763

1711 Formulæ Congregationum in quarta generali Congregatione confectæ et approbatæ, 12mo. 2*s.* 6*d.* *Antwerp.* 1635

1712 Formulaire de Prières, à l'usage des Pensionnaires des Religieuses Ursulines, 12mo. 3*s.* 6*d.* *Paris*, 1825

1713 France (la) Chevaleresque et Chapitrale, 18mo. 2*s.* *ib.* 1787

1714 Fodère (Jacques) Narration Historique et Topographique des Couvens de l'Ordre S. François, et Monastères S. Claire, erigez en la province ancienne-ment appellée de Bourgogne, à present de S. Bonaventure, enrichie des singularités plus remarquables des Villes et lieux où les dict Couvens sont situez, 4to. 7s. 6d.   *Lyon*, 1619

1715 François d'Assise (St.) Panégyrique de, par le Père Poisson, 4to. 4s.6d. *ib*.1733

1716 François de Sales (St.) Conduite pour la Confession et la Communion, 18mo. 3s. 6d.   *Besançon*, 1827

1717 —— Introduction à la Vie Dévote, 12mo. 3s. 6d.   *Paris*, 1824

1718 —— Vie de, par Marsollier, 2 vols. 12mo. 5s.   *ib*. 1789

1719 —— Lettres Diverses, 12mo.   *ib*. 1820

1720 —— Esprit de, recueilli de M. Camus, 12mo. 3s.   *Avignon*, 1770

1721 François Xavier (St.) Vie de, par Bouhours, 2 vols. 12mo. 5s.   *Paris*, 1825

1722 Francisci Xaverii (S.) Beneficia et Miracula Potami, Neapoli, et Alibi, facta annis 1652, 1656, 1658, 18mo. 4s.   *Antwerp*. 1658

1723 Frayssinous (M.) Les Vrais Principes de l'Eglise Gallicane sur la Puissance Ecclésiastique, &c. 8vo. 2s. 6d.   *Paris*, 1818

1724 Freville, Beaux Exemples de Piété Filiale, de Concorde Fraternelle, et de Respect envers la Vieillesse, 18mo. 3s.   *ib*. 1817

1725 Gallonius de SS. Martyrum Cruciatibus, cum figuris, per Ant. Tempestam, 4to. 8s. 6d.   *ib*. 1659

1726 Gavanti Thesaurus Rituum, seu Commentaria in Rubricas Missalis et Breviarii Romani, 2 vols. in 1, 4to. 12s.   *Antw*. 1634

1727 Gerson, (J.) Excellente Prédication du Grand Gerson, 8vo. 2s.6d. *Rouen*, 1622

1728 Gobinet, Instruction de la Jeunesse en la Piété Chrétienne, 12mo. 3s. 6d. *Paris*, 1825

1729 Godeau, Paraphrase des Pseaumes de David, 4to. 6s.   *ib*. 1648

1730 Gonnetieu, de la Présence de Dieu, qui renferme tous les Principes de la Vie Intérieure, 12mo. 3s. 6d.   *Lyon*, 1827

1731 Grancolas, (M. J.) les Catéchèses de Saint Cyrille de Jerusalem, avec des Notes et des Dissertations Dogmatiques, 4to. 7s. 6d.   *Paris*, 1715

1732 Granatensis, (Lodoici) libri iii. de Devotione, et necessitate orationis de Jejunio et Eleemosyna, ac de Eucharistia, 12mo. 6s.   *Colon*. 1600

1733 Gregorius Magnus (S.) a Criminationibus Casimiri Ordini Vindicatus; accessit dissertatio de nova S. Gregorii Magni editione a R.P.D. H. Gradonico, 8vo. 5s. 6d.   *Rome*, 1753

1734 Gregorii IX, P.M. Epistolæ Decretales Summorum Pontificum, 12mo. 3s. 6d. *Paris*, 1570

1735 Grou, Caractères de la Vraie Devotion, augmentée de la Paix de l'Ame, 32mo. bound, 1s.6d.   *Marseille*, 1830

1736 —— Intérieur de Jésus et de Marie, 2 vols. 12mo. 5s.   *Paris*, 1835

1737 Guicciardini (L.) Descrittione di tutti Paesi Bassi, altremente detti Germania Inferiori, folio, 70 *plans and maps of towns*, 10s. 6d.   *Anversa*, 1588

1738 Haller, Histoire de la Revolution Religieuse, ou la Reforme Protestante dans la Suisse Occidentale, 8vo. 6s.   *Paris*, 1818

1739 Harel (M. E.) l'Esprit du Sacerdoce, ou Recueil de Reflexions sur les Devoirs des Prêtres, 2 vols. 12mo. 8s.   *ib*. 1818

1740 Heures Canoniales contenues dans le Pseaume cxviii, avec un Commentaire, 12mo. 3s.   *ib*. 1684

1741 —— à l'Usage des Ecoliers qui étudient dans le Collège de la Compagnie de Jésus, 12mo. 2s.   *ib*. 1741

1742 Histoire abrégée et Morale de l'Ancien Testament, 12mo. 2s.   *ib*. 1737

1743 Histoire (Vénérable) du Très Saint Sacrement de Miracle, augmentée de plusieurs Preuves, Temoignages, et Circonstances Curieuses, par Pierre de Cafmeyer, folio, *boards, first edition, many plates*, 1l. 1s.   *Bruxelles*, 1720

1744 Histoire de France à l'Usage de la Jeunesse, avec Cartes Géographiques, 2 vols. 18mo. 3s. *Lyon*, 1820

1745 Histoire des Mœurs et depravée Religion des Taborites, anciens Hérétiques au Royaume de Bohème, 12mo. *rare, 5s. 6d.* *Paris*, 1569

1746 Histoire Générale de tous les Siècles de la Nouvelle Loy, par David l'Enfant, 6 vols. 12mo. 12s. *ib.* 1684

1747 Histoire de plusieurs Saints des Maisons des Comtes de Tonnère et de Clermont, 12mo. 2s. 6d. *ib.* 1698

1748 Histoire d'une Sainte et illustre Famille de ce Siècle, 12mo. 2s. 6d. *ib.* 1698

1749 Histoire Civile, Ecclésiastique, et Littéraire, de la Ville et du Doyenné de Montdidier, 12mo. 2s. 6d. *Amiens*, 1765

1750 Histoire de l'Eglise d'Arles, par M. Gilles du Port, 12mo. 3s. *Paris*, 1690

1751 Histoire des Principaux Hérésiarques, 18mo. 2s. *ib.* 1833

1752 Histoires Choisies, ou livre d'Exemples tirées de l'Ecriture,12mo.2s. *Toulouse,*1786

1753 Histoires abrégées des plus fameux Hérésiarques qui ont paru en Europe depuis l'année 1040, 12mo. 2s. 6d. *Rouen*, 1699

1754 Historia Divina y Vida de la Virgen Maria Madre de Dios manifestada por la Misma Señora a su esclaua la V.M. sor Maria de Jesus, 3 vols. folio, 1l. 7s.

1755 Historia Carthaginiensis Collationis, sive Disputationis de Ecclesia, olim habitæ inter Catholicos et Donatistas, Com. F. Balduini, 12mo. 2s. 6d. *Paris*, 1566

1756 Historia Heresiarcharum a Christo nato ad nostra usque tempora, authore A. Le Grand, 12mo. 4s. 6d. *Duaci*, 1725

1757 Historiæ Controversiarium de Divinæ Gratiæ Auxiliis sub summis Pontificibus Sixto V, Clemente VIII, et Paulo V, libri sex, folio, 12s. *Antverp.* 1705

1758 Historica Relatione del Regno di Cile, e delle Missioni e Ministerii che esercita in quella la Compagnia di Giesu, *with many curious plates,*folio, 12s. *Roma,*1646

1759 Hohenlohe (Prince de) le Fidèle au pied de la Croix, on Méditations sur les principaux sujets de Piété, 18mo. *bound, 2s. 6d.* *Paris*, 1828

1760 Holden (H.) Divinæ Fidei Analysis seu de Fidei Christianæ Resolutione, Libri Duo, 12mo. *ib.* 1767

1761 Homiliæ per Festivitates Sanctorum, per F. J. Royardum, 12mo. 1s. 6d.

1762 Horæ Diurnæ Breviarii Romani, 18mo. *5s. 6d. new and beautiful edition printed in red and black tyye* *Mechlin*, 1840

1763 Horæ in Laudem Beatissimæ Virginis Mariæ, Græca, secundum consuetudinem Romanæ Ecclesiæ, 18mo. 2s. 6d. *Paris*, 1538

1764 Horæ in Laudem Beatissimæ Virginis Mariæ, ad usum Romanum, 4to. *each page illuminated with beautiful woodcut borders,* only 1l. 4s. *ib.* 1543

1765 Hortus Pastorum Sacræ Doctrinæ Floribus Polymitus. Auctore J. Marchantio, folio, 18s. *ib.* 1651

1766 Hymni Sacri et Novi Autore Santolio Victorino, 12mo. 4s. *ib.* 1698

1767 Hymnes Nouvelles à l'usage du Diocèse de Rouen, notées, 12mo. 2s. *Rouen,*1730

1768 Idée du Bon Magistrat, en la Vie et en la Mort de M. de Cordes, 12mo. 1s. 6d. *Paris*, 1645

1769 Illustre Pénitente de Beziers, ou l'Histoire admirable de Mlle. Bachelier, du tiers ordre S. François, 12mo. 2s. 6d. *Rouen*, 1672

1770 Imitation de la Sainte Vierge, 32mo. *bound, 2s. 6d.* *Besançon*, 1835

1770*Imitation de la Sainte Vierge, 18mo. *bound, 3s. 6d.* *Tours*, 1832

1771 Introductio ad Sacram Scripturam, et Compendium Historiæ Ecclesiasticæ, 12mo. 3s. 6d. *Versailles*, 1820

1772 Introduction à la Philosophie, ou la Connaissance de Dieu et de Soi-même, 12mo. 2s. *Paris*, 1722

1773 Instruction Chrétienne sur les Huit Béatitudes, tirées de SS. Pères, 12mo. 4s. *ib.*1732

1774 Instruction sur les Spectacles, et sur la Danse, par l'Abbé Hulot, 2 vols. 18mo. 2s. 6d. *ib.* 1823

1775 Instruction sur le Chemin de la Croix, avec les Pratiques de cette Devotion, 18mo. *bound,* 2s. *Tours,* 1829

1776 Instruction Pastorale de Monseigneur l'Archevêque de Lyons sur l'Incredulité, 12mo. 3s. *Paris,* 1776

1777 Instructions Chrétiennes pour les Jeunes Gens, 12mo. 2s. *ib.* 1813

1778 Instructions Utiles au Chrétien et à l'Honnête Homme, en forme de Sentences, 12mo. 2s. *ib.* 1729

1779 Jansenii Paraphrasis in Omnes Psalmos cum Argumentis et Annotationibus, folio, 16s. *Antverpiæ,* 1614

1780 Jesuits. — Constitutiones Societatis Jesu cum eorum declarationibus, 8vo. 6s. *Romæ,* 1606

1781 Jeunes Martyres (les) de la Foi Chrétienne, 18mo. 12 *plates, bound,* 5s. *Paris,*

1782 Joannis (S.) Climaci, Scala Paradisi, 12mo. *very scarce,* 8s. *Colon.* 1583

1783 —— le même, traduit en François par Arnaud D'Andilly, 12mo. 5s. *Paris,* 1654

1784 Journée du Chrétien, sanctifié par la Prière et la Méditation, 12mo. *calf, neat, large type,* 5s. *ib.*

1785 Kempis (Thomas) l'Imitation de Jésus Christ, traduit et paraphrasée en Vers François par P. Corneille, 4to. 7s. *Rouen,* 1658

1786 —— Imitation de Jésus Christ, traduit par Gonnelleu, 18mo. 2s.6d. *Paris,* 1834

1787 —— le même, avec l'ordinaire de la Messe, 18mo. 2s. 6d. *Besançon,* 1838

1788 Kuinoel (C. T.) Libri Historici Novi Testamenti cum Commentariis, 3 vols. 8vo. *boards,* 15s. *Londini,* 1827

1789 Lambert, la Manière de bien instruire les Pauvres, 12mo. 3s. 6d. *Rouen,* 1740

1790 Lanuza (H. B.) Homiliæ Quadragesimales ex Hispanico Idiomate in Latinum editionem translatæ, 4 vols. folio, 1l. 10s. *Col. Ag.* 1686

1791 Lapide (Cornelius a) Commentaria in Vetus ac Novum Testamentum, 11 vols. in 10, folio, *fine copy,* 7l. 7s. *Antverp.* 1624-43

1792 —— another copy, 11 vols. in 10, 7l. 7s. *ib.* 1687-1714

1793 Laval, Premier Evêque de Quebec, Mémoires sur la Vie de, 12mo. 2s. *Col.* 1661

1794 Leçons Quotidiennes de Jésus Christ et des Saints, par l'Auteur de l'Ecole du Sauveur, 2 vols. 12mo. 5s. *Paris,* 1798

1795 Leguay, la Voie de la Véritable et Solide Vertu, ouvrage destiné aux Personnes du Monde, 12mo. 3s. 6d. *ib.* 1840

1796 Lettres de M. P. Godet du Marais (Evêque de Chartres) à Madame de Maintenon, 12mo. 4s. *Bruxelles,* 1755

1797 Lettres Pastorales de l'Evêque d'Arras, 12mo. 2s. 6d. *Orleans,* 1703

1798 L'Homond, Histoire abrégé de la Religion avant la venue de Jésus Christ, 12mo. *bound,* 4s. *Tours,* 1833

1799 —— Histoire abrégé de l'Eglise, pour servir de suite de la Religion avant Jésus Christ, 12mo. *bound,* 4s. *Paris,* 1833

1800 —— Doctrine Chrétienne, en forme de lecture et de piété, à l'usage des Maisons d'Education, 12mo. *bound,* 3s. 6d. *ib.* 1833

1801 Liber Psalmorum, additis Canticis, cum notis J. B. Bossuet, 8vo. 5s.6d. *Lugd.* 1691

1802 Liguori, Horloge de la Passion, ou Réflexions sur les Souffrances de Jésus Christ, 18mo. 2s. *Paris,* 1836

1803 —— l'Ame Fidèle au pied de la Croix, faisant suite à l'Horloge de la Passion, 18mo. 2s. 6d. *Lille,* 1835

1804 —— les Gloires de Marie, 2 vols. 18mo. *bound,* 5s. *Paris,* 1835

1805 —— Méditations pour Huit Jours d'Exercices Spirituels, et pieuses Aspirations sur la Passion de Jésus Christ, 18mo. *bound,* 2s. 6d. *Lyon,* 1828

1806 —— Visites au Sainte Sacrement, et à la Sainte Vièrge, 32mo. *bd.* 2s.6d. *Besançon*

1808 —— de l'Importance de la Prière, 18mo. 1s. *Avignon,* 1827

1809 Louis de Blois, le Guide Spirituel, ou le Miroir des Ames Religieuses, 12mo. 1s. 6d. *Paris,* 1809

1810 Louis de Gonzagues, (St.) Vie de, par Cepari, traduit par M. Calpin, 12mo.
4s. *Avignon*, 1820
1811 Ludolphi (de Saxonia) Vita Jesu Christi, e IV Evangeliis et Scriptoribus
orthodoxis concinnata, folio, 14s. *Antverp.* 1618
1812 Maimbourg, Histoire de la Décadence de l'Empire après Charlemagne, 2 vols.
18mo. 3s. *Paris*, 1710
1813 Malebranche, (N.) de Récherche de la Vérité, 2 vols. in 1, 4to. 12s. *ib.*1721
1814 Manière de conduire les Ames dans la Vie Spirituelle, par Père Guillore,
12mo. 2s. 6d. *ib.* 1676
1815 Manuale Sacerdotum per modum examinis Ordinandorum, ad curam animarum,
18mo. 1s. 6d. *Florent.* 1590
1816 Manuel (Nouveau) de Piété à l'usage des Ames Devotes, 32mo. *bound,*
3s. *Besançon*, 1834
1817 Manuel (Nouveau) des Associés du Saint Rosaire, 18mo. bd. 3s. *Paris*, 1834
1818 Manuel (Nouveau) du Rosaire Vivant, redigé par l'Abbé Berault des Billiers,
18mo. 6d. . *ib.* 1837
1819 Mariage Chrétien, ou Traité des Règles qu'ils doivent suivre pour s'y comporter
d'une Manière Chrétienne, 12mo. 2s. 6d. *ib.* 1715
1820 Martirologe, ou Mémoire de toutes les Fondations faites dans l'Eglise de S.
Germain la Vieille, 4to. 3s. 6d.
1821 Martyrologium Franciscanum, folio, 7s. *Parisiis*, 1653
1822 Martyrologium Romanum, Gregorii XIII jussu editum, C. Baronii Sorani
Notationibus illustratum, et Vetus Romanum Martyrologium Opera H.
Rosweydi (Soc. Jesu) folio, *vellum,* 1l. 1s. *Antverp.* 1613
1823 Martyrologium Romanum, Gregorii XIII jus. ed. 8vo. 7s. *Lugduni*, 1716
1824 Maslatrie, Chronologie Historique des Papes, des Conciles Généraux, et des
Conciles des Gaules et de France, 8vo. 8s. 6d. *Paris*, 1837
1825. Méditations pour tous les Jours de l'Année, 2 vols. 12mo. 4s. *ib.* 1736
1826 Mélanges Religieux, par Mlle. Natalie P * * *, 8vo. 4s. *ib.* 1833
1827 Mémoire fait en 1717, où l'on démontre que l'appel interjetté de la Bulle
Unigenitus au futur Concile, est manifestement nul et insoutenable, 4to.
4s. 6d. 1718
1828 Memorie Istoriche intorno alla Vita della Beata Elisabetta Picenardi, Nobile
Vergine Cremonese del ordine de' servi di Maria; raccolte dall' Abbate
Is. Bianchi, 4to. *fine plate*, 7s. 6d. *Rome*, 1803
1829 Mæratii (L. Soc. Jesu,) Disputationes in summa Theologicam S. Thomæ,
3 vols. folio, 1l. 7s. *Lutetiæ Parisiorum*, 1633
1830 Miræi Chronicon Cisterciensis Ordinis, 12mo. *scarce*, 5s. *Col. Ag.* 1614
1831 ——— Chronicon Præmonstatensis, 12mo. *scarce*, 6s. *ib.* 1613
1832 ——— Origines Benedictinæ, sive Exordia ac Progressus illustrium Cœnobiorum,
Ord. S. Benedicti, 12mo. *scarce*, 6s. *ib.* 1614
1833 Morel, Entretiens avec Jésus Christ dans le S. Sacrement de l'Autel, 12mo.
3s. *Paris*,1772
1834 Nayel, (J. J.) de l'Accord de la Philosophie avec Religion, 12mo. 1s.6d. *ib.*1801
1835 Natali, (H. Soc. Jesu,) Adorationes et Meditationes in Evangelia quæ in
Sacrosancto Missæ Sacrificio toto Anno leguntur, fol. 7s. *Antverp.* 1595
1836 Nepveu, Esprit de Christianisme, ou la Conformité du Chrétien avec Jésus
Christ, 12mo. 2s. 6d. *Lyon*, 1836
1837 ——— Méthode Facile d'Oraison réduite en Pratique, 12mo. 1s. *Paris*, 1600
1838 Nieremberg, Traité de la Difference du Tems et de l'Eternité,12mo.2s.6d. *ib.*1724
1839 Office Divin à l'usage de Rome, pour les Dimanches et les Fêtes de l'Année,
12mo. *bound*, 5s. *Limoges*, 1830
1840 Office de la Quinzaine de Pâques, à l'usage de Rome, 18mo. *plates, calf gilt,*
5s. 6d. *Paris*,
1841 Officia de SS. Eucharistiæ Sacramento, et de Conceptione B. V. M. 18mo.
3s. *Londini*, 1710

1842 Officium B. Mariæ Virginis, cum Indulgentiis et Calendario Gregoriano, 4to.
*beautiful edition, in large type, red and black, with a plate of the "Madonna
de Loretto,"* 1*l.* 1*s.*   *Venezia,* 1619
1843 Officium Hebdomadæ Sanctæ, *large type,* 12mo. 3*s.*   *Venetiis,* 1728
1844 Olier (M.) Catéchisme de la Vie Intérieure, 32mo. 1*s.* 6*d.*   *Paris,* 1837
1845 Pallu, des Fins Derniers de l'Homme, 12mo. 2*s.* 6*d.*   *ib.* 1825
1846 Paradisus Precum ex Lud. Granatensis Spiritualibus Opusculis, aliorumque
Patrum, concinnatus per M. ab Isselt, 12mo. 5*s.* 6*d.*   *Colon.* 1589
1847 Paradisus Puerorum, in quo primævæ honestatis totiusque pueritiæ rectæ
informatæ reperiuntur exempla, 8vo. 5*s.*   *Duaci,* 1618
1848 Paradisus Animæ Christianæ, Lectissimis omnivenæ pietatis deliciis amœnus:
studio et opera Jacobi Merlo Horstii, 1 vol. 24mo.   *Mechlin,* 1840
1849 Paulin, (St.) Lettres de, traduites en François, 8vo. 7*s.*   *Paris,* 1703
1850 Pélérinage d'une Jeune Fille du Canton d'Unterwalden à Jérusalem, 2 vols.
8vo. 7*s.*   *ib.* 1836
1851 Pellicia, (Alex.) de Christianæ Ecclesiæ Primæ Mediæ et Novissimæ Ætatis
Politia, libri vi. 3 vols. in 2, 8vo. 18*s.*   *Colon.* 1829
1852 Pellico, (Sylvio) Mes Prisons, 18mo. 3*s.*   *Paris,* 1833
1853 Pensées de la Solitude Chrétienne, sur l'Eternité, le Mépris du Monde, et la
Pénitence, 12mo. 2*s.* 6*d.*   *ib.* 1836
1854 Pensées Chrétiennes pour tous les Jours du Mois, 18mo. *bd.* 2*s.* *Besançon,* 1830
1855 Pensées de M. Massillon, 18mo. 2*s.*   *Paris,* 1787
1856 Pensez-y-bien, ou Réflexions sur les Quatres Fins Dernières, 24mo. 2*s.* 6*d.*
1857 Petit Trésor de l'Enfant Chrétien, 32mo. *bound,* 1*s.* 6*d.*   *Tours,* 1834
1858 Petites Pensées Chrétiennes, 32mo. *bound,* 3*s.*   *Paris,*
1859 Pointer, le Christianisme, ou Preuves et Caractères de la Religion Chrétienne,
12mo. *bound,* 3*s.* 6*d.*   *ib.* 1828
1860 Portrait (le) Sacré des Filles illustres de S. Benoist, avec les entretiens curieux
sur la Conduite de leur Vie, par F. Bachelard, 2 parts in 1 vol. 4to. *plates,*
7*s.* 6*d.*   *Lyon,* 1669
1861 Pouvoir du Pape sur les Souverains au Moyen Age, ou Recherches Historiques
sur le Droit Public de cette époque relativement à la Déposition des Princes,
8vo. 5*s.* 6*d.*   *Paris,* 1839
1862 Praxis et brevis declaratio Viæ Spiritualis, prout eam nos docet S. P. N.
Ignatius in suo libello Exercitiorum Spiritualium: auctore Lud. de Palma,
12mo. 3*s.* 6*d.*   *Antv.* 1634
1863 Précis de la Vie des Saints pour tous les Jours de l'Année, 18mo. 2*s.* 6*d.* *Paris*
1864 Principes de la Religion Naturelle, et de la Foi Chrétienne, expliqué en forme
de Catéchisme, 2 vols. 12mo. 5*s.*   *Londres,* 1799
1865 Pseautier pour le Chœur, 12mo. *sewed,* 2*s.* 6*d.*   *Paris,* 1788
1866 Quadrupani, Instructions pour éclairer les Ames pieuses dans leurs Doutes, et
pour les rassurer dans leurs Craintes, 32mo. 2*s.*   *Paris,* 1837
1867 Recueil de Prières tirées des Meilleurs Auteurs, suivies de la Messe et Vêpres,
18mo. *bound,* 3*s.*   *ib.* 1830
1868 Recueil de Cantiques Anciens et Nouveaux, 18mo. 2*s.*   *Londres,* 1798
1869 Réflexions Chrétiennes pour les Jeunes Gens qui entrent dans le Monde,
12mo. 1*s.* 6*d.*   *Paris,* 1714
1870 Régime de Vie Spirituelle pour conserver et augmenter le Fruit de la Mission,
12mo. 2*s.*   *ib.* 1680
1871 Règle de St. Benoît, 18mo. 3*s.* 6*d.*   *Bruxelles,* 1691
1872 Regnault, Instruction pour la Première Communion, 18mo. *bd.* 2*s.* *Lyon.* 1818
1873 —— Instruction pour la Confirmation, 18mo. *bound,* 2*s.*   *Paris,*
1874 Religion du Cœur, ou le Guide du Néophyte, par le Comte Rivallière Frauen-
dorf, 12mo. 2*s.* 6*d.*   *ib.* 1836

1875 Religion Chrétienne éclairée par le Dogme et par la Prophétie, 9 vols. 12mo. 18s. *Paris,* 1753
1876 Rénouard, Elements de Morale, 12mo. *bound,* 2s. 6d. *ib.* 1820
1877 Renversement (le) de la Morale de Jésus Christ par les Erreurs des Calvinistes touchant la Justification, par Arnaud d'Andilly, 4to. 6s. *Paris,* 1672
1878 Richard, Essai d'Annales de la Charité, ou de la Bienfaisance Chrétienne, 2 vols. 12mo. 5s. *Lille,* 1785
1879 Rodriguez, Abrégé de la Perfection Chrétienne, 2 vols. 12mo. *bd.* 7s. *Lyon,* 1818
1880 —— le même, 2 vols. 12mo. *sewed,* 4s. *ib.* 1818
1881 Romsee (T. J.) Praxis Celebrandi Missam tum privatam tum solemnem juxta Ritum Romanum, 5 vols. in 4, 12mo. 18s. *Mechlin,* 1838
1882 Roma.—Opere Pie di Roma descritte secondo lo stato presente dall' Abbate C. B. Piazza, 4to. 4s. 6d. *Roma,* 1679
1883 Royaumont, Histoire du Vieux et du Nouveau Testament, 12mo. 2s. 6d. *Par.* 1738
1884 Sage (le) réfléchissant sur l'Eternité, 24mo. 2s. *ib.* 1813
1885 Salutii (B.) Lux animæ ad perfectionem ambulantis, 18mo. 3s. 6d. *Colon.* 1607
1886 Salvien, de la Providence, traduction nouvelle, 12mo. 2s. *Paris,* 1701
1888 Schelstrate (Em.) Sacrum Antiochenum Concilium pro Arianorum conciliabulo passim habitum, nunc vero primum ex omni antiquitate restitutum, 4to. 5s. 1681
1889 Science du Confesseur, ou Conférences Ecclésiastiques sur le Sacrément de Péni-tence, par une Société de Prêtres Réfugiés, 5 vols. 12mo. 15s. *Lille,* 1830
1890 Segneri, Paraphrase du Miserere, en forme de Méditations, 12mo. 3s. *Par.* 1754
1891 Seneza (P. B.) Institutione Civile e Christiana per Uno, che desidere venere tanto in Corte, come altrare honoratamente e Christianamente, 4to. 5s. 6d. *Rome,* 1622
1892 Simonis (F.) de Fraudibus Hæreticorum ad Orthodoxos, Tractatio perutilis hoc Tempore, 12mo. 6s. *Mogunt.* 1677
1893 Soulas, du Pécheur recourant à la Vierge selon le Sentiment des SS. Pères, 12mo. 2s. 6d. *Douay,* 1669
1894 Stanihurst (G. Soc. Jesu) Dei immortalis in corpore mortali patientis Historia Moralis doctrinæ placitis et commentationibus illustrata, 12mo. *scarce,* 6s. *Colon.* 1674
1895 Stapletoni (*Thomas*) Tres Thomæ seu res gestæ S. Thomæ Apostoli, S. Thomæ Archiepiscopi Cantuariensis et Martyris, Thomæ Mori Angliæ quondam Cancellarii, 12mo. *very rare,* 1l. 4s. *Colon. Agr.* 1612
1896 Summula Perfectionis Christianæ: in qua brevissimus animæ cum Deo uniendæ modus traditur, 18mo. 3s. 6d. *Ant.* 1626
1897 Surin (P.) les Fondements de la Vie Spirituelle, tirés du Livre de l'Imitation de Jésus Christ, 18mo. 2s. 6d. *Paris,* 1824
1898 Tablettes du Clergé et des Amis de la Religion, Janvier 1822 à Juin 1823, 3 vols. 8vo. *bound,* 9s. *Paris,* 1823
1899 Testament (Nouveau) revu sur l'ancienne et vulgate édition Latine, collationnée exactement au Grec par François Véron, 4to. 4s. 6d. *Paris,* 1647
1900 Testament Nouveau de N. S. Jésus Christ, traduit par Amelote, 12mo. 3s. 6d. *Limoges,* 1793
1900*Testamentum Novum Latinum Vulgatæ Editionis, 18mo. 3s. 6d. *Paris,* 1695
1901 Theologia in tabulis compendiose depicta, 8vo. 2s. 6d. *ib.* 1669
1902 Thérèse (St.) Vie de, par M. de Villefore, avec Lettres choisies, 2 vols. 12mo. 5s. *ib.* 1818
1903 —— Méditations sur ses Vertus, précédées d'un Abrégé de sa Vie, 18mo. *bound,* 2s. *ib.* 1827
1904 Theresa (S.) Acta Canonizationis S. Virginis et Matris Theresiæ a Jesu Funda-tricis Reformationis Ordinis Virginis Mariæ de Monte Carmelo, 12mo. *scarce,* 7s. 6d. *Viennæ,* 1628
1905 Thomassin, Traité des Jeûnes de l'Eglise, 8vo. 4s. 6d. *Paris,* 1680

1906 Thomassin, Traité de l'Office Divin pour les Ecclésiastiques et les Laïques, 8vo. 4s. 6d.   *Paris,* 1693

1907 Thomas Aquinas (S.) Vita, Othonis Væni delineata, folio, 31 *plates,* 5s. 1778

1908 Toleti (Card.) Commentarii in Evangelium S. Lucæ, folio, 7s. 6d. *Col. Ag.* 1640

1909 Topographie des Saints, où l'on rapporte les Lieux devenus célèbres par la Naissance, la Demeure, la Mort, et le Culte des Saints, 8vo. 6s.   *Paris,* 1703

1910 Tournelly (H.) Prælectiones Theologicæ de Gratia Christi, 2 v. 8vo. 12s. *ib.* 1725

1911 Traité spirituel de l'excellente Dignité, Valeur et Bonheur de l'Etat dévôt des Filles et Vefues spirituelles dictes Filles de Sion, par A. de Nivelle, 12mo. *scarce,* 5s. 6d.   *Courtray,* 1625

1912 Traité des Saints Reliques, par l'Abbé de Cordemoy, 12mo. 2s.   *Paris,* 1719

1913 Trésor du Pieux Communicant, ou Manière de bien recevoir la Sainte Communion, 18mo. *bound,* 2s.   *Bruxelles,*

1914 Triomphe de l'Evangile, ou Mémoires d'un Homme du Monde, revenu des Erreurs du Philosophisme Moderne, 3 vols. 8vo. 7s. 6d.   *Lyon,* 1821

1915 Usure (l') considérée relativement au Droit Naturel, ou Réfutation de Grotius, &c. 2 vols. 12mo. 5s.   *Paris,* 1787

1916 Van Espen, Vie de, avec Eclaircissemens historiques sur tous ses Ecrits, 8vo. 5s. 6d.   *Louvain,* 1767

1917 Véritable Croyance de l'Eglise Catholique, et les Preuves de tous les Points de sa Doctrine, 12mo. 3s. 6d.   *Paris,* 1745

1918 Vertus du Christianisme, ou Recueil de Traits sublimes inspirés par la Religion, 12mo. 2s. 6d.   *ib.* 1818

1919 Vesperale pro Dominicis et Festis, 12mo. 5s.   *Lugduni,* 1730

1920 Vie de Jésus Christ, tirée de l'Evangile selon la Concorde, et mise dans la bouche de Jésus Christ ; suivie de Réflexions, et d'une Prière après chaque Lecture, 2 vols. 12mo. 5s.   *Paris,* 1808

1921 Vie de la Vénérable Mère Cathérine de Bar, Institutrice des Religieuses de l'Adoration Perpétuelle, 12mo. 4s. 6d.   *Nancy,* 1775

1922 Vie de Mademoiselle Marie Anne Du Val de Dampierre, ou l'Idée d'une Vierge Chrétienne consacrée à Dieu, 12mo. 3s.   *Liège,* 1684

1923 Vie de M. Delalande, Curé de Grigny, mort en odeur de sainteté, 12mo. 2s. 1773

1924 Vie de Madame de Beaufort Ferrand, ou l'Idée de la véritable et solide Dévotion, 8vo. 2s. 6d.   *Paris,* 1650

1925 Vie abrégée, Vertus et Miracles, du Bienheureux Pierre Fourier, Chanoine Régulier, avec l'Histoire de l'Institution de la Congrégation de Notre Dame, 2 vols. in 1, 12mo. 5s.   *Nancy,* 1731

1926 Vie de M. Gilles Marie, Curé de S. Saturnin, Supérieur des Religieuses de la Visitation, 3s.   *Chartres,* 1736

1927 Vie (la) de la Très-Illustre et Très-Religieuse Princesse Philippe de Gueldre, Epouse de Réné II, Roy de Jérusalem et de Sicile, depuis Religieuse de St. Claire, 12mo. 2s.   *Nancy,* 1721

1928 Vie (la) de Madame Helyot, 8vo. 5s. 6d.   *Paris,* 1697

1929 Vie (la) d'Isabelle de France, Sœur de Saint Louis, 12mo. 1s. 6d.   1772

1930 Vie et Tableau des Vertus de Benoit Joseph Labre, par Marconi, 12mo. 1s.6d. 1785

1931 Vie et Vertus de Mademoiselle Marie Joachim Elizabeth de Louvencourt, 12mo. 1s. 6d.   1779

1932 Vie du Vén. Père Dom Claude Martin, Religieux Bénédictin de St. Maur, 8vo. 3s. 6d.   *Tours,* 1697

1933 Vie de Mademoiselle De Meleun, Fondatrice des Religieuses Hospitalières de Baugé, 8vo. 5s. 6d.   *Paris,* 1687

1934 Vie (la) du Grand Apôtre de la Chine, le Vénérable Père Jean Baptiste de Moralis, 12mo. 1s. 6d.   *Cologne,* 1801

1935 Vie, Vertus, et Ecrits, de Mlle. Marguérite Pignier, ou l'Idée de la véritable Piété, par R. P. Paul du S. Sacrément, 8vo. 3s. 6d.   *Lyon,* 1669

1936 Vie de Mademoiselle Marguérite de Mesplet, Première Directrice des Filles Orphelines de Paris, 12mo. 2s. *Toulouse,* 1691
1937 Vie de M. Roy, Curé de Perse proche Tonnerre, 12mo. 2s. *Troyes,* 1702
1938 Vie de M. Charles de Saveuses, Prestre, Restaurateur des Ursulines de Magnay, 8vo. 2s. 6d. *Paris,* 1678
1939 Vie abrégée de Louis Stefanelli, mort à Rome en odeur de sainteté, 1737, 12mo. 2s. *Rome,* 1779
1940 Vie de Madame Marie Elizabeth Tricalet, 12mo. 2s. *Paris,* 1761
1941 Vie de M. Jean Antoine le Vachet, Prêtre, Instituteur des Sœurs de l'Union Chrétienne, 12mo. 2s. *Paris,* 1692
1942 Vie des Justes dans les plus humbles Conditions de la Société, par l'Abbé Carron, 12mo. 2s. 6d. *ib.* 1817
1943 Vie des Saints pour tous les Jours de l'Année, avec Réflexions, &c. 12mo. 375 *woodcuts,* 5s. *ib.* 1808
1944 Vincent de Paul (St.) Vie complète, par M. Collet, 2 vols. 8vo. 12s. *ib.* 1818
1945 —— Vie de, par Collet, 12mo. 3s. *ib.* 1819
1946 Vita Jesu Christi ex Evangelistarum verbis contexta, sive Unitas Evangelistarum, 12mo. 3s. *ib.* 1670
1947 Vita e dell' Istituto di S. Ignatio, Fondatore della Compagnia di Giesu, libri cinque, *P. D. Bartoli,* folio, 12s. *Roma,* 1650
1948 Vita di Santa Francesca Romana, Fondatrice dell' Oblate di Torre de' Specchi, 4to. 5s. 6d. *Roma,* 1675
1949 Voie de la véritable et solide Vertu ; ouvrage destiné aux Personnes du Monde, &c. par l'Abbé Leguay, 12mo. 3s. 6d. *Paris,* 1840
1950 Voyage sur la Mer du Monde, 12mo. 3s. 6d. *Lille,* 1834
1951 Voyage de Sophie et d'Eulalie au Palais du Vrai Bonheur, ouvrage pour servir de Guide dans les Voies du Salut, 12mo. 2s. 6d. *Paris,* 1789
1952 Vraie et la Fausse Religion, par forme d'entretiens entr'un Religieux et un Protestant, 12mo. 4s. 6d. *ib.* 1727

1953 Hofler, (C.) Die Deutschen Päpste, vols. 1 & 2, 8vo. 18s. *Regensburg,* 1839
1954 Klee, (Dr. H.) Katholische Dogmatik, 3 vols. 8vo. 1l. 5s. 6d. 1839
1955 Moehler, (A.) Patrologie, oder Christliche Literärgeschichte, vol. 1, 8vo. 18s. *Regensburg,* 1840
1956 Schmid, (F. X.) Liturgie der Christkatholischen Religion, vol. 1, 8vo. 5s. *Nassau,* 1840
1957 Thomas von Kempen, oder die vier Bucher von der Nachfolge Christi, von Dr. G. Görres, 8vo. *with beautiful engraved borders,* bds. 8s. 6d. *Wien,* 1839

New Works.

Just published, in post 8vo. price Six Shillings, cloth lettered,

A JOURNEY FROM LA TRAPPE TO ROME,

By the late Reverend Father MARIE JOSEPH DE GERAMB, Abbot and Procurator of La Trappe.

Also just published, in 18mo. price 2s. 6d. cloth lettered,

THE NEW MONTH OF MARY ;

Or, Reflections for each Day of the Month, on the different Titles applied to the Holy Mother of God, in the Litany of Loretto; principally designed for the Month of May.
By the Very Reverend P. R. KENRICK.

Also lately published, price 1s. in cloth,

FLOWERS OF PIETY ;

Selected from approved sources,& adapted for general use. Price 2s. 6d. bd. embossed roan, gt.-edg.

THE CATHOLIC FAMILY LIBRARY,
No. I, Price Five Shillings.
CONTAINING
SIR THOMAS MORE: HIS LIFE AND TIMES,
Illustrated from his own Writings and from Contemporary Documents.
BY W. JOS. WALTER,
LATE OF ST. EDMUND'S COLLEGE,
With a Portrait of Sir Thomas More.

*** No. II. of " The Catholic Library" will illustrate a portion of the reign of Queen Elizabeth, containing the journal of the twenty years' captivity, trial, and death, of Mary Queen of Scots.

Just Published, Price 1s. 6d. the Third Edition.
REASONS FOR BECOMING A ROMAN CATHOLIC.
Addressed to the Society of Friends, by Frederick Lucas, Esq. Barrister-at-Law.

Just Published, in 12mo. Price 4s. 6d. cloth lettered.
CONSIDERATIONS ON THE EUCHARIST,
Viewed as the Generative Dogma of Catholic Piety, Translated from the French of the Abbé Ph. Gerbet, by a Catholic Clergyman.

Lately Published, Price 4s. 6d. boards.
THE LIVES OF ST. ALPHONSUS LIGUORI, ST. FRANCIS DE
GIROLAMO, ST. JOHN JOSEPH OF THE CROSS, ST. PACIFICUS OF SAN SEVERINO, AND ST. VERONICA GIULIANI, whose Canonization took place on Trinity Sunday, 26th May, 1839. In 1 vol. 12mo.

Lately Published, a New Edition, in 1 vol. 12mo. Price 4s. 6d. cloth lettered.
THE SINNER'S COMPLAINTS TO GOD:
Being Devout Entertainments of the Soul with God, fitted for all States and Conditions of Christians; by the Rev. John Gother.

Just Published, in 8vo. Vols. I. and II. Price 9s. each, of
THE HISTORY OF THE CHURCH,
Translated from the German of the
REV. J. J. IG. DOLLINGER, D.D.
Professor of Theology in the Royal University of Munich,
By the Rev. Edward Cox, D.D. President of St. Edmund's College.
To be completed in Five Volumes.

We may safely state, that the appearance of any work of the learned Professor Döllinger, in the English language, would be most acceptable to our country. But the universally acknowledged want of an Ecclesiastical History in our Language, will, it is trusted, render the appearance of the present work the more acceptable to all who desire to become acquainted with the first Institution, and the many interesting events which have accompanied the progress of the Church of Christ.

Just Published, 2 vols. 12mo. price 7s.
THE TRUTHS OF THE CATHOLIC RELIGION,
Proved from Scripture alone, in a Series of Lectures, by Thomas Butler, D.D.

Just Published, in 8vo. cloth boards, price 6s.
SUMMARY OF THE CATHOLIC RELIGION,
Including its History, from the Birth of Our Saviour until the Present Time.
By Alexander Macdonald.
EXTRACT OF A LETTER TO THE AUTHOR.

" By your Work, just fresh from the Press, and entitled Summary of the Catholic Religion, I cannot but be pleased with the proof thus given of your attachment—founded on conviction—to the cause of Religious Truth, and of your zeal to promote its influence. Your sketches, however rapid and succinct they must be, by the nature of such a work, yet present to the Reader, whether within or without the pale of Catholic Unity, much both to instruct and interest. In my hasty view of the text, I have not noticed anything incorrect in the doctrinal and liturgical statements. The Publication will be the more acceptable as well as useful, that it is throughout of easy comprehension, and free from all complicated reasoning.

Edinburgh, 17th March, 1840.   And. Carruthers, V.A."

Just published, in 3 Vols. 12mo. price 18*s.* in boards,

INNISFOYLE ABBEY,

A Tale of Modern Times, by DENNIS IGNATIUS MORIARTY, ESQ. author of the
"WIFE HUNTER," "HUSBAND HUNTER," &c.

" A racy, vigorous, and entertaining tale."—*Dublin Morning Register.*
" This is one of the best novels of the season."—*Pilot.*
" An excellent and useful book."—*Freeman's Journal*
' Full of broad Irish humour."—*Dublin Review.*
" The author has a good idea of character."—*Sun.*
" The story is a real one, full of life and interest."—*Phœnix.*
" The work is a rare and valuable combination of sterling patriotism, controversial acumen, and keen observation of character and manners."—*Belfast Vindicator.*

Just published, in 18mo. price One Shilling,

A CATECHISM OF THE HISTORY OF ENGLAND,
FOR THE USE OF SCHOOLS, BY A LADY.

THE Publisher offers the above small work to the notice of the Catholic Public, as the first of a Series of " HISTORICAL CATECHISMS," which, in case he receives sufficient encouragement, it is his intention to continue and extend;—because almost every work for the instruction of youth in this country, is so imbued with prejudice and misrepresentation against " *Catholics and their religion,*" that such books cannot with any satisfaction be placed in the hands of children.

Just published, second edition, price 2*s.*6*d.* in boards,

CATECHETICAL INSTRUCTIONS
ON THE DOCTRINES AND WORSHIP OF THE CATHOLIC CHURCH,
BY JOHN LINGARD, D.D.

THE above work contains a short exposition of Catholic Doctrine, and Catholic practice, with the chief authorities on which that doctrine and practice are founded. To the well-informed it can offer nothing with which they are not already acquainted; but it is hoped it may prove useful to two classes of persons; to the young who are preparing themselves for their first communion, and to the more aged who have been suffered to grow up to manhood without a competent knowledge of their religion.

Lately published, price 6*s.* 6*d.* in sheep lettered, and 8*s.* in calf,

THE MISSAL FOR THE USE OF THE LAITY :

With the Masses for all the Days throughout the year, according to the Roman Missal; and those for the English Saints in their respective places. Newly arranged and in great measure translated by the REV. F. C. HUSENBETH. Third Edition, improved.

We approve of this Second Edition of the Missal for the use of the Laity, prepared by the Rev. F. HUSENBETH; and permit the use of it in our respective districts.

THOMAS, Bishop of Cambysopolis, V.A.M.D.	JOHN, Bishop of Trachis, V.A.N.D.
PETER AUGUSTIN, Bishop of Siga, V.A.W.D.	THOMAS, Bishop of Olena, V.A.L.D.

The Editor of this Missal has principally endeavoured to furnish his Catholic brethren, with an Edition correct in its contents and convenient in its arrangement. This volume will be found strictly conformable to the Roman Missal, as used by authority in this country; with the proper Masses of the English Saints, in their respective places, and the Communion of Saints restored to its appropriate place, after the proper Masses. Much care has been taken to give the proper Masses as free as possible from references. More Latin has been given, and one uniform plan observed in its insertion. Wherever Commemorations are to be made of Simple Feasts, they are carefully noted; and proper directions are given to find the Masses within the Octaves of all Festivals so celebrated. The Votive Masses of the B. Virgin are printed separately, and in their proper places, according to the Roman Missal. The Hymns, and Sequences, or Proses, have been newly translated with great care, and most of them in verse.

These are some leading features, which it is hoped will secure for this Edition a continuance of the approval and patronage bestowed on the former; especially as the work has been graciously approved, and its publication and use permitted, by the venerable authority of all our R. R. Vicars Apostolic.

N.B. The Missal may be had either with or without Plates, at the option of the Purchaser. Some copies are kept bound in the Ancient Monastic Style of the Middle Ages, from designs by A. Welby Pugin, Esq.; and adorned with brass corners and clasps in the same style; and also, some are splendidly bound in rich velvet, with metal gilt corners and clasps.

ILLUSTRATIONS TO THE MISSAL,

In six plates, Designed and Engraved by A. WELBY PUGIN, ESQ. Professor of Ecclesiastical Antiquities at St. Mary's College, Oscott.

A CATALOGUE OF BOOKS,

In Various Languages,

COMPRISING MANY

SCARCE & VALUABLE THEOLOGICAL WORKS,

Fathers of the Church, &c.

OFFERED FOR SALE AT THE PRICES AFFIXED,

BY

CHARLES DOLMAN,

No. 61, NEW BOND STREET, LONDON.

2000 ABELLY (L.) Episcopalis Solicitudinis Enchiridion, ex plurimorum Ecclesiæ Catholicæ antistitum, Sanctitate ac Pastorali vigilantiæ insignium, et præsertim D. Caroli Borromæi Theoria et Praxi accurate collectum : complectens summatim omnia, quæ ad sacri illius ministerii partes quascumque sedulo exsequendas requiruntur, cum appendice de iis, quæ ad Vicarii Generalis et Officialis munus pertinent; 4to, 14*s*.   *Vesontione*, 1837

2001 ACTA SANCTORUM quotquot toto Orbe coluntur, collegit, digessit, Notis illustravit JOANNES BOLLANDUS ; operum et studium contulit Godefr. Henschenius, &c. This copy is divided as follows:—January, 2 vols.; February, 3 vols.; March, 3 vols.; April, 3 vols.; May, 8 vols. (including the volume entitled "Propileum ad Acta Sanctorum Maii"); June, 7 vols.; July, 7 vols.; August, 6 vols.; September, 8 vols.; October, 5 vols. (being vols. 1, 2, 3, 4, and 6, wanting vol. 5, 1794); making in all, 52 vols. bound in 51, folio, *Antwerp*, 1643-1794.— Harpocrates Carmelitanus R. Pat. Papebrochio, ord. Carmel. Impugnatori loquens per Max. à S. Mariâ, *Coloniæ*, 1681.—Prodromus Carmelitanus, sive Papebrochii Acta SS. colligentis erga Elianum Carmeli ord. Sinceritas discussa, studio Val à S. Amando; 12mo, in 1 vol. vellum, *ib.* 1682.—[Seb. à St. Paulo] Exhibitio Errorum Papebrochii in notis suis ad Acta SS. commisit. *Colon.* 1693.—Motivum Juris pro lib. cui tit. " *Exhibitio Errorum.*" *Ant.* 1693. —Responsio D. Papebrochii ad exhibit Errorum. The 3 parts, 4to, together in 4 vols. *Antwerp*. 1696-8.—*A good copy of this valuable work ;* in all 57 vols. in 56, *only* £88. *v.y.*

2002 ADOLESCENS ACADEMICUS sub Institutione Salomonis. Authore C. Musart, *Soc. Jesu ;* 12mo, 16 *plates*, 7*s.* 6*d.*   *Duaci*, 1633

2003 ADVERTISSEMENT DES CATHOLIQUES ANGLAIS aux Français Catholiques, du Danger où ils sont de perdre leur Religion, en expérimenter, comme en Angleterre, la Cruauté des Ministres s'ils reçoivent à la Couronne un Roy qui soit hérétique ; 8vo, *rare*, 7*s.* 6*d.*,   *Louvain,* 1586

2004 ALFORDII Annales Ecclesiæ Britannicæ ubi potissimum Britannorum Catholica, Romana, et Orthodoxa Fides per quinque prima Sæcula, asseritur ; 4 vols. folio, *scarce*, 4*l.* 4*s.*   *Leodii,* 1663

2005 ALOYSII GONZAGÆ B. Vita, a R. P. V. Cepario; 12mo, portrait, 4*s.* 6*d.*   *Valencenis,* 1609

2005*AMBROSII (S.) OPERA omnia juxta editionem Monachorum S. Benedicti; 4 vols. 8vo. sewed, 1*l.*10*s.*   *Paris.* 1836

2006 AMEN. Pratique Angélique du mystérieux mot AMEN, par laquelle les personnes de toute sorte de condition et état peuvent aisément trafiquer avec Dieu, et se rendre participans de tout le bien qui se fait au ciel et en terre ; 12mo, scarce, 5*s.*6*d. Namur,*1674

2007 AMORIS DIVINI et Humani Antipathia sive affectus varii, e variis Sacræ Scripturæ locis de prompti emblematis suis expressi ; 12mo, *above* 80 *plates*, 7*s.* 6*d.* Antwerp. 1636

2008 AMORT (Euseb.) de Revelationibus, Visionibus, et apparitionibus privatis regulæ tutæ ex Scriptura, Conciliis, SS. Patribus aliisque authoribus collectæ ; 4to. 10*s.* 6*d.*   *Aug. Vindel.* 1744

2009 AMOUR DE LA CROIX (L') éclatant dans la Vie admirable de la très-vertueuse Mère Anne Catérine de la Croix de Sueilles, Religieuse de la Visitation ; 4to. 5*s.* 6*d. Pezenas,* 1687

2010 AMPHILOCHII, Methodii, et Andreæ Cretensis Opera omnia Gr. et Lat. cura F. Combefis ; folio, 1*l.* 11*s.* 6*d.*   *Paris.* 16*--*

2011 ANNUS APOSTOLICUS, seu Conciones tempore Quadragesimæ prædicabiles auctore F. L. Laselves; 3 vols. 12mo, 6s. *Leodii*, 1723

2012 ANTIPHONARIUM juxta Breviarium Romanum; 4to, 8s. 6d. *Lugduni*, 1699

2013 ARCA Honoraria Jesu Christi et Sanctorum ortum auctumque Zonigeræ sodalitatis S. P. Augustini continens; 12mo. 4s. *Antwerp.* 1628

2014 ARNAULD, le Renversement de la Morale de Jésus Christ par les Erreurs des Calvinistes touchant la Justification; 4to, 8s. 6d. *Paris*, 1672

2015 ANTIPHONARIUM Romanum; 12mo, 4s.6d. *Amsterdam*, 1769

2016 APOLOGIE CATHOLIQUE contre les Libelles, Déclarations, Advis, et Consultations faictes, escrites, et publiés par les Ligueurs, perturbateurs du repos du Royaume de France, par E. D. L. J. C.; 8vo, rare, 5s. 6d. 1585

2017 APOSTOLICÆ sedis definitiones veteres, de Gratia Dei; 12mo. 3s. 6d. *Duaci*, 1616

2018 ARINGHI (P.) Roma Subterranea Novissima, in qua post Bosium et alios Scriptores Antiqua Christianorum et præcipue Martyrum Cœmitaria, Titula ac Inscriptiones Sanctarum Sepulchra sex libris illustrantur; 2 vols. in 1, folio, 1l.11s. 6d. *Lut. Par.* 1659

2019 ART DE VÉRIFIER LES DATES, des Faits Historiques, des Inscriptions, des Chroniques, &c. avant et depuis l'Ere Chrétienne; 23 vols. 8vo. 5l. 15s. *Paris*, 1818-19

2020 AUGUSTINI (S.) de Doctrina Christiana lib. IV, et Enchiridion ad Laurentium ed. C. H. Bruder; 18mo, 2s. 6d. *Lipsiæ*, 1838

2021 ——— Confessiones, ed. C. H. Bruder; 18mo, 2s. 6d. *ib.* 1837

2022 AUGUSTINI Opera omnia, post Benedictinos; 12 vols. in 9, folio, calf, 9l. 9s. *Antwerp*, 1700-3

2023 AUGUSTINI OPERA OMNIA. Editio Benedictina recensita; 22 parts, imperial 8vo. sewed, 9l. 15s. *Paris*. 1837-40

2024 AVE MARIA. Banquete Espiritual, em favor das Almas do Purgatorio, e de todo o fiel Christao; por F. Bartholomen dos Martyres; 12mo, rare, 4s. *Lisboa*, 1751

2025 BASILII (S. *Magni*) Opera omnia Gr. et Lat. editio Benedictina recensita; 6 parts, imperial 8vo, sewed, 3l. 12s. *Paris*. 1839

2026 BEDÆ, Venerabilis Ecclesiasticæ Historiæ Gentis Anglorum lib. V; 18mo. 2 leaves slightly imperfect, 1s. 6d. *Col. Ag.* 1601

2027 BEDÆ (Ven.) Opera omnia; 8 vols. in 3, folio, 4l. 14s. 6d. *Coloniæ*, 1612

2028 ——— Idem; 8 vols. in 4, vellum, 6l. 6s. *ib.* 1688

2029 BELLARMINUS (Card.) De Arte bene moriendi; 12mo, 2s. 6d. *Paris*. 1620

2030 ——— De Ascensione mentis in Deum per Scalas rerum creaturum; 18mo. 2s. *Col.*1618

2031 BENEDICTI XIV. Doctrina de Servorum Dei Beatificatione et Beatorum Canonizatione in Synopsim redactæ ab Em. de Azevedo S. J.; royal 8vo, 8s. 6d. *Bruxellis*, 1840

THE BENEDICTINES.

2032 CALMET, Commentaire littéral, historique et moral, sur la Règle de St. Benoit; 2 vols. 4to. 16s. *Paris*, 1734

2033 CONSTITUTIONES Congregationis Anglicanæ, Ordinis Sancti Benedicti; 12mo, rare, calf neat, 8s. 6d. *Paris*. 1784

2034 MABILLON, Acta Sanctorum Ordinis S. Benedicti; 9 vols. folio, 5l.10s.

2035 ——— Annales Ordinis S. Benedicti; 6 vols. folio, *Lut. Par.* 1703.—ACTA Sanctorum Ordinis S. Benedicti; 9 vols. in 7, *Venet.* 1733.—15 vols. in 13, folio, uniform in calf, only 10l.10s.

2036 ——— Annales Ordinis S. Benedicti; 6 vols. folio, 4l. 4s. *Lucæ*, 1739

2037 BERNARDI Opera omnia editio Benedictina repetita; 4 parts, imperial 8vo. sewed, 2l.10s. *Paris*,

2038 BEVEREGII (G.) Codex Canonum Ecclesiæ Primitivæ Vindicatus ac illustratus; 4to. 7s. 6d. *Lond.* 1688

2039 BEYER (Gul.) Tractatus de auctoritate ac necessitate Episcoporum; cui adjuncti Tract. de Missionibus ad propag. fidem, &c.; 8vo, vellum, 4s. 6d. *Bruxellis*, 1669

2040 BIBLE (SAINTE) en Latin et Français, avec Notes critiques et historiques, Préfaces et Dissertations tirés de Calmet, par l'Abbe de Vence, &c.; 25 vols. 8vo. and atlas in 4to. sewed, 5l. 10s. *Paris*, 1829

2041 ——— traduite en Français par De Sacy; 12 vols. royal 8vo. with 300 plates by Marillier, calf gilt, 7l. 7s. *ib.* 1789

2042 ——— contenant l'Ancien et le Nouveau Testament, avec une Traduction Française en forme de Paraphrase, par le R. P. Carrières; 6 vols. 8vo, 1l.16s. *ib.* 1838

2043 BIBLIA MARIÆ, opus à B. Alberto Magno, conscriptum; in quo omniaferè, quæ in Sacris Bibliis continentur: accessit Vita B. Alberti, opera et studio R. P. F. Vincentii Justiniani; 12mo. rare, 4s.6d. *Col. Ag.* 1625

2044 BIBLIA SACRA vulgatæ editionis; 8vo, sewed, a new and very good edition, 12s. *Paris*, 1838

2045 BIBLIOTHECA ASCETICA Antiqua-Nova, hoc est: collectis veterum quorundam et recentiorum opusculorum asceticorum quæ hucusque in variis MSS. codicibus et Bibliothecis delituerunt R. P. Bernardi Pezii 8 vols. 12mo, 1l. 12s. *Ratisbon*, 1723-

2046 BIBLIOTHECA CLUNIACENSIS in qua SS Patrum Abb. Clun. Vitæ, Scripta, Statuta Privilegia, Chronologia quæ duplex, &c. Dom. Mart. Marrier; folio, rare, 1l. 11s. 6d *Lut. Par.* 161

2047 BIBLIOTHÈQUE CHOISIE des Pères d l'Eglise Grecque et Latine, ou Choix d'Eloquence Sacrée, par M. N. S. Guillon; 2 vols. 8vo. 4l. 14s. 6d. *Paris*, 182

2048 BIBLIOTHÈQUE SACRÉE, ou Dictionnaire Historique, Dogmatique, Canonique, Géographique, et Chronologique, des Sciences Ecclésiastiques; contenant l'Histoire de la Religion, les Papes, les Conciles, les Sièges Episcopaux, de *toute la Chrétienté*, et l'Ordre de leurs Prélats, Ordres Militaires et Religieux, des Schismes et des Hérésies, par Richard et Giraud; 29 vols. 8vo, 5l. 16s.
Paris, 1822

2049 BIBLIOTHÈQUE DES PRÉDICATEURS, qui contient les principaux sujets de la Morale Chrétienne, par le Père V. Houdry; 22 vols. 4to, scarce, 8l. 8s. *Lyon,* 1731

2050 BIBLIORUM CONCORDANTIÆ recensitæ atque emendatæ, ac plusquam viginti-quinque millibus versiculis auctæ, notis historicis, &c. curâ et studio F. P. DUTRIPON; royal 4to, sewed, 2l. 12s. 6d. *Paris.* 1838

2051 BIVERI (P.) Sacrum Sanctuarium Crucis et Patientiæ Crucifixorum et Cruciferorum emblematicis imaginibus ornatum: Artifices Gloriosi novæ artis bene vivendi et moriendi secundum rationem Regulæ et Circini; 4to. above 60 plates, fine copy, calf, gilt edges, 1l. 11s. 6d. *Antwerp,* 1634

2052 BLONDELL (David) de Joanna Papissa sive Famosæ Quæstionis, An fœmina ulla inter Leonem IV, et Benedictum III, Romanos Pontifices, media sederit. Authore *Davide Blondello*; 12mo, 6s. 6d. *Amst.*1657
Unknown to Brunet and Lowndes.

2053 BLOSII (LUD.) Institutio Spiritualis, non parum utilis iis, qui ad vitæ perfectionem contendunt: itemque Exercitium piarum precationum; *Lovanii*, 1553.—Tractatus Directorii Horarum Canonicarum et Exercitatorii Vitæ spiritualis, *Venetis*, 1555.—2 vols. in 1, 12mo, 6s.

2054 BLOSII Ludovici Opera, cura et studio Antonii de Winghe; fol. 1l. 10s. *Antw.* 1632

2055 BONA (Card.) Rerum Liturgicarum libri duo; 8vo. 7s. *Colon.* 1674

2056 BON MARIAGE, ou le moyen d'estre heureux, et faire son salut en estat de mariage, avec un Traité des Vefus, par CLAUDE MAILLARD, S. J.; 4to. rare, 12s. *Douay,* 1643

2057 BOSSUET, Vie de, par M. De Burigny; 12mo. 3s. 6d. *Bruxelles,* 1761

2058 BOUDART (J.) Catechismus Theologicus seu Compendium Manualis Theologici; 12mo. 4s. 6d. *Lovan.* 1725

2059 BOUDON (Hen.) Le Triomphe de la Croix, en la Personne de la Ven. Mère Marie Elisabeth de la Croix de Jésus; 12mo. 3s. 6d. *Liège,* 1686

2060 —— L'Homme de Dieu en la Personne du R. P. Jean Joseph Surin, S. J.; 2 vols. 12mo. 4s. *Lyon,* 1826
Vol. I wanting title.

2061 —— Vie de, par Collet; 12mo. portrait, 4s. 6d. *Paris,* 1762

2062 BOULOGNE (M. de, Evêque de Troyes) Sermons et Œuvres de; 8 vols. 8vo. half-bound, 1l. 4s. *Paris,* 1826

2063 BOURDALOUE, Œuvres Complètes, avec sa Vie et Table générale; 16 vols. 8vo. sewed, *fine paper*, 3l. 4s. *ib.* 1826

2064 BREVIARIUM ROMANUM; 4 vols. 4to. fine copy in black mor. gt. edg. 4l. 4s. *Ant.* 1751

2065 —— Idem; 4 vols. 12mo. 1l. 4s.
Bellovaci, 1830

2066 —— Idem, red and black type, with the "*Officia pro Anglia*;" 4 vols. 18mo, sewed, 1l. 10s. *Mechlin,* 1836

2067 —— Idem; complete in 1 vol. 12mo. sewed, 14s. *Ratisbon,* 1840

2068 BRIDGWATER (John) Concertatio Ecclesiæ Catholicæ in Anglia, adversus Calvino Papistas et Puritanos, à paucis annis singulari studio quorundam hominum doctrina et sanctitate illustrium renovata; small 8vo. first edition, rare, 1l. 4s. *August. Trev.* 1583

2069 —— the same, very much enlarged, the second edition; 3 parts in 4to. very scarce, 1l. 18s. *ib.* 1588
Among the additions is Cardinal ALLEN's reply to the "JUSTITIA BRITANNICA," by Lord Burleigh.

2070 BUSENBAUM (H.) Medulla Theologiæ Moralis; 12mo. 2s. 6d. *Insulis,* 1654

2071 CAMINO (EL) DEL CIELO allanado. Obra sacada del libro de los Exercicios de San Ignacio; 12mo. 2s. 6d. *Seville,* 1730

2072 CANISII (Petri) Opus Catechisticum sive summa Doctrinæ Christianæ; folio, scarce, 18s. *Colon.* 1596

2073 CARDINI (A. F. *S.J.*) Fasciculus e Japponicis Floribus, suo adhuc madentibus sanguine, 1646.—CATALOGUS REGULARIUM, et secularium qui in Japponiæ Regnis sub quatuor Tyrannis violenta morte sublati sunt, 1646.—Mors felicissima IV Legatorum et sociorum quos Japponiæ Imperator occidit in Odium Christianæ Religionis, 1646.—3 books in 1 vol. illustrated with 87 plates of the sufferings of the martyrs, exceedingly rare, 4to. vellum, 1l. 8s. *Rome,* 1646
A note on the flyleaf states it to be "livre très-rare, inconnu aux bibliographes."

2074 CARTUSIENSIS ORDINIS, Statuta a Domine Guigone Priore Cartusie edita:—et Privilegia Ordinis cum confirmationibus; *black letter,* with curious woodcuts, folio, russia, fine copy, 2l. 15s. *Basiliæ,* 1510
The following note in MS.—"Cet exemplaire est parfaitement conforme à la description qu'en donne De Bure dans la Bibliographie Instructive, Art. 994. Cailleau l'estime de 80 à 100 francs."
This volume, containing many woodcuts, is of the greatest rarity (the greater part of the edition having been withdrawn from circulation by the "Order"): it is quite perfect, and the interior in excellent condition, and contains in addition a Map of the "Grand Chartreuse."

2075 CARTHUSIANS.—Nova Collectio Statutorum Ordinis Cartusiensis. Accessit Directorium Novitiorum Ordinis Cartus; 4to. rare, 9s. 6d.   *Correriæ*, 1681

2076 CATÉCHISME de Persévérance, ou Exposé historique, dogmatique, moral et *liturgique*, de la Religion depuis l'Origine du Monde jusqu'à nos Jours, par l'Abbé J. Gaume; 8 vols. 8vo. 2l. 8s.   *Paris*, 1841

2077 CAVEA TURTURI malè contra Gementem Eminentissi Roberti Cardinalis BELLARMINI Columbam exultanti a Theologo veritatis vindice structa et a Geo. Riedelis publicata; 12mo. 3s. 6d.   *Monachi*, 1631

2078 CHESNEAU (A.) Orpheus Eucharisticus, sive Deus absconditus humanitatis illecebris illustriores Mundi partes ad se pertrahens, ultraneas arcanæ majestatis adoratrices; 8vo. illustrated with above 100 plates of emblems, *very scarce*, 15s.   *Paris.* 1657

2079 CHRYSOSTOMI (S.) Opera omnia, Gr. et Lat. Editio Benedictina emendata et aucta; 26 parts imp. 8vo, sewed, 18l. 18s. *Paris.* 1834-9

2080 —— de Sacerdotio, libri vi.—Juxta Editionem PP. Congregationis S. Benedicti; 32mo, 1s. 6d.   *Paris.* 1827

2081 CITÉ MISTIQUE DE DIEU, miracle de sa toute-puissance, Histoire divine et la Vie de la très Sainte Vièrge Marie Mère de Dieu, notre Reine et Maîtresse; manifestée dans ces derniers siècles par la Sainte Vièrge à la Sœur MARIE DE JESUS, Abbesse du Monastère de l'Immaculée Conception de la Ville d'Agreda; traduite de l'Espagnol par le P. Thomas Croset; 6 vols. 12mo. scarce, 18s.   *Brusselle*, 1717

2082 CLIMACI (S. Joannis) Opera omnia ed. Raderi; folio, scarce, 1l. 10s.   *Paris.* 1633

2083 COMBEFIS (F.) Historia Hæresis Monothelitarum, S. Asterii aliorumque plurimum Græcorum Patrum Opuscula; 2 vols. folio, scarce, 2l. 2s.   *Paris.* 1648

2084 —— Ecclesiastes Græcus, id est, Illustrium Græcorum Patrum ac Oratorum digesti Sermones et Tractatus; Basilius Magnus et Basilius Seleuciæ Isauriæ Episcopi, 8vo. 9s.   *Paris.* 1674

2085 COMMENTARIA in Regulas Cancellariæ Apostolicæ: authore Joanne a Chokier; 4to. 7s. 6d.   *Col. Ag.* 1674

2086 CONCILE DE TRENT, Lettres et Mémoires de François de Vargas et de quelques Evêques d'Espagne touchant le Concile de Trent, traduit par M. Le Nassor; 8vo. 5s. 6d.   *Amst.* 1700

2087 CONCILII TRIDENTINI Canones et Decreta, 32mo. 2s. 6d.   *Paris.* 1837

2088 —— Catechismus; 32mo. 3s. 6d.   *Paris.* 1830

2089 —— ex Actis, Christianorum Principum ad Sacrum Concil. Tridentinum Litera, et Mandata, Legatorumque ab iisdem missorum, habitæ Orationes, 12mo. 3s.   *Colon.* 1565

2090 CONCILII TRIDENTINI Monumentarum ad historiam amplissima Collectio, studio et opera J. Le Plat; 7 vols. 4to. 3l. 13s. 6d.   *Lovan.* 1781

2091 CONCORDE des Epitres de S. Paul et des autres Apôtres, par ordre des Matières: 12mo. 3s.   *Paris*, 1685

2092 COURONNE DES PLAYES très-sacrées de N. S. JESUS CHRIST, enrichie de xxxv considérations tirées de l'Ecriture sainte, des SS. Pères et de l'Histoire Ecclésiastique, par le R. P. Guil. de Wael (*Soc. Jesu*); 12mo. plates, 6s. 6d.   *Anvers*, 1651

2093 CROISADE du XIXᵉ Siècle, appel à la Piété Catholique à l'effet de reconstituer la Science Sociale sur une Base Chrétienne, par Louis Rousseau, 8vo. 8s. 6d. *Paris*, 1841

2094 DAVID (Joan, Soc. Jesu) Duodecim Specula Deum aliquando videre desideranti concinnata; 8vo. 13 plates, 7s. 6d. *Ant.* 1610

2095 —— Veridicus Christianus; containing 100 plates, scarce, 1l. 8s.   *ib.* 1601

2096 DE CULTU, Veneratione, intercessione, invocatione, meritis, festivitatibus, reliquiis et miraculis Sanctorum, Catholica assertio in quinque classes distributa: auctore F. Thomæ Beaux Amis Parasino; 12mo. 4s. 6d.   *Paris.* 1566

2097 DIONYSII AREOPAGITÆ Opera, Gr. et Lat. cum scholiis S. Maximi et Paraphrasi Pachymeræ, a B. Corderio notis illustrata, 2 vols. folio, 1l. 16s.   *ib.* 1634

2097* —— another copy, 2 vols. folio, boards, 1l. 10s.   *ib.* 1634

2098 DISSERTATIONS THEOLOGIQUES et Dogmatiques, sur les Exorcismes, sur l'Eucharistie, et sur l'Usuré; 12mo. 2s. 6d. *ib.* 1728

2099 DUGDALE and DODSWORTH, Monasticon Anglicanum, sive Pandectæ Cœnobiorum, Benedictinorum, Cluniacensium, Cisterciensium, Carthusianorum, a primordiis ad eorum usque dissolutionum; 3 vols. folio, russia, 13l. 13s.   *Lond.* 1665

2100 DU PLESSIS. LES ET CÆTERA de DU PLESSIS, parsémez de leurs *Qui pro quo*, avec autres de l'Orthodoxe mal-nommé, Rotan, Loque, Vignier, et quelques pretendus Ministres, sur les poincts de la *S. Messe*, *Eucharistie*, &c. 8vo. 5s. 6d. *Bourdeaux*, 1600

2101 EMBLEMES SACREZ sur le très-saint et très-adorable Sacrement de l'Eucharistie; illustrated with 100 plates of emblems, 9s. 6d.   *Paris*, 1667

2102 ENGELGRAVE (HEN.) Cœlum Empyreum, non vanis et fictis Constellationum Monstris belluatum, sed Divum Domus Domini Jesu Christi. — (*Partis primæ pars posterior.*) 12mo. plates, 4s. 6d.   *Coloniæ*, 1669

2103 ENTRETIENS de Piété, par J. P. Camus, Evesque de Belley; 2 vols. 12mo. 5s.   *Rouen*, 1641

2104 EXPLICATION des Cérémonies de l'Eglise, par Claude de Vert; 4 vols. 8vo. scarce, 1l. 8s.   *Paris*, 1720

2105 EXAMINATION bien ample faicte à Lambeth, de poinct en poinct selon le mandement de sa Majesté, de M. George Blackwell, faict Archi-prestre d'Angleterre, par Clement VIII. 12mo. very rare, 18s. *Amst.* 1609

2106 FILIUS PATIENS, et MATER COMPATIENS, sive Christi Domini Nostri passio, et Beatæ Mariæ Virginis Mariæ parallela compassio : piis affectibus et moralibus illustratæ, authore Jacobo à Passione Domini ; 12mo. 5s. 6d. *Ultrajecti,* 1678

2107 FISHER (Joannis *Epis. Roffensis*) Opera omnia ; folio, *rare,* 2l. *Wirceb.* 1597

2108 FLEURS DES EXEMPLES, ou Catéchisme Historial, contenant des Miracles, et beaux Discours, tirez de l'Ecriture Sainte, des SS. Pères, et anciens Docteurs de l'Eglise, &c., par Antoine d'Averoult ; 2 vols. 8vo. very scarce, 18s. *Duaci,* 1603

2109 FLEURY, Histoire du Christianisme, *(comme sous le nom d'Ecclésiastique)* augmentée de IV livres comprenant l'histoire du XVe siècle d'après un manuscrit de Fleury, et continuée à la fin du XVIIIe siècle, par l'Abbé O. Vidal ; 6vols. imp.8vo. 3l.12s. *Paris,* 1836

2110 FRANÇOIS de Sales (St.) Introduction à la Vie Dévote ; 18mo. sewed, 3s. *ib.* 1828

2110*—— INTRODUCTION à la Vie Dévote de S. FRANÇOIS DE SALES, par le R. P. Brignon, de la compagnie de Jésus ; 12mo. 3s. *Toulouse,* 1828

2111 FRANÇOIS DE SALES (St.) Œuvres Complètes, 16 vols. 8vo. sewed, 4l. *Paris,* 1821

2112 FULDENSIUM Antiquitatum, libri IV, auctore Christop. Brovero, Soc. Jesu ; folio, vellum, plates, 6s. *Antwerp,* 1612

2113 GARETII (Jo. *Lovanensis*) de Vera præsentia corporis Christi in Sacramento Eucharistiæ, Classes IX, contra Sacramentariam pestem ex omnibus fere Ecclesiasticis auctoribus summo studio collectæ ; 12mo. *scarce,* 6s. *ib.* 1561

2114 GARETIUS (I.) Omnium Ætatum, Nationum ac Provinciarum Corporis Christi in Eucharistia, consensus, per XVI. annorum Centenarios, Editio Tertia.— *Antv.* 1569.— Sacrificii Missæ, Precum, Cæremoniarumque, nec non et epithetorum ejus ex sanctis patribus et universa antiquitate collecta assertio ; 12mo. very scarce, 2vols in 1, 9s.6d. *ib.* 1569

2115 GAVANTI (B.) Thesaurus Sacrorum Rituum in Rubricas Missalis cum additionibus C. M. Merati ; 3 vols. in one, folio, vellum, 1l.18l. *Aug. Vind.* 1763

2116 GEBSON (J.) Apologia pro Joanne Gersonio pro suprema Ecclesiæ et Concilii Generalis auctoritate ; atque independentia Regiæ protestatis ab alio quam a solo Deo : adversus Scholæ Parisiensis ; 4to. 7s. *Lug. Bat.* 1676

2117 GERSONII (Joannes) Opera, folio, vellum, 12s. *Paris,* 1606

2118 GERTRUDIS (S.) Virginis et Abatissæ Ordinis S. Benedicti, Vita et Revelationes ; 8vo. scarce, 7s. *Paris,* 1662

2119 GRANATENSIS (Lodovici) Exercitia, in septem Meditationes matutinas, ac totidem Vespertinas, distributa ; 18mo. 3s. 6d. *Col.* 1698

2120 GRÉGOIRE (S.) Les Morales de S. Grégoire, Pape, sur le Livre de Job, traduites en Français ; 5 vols. 8vo. 1l. 5s. *Lyon,* 1692

2121 GREGORII MAGNI OPERA OMNIA ad manuscriptes codices Romanos, Gallicanos, &c. emendata, aucta et notis illustrata à D. Sammathano et Gul. Bessin, *Editio Benedictina ;* 4 vols. folio, 6l. 10s. *Paris,* 1705

2122 GREPPO (J. G.) Mémoires relatifs à l'Histoire Ecclésiastique des premiers Siècles, viz. Les Chrétiens de la Maison de Néron, de Domitien, et de quelques Empereurs ; 8vo. 6s. 6d. *ib.* 1840

2123 GUÉRANGER (Prosper, Abbé de Solesmes) Institutions Liturgiques,Vol.I; 8vo.7s.6d.1840

2124 GUIRAUD (Baron) Philosophie Catholique de l'Histoire, ou l'Histoire Expliquée ; 2 vols. 3vo. 16s. *ib.* 1841

2125 HARPSFELD (N.) Historia Anglicana Ecclesiastica, et CAMPIANI Narratio Divortionis Henrici VIII ; folio, 1l.11s.6d. *Duaci,*1622

2126 —— Dialogi sex contra summa Pontificatus, Monasticæ Vitæ, Sanctorum, S. Imaginum Oppugnatores et pseudo-Martyres ; 4to, scarce, 1l. 10s. *Antwerp,* 1566
Charles Butler's copy.

2127 HAVENSII (A.) Speculum Hæreticæ Crudelitatis ; 12mo. scarce, 4s. 6d. *Colon.* 1608

2128 HEBDOMADA SANCTA, seu Christus Rex, Index, Mediator, Pater, Benefactor, Redemptor, et Sponsus. Auctore S. Niwicki ; 4to. many plates, 7s. 6d. 1692

2129 HEURES NOUVELLES, Paroissien Complet, Latin-Français, à l'Usage de Paris et de Rome, par M. l'Abbé Dassance, avec Dessins de FRED. OVERBECK ; 8vo, sewed, 1l. 11s. 6d. *Paris,* 1841
This is one of the most beautiful books ever offered to the public ; nearly every page is adorned with engraved borders, and it is enriched with twelve beautiful plates designed by OVERBECK.

2130 HEURES NOUVELLES, tirées de la Sainte Ecriture, écrites et gravées par L. Senault, the whole beautifully engraved in 260 pages, with very numerous illustrations ; 8vo. red morocco, G. L. 18s. *ib.*

2131 HISTOIRE DE DANTE Alighieri, par M. le Chevalier Artaud de Montor ; 8vo. sewed, 12s. *ib.* 1841

2132 HISTOIRE (Vénérable) du Très-Saint Sacrement de Miracle ; 8vo, with above 20 plates engraved by J. Harrewyn, scarce, 5s. 6d. *Bruxelles,* 1720
Every page adorned with beautiful woodcut borders and plates.

2133 HORÆ in laudem Beatissimæ Virginis Mariæ ad Usum Romanum ; 4to. yellow morocco, rare, 1l. 4s. *Paris,* 1543

2134 HUBY (Père Vincent, de la Compagnie de Jésus) Œuvres Spirituelles; 12mo. sewed, 3*s.* 6*d.* *ib.* 1772

2135 HUGO (Her.) De prima scribendi origine et universa Rei literariæ antiquitate; 8vo, 3*s.* 6*d.* *Antwerp*, 1617

2136 IGNATII (S.) Sententiæ et Effata per singulos anni dies distributa; 12mo. 3*s.* *Mogunt.* 1841

2137 INSTRUCTIONS SUR LE RITUEL, contenant la Théorie et la Pratique des Sacremens et de la Morale, et tous les Principes et Décisions nécessaires aux Curés, Confesseurs, Prédicateurs, Prêtres, ou Clercs, par Louis Albert Joly de Choin, Evêque de Toulon; 3 vols. 4to. 1*l.* 11*s.* 6*d.* *Lyon*, 1780

IRELAND.

2138 TRIADIS THAUMATURGÆ, seu Divorum Patricii, Columbæ, et Brigidæ trium veteris et majoris SCOTIÆ seu HIBERNIÆ Sanctorum Insulæ communium patronorum ACTA; Scripta et studio Joannis Colgani, Tomus Secundus; folio, very rare, 6*l.* 6*s.* *Lovanii*, 1647

2139 DE BURGO (Thoma, Epis. Ossor.) Hibernia Dominicana sive Historia provinciæ Hiberniæ Ordinis Prædicatorum,1762. —Supplementum Hiberniæ Dominicanæ, 1772.—4to. russia extra, *Col. Agr.* 1762

This work is of great rarity, and is quite complete, containing the supplement as well as the usually castrated leaves in the VIIth chapter relating to the state of the Catholics in Ireland in the time of James II, and to the appellation of "Duke of Hanover" given to George I and II.

This work, though bearing the imprint of Cologne, was executed by Edmund Finn at Kilkenny, under Burgh's own inspection.

N.B. This copy belonged to Mr. Hanrott and to Mr. James Weale, at whose sale it was purchased.

2140 ROTH, Analecta Sacra Nova et Mira de rebus Catholicorum in Hibernia pro fide et religione gestis, divisa in tres partes, 2 vols. 12mo. red morocco, bound by *Lewis*, very rare *Coloniæ*, 1617

2141 JANSSONII (J.) In Sacrum Missæ Canonem, quo Romana utitur Ecclesia, expositio. Authore Jacobo Janssonio Amsterdamensi, Sacræ Theologiæ Lovanii professore; 12mo. rare, 3*s.* 6*d.* *Lovanii*, 1586

JESUITS.

2142 ANNUS SECULARIS Societatis Jesu adumbratus ex anno tempora et a Gymnasio Tricoronato Ubiorum; 4to. plates, scarce, 8*s.* 6*d.* 1640

2142*BECANI (M.) Jacobi Angliæ Regis Apologiæ Refutatio, *Moguntiæ*, 1610.— GRETSERI (J.) Relatio de Studiis Jesuitarum abstrusioribus, *Ingolst.* 1609.—2 vols. in 1, 12mo. 5*s.* 6*d.*

2143 DICTIONNAIRE des Livres opposés à la Morale de la Société des soy-disant Jésuites; 4 vols. 12mo. calf, 12*s.* *Brux.*1761

JESUITS.

2144 DE CHRISTIANA EXPEDITIONE apud Sinas suscepta ab Societate Jesu, à PP. Matthæo Ricio, et Nicolas Trigault conscriptum; 4to. 8*s.* 6*d.* *Aug. Vind.* 1615

2145 DIRECTORIUM Exercitiorum spiritualium B. P. N. Ignatii; 18mo. 2*s.* 6*d.* *Antwerp*, 1600

2146 ELOGIA SOCIETATIS JESU, sive propugnaculum, Pontificum, Conciliorum, Cardinalium, &c. testimoniis quà expressis verbo, quà scripto consignatis constructum : per A. P. Christop. Gomez *ejusdem Societatis;* 4to, rare, 14*s.* *ib.* 1681

2147 EPISTOLÆ præpositorum Generalium ad Patres et Fratres Societatis Jesu; 8vo, scarce, 9*s.* 6*d.* *Pragæ*, 1711

2148 FLORUS ANGLO-BAVARICUS, seu Historia Fundationis Collegii Anglorum Soc. Jesu Leodii sub Maximiliano et Maria Bavariæ Ducibus ad hæc tempora gesta sunt complectens, et in nupera procella contra Catholicos ac præsertim PATRES SOCIETATIS JESU in Anglia a TITO OATE excitata, paucis exponens; 4to, very rare, 1*l.* 1*s.* *Leodii*, 1685

2149 —— Another copy; on large paper, and partly in different type, 1*l.*5*s.* *ib.* 1685

2150 GARNET. Actio in Hen. Garnetum Societatis Jesuiticæ in Anglia superiorem et cæteros qui proditione longè Brit. Mag. Regem et Regni Angliæ. adjectum est Supplicium de Hen. Garneto; 4to. 7*s.* 6*d.* *Lond.* 1607

2151 HISTORIA Provinciæ Paraquariæ Societatis Jesu. Authore P. Nicolao del Techo; folio, rare, 1*l.* 1*s.* *Leodii*, 1673

5152 IGNACE (Saint) Exercices Spirituels, traduits en Français par l'Abbé Clément; 18mo, sewed, 1*s.* 6*d.* *Paris*, 1840

2153 IGNATII LOYOLÆ Exercitia Spiritualia; 18mo. 3*s.* 6*d.* *Andomaropoli*, 1610

2154 —— EXERCITIA Spiritualia S. P. cum Bullis Pontificum, tum approbationis Exercitiorum; tum Indulgentiæ plenariæ, pro omnibus, qui octiduo illis vacant in domibus Societatis; 8vo. illustrated with above 50 plates, 10*s.* 6*d.* *Antwerp*, 1676

2155 —— EXERCITIA Spiritualia cum sensu eorumdem explicatio a P. Ignatio Diertins (*Soc. Jesu*); 12mo. 4*s.* 6*d.* *ib.* 1693

2156 —— EXERCITIA Spiritualia Accuratiori quam hactenus ab aliis factum et menti ejus propriori methodo explanata; accedit triduum sacrum, &c. Auctore R. P. Aloysio BELLECIO (*Soc. Jesu*); 8vo. 6*s.* 6*d.* *Paris*, 1836

2157 IMAGO primi Seculi Societatis Jesu, a provincia Flandro-Belgica ejusdem Societatis representa; folio, scarce, many plates, 1*l.* 11*s.* 6*d.* *Antwerp*, 1640

2158 INSTITUTUM SOCIETATIS JESU ex Decreto Congregationis Generalis Decimæ

JESUITS.

Quartæ meliorem in ordinem digestum, Auctum, ac denuo recusum ; 2 vols. folio, vell. good copy, scarce, 3*l.*3*s. Pragæ,* 1705

2159 —— Another copy ; 2 vols. in 1, 2*l.* 15*s. ib.* 1705

2160 JAPAN. Rerum Memorabilium in Regno Japoniæ gestarum Litteræ annis 1619, 1620, 1621, Societatis Jesu ; 12mo, scarce, 5*s. Antwerp,* 1625

2161 LITTERÆ Societatis Jesu, anno 1602 et 1603, e Sinis, Molucis, Japone datæ progressum Rei Christianæ in iis oris ; 12mo. 3*s.* 6*d. Mogunt.* 1607

2162 LITTERÆ APOSTOLICÆ, quibus Institutio, Confirmatio et varia privilegia continentur Societatis Jesu, 1635.—CONSTITUTIONES Societatis Jesu et Examen cum declarationibus,1635.—REGULÆ Societatis Jesu, auctoritate septimæ Congregationis Generalis auctæ ; 3 vols. in 1, 12mo. rare, 9*s.* 6*d. Antwerp,* 1635

2163 ORDINATIONES Præpositum Generalium. Instructiones et Formulæ communes toti societati ; 8vo. scarce, 6*s. Romæ,* 1606

2164 PASCAL, Les Provinciales, ou Lettres écrites par Louis de Montalte à un Provincial de ses Amis et aux RR. PP. Jésuites ; 12mo. 2*s.* 6*d. Cologne,* 1785

2165 —— Another copy ; sewed, 3*s.* 6*d. ib.* 1698

2166 RERUM A SOCIETATE JESU in Oriente gestarum ad annum 1568, Commentarius Eman. Acostæ. Accessere de Japonibus rebus Epistolarum libri IV ; 12mo. rare, 5*s.* 6*d. Dilingæ,* 1571

2167 RIBADENEIRA (P.) Illustrium Scriptorum Religionis Societatis Jesu Catalogus ; 8vo. 4*s.* 6*d. Antwerp,* 1608

2168 JOURNÉE DU CHRÉTIEN, par l'Abbé de la Hogue ; 18mo, in 180 engraved plates with pictorial borders, red morocco, 9*s.* 6*d. Paris*

2169 KEMPIS (Thomas à) Soliloquia, adjectus Hortulus Rosarum ; 18mo. 2*s.*6*d. Lovan.*1600

2170 —— Viator Christianus recta ac regia in cœlum via tendens, aucta Thomæ de Kempis, cujus De Imitatione Christi aliaque piissima Opuscula, notis J. B. Horstii ; 32mo. rare, 4*s.* 6*d. Col. Ag.* 1643

2171 —— Opera omnia studio H. Sommalii, *(Soc. Jesu)* ; 4to. neat, 14*s. Antwerp,* 1607

2172 LADVOCAT, Dictionnaire Historique et Bibliographique ; 5 vols. 8vo. 15*s. Par.* 1822

2173 LAPIDE (Cornelius à) Commentaria in Quatuor Prophetas Majores ; folio, 8*s. Lugduni,* 1622

2174 —— Commentarius in Vetus ac Novum Testamentum ; 10 vols. folio, bd. 6*l.* 16*s.* 6*d. Antwerp,* 1630

2175 LE BRUN, Explication Historique et Dogmatique des Prières et des Cérémonies de la Messe, suivant les anciens Auteurs, et les Monumens de toutes les Eglises du Monde Chrétien, avec des Notes sur l'Origine des Rits ; 8 vols. 8vo. scarce, 1*l.*16*s. Paris,* 1726

2176 —— le même ; 8 vols. bound in 4, scarce, 2*l.* 2*s. ib.* 1726

2177 LE GRAND, Histoire du Divorce de Henry VIII, Roy d'Angleterre, et de Cathérine d'Arragon : avec la Défense de Sanderus : la Réfutation de M. Burnet : et les Preuves ; 3 vols. 12mo. very scarce, 1*l.* 4*s. Paris,* 1788

2178 **Le Grand Martial** de la Mère de Dieu, des Oracles, mérites, louenges, hystoires, et prérogatives de la très sacrée Vierge Marie, Mère de Dieu, Dame des Anges, Royne de Miséricorde, &c. 4to. BLACK LETTER.—De la très-pure immaculé conception de la Vierge Sacrée Marie, très-digne Mère de Dieu, que est le second livre du grand Marial de la Mère de Vie ; 2 vols. in one, *very rare and curious,* 18*s. ib.* 1539

2179 LEONIS Magni Opera omnia, acced. S. Hilarii Opuscula, ed. P. Quesnel ; 2 vols. 4to. neat, 1*l.* 8*s. Lut. Par.* 1675

2180 LESLEY (John) *Bishop of Ross in Scotland.* De titulo et Jure Serenissimæ Principis MARIÆ SCOTORUM REGINÆ, quo Regni Angliæ successionem sibi juste vendicat libellus. Opera Jo. Leslæi, 1580.—Parænesis ad Anglos, et Scotos, ut perpetuâ amicitiâ coalescant, 1580.—De illustrium Fæminarum, in republica administranda, et ferendis legibus, authoritate : 1580 ; 4to. *very rare,* 2*l.*2*s. Rhemes,* 1580.

This copy contains the Table of Genealogies.

2181 LETTRES EDIFIANTES et Curieuses écrites par des Missionnaries de la Compagnie de Jésus, enrichies de nouvelles notes ; 40 vols. 18mo. sewed, 2*l.* 8*s. Paris,* 1829

2182 LETTRES de St. François Xavier, précédées d'une notice historique sur la vie de ce Saint et sur l'établissement de la Compagnie de Jésus ; 2 vols. 12mo, sewed, 7*s. Bruxelles,* 1838

2183 LIBER VITÆ, seu Expositio litteralis in sacram Regulam S. Francisci, ordinis Fratrum Minorum Fundatoris ; 12mo. 4*s. Augustæ,* 1734

2184 LIVRE DES PEUPLES et des Rois, par Charles Sainte-Foi : second édition, augmentée ; 8vo. 8*s. Paris,* 1839

2185 LUTHER. Septiceps Lutherus ubique sibi suis Scriptis contrariis, in visitationem Saxonicam : per D. Jo. Cochlæum ante annos 44 æditus ; 8vo. rare, 8*s.* 6*d. ib.*1564

On the title is the figure of Luther with seven heads.

2186 —— Historia Joannis Cochlæi de actis et scriptis Martini Lutheri ab 1517 ad 1546, inclusive conscripta ; 8vo. 4*s.* 6*d. ib.* 1565

2187 —— Historia de Vita, moribus, rebus gestis, studiis ac denique morte DOCT. MARTINI LUTHERI : authore D. Caspar Vlenbergio ; 12mo. rare, 5*s.* 6*d. Col. Agr.* 16??

2188 LA LITURGIE SACRÉE, ou toutes les parties de la Sainte Messe sont expliquées, avec leur Mystères et Antiquitez, par G. Grimaud, *Prestre; 4to. scarce,* 12s.
Lyon, 1666

2189 MABILLON (J.) De Liturgia Gallicani, libri III. accedit Disquisitio de Cursu Gallicano; 4to. scarce, 15s. *Paris.* 1729

2190 MAGUIN (Abbé) La Papauté considérée dans son origine, dans son développement au moyen age, et dans son état actuel, aux prises avec le Protestantisme; 8vo. 7s. 6d.
ib. 1841

2191 MANIERE de donner l'Habit aux Soeurs de Sainct Marie; 8vo. 2s. 6d. *Lyon,* 1666

2192 MANSI (Jos.) Locupletissima Bibliotheca Moralis Prædicabilis, hoc est, Discursus varii exquisiti, in quibus per tractatus ordine digestos ad verbum Dei fructuose et faciliter prædicandum, de virtutibus et vitiis copiosissimæ materiæ morales subministrantur, et ad plenum digeruntur; 4 vols. folio, scarce, 3l. 18d. *Aug. Vindel.* 1732

2193 MANUEL du Chrétien, contenant les Pseaumes, le Nouveau Testament, l'Imitation; précédé des Prières pour la Messe, des Vépres, et des Complies; 32mo. 4s. 6d.
Paris, 1841

2194 MARGARITA EVANGELICA, sive JESU CHRISTI D. N. Vita, Doctrina, Historiaque universa, e S. S. quatuor Evangeliorum dispositione concordi, ordine temporum novaque methodo descripta et explanata, per P. Joannem de Paris, 4to. vellum, 9s. 6d.
Antwerp, 1657

2195 MARIN, Lettres Ascétiques et Morales, 2 vols. 12mo. 4s. *Avignon,* 1769

2196 MARTENE (E.) De Antiquis Monachorum Ritibus, libri v. 2 vols. 4to. 1l. 1s. *Lug.* 1690

2197 MARTYROLOGIUM Romanum Gregorii XIII et Clementis X, auct. recog. 8vo. 9s. 6d.
Antwerp, 1723

2198 MARTYROLOGIUM ROMANUM, Gregorii XIII jussu editum, editio nova a Benedicto XIV aucta et castigata; 4to. 10s. 6d.
Venetiis, 1749

2199 MARTYROLOGIUM Reveren. Domini Francisci Maurolyci Abbatis Messanensis: in quo addita sunt locorum nomina in quibus Martyres passi sunt: atque eorum corpora in præsentiarum requiesount; 4to. 6s. 6d.
ib. 1568

MARY QUEEN OF SCOTS.

2200 MARIA STUARTA, Regina Scotiæ, Dotaria Franciæ, Hæres Angliæ et Hyberniæ; Martyr Ecclesiæ Innocens à cæde Darleana; vindice Oberto Barnestapolio; 12mo. *very rare,* morocco, gilt edges, 15s.
Coloniæ, 1627

2201 —— Summarium Rationum, quibus Cancellarius Angliæ et Prolocutor Puckeringius Elizabethæ Angliæ Reginæ persuaserunt occidendam esse Serenissimam Principem Mariam Stuartam Scotiæ Reginam: una cum responsionibus Reginæ Angliæ et Sententia mortis, additum est Supplicium et Mors Reginæ Scotiæ. Opera Romoaldi Scoti; 12mo. *rare,* morocco, gilt edges, 12s. 6d. *Coloniæ,* 1627

2202 MASON (N.) CERTAMEN SERAPHICUM PROVINCIÆ ANGLIÆ PRO SANCTA DEI ECCLESIA. OPERE R. P. F. ANGELI A S. FRANCISCO; 4to. *very rare,* contains all the portraits, fine copy in vellum, 7l. 7s. *Duaci,* 1649

2203 —— APOLOGIA PRO SCOTO ANGLO, in qua defenditur D. Joannes Pitseus in sua relatione, de loco nativitatis subtilis Doctoris F. Joannis Scoti: et rejectis argumentis adversæ partis, maximè R. P. JOANNIS COLGANI HIBERNI, Scotum fuisse Anglum natione ostenditur. Per F. ANGELUM A S. FRANCISCO, *Anglum;* 12mo. *cæceedingly rare,* 12s. *ib.* 1656

2204 —— Sacrarium privilegiorum quorundam Seraphico S. Francisco, in gratiam observantium regulam, eumque vel suos amantium à Deo O. M. Indultorum, in quo eorum veritas elucidatur, comprobatur, ac defenditur. *Duaci,* 1636.—Statuta FF. Minorum Recollectorum provin. inf. Germaniæ à capitula provin. in Conventu Mechlin. 1672.—Tabula Capituli Generalis celebrati, *Romæ,* An. 1651.—Statuta Generalia Ord. Frat. Min. edita in Capit. Gen. celeb. *Romæ,* 1651 —et revisa reformata in Capit. Gen. *Toletani,* 1658.—Tabula et Constitutiones celeb. Con. Gen. totius Cismontanæ familiæ ordinis Frat. Min. 1662; all in 1 vol. 12mo. very rare, 8s. 6d. *v. y.*

2205 MASSILLON, Œuvres complètes; 2 vols. imp. 8vo. 1l. 10s. *Paris,* 1838

2206 MAXIMES Chrétiennes et Morales, par l'Abbé de Rance; 2 vols. 12mo. 4s. *ib.* 1702

2207 MEL DE PETRA, Devotæ Animæ dulcedo, sive Exercitia Sacrarum Precum præcipuis Christianæ Religionis officiis; 8vo. 3s. 6d.
Bamberge, 1769

2208 MESSINGHAMI *(Sacer. Hibern.)* Florilegium Insulæ Sanctorum, seu Vitæ et Actæ Sanctorum Hiberniæ, quibus accesserunt S. Patricii purgatorium; S. Malachiæ Prophetia de summis Pontificibus, &c. folio, *very rare,* 2l. 10s. *Par:* 1624

2209 MIRÆI (A.) Ordinis Præmonstatensis Chronicon; 12mo. 3s. 6d. *Col. Ag.* 1613

2210 MIRÆI Originum Monasticarum, libri IV, in quibus ordinum omnium Religiosorum initia ac progressus breviter describuntur; 12mo. 3s. 6d. *ib.* 1620

2211 MIROIR des Domestiques Chrétiens; 18mo. 2s. *Tours,* 1838

2212 MIROIR DU PECHEUR pénitent, ou explication du *Miserere,* par figures tirées et comparées de la Vie et Passion de N. S. J. C. avec Méditations et Prières; 12mo. 25 plates, 9s. 6d. *Louvain,* 1627

2213 MISSA APOSTOLICA, sive Divinum Sacrificium Sancti Apostoli Petri, cum apologia Wil. Lindani (Epis. Gand.) pro eadem D. Petri Apostoli Liturgia; 8vo. scarce, 7s. 6d.
Antwerp, 1589

2214 —— seu Divinum Sacrificium S. Apostoli Petri, cum Canone Lat. S. Ecclesiæ Rom. et notis: *Lutetiæ,* 1595.—S. GREGORII PAPÆ quem Dialogum Græci cognominant, divinum officium, sive MISSA, cum interpretatione Græca, *Lutetiæ,* 1595.—CONSTANTINI Imp. Rescriptum ad Arium et Arianos, Græce et Latine: *Lutetiæ,* 1595; 3 vols. in one, 8vo. 10s. 6d.

2215 𝕸𝖎𝖘𝖘𝖆𝖑𝖊 𝕮𝖆𝖗𝖙𝖍𝖚𝖘𝖎𝖊𝖓𝖘𝖊, black letter; 8vo. many woodcuts (*one leaf wanting*) 9s. 6d.
Printed by T. Kerver, Paris, 1541

2216 MISSALE ROMANUM; folio, sewed, red and black type, 2l. 10s.
Rome, 1826

2217 —— Idem, with the " Missæ propriæ pro Anglia;" folio, morocco, gilt edges, 5l. 5s.
Mechlin, 1836

2218 —— Idem, red and black type; 12mo. sewed, 10s. 6d.
ib. 1840
A most beautifully printed work.

2219 —— Idem, black type only; 12mo. sewed, 10s. 6d.
Berolini, 1841

2220 𝕸𝖎𝖘𝖘𝖆𝖑𝖊 𝖆𝖉 𝖚𝖘𝖚𝖒 𝖎𝖓𝖘𝖎𝖌𝖓𝖎𝖘 𝕰𝖈𝖈𝖑𝖊𝖘𝖎𝖆𝖊 𝕻𝖆𝖗𝖎𝖘𝖇𝖚𝖗𝖎𝖊𝖓𝖘𝖎𝖘, folio,
Paris. 1555
A most beautiful copy of this rare book, as perfect and clean as if just issued from the press: filled with a profusion of woodcut illustrations, besides two large plates on vellum; bound in the ancient style in velvet, with brass ornaments, corners, bosses, and clasps; the edges gilt and tooled.

2221 MOELLER (J.) Précis de l'Histoire du Moyen Age, depuis la chûte de l'Empire Romain d'Occident jusqu'à la naissance du Protestantisme, (476-1517) 8vo. 7s. 6d.
Louvain, 1841

2222 MOEHLER (J. A.) Athanase le Grand et l'Eglise et son temps en lutte avec l'Arianisme, traduit de l'Allemand, avec une notice historique par J. Cohen; 3 vols. 8vo. 18s.
Paris, 1840

2223 MOLANI. De Historia S. S. Imaginum et Picturarum, pro vero earum usu contra abusus, libri IV; ejusdem Oratio De Agnus Dei et alia quædam: recensuit J. H. Paquot; 4to. 12s.
Lovan. 1771

2224 MONTALEMBERT (Comte de) Du Vandalisme et du Catholicisme dans l'Art; 8vo. 6s. 6d.
Paris, 1839

2225 —— Histoire de Saint Elisabeth de Hongrie, Duchesse de Thuringe—1207-1231 —troisième édition avec plusieurs additions; royal 8vo. plates, 14s.
ib. 1841

2226 MORINI Antiquitates Ecclesiæ Orientalis, præfixa est J. Morini Vita; 12mo. 4s. 6d.
Lond. 1682

2227 MUIS (Simeonis de) Commentarius in omnes Psalmos Davidis, et selecta veteris Testamenti Cantica. Accesserunt J. B. BOSSUET

Notæ in Psalmos et aliquot Cantica: ejusdem supplenda in Psalmos, et dissertatio Gallica in Psalmum XXI; 2 vols. 4to. 18s.
Lovan. 1770

2228 MYSTICA Theologia do Serafico S. Boaventura; 12mo. 2s.

2229 NICOLE (M.) Ouvres complètes; 25 vols. 12mo. sewed, 2l. 12s. 6d.
Paris, v. y.
viz.—Essais de Morale, 14 vols. in 15 Vols.
Instructions sur le Symbole, 2
—— sur les Sacremens - 2
—— le Décalogue . . - 2
—— la Prière . . . - 2
—— Oraison Dominicale, 1
Esprit - - - - - - - 1

2230 NOVA Collectio Decretorum Sacræ Rituum Congregationis Notis illustrata juxta editionem Romanam cum appendice, &c. 13mo. 3s. 6d.
Lovan. 1788

2231 OPTATI, Sancti, Opera, cum notis Albaspinæi, accedit S. Facundi Hermianensis Episcopi, pro tribus Capitulis Concilii Chalcedonensis, lib. XII, cum notis Albaspinæi et variorum, curis J. Priorii et J. Sirmondi, folio, neat, 1l. 1s.
Paris. 1679

2232 —— another copy, ed. L. E. Dupin; folio, calf, neat, 1l. 11s. 6d.
ib. 1700

2233 ORDO perpetuus Divini Officii juxta ritum Breviarii ac Missalis Sanctæ Romanæ Ecclesiæ. Nova editio; 12mo. 4s. 6d.
ib. 1834

2234 PALLADII Dialogus de Vita S. Johannis Chrysostomi, Gr. et Lat., curâ Bigotii; 4to. 6s.
Lut. Par. 1680

2235 PARADISUS Animæ Christianæ, studio et opera J. M. Horstii; 24mo. 4s. 6d.
Mechlin, 1840

2236 PARADISUS PUERORUM, per Phil. de Berlaymont, Soc. Jesu, 8vo. scarce, 5s. 6d.

2237 PARADISUS SPONSI ET SPONSÆ: in quo Messis myrrhæ et aromatum, ex instrumentis ac mysteriis Passionis Christi colligenda, ut ei commoriamur; et Pancarum Marianum, Septemplici Titulorum serie distinctum: auctore P. J. David; 8vo. *rare*, 7s. 6d.
Antwerp, 1707

2238 PERPETUITÉ de la Foi de l'Eglise Catholique touchant l'Eucharistie, défendue contre le livre du Sieur Claude de Charenton; 4to. scarce, 18s.
Paris, 1669

2239 PERPETUITE DE LA FOY de l'Eglise Catholique touchant l'Eucharistie defendue contre Claude, &c. par Arnauld, Nicole, &c. 4 vols. 4to. boards, *scarce*, 2l. 8s.
ib. 1704

2240 —— another copy, 4 vols. 4to. calf, neat, 2l. 14s.
ib. 1704

2241 PERSONS, Robert, *Soc. Jesu*, Elizabethæ Angliæ Reginæ Hæresim Calvinianam propugnantis, sævissimum in Catholicos sui regni edictum, promulgatum Lond. 29 Nov. 1591, cum responsione ad singula capita, per D. And. Philopatrum; 8vo. first edition, *rare*, 9s. 6d.
Augustæ, 1592

2242 —— the same, second edition, 8s. 6d. 1593

2243 PICART, Cérémonies et Coûtumes de tous les Peuples du Monde, with the "Supplement" and the "Superstitions ;" 11 vols. folio, calf, 13l. 13s.   *Amst.* 1723

2244 PONTIFICALE Romanum, Clementis VIII. Pont. Max. jussu restitutum atque editum ; folio, 1l. 11s. 6d.   *Paris.* 1615

2245 —— Clementis VIII et Urbani VIII, recog. cum figuris ; 8vo. 15s. *Bruxellis*

2246 —— ex recognitione Benedicti XIV, cum additionibus ; 4 vols. in one, large folio, many plates, 5l. 5s.   *Urbini,* 1818

2247 POLE, CARDINAL. *Epistolarum* REGINALDI POLI S. R. E. *Cardinalis et aliorum ad ipsum ;* 5 vols. 4to. vellum, fine copy, *very scarce,* 5l. 15s. 6d.   *Brixiæ,* 1744-57

2248 POSSEVINI, Ant. *(Soc. Jesu)* Apparatus Sacer. 3 vols. in 2, folio, neat copy, 1l. 8s.   *Venet.* 1603

2249 —— Bibliotheca Selecta de Ratione Studiorum ; 2 vols. in one, folio, neat, 18s.   *ib.* 1603

2250 QUADRUPANI, Instructions pour Vivre Chrétiennement dans le Monde ; 32mo. 2s.   *Paris,* 1840

2251 —— Instructions pour éclairer les Ames pieuses dans leurs Doutes, et pour les rassurer dans leurs Craintes ; 32mo. 2s. *ib.*1837

2252 REPRESENTACION de la Vida del Padre Fray Joan de la Cruz, por el Rev. Fray Gaspar ; 8vo. above 70 plates, *very curious,* title wanting, 6s. 6d.   *Bruselas,* 1677

2253 REYNERI, Clementis, Apostolatus Benedictinorum in Anglia, sive Historia de Antiquitate Ordinis S. Benedicti in Regno Angliæ ; folio, *rare,* 1l. 16s.   *Duaci,* 1626

2254 REYRE, Abbé, Année Pastorale, ou Prônes nouveaux en forme d'Homélies, contenant une explication de l'Evangile de tous les Dimanches de l'Année, et de tous les jours de Carême ; 3 vols. 12mo. 8s. 6d.   *Paris,* 1835

2255 REVELATIONS faites en faveur de la France, par l'entremise de Thomas Martin en 1816 ; 12mo. 2s.   *ib.* 1827

2256 ROME ET JERUSALEM, par J. D'Avenel ; 8vo. 7s. 6d.   *ib.* 1841

2257 ROME. Des Institutions de Bienfaisance publique, et d'instruction primaire à Rome, Essai historique et statistique traduit de l'Italien de M. Morichini, par M. E. De Bazelaire ; 8vo. 7s. 6d.   *ib.* 1841

2258 ROMÉCOURT, Baron de, Aperçus Philosophiques sur le Christianisme ; 8vo. 5s.   *ib.* 1841

2259 ROSARIUM AUREUM Mysticum nuper editum per Rev. G. Pepin, *Ord. Præd.* 12mo. BLACK LETTER, rare, 8s. 6d.   *ib. Jean Petit, circa* 1518

2260 ROSELINE, ou la Nécessité de la Religion dans l'Éducation des Femmes ; 8vo. 5s.   *Paris,* 1840

2261 SALMASII, Cl., Librorum de Primatı Papæ, cum apparatu Nili *(Archiepis. Thes sal.)* et Barlaami Tractatus ; 4to. *good cop*ı calf, 20s.   *Lug. Bat.* 164ı

2262 SANDERI, N., De Origine ac progress Schismatis Anglicani libri tres ; cum appen dice R. P. PETRI RIBADANEIRÆ *(Soc. Jesu* 12mo. *rare,* 8s. 6d.   *Col. Ag.* 161(

2263 —— Vera et Sincera Historia Schisma tis Anglicani, de ejus origine ac progressu aucta per E. Rishtonum, cum appendicı Petri Ribadeneira ; 12mo.*rare,*8s.6d. *ib.*162?

2264 —— De Origine ac Progressu Schisma tis Anglicani, libri III, aucti per Ed. Rish tonum ; 8vo. rare, 8s. 6d.   *Ingolst.* 1588

2265 SANDERUS Histoire du Schisme d'Angle terre, traduit en Français par Maucroix 12mo. seconde édition, 5s. 6d.   *Paris,* 1678

2266 —— Histoire du Schisme d'Angleterre, traduite en Français par Maucroix ; troisième edition, 12mo. 5s. 6d.   *ib.* 1683

2267 SANDERUS, N., De Clave David seu Regno Christi, libri VI, contra calumnias Acleri pro visibili Ecclesiæ Monarchia ; 4to. scarce, 8s. 6d.   *Rome,* 1588

2268 —— De Visibili Monarchia Ecclesiæ ; first edition, folio, 1l. 6s.   *Lovan.* 1571

2269 —— Idem, access. libri VI, de Clave David, seu de Regno Christi ; folio, scarce, 1l. 18s.   *Wirceb.* 1592

2270 SCHALL, J., Historica Relatio de Ortu et progressu Fidei Orthodoxæ in Regno Chinensi, per Missionarios Societatis Jesu, ab 1581 ad 1669 ; 8vo. scarce, 6s.   *Ratisbon,* 1672

2271 SERGEANTII, Joannis, Vindiciæ. Tribunalibus Romano et Parisiensi, ubi ab Ill. PETRO TALBOTO, Archiepiscopo Dubliniensi, de doctrinâ pravâ accusatus fuit, in Librorum suorum Defensionem exhibitæ ; 12mo. *very rare,* 7s. 6d.   1678

2272 SERMONS du R. Père Elisée, Carme Déchaussé ; 4 vols. 12mo. 12s.   *Paris,* 1785

2273 SERMONS du Rev. Père de Maccarthy, de la Compagnie de Jésus ; 4 vols. 12mo. sewed, 14s.   *ib.* 1840

2274 SIRMONDI, J. *(Soc. Jesu)* Opera Varia, seu Opuscula S.S. Patrum et Auctorum Ecclesiasticorum ; edidit J. de la Beaume ; 5 vols. folio, *large paper,* calf gilt, 4l.   *ib.* 1696

2275 SMYTH (Richard) De Missæ sacrificio, succincta quædam enarratio, ac brevis repulsio præcipuorum argumentorum, quæ Philippus Melanchthon, Joannes Calvinus, et alii sectarii objecerunt adversus illud et Purgatorium ; 8vo. *Lovan.* 1562.—Confutatio eorum, quæ Philippus Melanchthon objicit contra Missæ sacrificium propitiatorum ; 8vo. *ib.* 1562.—Refutatio luculentæ, crassæ, et exitiosæ, hæresis Joannis Calvini, et Christ. Carlili, Angli, qui astruent Christum non descendisse ad inferos alios, quam ad infernum infimum, qui est locus damnatorum perpetuus, aut ad sepulchrum; 8vo. *ib.* 1562.—De Infantium Baptismo, contra Joannem Calvinum, ac de operibus supererogationis, et merito mortis Christi adversus eundem Calvinum et ejus discipulos; 8vo. *ib.* 1562.—Defensio comprehendiaria, et orthodoxa, sacri, externi et visibilis Jesu Christi sacerdotii. Cui addita est sacratorum Catholicæ Ecclesiæ altarium propugnatio ac Calvinianæ Communionis succincta refutatio; 8vo. *ib.* 1562.—5 treatises in 1 vol. very rare, 18*s.*

2276 SMYTH (Richard) Defensio Compendiaria et orthodoxa, sacri, externi et visibilis Jesu Christi Sacerdotii. Cui addita est sacratorum Catholicæ Ecclesiæ altarium propugnatio, ac Calvinianæ Communionis succincta refutatio; 8vo. rare, 7*s.* 6*d.* *ib.* 1562

2277 —— Refutatio Locorum Communium Theologicorum Philippi Melanchthonis, Germani, M. Lutheri Discipuli primarii; 8vo, very rare, 10*s.* 6*d.* *Duàci,* 1563

2278 SOUFFRANCES DE N. S. JÉSUS CHRIST, par le Père Thomas de Jésus, traduit par le Père Alleaume; 2 vols. 12mo. sewed, 5*s.* *Paris,* 1833

2279 STANIHURST (Guil.) Veteris Hominis per expensa quatuor novissima Metamorphosis, et novi Genesis; 12mo. 5*s.* *Antwerp,* 1661

2280 STAPLETONI (Th.) Antidota Apostolica contra nostri temporis hæreses (maxime Calvinus et Beza; 8vo. very scarce, 15*s.* *ib.* 1595

2281 —— Apologia pro Rege Catholico Philippo II Hispaniæ, &c. Rege, contra varias et falsas Accusationes Elisabethæ Angliæ Reginæ, per edictum suam 18 Oct. 1591; 8vo. very rare, 1*l.* 1*s.* *Constantia,*

2282 —— TRES THOMÆ seu Res gestæ S. Thomæ Apostoli, S. Thomæ Arch. Cant. et Thomæ Mori Angliæ Cancell.; 12mo, very scarce, 1*l.* 4*s.* *Col. Ag.* 1612

2283 STEYARTII, Martini, in Propositionibus damnatis annotationes omnes jam collectæ et ab authore illustratæ; 12mo. 3*s.* *Lovan.* 1736

2284 SUMMA Constitutionum summorum Pontificum, et rerum in Ecclesia Romana gestarum à Gregorio IX usque et Sixtum V, per P. Matthæum; 4to. scarce, 1*l.* 11*s.* 6*d.* *Lugduni,* 1589

2285 SYNTAGMA de Annulis, sive Tractatus Annularis de Annulorum origine, virtute, et dignitate; 8vo. plates, 5*s.* 6*d.* *Antwerp*

2286 Summa Angelica Reverendi Patris Fratris Angeli de Clavasio: per necessaria sacerdotibus et maxime animarum curam habentibus: casus conscientiæ et vitiorum remedia continens; 12mo, rare, 7*s.* 6*d.* *Paris, J. Petit,* 1519

A good specimen of the press of "Jean Petit."

2287 SUTORI, P. De Vita Cartusiana lib. duo, accessit Bostius de illustribus aliquot ejusdem ordinis viris; 12mo. 5*s.* 6*d.* *Col. Ag.* 1609

2288 TAXA S. CANCELLARIÆ ROMANÆ in lucem emissa, et notis illustrata; 12mo, scarce, 12*s.* *Franckeræ,* 1651

2289 THEOPHYLACTI (Archiepisc. Bulgariæ) Commentarii in IV Evangelia, Gr. et Lat. cura C. Morell, 1631.—Commentarii in S. Pauli Epistolas, Gr. et Lat. cura A. Lindsell, 1635.—2 vols. folio, 1*l.* 18*s.*

2290 TIRINI, J. Commentarius in Vetum et Novum Testamentum; 2 vols. in 1, folio, 1*l.* 1*s.* *Lugduni,* 1683

2291 —— Idem; best edition, 2 vols. calf neat, fine copy, 1*l.* 12*s.* *Antwerp,* 1729

2292 —— Idem; 2 vols. folio, 1*l.* 1*s.* *Lugduni,* 1736

2293 TOURNELY, Prælectiones Theologicæ de Gratia; 12mo, 4*s.* 6*d.* *Paris,* 1742

2294 TOMBEAU (Le) des Hérétiques, par George l'Apostre. Où le faux masque des Huguenots est découvert; 12mo. 4*s.* *Thurin.* 1602

2295 TRAITÉ de la Vocation à l'Etat Ecclésiastique, *Paris,* 1695.—Des Vertus Théologales et Cardinales, par I. G. De Ville Thierry, *Par.* 1710.—12mo. 4*s.* 6*d.* *ib.* 1695-1710

2296 TRANSITUS Animæ revertensis ad jugum sanctum Christi Jesu, auctore Lud. Besombes de St. Genies; 12mo. 5*s.* 6*d.* *Montalbani,* 1788

2297 VADE MECUM piorum Sacerdotum, sive Exercitia et Preces Matutinæ, Vespertinæ, ante et post Missam, &c.; 12mo. 2*s.* *Preston,* 1774

2298 VARII Fasciculi Myrrhæ et Aromatum ex Passione Domini collecta; 12mo. plates, 3*s.* 6*d.* *Aug. Vindel.* 1658

2299 VERSTEGANI, Richardi, Theatrum Crudelitatum nostri temporis, 29 plates *of the horrid cruelties exercised towards the Catholics, including a plate of the execution of Mary, Queen of Scots, and others in England;* 4to. half-bound, good copy, 18*s.* *Antwerp,* 1594

2300 VERNAZZA, Battista, Opere Spirituali della Venerabile Serva di Dio Madre Donna Battista Vernazza Canonichessa Regolare nel Monistero di S. Maria delle Grazie di Genova; 6 vols. in 3, 4to, vel. 18*s.* *Genova*

2301 VIE de Dom Augustin de l'Estrange, Abbé de la Trappe; 12mo. 2*s.* 6*d.* *Paris,* 1829

2302 VIE du Père Bernard Colnago de la Comp. de Jésus; 12mo. 3*s.* 6*d.* *Douay,* 1665

2303 VIE du Cardinal Jean François Commendon, par M. Fléchier; 12mo. 3*s.* *Paris,* 1695

2304 VIE de St. Jean de la Croix, Confesseur de Ste. Thérèse; 12mo. 3*s.* 6*d.* *ib.* 1810

2305 VIE de Marie Lumague, Veuve Institutrice des Filles de la Providence, sous la Conduite de St. Vincent de Paul, par Collin, 12mo. 3*s.* *ib.* 1744

2306 VIE et Instructions de la Vénérable Mère Anne de S. Barthélémy, Compagne et Coadjutrice de St. Thérèse, et Fondatrice des Carmélites Déchaussées; 8vo. portrait, 6*s.* *Bruxelles,* 1708

2307 VIE de Mademoiselle de Meluen, Fondatrice des Religieuses Hospitalières, par J. Grandet, Prêtre; 8vo. 4s. 6d. *Paris*, 1703

2308 VIE de Ste. Thérèse, par Villafore; 2 vols. 12mo. 4s. *ib.* 1820

2309 VIA del Paradiso, con l'Uffizio della Madonna e dei Morti; 32mo. 3s.6d. *Livorno*,1833

2310 VIRIDARIUM MARIANUM variis Rosariorum, exercitiorum, exemplorumque Plantationibus peramœnum, auctore F. Vin. Hensbergio; 12mo. many plates, *rare*, 7s. *Antwerp*, 1626

2311 VIVIS LUDOVICI, de Officio Mariti liber unus. De Institutione Fœminæ Christianæ libri tres. De Ingenuorum Adolescentum ac puellarum Institutione libri duo, 12mo. *scarce*, 4s. 6d. *Basileæ*

2312 VITA del Ven. Padre Pietro Canisio, della Compagnia di Gesù, scritta da Longaro degli Oddi della medesima compagnia: 4to. 6s. 6d. *Napoli*, 1755

2313 WILKINS, DAVID, CONCILIA MAGNÆ BRITANNIÆ ET HIBERNIÆ, ab anno 1446 ad 1717; accedunt CONSTITUTIONES et alia ad Historiam Ecclesiæ Anglicanæ Spectantia; 4 vols. folio, *fine tall copy, half-bound*, 36l. *Lond.* 1737

This valuable work, without which no English library can be complete, is now of great rarity, and it is but very seldom that a copy is offered for sale.

2314 WHITE, A., Schismatis Anglicani Redargutio. Authore Alexandro White, ex eodem schismate, per Dei gratiam ad fidem Catholicam converso; 12mo. very rare, vellum, 10s. 6d. *Lovan.* 1661

OMISSIONS.

2322 Allen (Cardinal) Ad persecutores Anglos pro Catholicis Domi forisque persecutionem sufferentibus; contra falsum, seditiosum, et contumeliosum Libellum, inscriptum:—JUSTITIA BRITANNICA; 8vo. very rare, 18s. *Ingolst.* 1584

2323 BENEDICTI, D. Patris, Regula et Constitutiones Montis Oliveti; 4to, rare, 8s. 6d. *Romæ*, 1573

2324 HISTOIRE de Saint François d'Assise, 1182-1226, par François Emile Chavin; 8vo. 8s. 6d. *Paris*, 1841

IRELAND.

2325 Histoire de la Vie et du Purgatoire de St. Patrice, Archévêque et Primat d'Hybernie, mise en Français par François Bouillon; 12mo. rare, 9s. 6d. *Rouen*, 1661

2326 PATRICII S. *In Nomine Jesu*, Opusculum de Purgatorio Sancti Patritii Hyberniæ Patroni, scriptum per Rev. Patrem Dom. Brullanghan S. Ord. Præd. Miss.; 8vo. very rare, 5s. 6d. *Lovanii*, 1735

Dedicated to Dr. M'Mahon, Bishop of Clogher.

2327 ITINERARIUM Thomæ Carve, Tipperariensis in fortissima juxta et nobilissima Legione strenuissimi Domini Colonelli D. Walteri Deverous, cum Historia Butleri, Gordon, Lesly, et aliorum; FIRST EDITION, 12mo. rare, 13s. 6d. *Moguntiæ*, 1639

A copy was sold for £20.12s. at Col. Stanley's sale.

2328 JESUITS. Nuove lettere delle cose del Giappone, paese del mondo novo, dell' anno 1579 al 1581, con la morte d'alcuni Padri della Compagnia di Giesu; 8vo. scarce, 5s. *Venetia*, 1585

2329 MANUEL de la Messe, ou Explication des Prières et des Cérémonies du Saint Sacrifice, par M. Le Courtier; 12mo. 4s. *Paris*, 1841

2330 POLI, Reginaldi Cardinalis, Sedis Apostolicæ legati, Reformatio Angliæ, anno 1556; 4to. rare, 8s. 6d. *Romæ*, 1562

2331 ROMA Triumphans Septicollis, qua nova hactenus, et insolita methodo comparativa: tota fides Romano-Catholica clarissime demonstretur: atque infidelium omnium argumenta diluantur. Authore FR. RAYMUNDO CARONO Hiberno.—APOSTOLATUS Evangelicus Missioniarum per universum mundum expositus, per RAYMUNDO CARONO Hiberno: 2 works in 1 vol. 8vo. very scarce, 18s. *Antwerp*, 1653

2332 SANDERS, Nicholas, Trois Livres touchant l'Origine et Progrès du Schisme d'Angleterre, augmenté par E. Rishton; 8vo. scarce, 9s. 6d. 1587

2333 TAXE de la Chancellerie Romaine et la Banque du Pape; 8vo. sca. 5s. *Lond.* 1701

2334 VIE de Saint Hugues, Evêque de Grenoble, suivie d'une Notice Chronologique sr les Evêques de Grenoble, par Albert Du Boys; 8vo. 8s. *Grenoble*, 183?

A SELECTION

OF

CURIOUS & INTERESTING ENGLISH BOOKS,

Chiefly Catholic,

ON SALE AT THE PRICES AFFIXED,

BY

CHARLES DOLMAN, 61, NEW BOND STREET.

2335 ABRIDGMENT of Christian Doctrine, with Proofs of Scripture for Points controverted, by H[enry] T[urberville], dedicated to the Lady E. B[edingfeld]; 32mo. scarce, 5s. *Permissu Superiorum*   *Douay*, 1648

2336 AINSWORTH, (H.) The Communion of Saincts. A Treatise of the Fellowship that the Faithful have with God and his Angels, and one with another, in this present Life. Gathered out of the Holy Scriptures; 12mo. rare, 7s. 6d.   *Reprinted* 1615

2337 ALLEN (Cardinal) A true sincere and modest defence of English Catholiques that suffer for their Faith both at home and abrode: against a false, seditious and slanderous libel intituled;
THE EXECUTION OF JUSTICE IN ENGLAND. *Wherein is declared, how unjustlie the Protestants doe charge Catholiques with treason; how untrulie they deny their persecution for religion; and how deceitfullie they seeke to abuse strangers about the cause, greatnes, and maner of their sufferinges, with divers other matters perteining to this purpose;* 8vo. very rare, 1l. 4s.   *Ingolst.* 1584

2338 ANN (St.) An Abridgment of the Prerogatives of St. Ann, Mother of the Mother of God, by William Claget, D.D.; 4to. 3s. 6d.   *London*, 1688

2339 ANNALS of the Church from the Death of Christ during the first five Centuries; 5 vols. 8vo. 1l. 10s.   *ib.* 1738

2340 ——— DITTO; fine paper, 5 vols. 8vo. 1l. 15s.   *ib.* 1738

2341 ANTIQUITIES of the English Franciscans, or Friers Minors, commonly called Gray Friers, in 2 parts, with an Appendix concerning the English Nuns of the Order of St. Clare, compiled and collected by A. P.; 4to. rare, 18s.   *ib.* 1726

2342 APOLOGY (the late) in Behalf of the Papists, reprinted and answered in Behalf of the Royalists; fourth edition, 4to. 4s. *ib.* 1675

2343 ARIAS (Francis) The little Memorial, concerning the good and fruitfull Use of the Sacraments; 18mo. 3s. 6d.   *Roan*, 1602

2344 APPLETON (Rev. Mr.) Collection of Discourses on the Duties of Religion; 8vo. 6s.   *Dublin*, 1790

2345 AUGUSTINE (S.) of the Citie of God: with the learned Comments of Jo. Ludovicus Vives; folio, second edit. 15s. *London*, 1620

2346 AUSTIN (John) Devotions in the Ancient Way of Offices; containing Exercises for Every Day in the Week and Every Holiday in the Year; 8vo. calf neat, scarce, 10s. 6d.   *Edinburgh*, 1789

2347 AUSTIN (William) Devotionis Augustinianæ Flammæ, or Certaine Devout, Godly, and Learned Meditations; folio, 8s. 6d.   *London*, 1637

2348 BAYLIE (Tho.) Certamen Religiosum: or a Conference between His late Majestie Charles, King of England, and Henry, Marquis of Worcester, concerning Religion, 1646; 8vo. scarce, 4s. 6d.   *ib.* 1649

2349 ——— An End to Controversie between the Romane Catholique and the Protestant Religions, justified by all the severall manner of wayes, whereby, all kind of Controversies are usually determined; 4to. very scarce, 18s.   *Douay*, 1654

2350 BELSON (John) Tradidi Vobis; or the Traditionary Conveyance of Faith, cleered in the Rational Way, against the Exceptions of a Learned Opponent, by J. B.; 12mo. scarce, 5s.   *London*, 1662

2351 BENEDICT (St.) Statutes for the better Observation of the Holy Rule of the most Glorious Father and Patriarch *St. Benedict:* confirmed by the Archbishop of Mechlin, and by him delivered to the English Religious Women of the Monastery of Our Blessed Lady the perpetuall Virgin Mary in Bruxelles, and to all their Successours; 12mo. very rare, 12s.   *Gant*, 1632

2352 BERNARD (Francis, Student in Divinity) The Christian Duty, in 51 Discourses on the Creed, Sacraments, Commandments, &c.; 4to. scarce, 6s. 6d.   *Aire*, 1684

BIBLES & TESTAMENTS.

2353 THE HOLIE BIBLE faithfully translated into English out of the authentical Latin, with Annotations, &c. by the English 'College of Douay, *Douay,* 1609-10.—THE NEW TESTAMENT translated faithfully into English, with Annotations, &c. by the English College of Rhemes, *Rhemes,* 1682. —4to. fine copy, calf lettered, uniform, 4l. 14s. 6d.   *v. y.*

2354 —— Another copy; 3 vols. 4to. original edition, 4l. 4s.

2355 THE NEW TESTAMENT; first edition, 4to. calf lettered, 1l.11s. 6d. *Rhemes,* 1582

2356 —— Ditto; second edition, scarce, 18s.   *Antwerp,* 1600

2357 —— Ditto; third edition, 18mo. very rare, 14s.   *ib.* 1621

2358 —— Ditto; fifth edition, first in folio, scarce, calf neat, 1l. 4s. *Permis. Sup.* 1738

2359 THE NEW TESTAMENT, with Annotations by R. Witham; 2 vols. 8vo. 16s. 1730

2360 —— Another copy; 2 vols. in 1, half-bound, 12s.   1730

2361 THE NEW TESTAMENT of Our Lord and Saviour Jesus Christ, newly translated out of the Latin Vulgate, together with Annotations by C. NARY; 8vo. rare, 12s.

2362 THE HOLY BIBLE and NEW TESTAMENT, with Useful Notes, Critical, Historical, and Controversial, &c. by the Rev. Geo. Leo. Haydock; 2 vols. folio, rough calf, 3l. 13s. 6d.   *Manchester,* 1811

2363 —— Another copy; in calf extra, 4l. 4s.   *ib.* 1811

2364 THE HOLY BIBLE and NEW TESTAMENT, with Annotations and Historical Index, &c. published by Syers; folio, calf, 2l. 2s.   *ib.* 1813

2365 —— Another copy; good condition, rough calf, 2l. 12s. 6d.   *ib.* 1813

2366 THE HOLY BIBLE and NEW TESTAMENT, with Annotations and Historical Index, approved by the Most Rev. Dr. Troy; 4to. scarce, morocco, 2l.12s.6d.*Dubl.*1816

2367 THE HOLY BIBLE and NEW TESTAMENT, newly revised and corrected, with Annotations, &c.; 5 vols. 12mo. scarce, calf neat, 1l. 5s.   *Edinburgh,* 1796

2368 —— ANOTHER COPY; 5 vols. 12mo. 1l. 1s.   *ib.* 1805

2369 THE HOLY BIBLE, according to the Vulgate; stereotype edition, 8vo. sheep, 9s.   *Dublin,* 1840

2370 —— the same; on fine paper, in royal 8vo. calf gilt, 1l. 1s.   *ib.* 1840

2371 —— the same; worked in 4to. paper, with large margins for notes and remarks, scarce, 2l. 2s.   *ib.* 1833

2372 THE HOLY BIBLE, according to the Latin Vulgate, published with the Approbation of the Rt. Rev: Dr. Denvir; 18mo. cloth, 6s.   1838

2373 BLYTH (F.) A Devout Paraphrase on the Seven Penitential Psalms, or a Practical Guide to Repentance; 12mo. 3s. 1741

2374 —— Devout Paraphrase on the Seven Penitential Psalms, or a Practical Guide to Repentance; 8vo. *scarce,* 4s. 6d. *London,* 1742

2375 —— An Explanation of the Adoration of the Holy Cross; 8vo. 1s. 6d.   1766

2376 Sermons for every day in the Year; 2 vols. in one, 4to. scarce, 18s.   *Dublin,* 1763

2377 BISHOP WILLIAM (Dr.) Reproof of Dr. Abbot's Defence of the Catholic Deformed: 4to. (title and a few leaves at the end wanting) 3s. 6d.   1608

2378 BOSSUET. Conference with Claude on the Authority of the Church, 1687.—Exposition of the Doctrine of the Church, 1685.— Treatise of Communion under both kinds, 1687.—Answers to a Discourse against Transubstantiation (*supposed by Gother*) 1687: 4 pieces in 1 vol. 4to. *rare,* 8s. 6d.
London, 1685-7

2379 —— An Exposition of the Doctrine of the Catholike Church, in the points of Controversie with those of the pretended Reformation; translated into English by W. M. (WALTER MONTAGUE, *Abbot of St. Martin's*); 12mo. *rare,* 5s.   *Paris,* 1672

2380 BOSSUET, History of the Variations of the Protestant Churches; 2 vols. 8vo. 8s.
Antwerp, 1742

2381 —— New edition, 2 vols. 8vo. bds. 10s.
Dublin, 1836

2382 —— A Treatise of Communion under both Species; 12mo. scarce, 5s. *Paris,* 1685

2383 —— Treatise of Communion under both kinds; translated by Jo. Davis, dedicated to Thomas Lord Petre; 4to. 3s. 6d. *Lond.* 1687

3384 A BRIEF HISTORIE of the Glorious Martyrdom of XII Reverend Priests, executed within these twelvemonths for Confession and Defence of the CATHOLIKE FAITH; but under the false pretence of Treason, with a note of sundry things that befel them in their life and imprisonment, and a preface declaring their innocencie; sm. 8vo. *exceedingly rare,* red morocco, bound by Lewis, 2l.2s.
1581

2385 BRISTOW (Richard) A Briefe Treatise of divers plaine and sure waies to find out the Truth in this doubtful and dangerous time of Heresie, conteyning sundrie worthy motives unto the Catholike Faith; 8vo. very rare, 10s. 6d.   *Antwerp,* 1599

2386 BRITANNIA Sancta, or the Lives of the most Celebrated British, English, Scottish and Irish Saints, who have flourished in these Islands, collected from their Acts and Records by the Right Rev. Richard Challoner; 2 parts in 1 vol. 4to. scarce, 1l. 1s.
London, 1745

2387 Ditto, Large Paper, *very scarce,* roy. 4to. half russia, 1l. 11s. 6d.   *ib.* 1745

2388 BROOKE (Mr.) The Tryal of the Roman Catholics; 8vo. 3s. 6d. *Dublin,* 1761

2389 BROUGHTON, Richard, A True Memorial of the Ancient, most Holy and Religious State of Great Britain in the time of the Britains; and Primitive Church of the Saxons; 8vo. rare, calf gilt, fine copy, 16s. *Permissu Superiorum* 1650

2390 BUTLER (Rev. Alban) Lives of the Fathers, Martyrs, and other principal Saints; first edition, 6 vols. 8vo. 1l. 16s. *Lond.* 1756

2391 —— Lives of the Fathers, Martyrs, and other principal Saints; the third edition, 12 vols. 8vo. bd. 2l. 14s. *Edin.* 1798

2392 —— Lives of the Fathers, Martyrs, and other principal Saints, *reprinted,* with a preface by the Right Rev. Dr. Doyle; in 2 vols. roy. 8vo. cloth, 1l. 10s. 1833

2393 —— DITTO. Large and fine Paper; 2 vols. imp. 8vo. cloth, 2l. 2s.

2394 —— Lives of Saints, selected from the original work; 2 vols. 8vo. 14s. *Newcastle,* 1799

2395 —— Meditations and Discourses on the Truths and Duties of Christianity; original edition, good type, 3 vols. 8vo. 1l. 1s. *Lond.* 1791

2396 —— The Moveable Feasts, Fasts, and other Annual Observances of the Catholic Church; 8vo. original edition, good type, 7s. 6d. *ib.* 1774

2397 —— Remarks on the two first volumes of the late Lives of Popes; 8vo. scarce, 2s. 6d. *Douay,* 1764

2398 —— Account of the Life and Writings of, by Charles Butler, bound together with the Chronological Index to the Saints' Lives; 8vo. calf, 5s. *Edin.* 1800

2399 BUTLER (Charles) A continuation of the Lives of the Saints to the present time; 8vo. bds. 5s. 6d. *Lond.* 1833

2400 —— Notes on the Chief Revolutions of the Germanic Empire; royal 8vo. 7s. *Lond.* 1807

2401 —— Biographical and Philological works: viz. Horæ Biblicæ and Juridicæ—History of the Germanic Empire—Church of France —Confessions of Faith—and Lives of Eminent Persons; 5 vols. 8vo. bds. 1l. 15s. *ib.* 1817

2402 —— Reminiscences; 2 vols. 8vo. calf extra, 18s. *ib.* 1824

2403 —— The Book of the Roman Catholic Church, in letters to R. Southey, with the Vindication, 2 vols. 8vo. calf neat, scarce, 1l. 1s. *ib.* 1826

2404 —— Vindication of the Book of the Roman Catholic Church, 8vo. bds. 6s. 6d. *ib.* 1826

2405 CALDERBANK (Rev. J.) Observations, in letters, in Answer to certain Questions relating to various subjects of Religion proposed by a Clergyman of the Established Church to a Catholic Convert. 8vo. 3s. 6d. *Bath.* 1814

2406 CAMUS (John Peter, Bishop of Belley) The Spirituall Director disintressed according to the Spirit of B. FRANCIS DE SALES; 18mo. title wanted, 4s. 6d. *Paris,* 1631

2407 CANES (John Vincent) Fiat Lux, or a General Conduct to a Right Understanding in the great Combustions and Broils about Religion here in England, betwixt Papist and Protestant, Presbyterians and Independents; 18mo. 8vo. rare, 6s. 6d. 1661

2408 —— The Reclaimed Papist, or the Process of a Papist Knight reformed by a Protestant lady, with the assistance of a Presbyterian minister and his wife; 8vo. rare, 5s. 6d. 1665

2409 CARRE (Thomas) Pietas Parisiensis, or a Description of the Pietie and Charitie commonly exercised in Paris, which represents, in short, the pious practises of the whole Catholic Church; 18mo. rare, 4s. *Paris,* 1666

2410 —— A Spirituall Exercise according to the custom of Windesem. 1400: with Meditations of Sin, Death, Heaven, and Hell; 12mo. scarce, 3s. 6d. *ib.* 1658

2411 THE CATHOLIC Naked Truth, or the Puritan Convert to Apostolical Christianity; signed with the initials W. H. 4to. rare, 3s. 6d. *Permissu Sup.* 1676

2412 THE CATHOLIC Letter to the Seeker, or a Reply to the Protestant Answer, showing that Catholicks have express Scriptures for believing the Real Presence, and that Protestants have none at all for denying it, by N. N. 1688.—Also, Advice to Protestants, at the end, 4 pages, 1687; 4to. rare, 3s. 6d. *Lond.* 1688

2413 THE CATHOLIC MODERATOR, or a Moderate Examination of the Doctrine of the Protestants; 4to. rare, 6s. *ib.* 1623

2414 CATHOLIC Vindicator, edited by W. E. Andrews; 8vo. bds. 2s. *ib.*

2415 CARY (Edward) The Catechist Catechiz'd, or Loyalty Asserted, in vindication of the Oath of Allegiance against a new Catechism set forth by a Father of the Society of Jesus; 8vo. scarce, 5s. 6d.

2416 CAUSSIN (N.) Entertainments for Lent; 12mo. 2s. 6d. *Lond.* 1741

2417 —— The Holy Court, or Motives to excite Men to Christian perfection, &c. folio, first edition in English, 12s. *ib.* 1650

2418 —— The same; third edition, folio, 14s. *ib.* 1663

2419 CHALLONER (Rt. Rev. Dr.) Memoirs of Missionary Priests, as well Secular as Regular, and of other Catholics of both Sexes that have suffered Death in England on Religious accounts from 1577 to 1684; 2 vols. 8vo. original edition, scarce, 1l. 4s. 1741

2420 CHALLONER (Richard, Bishop of Debra) Life of, by James Barnard; 12mo. 2s. 6d. *Lond* 1784

2421 CHAMPNEY (Anthony) A Treatise of the Vocation of Bishops, and other Ecclesiasticall Ministers, proving the Ministers of the pretended Reformed Churches in generall to have no calling, and in particular the pretended Bishops in England to be no true Bishops ; against Mr. Mason ; very rare, 1l. 4s.   *Douay*, 1616

2422 CLAGET (William D.D.) A Discourse concerning the Worship of the Blessed Virgin and the Saints, in Answer to Bossuet; 4to. 4s. 6d.   *London*, 1686

2423 CHRISTIAN RULES, proposed to the Vertuous Soul aspiring to holy perfection, third edition, renewed by W. C. (WILLIAM CLIFFORD) 8vo. calf neat, scarce, 6s. 6d.   1665

2424 —— Ditto, fourth edition, reprinted for M. M. 8vo. fine edition, 7s. 6d.   *Birmingham*, 1801

2425 COUNCIL OF TRENT, A large Summary of the Doctrines contained in the Catechism published by the Decree of the C. of Trent ; 8vo. scarce, 5s. 6d.   1675

2426 CRESSY (Hugh-Paulin) Exomologesis, or a Faithful Narration of the Occasion and Motives of his Conversion unto Catholike Unity.—*Second edition*, containing an Appendix in Reply to Chillingworth, and to J. P.'s Preface to Lord Falkland's Discourse touching Infallibility ; 12mo. rare, 8s. 6d.   *Paris*, 1653

2427 —— A NON EST INVENTUS returned to Mr. Edward Bagshaw's Enquiry and vainly boasted Discovery of Weakness in the Grounds of the Churches Infallibility, by a Catholic Gentleman; 12mo. rare, 5s. 6d. 1662

2428 —— *First Question :* Why are you a Catholic? the answer follows. *Second Question :* But why are you a Protestant? an answer attempted (*in vain*); 4to. very scarce, 5s. 6d.   *London*, 1686

2429 —— XVI Revelations of Divine love shewed to a devout servant of Our Lord, called MOTHER JULIANA, an Anchorite of Norwich, who lived in the dayes of King Edward the Third, dedicated to Lady Mary Blount of Sodington ; 8vo. rare, 7s. 6d.   *Permissu Super.* 1670

2430 CROSS (John, D.D.) Contemplations on the Life and Glory of Holy Mary, the Mother of Jesus, with a daily office agreeing to each Mystery thereof, by J. C.—An Apology for the Contemplations, shewing the Innocency and Antiquity of the Honor and Veneration given to the Blessed Virgin Mother by the Catholic Church, by J. C. 12mo. scarce, 9s. 6d.   *Lond.* 1687

2431 —— The Apology, separate ; 12mo. 5s.6d.   *ib.* 1687

2432 CROSS (Nicholas) The Cynosura, or a Saving Star that leads to Eternity, discovered amidst the celestial orbs of David's Psalms, by way of paraphrase upon the MISERERE,

dedicated to the Countess of Shrewsbury; folio, scarce, 12s.   *Lond.* 1670

2433 DAILY Exercises of a Christian Life, or the interiour Spirit with which we ought to animate our actions throughout the whole day, translated from the French by N. N. scarce, 4s. 6d.   *Paris*, 1684

2434 DANIEL, Rev. John, Ecclesiastical History of the Britons and Saxons, 8vo. 2s. 6d.   *Lond.* 1815

2435 DECLARATION of the Principall Pointes of Christian Doctrine, gathered out of diverse Catechismes, and set forth by the English Priests dwelling in TOURNAY Colledge; hf-bd. neat, scarce, 8s. 6d.   *Paris*, 1647

2436 DEFENCE OF CATHOLIKES persecuted in England, invincibly proving their holy Religion to be that which is the only true Religion of Christ, and that they, in professing it, are become most faithfull, dutifull, and loyal subjects to God, their king, and country ; 8vo. *very rare*, 15s.   *Douay*, 1630

2427 DIVINE OFFICE, containing Devotions for the Canonical hours of prayer, to be used by all Religious Societies where there is a Priest, and in the houses of the Clergy ; 8vo. 4s. 6d.   1761

2438 DIVINE OFFICE for the use of the Laity, 4 vols. 12mo. *good copy*, 1l. 10s. *Lond.* 1763

2439 DODD (Charles, alias Hugh Tootle) A Modest Defence of the Clergy and Religious, in a Discourse directed to R. C. (CH. DODD) about his History of DOUAY COLLEGE, with an account of the matters of Facts misrepresented in the said History, by HUNTER; 8vo. rare, 9s. 6d.   1714

2440 DONLEVY (Andrew) The Catechism, or Christian Doctrine by way of Question and Answer; 8vo. 3s. 6d.   *London*, 1791

2441 DREXELIUS. Nicetas, or the Triumph over Incontinencie, translated by R. S. 12mo. scarce, 6s. 6d.   1633

2442 DRYDEN (John) A Defence of the Papers written by the late King of blessed memory and Duchess of York against the Answer made to them ; 4to. rare, 6s. *London*, 1686

2443 —— A Reply to the Answer made upon the Three Royal Papers ; 4to. 4s.   *ib.* 1686

2444 —— Life of St. Francis Xavier of the Society of Jesus; 8vo. scarce, 9s. *Dublin*, 1812

2445 DUQUENE (Abbé) Devout Meditations on the Gospel for Every Day in the Year, abridged from the French ; 4 vols. 8vo. half-bound calf, nt. scarce, 1l. 10s. *Reading*, 1821

2446 DURHAM. The Antiquities of the Abbey or Cathedral Church of Durham, to which is added the Succession of the Bishops, Deans, and Prebends, &c. ; 12mo. scarce, 6s. 6d.   *Newcastle*, 1767

2447 EPISTLE of Consolation from a Banished Priest now at *Roane*, to the Catholicks of England ; 8vo. very rare, 9s. 6d.   *Roane*, 1663

2448 ESSAY towards a proposal for Catholic Communion, by a Minister of the Church of England ; 12mo. 3s. *London,* 1704

2449 EXERCISE of a Christian Life; dedicated to the Fathers of the Society of Jesus, by James Sancer ; title wanted, 12mo. 2s. 6d. *Paris,* 1597

2450 FISHER (John, Bishop of Rochester) The Funeral Sermon of Margaret Countess of Richmond, mother to King Henry VII : with a Preface, containing an account of her Charities and Foundations, 8vo. scarce, 7s. 6d. *London,* 1708

2451 —— Life and Death of, selected from Records by Thomas Baily ; 8vo. portrait, rare, 8s. 6d. *ib.* 1655

2452 FITZHERBERT (Thomas) A Treatise concerning Policy and Religion, wherein the necessity of Christian Religion in Commonwelth is shewed, &c.—and also wherein is proved that the Catholique Religion only doth make a happy commonwelth, 2 vols. 4to. very scarce, 1l. 18s. *Douay,* 1606-10

2453 —— A Treatise of Policy and Religion, Part I. Third edition, 8vo. 5s. 6d. *Lond.* 1695

2454 FLEETWOOD (William) An Account of the Life and Death of the Blessed Virgin, according to Romish writers, with the grounds of the Worship paid to her; 4to. 4s. 6d. *ib.* 1687

2455 FRANCIS XAVIER (St.) Life, translated from the French of Bouhours by Mr. Dryden ; 8vo. calf neat, scarce, 10s. 6d. *ib.* 1688

2456 —— Devotion of Ten Fridays in honour of St. Francis Xaverius, with an Epitome of his Life, dedicated to Lady Mary Caryll, Abbesse of the English Benedictine Dames at Dunkerque, by N. N. 18mo. (title wanted) rare, 4s.

2457 FREE Examination of the Impolitic and unwise Methods employed to prevent the growth of Popery; 12mo. 5s. *Cork,* 1808

2458 FRIENDLY and Seasonable Advice to the Roman Catholicks of England, by a Charitable Hand; 12mo. 3s. 6d. *London,* 1677

2459 GANDOLPHY (Rev. Peter) Defence of the Ancient Faith, or a full exposition of the Christian Religion, in a series of Controversial Sermons ; vols. 1 and 2, 8vo. calf, scarce, 18s. *ib.* 1813

2460 GENINGS, John, The Life and Death of Mr. Edmund Geninges, Priest ; crowned with martyrdome at London the 10th day of November, in the yeare MDXCI ; 4to. *illustrated with* 12 *plates,* bound in morocco extra, 3l. 13s. 6d. *St. Omers,* 1614
A fine copy of one of the rarest books of English Catholic Biography.

2461 GILBERT, Rev. N. The Catholic Doctrine of Baptism proved from Scripture and Tradition ; 12mo. 4s. 6d. *Berwick,* 1802

2462 THE GODLY GARDEN of Gethsemani, furnished with holsome fruites of MEDITACION and PRAYER: UPON THE BLESSED PASSION OF CHRIST OUR REDEEMER ; 1 volume, black letter, many woodcuts, the last page supplied in MS. very rare, 9s. 6d. *circa* 1487

2463 GOTHER, John, Good Advice to the Pulpits, delivered in a few cautions for the keeping up the reputation of those Chairs, and preserving the Nation in peace ; 4to. rare, 4s. 6d. *Lond.* 1687

2464 —— Nubes Testium, or a collection of the Primitive Fathers, giving testimony of the Faith once delivered to the Saints. Being a full discovery of the Sentiments of the Ancient Fathers in the chief points of Controversie at present under debate ; with an Appendix containing the appendix of many eminent Protestants; 4to. *Lond.* 1686.—Discourse on the Use of Images: in relation to the Church of England and the Church of Rome, in vindication of *Nubes Testium ;* 4to. 1687.—The Primitive Fathers no Protestants: or a Vindication of *Nubes Testium* from the cavils of the Waverer; 4to. 1687.— The Pope's Supremacy asserted, from the considerations of some Protestants, and the practise of the primitive Church, in vindication of *Nubes Testium,* 1688 : all in 1 vol. 4to. very rare, hf.-bd. 1l. 1s. *ib.* 1686-8

2465 —— Nubes Testium, separate ; 4to. very rare, 9s. 1686

2466 —— A Papist Misrepresented and Represented, 1686.—Doctrines and Practices of the Church of Rome truly represented, 1686.—A Papist not Misrepresented by Protestants, 1686.—Remarks upon the Reflections of the Author of Popery Misrepresented, 1686.—Papists Protesting against Protestant Popery, 1687.—Answer to the same, 1686.— Amicable Accommodation of the Difference between the Representers, 1686.—Answer to the Amicable Accommodation, 1686.—Reply to the Answer, 1686.—View of the Whole Controversy ; 1 thick volume, 4to. neat, 16s.

2467 —— A Papist Mis-represented *and* Represented : or a twofold character of Popery, by J. L. to which is annexed, Roman Catholic Principles, in reference to God and the King, 1685.—The Catholic Representer, or the Papist Misrepresented and Represented, second part, 1687.—The Papist Misrepresented and Represented, third part, with a Preface containing Reflections upon two Treatises, 1687.—Papists protesting against Protestant Popery, being a vindication of the Papist Misrepresented, *London,* 1686 ; all in 1 vol. 4to. hf.-bd. very rare, 14s.

2468 —— Pope Pius his Profession of Faith Vindicated from Novelty in additional articles ; 4to. 3s. *Lond.* 1687

2469 —— The Pope's Supremacy Asserted from the considerations of some Protestants and the practice of the Primitive Church, in a Dialogue between a Church Divine and a Seeker : in vindication of Nubes Testiur 4to. scarce, 4s. 6d. *ib.* 16

2470 GOTHER, John, The Primitive Fathers no Protestants : or a Vindication of Nubes Testium from the Cavils of the Answerer; 4to. scarce, 4*s.* 6*d.*   *London,* 1687

2471 —— Pulpit Sayings, or the Characters of the Pulpit-Papists examined, in answer to the Apology for the Pulpits, and in vindication of the *Representer* against the *Stater* of the Controversie ; 4to. 4*s.* 6*d.*
        ib. 1688

2472 —— Transubstantiation Defended, and proved from Scripture: in answer to the first part of a Treatise intituled ' a Discourse against Transubstantiation ;' 4to. rare, 5*s.* 6*d.*
        ib. 1687

2473 —— The Sinners Complaints to God, being Devout Entertainments of the Soul with God ; 8vo. large print, scarce, 8*s.* 6*d.*
        Birmingham, 1770

2474 —— Sinners Complaints to God ; new edition, 12mo. cloth, 4*s.* 6*d.*   *Lond.* 1839

2475 —— Works, consisting of his moral and devotional writings in 16 vols. 12mo. *scarce,* calf neat, 4*l.* 4*s.*   *Newcastle,* 1790

2476 GREGORIE THE GREAT. The Second booke of the Dialogues, containing the Life and Miracles of Our Holie Father *St. Benedict,* translated by B. E. T. 18mo. 3*s.* 6*d.*
        Permissu Superiorum 1638

2477 GUEVARA, Sir Anthonie, Preacher to Charles V, The Familiar Epistles of, translated by Edward Hellowes, Groom of the Leash ; 4to. BLACK LETTER, 12*s.* *Lond.* 1577

2478 HARMER, Anthony *(H. Wharton)* A Specimen of some errors and defects in the History of the Reformation of the Church of England, wrote by Gilbert Burnet ; 8vo. 3*s.* 6*d. ib.* 1693

2479 HAWARDEN, Edward, Charity and Truth, or Catholics not uncharitable in saying, that none are saved out of the Catholic Communion; 8vo. scarce, 8*s.* 6*d.*   *Brussells,* 1728

2480 —— The True Church of Christ shewed by concurrent testimonies of Scripture and primitive Tradition, in anser to *Lesley's case stated,* &c. three parts in 2 volumes, 1714.—
CHARITY AND TRUTH, or Catholics not uncharitable in saying that none are saved out of the Catholic Communion, 1 vol. 8vo. 1728 ; in all 3 vols. fine copies, *scarce,* 1*l.* 4*s. Lond. v.y.*

2481 —— The Rule of Faith truly stated in a new and easy method ; or a Key to Controversy ; 18mo. scarce, 4*s.* 6*d.*   *ib.* 1721

2482 HAY, Bishop, Scripture Doctrine of Miracles displayed ; 2 vols. 12mo. 9*s. ib.* 1775

2483 HEATH, Nicholas, Archbishop of York, Speech in the Upper House of Parliament, 1555, on occasion of the Supremacy, with proofs from Scripture and the Fathers that there is no Salvation out of the Catholic Church, with other tracts ; 12mo. rare, 4*s.* 6*d*
        ib. 1688

2484 HEIGHAM, John, The Life of Our Lord and Saviour Jesus, gathered out of Saint Bonaventure, augmented, the second edition, 18mo. scarce, 6*s.* 6*d.*   *St. Omers,* 1622

2485 HILTON, Walker, *(a Carthusian)* The Scale or Ladder of Perfection, first published 1494, revised by *Abraham Woodhead,* 8vo. scarce, 10*s.* 6*d.*   *London,* 1659

2486 HORNIHOLD, James, The Grounds of the Christian's Belief, or the Apostle's Creed explained, in a concise and easy manner, in 23 discourses: 8vo. 3*s.* 6*d. Birmingham,* 1771

2487 — — The Sacraments explained, in 20 Discourses, 8vo. 3*s.* 6*d.*   *London,* 1747

2488 HOWARD, William, (afterwards VISCOUNT STAFFORD) A Paterne of Christian Loyalty: whereby any prudent man may clearly perceive, in what manner the *New Oath of Allegiance,* and every clause thereof, may in a true, and Catholike sense, without danger of perjury, be taken by Roman Catholikes ; 4to. very rare, 9*s.* 6*d.*   *ib.* 1634

2489 How the Members of the CHURCH OF ENGLAND ought to behave themselves under a ROMAN CATHOLIC KING, with reference to the Test and Penal Laws; 12mo. 5*s.* 6*d.*
        ib. 1687

2490 HUGO, Herm, Pia Desideria: or Divine Addresses, in 3 books, illustrated with 47 plates; Englished by EDM. ARWAKER, M.A. Second edition, 8vo. 7*s.* 6*d.*   *ib.* 1690

2490*—— Another copy, Fourth edition, 7*s.* 6*d.*
        ib. 1712

2491 THE HUMBLE PETITION of the Lay Catholiques Recusants of England, with the answer to the Recusants petition ; 4to. rare, 2*s.*   *ib.* 1641

2492 IMPORTANT Inquiry; or the Nature of a Church Reformation fully considered ; wherein is shewn, from Scripture, Reason, and Antiquity, that the late pretended Reformation was groundless in the attempt, and defective in the execution ; 8vo. 7*s.* 6*d.*   *ib.* 1758

IRELAND.

2493 DUNLEVY, Andrew, The Catechism, or Christian Doctrine by way of Question and Answer, in IRISH and ENGLISH ; 8vo. scarce, 9*s.* 6*d.*   *Paris,* 1742

2494 HISTORY of the Irish Catholics from the settlement in 1691, by MATHEW O'CONOR, Part I, scarce, 7*s.* 6*d.*
        Dublin, 1813

2495 PLOWDEN, Francis, An Historical Review of the State of Ireland from Henry the Second until the Union in 1801, 3 vols. 4to. calf extra, fine copy, 3*l.* 3*s. Lond.* 1803

2496 —— Ditto, 3 vols. 4to. in boards, 2*l.* 2*s.*   *ib.* 1803

2497 A Statement of the Penal Laws which aggrieve the Catholics of Ireland ; with commentaries, in two parts, 8vo. scarce, 9*s.*   *ib.* 1812

2498 WALSH, Peter, the History and Vindication of the LOYAL FORMULARY, or IRISH REMONSTRANCE received by his Majesty,

IRELAND,

anno 1661, against all Calumnies and Censures, in several treatises, with a true account of the DELUSORY IRISH REMONSTRANCE, and other papers, framed and insisted on by the National Congregation at Dublin 1666, and presented to his Majesties Lord Lieutenant, the Duke of Ormond; but rejected by his Grace; to which are added Three Appendices: whereof the last contains the Marquess of Ormond's letter of the 2d December 1650, in answer to the Declaration and Excommunication of the Bishops, &c. at Jamestown, folio, *very rare*, 8*l.* 18*s.* 6*d.*　　　*Anno* 1674

2499 JAMES II. Directions to the Archbishops of Canterbury and York concerning Preachers, 4to. rare, 2*s.* 6*d.*　　　　　1685

2500 —— Abridgment of the Life of James II, extracted from an English manuscript of Father Sanders, by Father Francis Brettonneau; 8vo. scarce, 4*s.* 6*d.*　　*London*, 1704

2501 JANSENISTS. The Secret Policy of the Jansenists and the present state of the Sorbon discovered by a converted Doctor of that Faculty; 12mo. Second edition, scarce, 3*s.* 6*d.*　　　　　　　1703

JESUITS.

2502 An Answer to the Provinciall Letters published by the Jansenists under the name of Lewis Montalt against the doctrine of the Jesuits: made by some Fathers of the Society in France; 12mo. rare, 5*s.* 6*d.*　　　　*Paris*, 1659

2503 A True and perfect Relation of the whole proceedings against GARNET and his Confederates, &c. with all that passed at Garnet's execution; 4to. 6*s.* 6*d.* *London*, 1606

2504 A JUST and Moderate Answer to a most injurious and slanderous Pamphlet, intituled, '*An Exact Discovery of Romish Doctrine in case of Conspiracie and Rebellion,*' wherein the innocency of Catholike Religion is proved, and every objection returned upon the Protestant accuser, and his owne profession; with licence of Superior. ' Dedicated to King James;' 4to. rare, 7*s.* 6*d.*

2505 KELLISON, Mathew, A survey of the New Religion, detecting manie grosse absurdities which it implieth; 8vo. rare, 9*s.* 6*d.* *Douay*, 1603

2506 LASSELS, Richard, The Voyage of Italy, with Characters of the People, Descriptions of the Chief Towns, Churches, Libraries, and Antiquities, &c. corrected and set forth by S. Wilson; 2 parts, 8vo. 5*s.*　*Paris*, 1670

2507 LECHMERE, Edmund, A Disputation of the Church, wherein the Old Religion is maintained; 8vo. scarce, 8*s.* *Douay*, 1632

2508 —— Another copy; second edition, enlarged, 8vo. 3*s.* 6*d.*　　　　*ib.* 1640

2509 LETTER concerning the Council of Trent, *no title*, but signed with the initials N. N. ' 12mo. 2*s.* 6*d.*　　　　　*Sept.* 1686
　N.B. The same initials are used by the Rev. Edward Scarisbrick in his Life of Lady Warner.

2510 LEYBURN, George, Holy Characters, containing a Miscellany of Theologicall Discourses, that is Theology; 8vo. rare, 15*s.*　　　　　　　　*Douay*, 1662

2511 LIVES OF SAINTS, collected from authentic Records of Church History, with a full Account of the Festivals of the Year, with Reflections; 4 vols. 4to. half-bound calf, neat, 1*l.* 16*s.*　　　　*London*, 1750

2511* —— Another copy; 4 v. 4to. 1*l.* 4*s.* 1750

2512 LOVE OF JESUS. A sure and short pleasant and easie Way to Heaven, in Meditations and Resolutions; 2 parts, 12mo. 4*s.* 6*d.*　　　　　　　*London*, 1677

2513 LUTHER'S ALCORAN, being a Treatise first written in French by Cardinal Peron, against the Huguenots of France, and translated into English by N. N. P.; 8vo. rare, 9*s.* 6*d.*　　　*With license*, 1642

2514 MANNING, Robert, England's Conversion and Reformation compared, or the Young Gentleman directed in the Choice of his Religion; 8vo. first edition, 4*s.* 6*d.* *Antw.* 1725

2515 —— Plain and Rational Account of the Catholic Faith, with a Preface and Appendix in Vindication of Catholic Morals from Old Calumnies revived:—to which is annext the Reformed Churches proved destitute of a Lawful Ministry; 8vo. third edition, scarce, 6*s.* 6*d.*　　　　　　*Rouen*, 1721

2516 —— The Rise and Fall of the Heresy of Iconoclasts, or Image Breakers; 8vo. scarce, 5*s.*　　　　　*London*, 1731

2517 —— A Single Combat between Mr. Trapp and his Anonymous Antagonists; 8vo 3*s.* 6*d.*　　　　　*Antwerp*, 1728

3518 MANUELL of the Arch-Confraternitie of the Cord of the Passion, instituted in the seraphicall Order of S. FRANCIS, by Br. Angelus Francis; 18mo. rare, calf neat, 6*s.* 6*d.*　　　　　　　　*Douay*, 1654

3519 MARTIN, Gregory, A Discoverie of the manifold Corruptions of the Holy Scriptures by the Heretikes of our daies, specially the English Sectaries, and of their foul dealing therein by partial and false Translations; 8vo. very rare, 1*l.* 1*s.*　　*Rhemes*, 1582
　Dr. Gregory Martin was one of the Professors in the English College at *Rhemes*, and was concerned in the translation of the Testament published in 1582.

2520 MEMORIAL of Ancient British Piety: or a British Martyrology, giving an Account of all such Britons as have been honoured of old amongst the Saints:—and a Translation of two Saxon Manuscripts, relating to the burying places of the English Saints, by the Rt. Rev. Rd. Challoner; 12mo. 4*s.* *Lond.* 176

2521 MASS. 𝖙𝖍𝖊 𝕴𝖓𝖙𝖊𝖗𝖕𝖗𝖊𝖙𝖆𝖈𝖕𝖔𝖓, 𝖆𝖓𝖉 𝕾𝖞𝖌𝖓𝖞= 𝖙𝖞𝖊𝖆𝖈𝖞𝖚𝖓 𝖔𝖋 𝖙𝖍𝖊 𝕸𝖆𝖘𝖘𝖊, a good devoute Boke to the honoure of God, of Our Lady his Mother, and of all sayntes, and ryght profytable to all good Catholyke persones, to knowe howe they shall devoutly here Masse. And how salutaryly they shal confesse them, &c.; small 8vo. black letter, 1*l*. 11*s*. 6*d*.
Imprynted by Robert Wyer, 1532

2522 MATTHEWS', Sir Toby, The Penitent Bandito: or the History of the Conversion and Death of Signor Troilo Savelli, a Baron of Rome; second edition, 12mo. 3*s*. 6*d*. 1663

2523 MENTAL PRAYER, Method of, rendered practical and easie for all sorts of Persons; 12mo. 2*s*. 6*d*.   *ib*. 1694

2524 MILNER, John, History of Winchester; 2 vols. 4to. plates, first edition, boards, 1*l*. 8*s*.
Winchester, 1798

2525 —— Ditto; new edition in royal 8vo. cloth, 1*l*. 4*s*.   *ib*. 1840

2526 —— An Inquiry into certain Vulgar Opinions concerning the Catholic Inhabitants and Antiquities of Ireland; 8vo. half-morocco, 10*s*. 6*d*.   *London*, 1808

2527 MILNER, Rev. John, Supplementary Memoirs of English Catholics, addressed to Chas. Butler, Esq.; 8vo. scarce, 9*s*. *ib*. 1820

2528 MISSALE ROMANUM Vindicatum, or the Mass vindicated from D. Daniel Brevent's Calumnious and Scandalous Tract, by R. F. 12mo. rare, 4*s*. 6*d*.   1674

2529 MODEST AND TRUE ACCOUNT of the Chief Points in Controversy between the Roman Catholicks and the Protestants, by N. C.; 12mo. 4*s*. 6*d*.   *Antwerp*, 1705

2530 MONTAGU, Walter, Miscellanea Spiritualia, or Devout Essaies, composed by the Honourable Walter Montagu, Esq. in 21 Treatises; 4to. rare, mor. 8*s*. 6*d*. *Lond*. 1648

2531 MORE, Sir Thomas, A Dialogue of Cumfort against Tribulation, made by the right vertuous, wise and learned man Sir Thomas More, Lord Chancellor of England, which he wrote in the Tower of London, 1534; small 8vo. black letter, rare, 1*l*.1*s*. *Antw*.1573

2532 MUMFORD, James, The Question of Questions; 2nd edition, 12mo. 3*s*. 6*d*. *Lond*. 1686

2533 NARY, C. A Letter to His Grace Edward Lord Archbishop of Tuam, in Answer to his Charitable Address, to all who are of the Communion of the Church of Rome; 8vo. scarce, 6*s*. 6*d*.   *Dublin*, 1728

2534 OFFICE of the B. V. MARY, to which is added the Method of saying the Rosary, &c.; 12mo. 1*s*. 6*d*.   1770

2534* —— the same, calf gilt, 4*s*.   1770

2535 OLD-FASHIONED FARMER'S Motives for leaving the Church of England and embracing the Catholic Faith; 8vo. first edition, 2*s*. 6*d*.   1778

2536 O'LEARY, Rev. Arthur, Miscellaneous Tracts; 8vo. 7*s*.   *Dublin*, 1781

2537 THE OLD RELIGION demonstrated in its Principles, and described in the Life and Practise thereof; 12mo. scarce, 4*s*. 6*d*.
London, 1684

2538 ORTHODOX JOURNAL of Useful Knowledge, edited by W. E. Andrews, Vols. I to IV, from July 1835 to June 1837; bound in 2 vols. 8vo. 12*s*.   *London*

2539 PALME OF CHRISTIAN FORTITUDE, or the glorious Combats of Christians in Japonia, taken out of Letters of the Society of Jesus from thence, Anno 1634; 8vo. scarce, 8*s*. 6*d*.
With Permission, 1630

2540 PASTORAL INSTRUCTIONS of the Bishop of Troyes, translated by Abbé Cummins; 8vo. half-bound, 4*s*.   *Kilkenny*, 1822

2541 PASTORAL LETTER of the Archbishop of Treves to his Church of Ausbourg; 8vo. 2*s*. 6*d*.   *London*, 1796

2542 PATTENSON, Matthew, The Image of bothe Churches, Hierusalem and Babel, Unitie and Confusion, Obedience and Sedition; 12mo. rare, 7*s*. 6*d*.   *Tornay*, 1623
Dedicated to Charles the First, when " Prince of Wales," by Pattenson, his physician.

2543 —— Another copy, stained, 5*s*. 6*d*.
ib. 1623

2544 —— Jerusalem and Babel, or the Image of both Churches, being a Treatise historically discussing, whether Catholikes or Protestants be the better Subjects; the second edition, 18mo. 5*s*. 6*d*.   *London*, 1653

2545 PAX VOBIS. An Epistle to the Three Churches; with an Addition of a Preface and Postscript, setting forth the Rule for the Truth and true Sense of Scriptures, &c.: 8vo. very rare, 10*s*. 6*d*.   *ib*. 1721
A note on the fly-leaf states this to be written by Hugh Tootle, *alias* Dodd.

2546 PEACH, Rev. E. Sermons for Every Sunday and Festival, chiefly taken from Masillon; 3 vols. 12mo. half-bound, 12*s*. *ib*. 1807

2547 PEMBRIDGE, Michael, The Roman Catholic Church and Religion vindicated, and deduced from the Bible and Tradition; 8vo. scarce, 9*s*. 6*d*.   *Bath*, 1806

2548 PERSONS, Robert, A Briefe Apologie, or Defence of the Catholike Ecclesiastical Hierarchie, and Subordination in England, erected these later yeares by our holy Father Pope Clement the eyght; and impugned by certayne libels printed and published of late both in Latyn and English; by some unquiet persons under the name of Priests of the Seminaries. Written and set forth for the true information of all good Catholikes, by Priests united in due subordination to the Right Reverend Archpriest, and other their Superiors, *Permissu Superiorum*; 8vo. very rare, 1*l*.4*s*.

2549 —— An Answere to the Fifthe Part of Reportes lately set forth by Sir Edward Coke,

Knight, concerning the ancient and moderne Municipall Lawes of England which do apperteyne to Spirituall Power and Jurisdiction; 4to. scarce, 14s. 1606
One leaf of the Index wanting.

2550 —— A Christian Directory guiding Men to their Eternal Salvation; 8vo. 7s. 6d. *Dublin,* 1820

2551 —— A Conference about the next Succession to the Crown of England, *under the name of* R. DOLEMAN; 8vo. rare (wanting the Genealogical Table), 8s. *Reprinted* 1681

2552 —— The Jesuit's Memorial for the intended Reformation of England, published from the Copy that was presented to King James II, with an Introduction and Notes, &c. by E. Gee; 8vo. 9s. 6d. *London,* 1690

2553 PILGRIMAGE to the Monastery of La Trappe; 8vo. 2s. *Havant,* 1815

2554 POLE, Cardinal, Some Observations upon the Life of REGINALDUS POLUS, Cardinal of the Royal Bloud of England. Sent in a pacquet out of Wales by G. L. [William Joyner *alias* Lyde]; 12mo. scarce, 5s. 6d. *London,* 1686

2555 —— History of the Life of, by Thomas Phillips; 2 parts, 4to. portrait, calf neat, 15s. *Oxford,* 1764

2556 —— History of the Life of, by Thomas Phillips; 2 vols. 8vo. portr. 12s. *Dubl.* 1765

2557 POPISH PAGAN, A, the Fiction of a Protestant Heathen; 8vo. 5s. 6d. *London,* 1743

2558 PORTER, Jerome, The Flowers of the Lives of the most renowned Saincts of the Three Kingdoms, England, Scotland, and Ireland, collected out of the best Authors and Manuscripts of our Nation. The first tome, January to June; 4to. plates, very rare, 1l. 4s. *Douay,* 1632
N.B. The first volume was all that was ever published.

2559 PRACTICAL METHODS of performing the Ordinary Actions of a Religious Life, with Fervour of Spirit; 12mo. scarce, 5s. 6d. *London,* 1718

2560 PRIMER, the, or Office of the B. Virgin Mary revived: with a New Version of the Church Hymns; 12mo. scarce, 7s. 6d. 1706

2561 PRIMITIVE CHRISTIAN DISCIPLINE not to be slighted: or Man look home and know thyself; 12mo. 5s. 1658

2562 PROTESTANT APOLOGY for the Roman Catholic Church; or the Orthodoxy of her Faith proved from the Testimony of her most learned Adversaries, to which is prefixed an Introduction concerning the Present State of the Church of England; 8vo. scarce, 7s. 6d. *Dublin,* 1809

2563 PUENTE, Luys de la, Meditations upon the Mysteries of our Faith, corresponding to the three Wayes, Purgative, Illuminative, and Unitive; 12mo. 7s. *Permissu Super.* 1624
One leaf of the Index wanting.

2564 PROTESTANT RULE OF FAITH, a full and clear Exposition of, with a Dialogue laying forth the large Extent of true Protestant Charity against the Uncharitable Papists; 4to. 2s. 6d.

2565 QUIS DIVES SALVUS. How a rich Man may be saved, written by Salvianus, Bishop of Massilia, translated into English by N. T.; 12mo. 3s. 6d. *Permissu Sup.* 1618

2566 RADFORD, John, A Directorie teaching the Way to the Truth, in a briefe and plaine Discourse against the Heresies of this Time, dedicated to Blackwell the Archpriest; 12mo. rare, calf neat, 12s. 1605

2566* —— Another copy; *title wanting,* 7s.

2567 RAINOLDS, William, A Refutation of sundry reprehensions, cavils, and false sleightes, by which M. Whitaker laboureth to deface the late English Translation, and Catholike Annotations of the New Testament, and the Booke of Discovery of Heretical Corruptions; 8vo. very rare, fine copy, 1l. 1s. *Paris,* 1583

2568 REMONSTRANCE of Piety and Innocence: containing the last Devotions and Protestations of several Roman Catholics condemned and executed on Account of the Plot; 12mo. rare, 5s. 6d. *London,* 1683

2569 RODRIGUEZ. A Treatise of Humility, translated into English; 12mo. scarce, 5s. 6d. *Permissu Sup.* 1632

2570 ROMAN Catholic Principles, in reference to God and the King, explained in a Letter to a Friend, now made public to shew the Connexion between the said Principles and the late POPISH PLOT; 4to. 2s. 6d. *Lond.* 1680

2571 ROMAN MISSAL, in Latin and English; 4 vols. 12mo. rare, 1l. 1s. 1737

2572 ROSARY. The Nature and Practise of the celebrated Devotion of the Holy Rosary: plainly illustrated, and orderly disposed, for the use of all pious Christians, illustrated with 15 plates of the Mysteries; 12mo. very scarce, 8s. 6d. *London,* 1754

2573 SANDERS, Nicolas, D.D. The Rocke of the Churche, wherein the Primacy of St. Peter and of his Successours the Bishops of Rome is proved out of God's worde; 8vo. rare, 15s. *Lovanii,* 1567

2574 SAVONAROLA, The Verity of Christian Faith; 18mo. 2s. *London,* 1651

2575 SCLATER, Edward, Minister of Putney, Consensus Veterum: or the Reasons for his Conversion to the Catholic Faith; 4to. rare, 5s. *ib.* 1686

2576 SCOT, Philip, A Treatise of the Schism of England, wherein particularly Mr. Hales and Mr. Hobbs are modestly accosted; 12mo. scarce, 4s. 6d. *Amsterdam,* 1650

2577 SERGEANT, John, Errour Nonplust, or Dr. Stillingfleet shown to be the Man of no Principles, with an Essay how Discourses concerning Catholic Grounds bear the high^est Evidence; 12mo. rare, 6s. 6d. 16?

2578 SERGEANT, John, A Discovery of the Groundlessness and Insincerity of my Lord of Down's Dissuasive, being the Fourth Appendix to SURE-FOOTING, with a Letter to Dr. Casaubon, and another to his answerer; ·8vo. 3s. 6d. *London*, 1665

2579 —— Schism Disarmed of the defensive Weapon lent it by Dr. Hammond, and the Bishop of Derry; 8vo. (title and 2 pages at the end wanting), rare, 2s. 6d. *Paris*, 1655

2580 —— Schism Dispatch't, or a Rejoynder to the Replies of Dr. Hammond and the Lord of Derry; 8vo. scarce, 9s. 6d. 1557

2581 —— The SECOND Catholic Letter, or Reflections on the Reflector's Defence of Dr. Stillingfleet, 1687.—THIRD Catholic Letter in answer to the arguing part of Dr. S.'s Second Letter, 1687.—The FIFTH Catholic Letter, in reply to Stillingfleet's *(pretended)* Answer, 1688.—The Reflector's Defence of his Letter to a Friend, against the furious assaults of Mr. S. in his Second Catholic Letter, 1688.—A Letter to Mr. G. giving a true account of a late Conference at the D. of P. 1687.—A Letter to the D. of P. in answer to the arguing part of his First Letter to Mr. G. 1687.—A Letter to a Friend in answer to the arguing part of his (D. of P.) First Letter to Mr. G.—A Second Letter to Mr. G. in answer to Two Letters on the Conference at the D. of P. 1687.—Letter to Dr. E. S. concerning his Letter to Mr. G. 1687.— Eight pieces in 4to. rare, 10s. 6d.

2582 —— The Rehearsal transprosed: or Animadversions upon a late Book, intituled, a Preface shewing what grounds there are of Fears and Jealousies of Popery; second edition, corrected, 12mo. 3s. 6d. *London*, 1672

2583 —— Another edition; with Additions and Amendments; 8vo. scarce, 5s. 6d. 1672

2584 SERMONS preached before King James II, the Queen, and the Queen Dowager, at St. James, at Windsor, and at other places, by W. Hall, Lewis Sabran, John Crosse, James Ayray, Edward Scarisbrike, Phil. Ellis, and Nicholas Cross; also Bossuet's Funeral Oration upon Maria Theresa,—nine sermons; 4to. scarce, 7s. 6d. *Lond. v.y.*

2585 SMITH, Richard, Bishop of Chalcedon, A Treatise of the best kinde of Confessors, by which Priests in England may see how they may be, and lay Catholiks see how they may choose the best kind of Confessors; 12mo. rare, 7s. 6d. 1651

2586 SOUTHWELL, Robert, Prose Works of, viz. Mary Magdalen's Funeral Tears — The Triumphs over Death - An Epistle of Comfort; edited by W. J. Walker; 12mo. bds. scarce, 6s. *Lond.* 1822

2587 —— Marie Magdalen's Funerall Teares for the Death of Our Saviour; 8vo. bds. 5s. *Reprinted* 1823

88 —— Ditto, 18mo. 1s. 6d. *London*,

2589 SPIRITUAL RETREAT, for one day in every month, *by a Priest of the Society of Jesus*, 12mo. 4s. 6d. 1698

2590 STAFFORD'S MEMOIRES, or a brief and impartial account of the Birth and Quality, imprisonment, tryal, principles, declaration, comportment, devotion, last speech and final end of WILLIAM late LORD VISCOUNT STAFFORD, beheaded on Tower Hill 29 December 1680; folio, red morocco, scarce, 15s. *Printed in the year* 1681

2591 STAPLETON, Thomas, The Apologie of Fred. Staphylus, treating of the Scriptures and disagreement in Doctrine amongst the Protestants, translated from the Latin; 8vo. scarce, 12s. *Antwerp*, 1565

2592 St. TERESA, Life of the Holy Mother St. Teresa, foundress of the Reformation of Discalceate Carmelites, with an Account of the Foundations she made; 8vo. calf, scarce, 10s. 6d. *London*, 1757

2593 TOUCHSTONE of the Reformed Gospels · wherein the Heads and Tenets of the Protestant Doctrine (objected against Catholicks) are briefly refuted, by texts of the Protestants' own Bible, &c. 18mo, scarce, 2s. 6d. 1678

2594 THE TRIUMPHS of the Cross; or the Penitent of Egypt, in 8 books; 8vo. scarce. 6s. *Birmingham*, 1775

2595 VALSECCHI's Foundations of Religion and the Fountains of Impiety: translated by the Rev. T. Carbry; 3 vols. 8vo. 9s. 1800

2596 VANE, Thomas, A Lost Sheep returned Home; or the motives of the Conversion to the Catholike Faith of THOMAS VANE, second edition; 12mo. rare, 7s. 6d. *Paris*, 1648

2597 VIEW of the real Power of the POPE, and of the power of the Priesthood over the Laity, with an Account how they use it, by T. Hart, 8vo. scarce, 8s. 6d. *Lond.* 1733

2598 VISITATION! The Rules of St. Augustin; with the Constitutions and Directory composed for the Religious Sisters of the VISITATION, by St. Francis de Sales; 18mo. rare, 6s. 6d. *London*, 1803

2599 WALSH, Peter, Four Letters on several subjects to Persons of Quality, the fourth being an answer to the Lord Bishop of Lincoln's book; 8vo. rare, 16s. 1686

2600 WALMESLEY, Bishop, The General History of the Christian Church, chiefly deduced from the Apocalypse of St. John, second edition, with remarks by Sig. Pastorini; 8vo. bds. 8s. 6d. *Lond.* 1798

2601 —— Another copy, fifth edition, 8vo. bound, 9s. *Dublin*, 1812

2602 WARD (Thomas) England's Reformation from the time of King Henry the VIIIth to the end of Oates' plot, a poem; 4to. first edition, *rare*, 18s. *Hambourgh*, 1710

2603 —— Another edition, adorned with copper plates; 2 vols. in 1, 12mo. scarce, russia, fine copy, 15s. *London*, 1747

2604 WARD, T. The Errata of the Protestant Bible; or the truth of the English translations examined: a new edition, to which are added the Preface of the Rev. Dr. L * *, and a Vindication by Dr. MILNER in reply to GRIER; royal 8vo. 5s. *Dublin*, 1841

2605 —— An Interesting Controversy with Mr. Ritschell, Vicar of Hexham, whether the established Church of England, or that of Rome, be the true Church of Christ: 8vo. bds. 7s. 6d. *Manchester*, 1819

2606 —— Ditto, the Original Manuscript in the hand-writing of THOMAS WARD; folio, 3l. 3s.

2607 WARNER (John) A Defence of the Doctrine, and Holy Rites of the Roman Catholic Church, from the Calumnies and Cavils of Dr. Burnet's Mystery of Iniquity Unveiled; the second edition; 8vo, scarce, 6s. 6d. *Lond.* 1688

2608 WINEFREDE (St.) The Life and Miracles of, together with her litanies: with some Historical Observations made thereon; 8vo. rare, 7s. 6d. *London*, 1713

2609 WESTMINSTER. The Antiquities of St. Peter's, or the Abbey Church of Westminster; 2 vols. 8vo. plates, 15s. *ib.* 1722

2610 WESTON (John Baptist) An Abstract of the Doctrine of Jesus Christ, or the Rule of the FRIER MINORS: literally, morally, and spiritually expounded, by Brother John Baptist Weston; 4to. rare, 12s. *Douay*, 1718

2611 WILSON (John) The English Martyrologe, conteyning a Summary of the lives of the Glorious and Renowned Saintes, of the three Kingdomes, England, Scotland, and Ireland, whereunto is added a catalogue of those who suffered for defence of the Catholike cause; sm. 8vo. vellum, *very rare*, 15s. *Permissu Superiorum*, 1608

2612 —— The Roman Martyrologe, according to the Reformed Calendar, translated out of Latin into English by G. K. of the Soc. of Jesus; 12mo. first edition, very scarce, (stained at the end) 7s. 6d. *With license*, 1627

2613 —— Another copy, second edition, to which are added divers Saints; 12mo. rare, 9s. 6d, *St. Omers*, 1667
The Epistle to the Catholick Reader is signed with the Initials W. B.

2614 WOODHEAD (Abraham) A Brief Account of Ancient Church-Government, with a Reflection on several modern writings of the writings of the Presbyterians; second edition, in four parts, 4to. scarce, 9s. 6d. *Lond.* 1685

2615 WOODHEAD, A. Animadversions on the Eight Theses entitled 'Church Government,' Part v, lately printed at Oxford by 'George Smallridge;' 4to. 4s. *Oxford*, 1687

2616 —— An Historical Narration of the Life and Death of Our Lord Jesus Christ, in two parts; 4to. scarce, 9s. 6d. *ib.* 1685
Printed and Published by Obadiah Walker, and and was owned by him, before the House of Commons.

2617 —— Motives to Holy Living, or Heads for Meditation, divided into Considerations, Counsels, and Duties, together with some forms of Devotion; 4to. scarce, 6s. 6d. *ib.* 1688

2618 —— Pietas Romana, et Parisiensis, or a faithful relation of the several sorts of Charitable and Pious Works eminent in the cities of Rome and Paris; 8vo. 3s. 6d. *ib.* 1687

2619 —— Two Discourses, *the first*, concerning the Spirit of MARTIN LUTHER and the original of the Reformation, *the second*, concerning the Celibacy of the Clergy; 4to. rare, 6s. 6d. *ib.* 1687

2620 —— A Reply to two Discourses on the Adoration of Our B. Saviour in the Holy Eucharist, by *Henry Aldrich*; 4to. 4s. *ib.* 1685

2621 —— An Answer to some Considerations on Martin Luther, by '*Francis Atterbury*;' 4to. scarce, 4s. *ib.* 1687

2622 —— An Answer to a Discourse concerning the Celibacy of the Clergy, by '*George Tully*;' 4to. scarce, 4s. 1688

2623 —— Dr. Stillingfleet's Principles, giving an account of the Faith of Protestants, considered: *Paris*, 1671.—The Roman Church's Devotions Vindicated from Dr. Stillingfleet: 1672.—The Doctrine of Repentance and Indulgences Vindicated from Stillingfleet: 1672.—Fanaticism imputed to the Catholic Church by Dr. Stillingfleet, by S. C. (HUGH PAULIN CRESSY) 1672; 4 tracts in 1 vol. 8vo. very scarce, 10s. 6d. 1672

2624 WORSLEY (Edward) A Discourse of Miracles wrought in the Roman Catholick Church, or a full refutation of Dr. Stillingfleet's unjust exceptions against Miracles, &c. 8vo. scarce, 9s. 6d. *Antwerp*, 1676

2625 —— Reason and Religion, or the certain Rule of Faith, where the infallibility of the R. C. Church is asserted, with a Refutation of Stillingfleet's gross errours; 4to. rare, 18s. *ib.* 1672

2626 WORTHINGTON, Thomas, The Anker of Christian Doctrine, Vol. 1, wanting the title and the first 10 pages, and also the Index, &c. 4to. 6s. *Douay*, 1622

ADDENDA.

2627 AMMAESTRAMENTI e preci tratte dalle sa-scritture e dai Santi Padri per Cura Melchior Missirini; 12mo. 4s. 6d. *Firenze*, 1840

2628 BAYLY, Thomas, D.D. Herba Parietis: or the Wall Flower, as it grew out of the Stone Chamber belonging to the Metropolitan Prison of London called NEWGATE, with the frontispiece; folio, rare, 1l. 1s. *London*, 1650

2629 CATHOLIKE'S SUPPLICATION unto the

King's Majestie, for Toleration of Catholike
Religion in England, whereunto is annexed
a Supplicatorie Counterpoyse of the Protestants, by Gabriel Powell ; 4to. rare, *Lond.*1603
2630 MARTYROLOGIUM Metricum Ecclesiæ
Græcæ ex Menæis, Cod. Chiffletiano actis-

que Sanct. Gr. et Lat. nunc primum collig
G. Siberus ; 4to. scarce, 8*s.* 6*d. Lipsiæ,*17?
2631 WHITE, Thomas, Villicationis suæ (
medio animarum statu Ratio Episcopo Cha
cedonensi reddita, à THOMA ANGLO; 12m
rare, half-bound, 5*s.*   *Paris,* 165

VALUABLE WORKS PUBLISHED BY CHARLES DOLMAN.

Just published, Volumes First, Second, Third, and Fourth, price 12s. each, in cloth,

THE CHURCH HISTORY OF ENGLAND

FROM THE YEAR 1500 to 1688,
CHIEFLY WITH REGARD TO CATHOLICS,
BY CHARLES DODD,

WITH NOTES, AND A CONTINUATION TO THE BEGINNING OF THE PRESENT CENTURY,

By the REV. M. A. TIERNEY, F.S.A.

To be completed in Fourteen Volumes.
FIFTY Copies printed on LARGE PAPER in royal 8vo. price One Guinea each volume, in cloth.

Just published, a new edition, in 1 Vol. foolscap 8vo. uniform with the STANDARD NOVELS, &

GERALDINE: A TALE OF CONSCIENCE,
BY E. C. A.

Just published, in One Volume, price Twenty Shillings, hf.-bd.

Illustrations of the Corporal & Spiritual Works of Mercy,

IN SIXTEEN DESIGNS, ENGRAVED IN OUTLINE,

With Descriptive Anecdotes in Four Languages, and a Sketch of the ORDER OF MERCY, by a SISTER of the
Religious Order of OUR LADY OF MERCY.

Just published, in 18mo. price 2s. cloth,

THE YOUNG COMMUNICANTS,

Written for the Use of the Poor School, Bermondsey, and respectfully dedicated to the Rev. Peter Butler, by the
Authoress of "Geraldine," with the approbation of the Rt. Rev. Dr. Griffiths, V.A.L.

Just published, second edition, price 2s. 6d. in boards,

CATECHETICAL INSTRUCTIONS,
ON THE DOCTRINES AND WORSHIP OF THE CATHOLIC CHURCH,
BY JOHN LINGARD, D.D.

Now ready, in One Volume, 4to. the second edition, enlarged,

CONTRASTS:

OR A PARALLEL BETWEEN THE NOBLE EDIFICES OF THE MIDDLE AGES AND
CORRESPONDING BUILDINGS OF THE PRESENT DAY.

Shewing the Present Decay of Taste, accompanied by appropriate Text.

BY A. WELBY PUGIN, ARCHITECT.

Illustrated with TWENTY PLATES.

CPSIA information can be obtained
at www.ICGtesting.com
Printed in the USA
LVHW082341250619
622382LV00002B/32/P

9 780342 129270